CHARTER OF THE UNITED NATIONS
COMMENTARY AND DOCUMENTS

WORLD PEACE FOUNDATION

40 Mt. Vernon Street, Boston, Massachusetts

Founded in 1910

THE World Peace Foundation is a non-profit organization which was founded in 1910 by Edwin Ginn, the educational publisher, for the purpose of promoting peace, justice and good-will among nations. For many years the Foundation has sought to increase public understanding of international problems by an objective presentation of the facts of international relations. This purpose is accomplished principally through its publications and by the maintenance of a Reference Service which furnishes on request information on current international problems. Recently increased attention has been focused on American foreign relations by study groups organized for the consideration of actual problems of policy.

CHARTER
OF THE
UNITED NATIONS
COMMENTARY AND DOCUMENTS

LELAND M. GOODRICH

Director, World Peace Foundation

AND

EDVARD HAMBRO

*Director of the Department of International
Relations of the Chr. Michelsen Institute
Bergen, Norway*

WORLD PEACE FOUNDATION

BOSTON

1946

PREFACE

The idea of preparing a commentary on the United Nations Charter, and of publishing it along with a compilation of relevant documents, originated in San Francisco where Dr. Hambro and I were engaged in the work of the Conference, he as a member of the technical staff of the Norwegian Delegation and member of the Committee on Pacific Settlement of Disputes, and I as a member of the Conference Secretariat, more particularly, as Secretary of the aforementioned Committee. The original plan has somewhat changed in character in the course of its realization. Its consummation has been delayed far beyond our original intention by various circumstances. For one thing, collaboration across the far reaches of the Atlantic under prevailing conditions has not been as easy as we were perhaps tempted to believe when we were together in San Francisco.

It was not and is not our intention that this is to be regarded as a thorough work of scholarship. Our purpose is much more modest. We hope that this Commentary and the assembled documents will be of some assistance to the student and layman desiring a better understanding of the Charter as drafted at San Francisco. We have made use of the League of Nations experience and of the discussions at San Francisco to throw further light on the intent and meaning of the Charter.

By the very force of circumstances, I have had to assume special responsibility for deciding questions of form and substance which collaboration under more ideal conditions would not have required. Consequently, there are probably things said and unsaid for which Dr. Hambro would prefer not to assume full responsibility. Because of the physical difficulties under which we have labored, he has been generous in accepting my judgment in many matters and it is only right that I should shoulder more than an equal part of the blame for errors of omission and commission. It is of course understood that he has collaborated wholly as a private individual, and I have done likewise.

We have had valuable assistance in our work. Professor Clyde Eagleton of New York University, who was at San Francisco as a member of the United States technical staff and who participated in the preparatory work in the Department of State, read our first draft and made

v

some valuable suggestions, though of course he assumes no responsibility for what appears. Miss Marie J. Carroll has been of invaluable assistance in many ways, in the preparation of the bibliography, in checking our factual statements and documentary references, and in taking care of all the technical details in connection with publication.

It is hardly necessary to say that the Trustees of the World Peace Foundation, while making possible the publication of this book, assume no responsibility for opinions expressed.

LELAND M. GOODRICH
Director

January 30, 1946

CONTENTS

CONTENTS xiii

PART I

DEVELOPMENT AND GENERAL PLAN

DEVELOPMENT AND GENERAL PLAN

The Charter of the United Nations, signed at San Francisco on June 26, 1945 by the representatives of fifty nations, was the product of an evolutionary development extending over a period of many decades, even centuries. It was the immediate result of proposals emanating from the careful study of the experience of the past, and of exchanges of views between the representatives of governments leading to the narrowing and final elimination of areas of disagreement. These preliminary studies were both official and unofficial. It is impossible accurately to evaluate the contributions made by private groups and organizations such as the League of Nations Union (London) and the Commission to Study the Organization of Peace. Their influence was undoubtedly considerable. However, the Charter would not have been possible if the peoples and governments which participated in the making of the Charter had not been motivated by a common desire to maintain peace and security in a world devastated by war. That war has unleashed its forces for the second time within the memories of most of us and that by virtue of the miracles of modern science it has shown itself increasingly destructive to the point where it threatens the continued existence of civilization have undoubtedly strengthened this common purpose. It was the unity born of the experiences of war which in the last analysis produced this common effort in the cause of peace.

FAILURE OF THE LEAGUE EXPERIMENT

At the conclusion of the First World War an attempt was made, under the leadership of Woodrow Wilson, to organize the vital forces of the world in support of peace, security and human welfare. The Covenant of the League of Nations was the product of this great effort. The League experienced an initial setback when the United States failed to become a member. Yet for a decade and a half people throughout the world looked to the League as the instrument by which it might be possible to establish peace and stability in the world and to assist mankind in its uneven progress toward greater freedom and happiness.[1] The world-wide economic collapse of the late twenties and the early thirties, the rise in popularity of anti-democratic and nationalistic doctrines, and the unwillingness of peace-loving peoples to assume necessary responsibilities for the maintenance of peace resulted in the disintegration

---

[1] On the work of the League and the causes of its failure see Rappard, W. E., *The Quest for Peace since the World War*, Cambridge, Harvard Univ. Press, 1940.

3

and collapse of the League system. Into the vacuum produced by the lack of vision and power of decision of the peace-loving peoples of the world stepped the confident and aggressive forces of Italian Fascism, German Nazism and Japanese Militarism.

The failure of League sanctions against Italy in 1935 and 1936, accompanied by the rearmament of Germany, and particularly by the remilitarization of the Rhineland in 1936, made it morally certain that the peace-loving peoples of the world, unless they were to surrender to the forces of aggression without resistance, would sooner or later have to take up the challenge again, with bloodshed and wanton destruction as the inevitable consequences. The challenge was accepted in September 1939, and by the end of 1941 the war had spread to all continents and all the major powers of the world were involved. The final alignment of forces had taken place.

THE UNITED NATIONS — FOR WAR

The signing of the Declaration by United Nations on January 1, 1942,[1] was an important landmark in the evolution of the United Nations. By the terms of the Declaration a wartime coalition was formed. The signatories accepted the principles of the Atlantic Charter, signed by President Roosevelt and Prime Minister Churchill on August 14, 1941.[2] They thereby subscribed to the hope expressed in the Charter "to see established a peace which will afford to all nations the means of dwelling in safety within their own boundaries, and which will afford assurance that all the men in all the lands may live out their lives in freedom from fear and want." Furthermore, they expressed the belief that the disarmament of aggressor nations was essential "pending the establishment of a wider and permanent system of general security."

The signatories asserted their conviction "that complete victory over their enemies is essential to defend life, liberty, independence and religious freedom, and to preserve human rights and justice in their own lands as well as in other lands, and that they are now engaged in a common struggle against savage and brutal forces seeking to subjugate the world." By the Declaration, each signatory government pledged itself "to employ its full resources, military or economic, against those members of the Tripartite Pact and its adherents with which such government is at war" and "to cooperate with the Governments signatory hereto and not to make a separate armistice or peace with the enemies."

Beyond the general principles set forth in the Atlantic Charter and accepted in the Declaration by United Nations, together with those expressed in the declarations of the leading statesmen of the United Nations, no important statement of United Nations policy with respect

[1] See this volume, p. 306.   [2] *Ibid.*, p. 305.

to the establishment of an international organization to maintain peace and security was made until the Moscow Conference of October 19–30, 1943. At that time the representatives of the four principal United Nations — China, the Soviet Union, the United Kingdom and the United States — recognized "the necessity of establishing at the earliest practicable date a general international organization, based on the principle of the sovereign equality of all peace-loving states, and open to membership by all such states, large and small, for the maintenance of international peace and security." [1] They also agreed that "for the purpose of maintaining international peace and security pending the re-establishment of law and order and the inauguration of a system of general security" they would consult "with one another and as occasion requires with other Members of the United Nations with a view to joint action on behalf of the community of nations," and that they would "confer and cooperate with one another and with other Members of the United Nations to bring about a practicable general agreement with respect to the regulation of armaments in the post-war period."

At Tehran, on December 1, 1943, the President of the United States, the Prime Minister of the United Kingdom and the Premier of the Soviet Union recognized fully "the supreme responsibility resting upon us and all the United Nations to make a peace which will command the good will of the overwhelming mass of the peoples of the world and banish the scourge and terror of war for many generations." They also agreed to seek the "cooperation and active participation of all nations, large and small, whose peoples in heart and mind are dedicated, as are our own peoples, to the elimination of tyranny and slavery, oppression and intolerance," and stated that they would welcome them, "as they may choose to come, into a world family of Democratic Nations." [2]

THE DUMBARTON OAKS PROPOSALS

The first important step in the direction of the actual creation of a general international organization of the kind envisaged in the Moscow Declaration was taken in the late summer of 1943 when representatives of the Governments of China, the Soviet Union, the United Kingdom and the United States met at Dumbarton Oaks for exploratory conversations. In preparation for such an exchange of views, the Department of State had undertaken, and carried out over a period of two years, careful studies and wide consultations, with a view to the elaboration of a plan which would take into account the experience of the past and which would be acceptable to American public opinion and to the Congress. Preparatory studies were also made in the foreign offices of the

---

[1] For text of Moscow Four-Power Declaration, see *ibid.*, p. 307.
[2] Department of State, *Bulletin*, IX, p. 409.

other participating governments. Each of the four governments, as a result of these preliminary studies, was able to present a draft proposal of its own for consideration.

The Conversations were in two phases. In the first phase, which extended from August 21 to September 28, 1944, the representatives of the Soviet Union, the United Kingdom and the United States were participants. The second phase, to which representatives of China, the United Kingdom and the United States were parties, was held from September 29 to October 7. The results of the agreements reached in these two series of exploratory conversations were embodied in the Dumbarton Oaks Proposals which were submitted to the four governments represented as the unanimously agreed recommendations of the four delegations.[1]

The Proposals in themselves did not constitute a charter for the proposed world organization. They were not presented in charter language, and there were important matters which they did not cover. They were submitted, as their name suggested, as tentative proposals of the four governments for a general international organization. It was the purpose of the four governments that these tentative proposals should be widely discussed and carefully considered, and that, together with such suggestions as they might elicit, they should be the basis of discussion at a general conference of the United Nations, called to frame a definitive charter.

The Proposals stated in Chapter I what the purposes of the Organization should be. These included the following: (1) "to maintain international peace and security"; (2) "to develop friendly relations among nations and to take other appropriate measures to strengthen universal peace"; (3) "to achieve international cooperation in the solution of international economic, social and other humanitarian problems"; and (4) "to afford a center for harmonizing the action of nations in the achievement of these common ends." The Proposals then went on to enumerate certain principles in accordance with which the Organization and its Members were to act in carrying out these purposes.[2] Of these principles the first to be stated and the one presumably of basic importance was that of "the sovereign equality of all peace-loving states." That determined the fundamental character of the proposed organization and made it inevitable that in its essential features the organization proposed should resemble closely the League of Nations.

The Organization envisaged in the Proposals was not to be universal in membership, at least in the beginning. Membership, it was stated, "should be open to all peace-loving states." [3] New members were to be admitted by two-thirds vote of the General Assembly upon the recom-

[1] See this volume, p. 308.   [2] Chapter II, *ibid.*   [3] Chapter III, *ibid.*, p. 309.

mendation of the Security Council, but no criteria were laid down governing qualifications for membership other than that referred to above.

The Proposals were mostly concerned with defining the organizational framework of the proposed Organization, and the basic obligations and responsibilities which members were to assume in order that the Organization might be able to carry out its purposes. The organizational framework proposed differed only in one significant respect from that of the League of Nations. As under the Covenant, provision was made for an assembly (called General Assembly) in which all members would be represented equally, a council (called Security Council) on which the great power members would have permanent representation and the smaller power members only occasional representation, an international court of justice and a secretariat. Differing from the Covenant, the Proposals envisaged two councils to perform the functions vested in the League Council: the Security Council primarily responsible for taking measures necessary to the maintenance of peace and security, and the Economic and Social Council responsible for carrying out the functions of the Organization in achieving international economic and social cooperation. In making this proposal, the Dumbarton Oaks conferees were largely following the recommendations of the Bruce Committee to the League Assembly in 1939.[1]

What distinguished the plan of the Proposals from the League system was not so much the organizational framework or the basic principles, as the manner in which the functions of the organs and the obligations of members were defined. Thus under the Proposals a clear-cut distinction was attempted between the functions of the General Assembly and those of the Security Council. Under the Covenant, the Assembly and the Council were equally empowered to deal with "any matter within the sphere of action of the League or affecting the peace of the world."[2] The Proposals attempted to delimit the functions of the two organs by making the General Assembly primarily the body for discussion and for dealing with matters of general welfare and the Security Council the body for action in the limited field of maintaining international peace and security. In fact it was proposed that the members of the Organization should confer on the Security Council "primary responsibility for the maintenance of international peace and security"[3] and that the General Assembly should not on its own initiative make recommendations on any matter relating to the maintenance of international peace and security which was being dealt with by the Security Council.

---

[1] *The Development of International Cooperation in Economic and Social Affairs.* (Bruce Report). Geneva, 1939, League of Nations Document 1939. General. 3.

[2] *Covenant of the League of Nations*, Articles 3 and 4, reprinted by World Peace Foundation, 1945.

[3] Chapter VI, Section B, par. 1, see this volume, p. 311.

This delimitation of functions, taken together with the proposal governing Council voting procedure which was agreed to at the Yalta Conference in February 1945, had the effect of establishing the permanent members of the Security Council, the so-called great powers, in a much more firmly entrenched position of dominant influence than they occupied under the Covenant. Each Member State of the League had a theoretical veto, but in practice this right of veto was considerably modified by procedures and understandings which were developed in the course of the League's experience. Under the Proposals, as completed at Yalta, the great powers alone were to enjoy this so-called right of veto, and with respect to those matters falling exclusively within the Council's competence, there was to be no possibility of appeal to the General Assembly.

In another important respect the Dumbarton Oaks plan differed from the League system. It gave to the Security Council enforcement powers which the League Council never possessed and provided for placing forces and facilities at the disposal of the Council to an extent which the Covenant had never approached. If the Security Council were able to come to a decision, it would have at its disposal under the Proposals means of action which were never available to the Council. On the other hand the Proposals made no provision for "automatic sanctions," that is, the application of sanctions by Members immediately upon the commission of an act of aggression, as had been provided in Article 16 of the Covenant. Under the Proposals no obligation to take enforcement action was to exist except as the result of a decision of the Security Council.

While placing major emphasis upon the maintenance of international peace and security by methods of peaceful settlement and enforcement action, the Proposals also recognized the desirability of creating by positive action those "conditions of stability and well-being" under which peace would be most likely to prevail. In Chapter IX, therefore, provision was made for facilitating "solutions of international economic, social and other humanitarian problems" and promoting "respect for human rights and fundamental freedoms." Responsibility for the discharge of these functions was vested in the General Assembly, and, under the authority of the General Assembly, in an Economic and Social Council consisting of eighteen members elected by the General Assembly. The provisions of the Dumbarton Oaks Proposals for facilitating economic and social cooperation were much more detailed and carefully thought out than the corresponding provisions of the Covenant. They reflected the generally held view that successful cooperation in this field was particularly necessary if the Organization was to succeed in its major objective of maintaining peace and security.

The arrangements for international economic and social cooperation which were adopted at Dumbarton Oaks were based on the assumption that by the time the Charter came into force there would already be in existence or in the process of establishment a number of specialized organizations and agencies such as the International Labor Organization, the Food and Agriculture Organization and the International Bank for Reconstruction and Development which would assume primary responsibility for dealing with matters within their respective spheres of activity. Thus it was provided that these various specialized organizations and agencies "would have responsibilities in their respective fields as defined in their statutes." [1] Each such organization or agency was to be brought into relationship, however, with the general organization on terms to be defined by agreement between the Economic and Social Council and the appropriate authority of the organization or agency in question, subject to approval by the General Assembly. Thus it was not proposed that the numerous organizations should develop and function independently of each other and without regard to common interests and purposes.

The Dumbarton Oaks Proposals left a number of matters unresolved. Until the Crimea Conference, there was no agreement on the matter of the Council's voting procedure. It was agreed that there should be an international court of justice, but the Proposals left wholly unanswered the question whether this court was to be the Permanent Court of International Justice or an entirely new court. Nor was the nature of the court's jurisdiction decided. There were no provisions included with respect to the administration of non-self-governing territories, though this matter had been the subject of an important article of the Covenant. The question of the relation of the proposed Organization to the League of Nations was left unanswered. A number of other matters, such as the registration of treaties, were not touched upon. Some of these, it was anticipated, would be covered by later proposals of the four governments; others would presumably be left open until the United Nations Conference met.

THE YALTA AGREEMENT

The question of voting procedure in the Security Council was taken up at the Crimea (Yalta) Conference of February 3–11, 1945.[2] At this Conference, attended by the heads of the Governments of the Soviet Union, the United Kingdom and the United States and their advisers, agreement was reached on the formula which was subsequently included in the Dumbarton Oaks Proposals as Section C of Chapter VI. The agreement provided that all decisions on questions of procedure should be taken by a special majority of seven votes, and that decisions on

[1] *Dumbarton Oaks Proposals*, Chapter X, Section A, par. 2, see this volume, p. 317.
[2] See this volume, p. 318.

other questions should be taken by a like majority, with the added requirement of unanimity of the permanent members. It was provided, however, that in the case of decisions under Chapter VIII, Section A, and the second sentence of paragraph 1 of Chapter VII, Section C, a party to a dispute should abstain from voting.

It was also announced at the conclusion of the Crimea Conference that the three governments had agreed that a conference of the United Nations should be called to meet at San Francisco on April 25, 1945 "to prepare the charter of such an organization, along the lines proposed in the informal conversations at Dumbarton Oaks." The Government of China subsequently accepted the invitation to become a sponsor of the Conference, but the Provisional Government of France, while agreeing to participate in the Conference, chose not to become one of the Sponsoring Governments.[1]

The United Nations Conference on International Organization

Invitations to the Conference were issued on March 5 by the Government of the United States in the names of the four Sponsoring Governments.[2] The complete list of the Sponsoring Governments and the Governments invited by them to attend the Conference follows:

Australia	Iraq
Belgium	Lebanon
Bolivia	Liberia
Brazil	Luxembourg
Canada	Mexico
Chile	Netherlands
China	New Zealand
Colombia	Nicaragua
Costa Rica	Norway
Cuba	Panama
Czechoslovakia	Paraguay
Dominican Republic	Peru
Ecuador	Philippine Commonwealth
Egypt	Saudi Arabia
El Salvador	Syria
Ethiopia	Turkey
France	Union of South Africa
Greece	Union of Soviet Socialist Republics
Guatemala	United Kingdom
Haiti	United States of America
Honduras	Uruguay
India	Venezuela
Iran	Yugoslavia

[1] Department of State, *Bulletin*, XII, p. 394.
[2] See this volume, p. 320.

In the invitation, it was suggested that the Conference consider the Dumbarton Oaks Proposals "as affording a basis" for the proposed charter. It was also indicated that in the event the invited government desired "in advance of the Conference to present views or comments concerning the proposals," the Government of the United States would "be pleased to transmit such views and comments to the other participating Governments."

The Conference convened at San Francisco on April 25, 1945, with all the sponsoring and invited governments represented. Subsequently the Governments of Argentina, the Byelorussian Soviet Socialist Republic, the Ukrainian Soviet Socialist Republic and Denmark were invited to send representatives, bringing the total of participating governments up to 50.[1]

The agenda of the Conference was agreed to at a meeting of the Heads of Delegations on April 27, 1945.[2] The meeting approved a recommendation of the temporary Secretary-General that the agenda should be "the Dumbarton Oaks Proposals, as supplemented at the Crimea Conference, and by the Chinese proposals agreed to by the Sponsoring Governments, and the comments thereon submitted by the participating countries." It was also agreed that a time limit of one week (until midnight of May 4) should be set for the submission of proposed amendments and comments to the Secretary-General. It was understood, however, that this did not apply to trusteeship matters since the Conference had no formal proposals on this subject before it at that time. The comments and proposed amendments which were thus presented were printed as Conference documents and were brought together in a loose-leaf volume with the title, *Comments and Proposed Amendments Concerning Dumbarton Oaks, Submitted by the Delegations to the United Nations Conference on International Organization, May 7, 1945*. The Secretariat of the Conference later prepared a *Guide to Amendments, Comments and Proposals Concerning the Dumbarton Oaks Proposals for a General International Organization*,[3] which contained the texts of the Dumbarton Oaks Proposals and the amendments agreed to by the Sponsoring Governments, and an index to the proposals and comments of the other participating governments.

ORGANIZATION OF THE CONFERENCE

At the fifth plenary session on April 30, the Conference adopted a report, introduced by the Rapporteur of the Steering Committee, defin-

---

[1] Provision was made at the Conference for Poland to sign as an original Member of the U.N.O., and on October 15, 1945 the Foreign Minister of the Polish Provisional Government signed the Charter on behalf of Poland, thus making 51 signatories to the instrument. Department of State, *Bulletin*, XIII, p. 627.

[2] UNCIO, *Meeting of the Heads of Delegations to Organize the Conference, April 27, 1945*, Doc. 30, DC/5 (1).   [3] *Ibid.*, Doc. 288, G/38.

ing the permanent organization of the Conference.[1] This provided for the organization of the Conference into four general committees, four commissions and twelve technical committees. The general committees included the Steering Committee, consisting of the chairmen of all the Delegations; the Executive Committee, consisting of the chairmen of the Delegations of the Sponsoring Governments, and ten other governments, including that of France [2]; the Coordination Committee, composed of one representative of each state represented on the Executive Committee; and the Credentials Committee. The meetings of the Conference in plenary session and of the Commissions were open to the public; the meetings of the committees and subcommittees were open only to those with proper credentials.

The four Commissions were set up to develop general principles to guide the technical committees and subcommittees included within each Commission, to consider the recommendations of their technical committees and the relationships of such recommendations to those made by the technical committees of other Commissions, and to "recommend to the Conference in Plenary Session proposed texts for adoption as parts of the Charter."[3] All Delegations were entitled to representation on each Commission. The four Commissions were set up with the following titles: Commission I (General Provisions); Commission II (General Assembly); Commission III (Security Council); and Commission IV (Judicial Organization).

The technical committees were set up within the Commissions to formulate recommendations on the various parts of the agenda assigned to them. More specifically the technical committees were given the function of preparing and recommending to their respective Commissions draft provisions for the Charter of the United Nations relating to the matters dealt with in those parts of the Dumbarton Oaks Proposals referred to them and to the comments and suggestions relevant thereto submitted by the governments participating in the Conference. The following table gives the organization of technical committees according to Commission, subject matter and specific provisions of the Dumbarton Oaks Proposals which were referred to each:

COMMITTEE [4]	TITLE	PROVISIONS OF DUMBARTON OAKS REFERRED TO COMMITTEE
Commission I:	*General Provisions*	
Committee I/1	Preamble, Purposes and Principles	Chapters I and II

[1] *Ibid., Addendum to Verbatim Minutes of the Fifth Plenary Session, April 30, 1945,* Doc. 42, P/10 (a).

[2] The following governments were represented on the Executive Committee: Australia, Brazil, Canada, Chile, China, Czechoslovakia, France, Iran, Mexico, Netherlands, Union of Soviet Socialist Republics, United Kingdom, United States and Yugoslavia.   [3] *Ibid.,* Doc. 42, P/10 (a), cited above, p. 2.

[4] The Roman numeral was used to indicate the Commission within which the Committee was set up, and the Arabic numeral, the number of the Committee within the Commission.

COMMITTEE	TITLE	PROVISIONS OF DUMBARTON OAKS REFERRED TO COMMITTEE
Committee I/2	Membership, Amendment and Secretariat	Chapters III, IV, X and XI
Commission II:	*General Assembly*	
Committee II/1	Structure and Procedures	Chapter V, Sections A, C, D, and the pertinent paragraphs of Section B
Committee II/2	Political and Security Functions	Chapter V, esp. Section B
Committee II/3	Economic and Social Cooperation	Chapter IX, and pertinent paragraphs of Chapter V
Committee II/4	Trusteeship System	The terms of reference of this Committee were "to prepare and recommend to Commission II, and to Commission III as necessary, draft provisions on principles and mechanism of a system of international trusteeship for such dependent territories as may by subsequent agreement be placed thereunder." [1]
Commission III:	*Security Council*	
Committee III/1	Structure and Procedures	Chapter VI, Sections A, C, and D, and the pertinent paragraphs of Section B [2]
Committee III/2	Peaceful Settlement	Chapter VIII, Section A
Committee III/3	Enforcement Arrangements	Chapter VIII, Section B and Chapter XII
Committee III/4	Regional Arrangements	Chapter VIII, Section C
Commission IV:	*Judicial Organization*	
Committee IV/1	International Court of Justice	Chapter VII
Committee IV/2	Legal Problems	The terms of reference of this Committee were "to prepare and recommend to Commission IV draft provisions for the Charter of the United Nations relating to matters dealt with in connection with the functioning of the United Nations Organization, such as registration of treaties, treaty obligations inconsistent with the Charter, the juridical status of the Organization, and privileges and immunities of officials of the Organization." [3]

[1] *Ibid.*, p. 4.   [2] All of Section B was subsequently referred to Committee III/1.
[3] *Ibid.*, p. 5.

CONFERENCE PROCEDURE

The Committees followed no uniform pattern of operation in the performance of their functions. All faced the necessity of introducing some systematic order into the mass of proposals and comments which were before them for consideration. Each Committee dealt with this problem in its own way. The common practice was for the Committee to prepare, usually through a subcommittee, a working document or paper which would be the basis for the Committee's subsequent discussions and decisions. Furthermore, there was no uniformity in the manner in which these discussions were organized and the decisions taken. In one Committee, the work of examination and detailed consideration was turned over to a subcommittee whose recommendations were then discussed and acted upon by the full Committee. In another case, the Committee considered and gave answers to general questions which were suggested by the detailed proposals and comments, referred to a drafting subcommittee the task of translating these general propositions into specific texts, and then considered and acted upon the texts proposed. In still another case, the Committee considered the amendments proposed, indicated its approval of certain of these amendments in principle or as to their general ideas, and then referred to a drafting subcommittee the task of preparing a final text, which was then submitted to the full Committee for final approval.

The work of the Committees extended over a period of about a month and a half, with numerous periods of relative inactivity due to disagreements which had to be eliminated by direct negotiations between governments. Some idea of the activity of the Committees is given by the following statistics on the number of meetings held:

Committee I/1 — 17 meetings	Committee III/1 — 27 meetings
Committee I/2 — 29 meetings	Committee III/2 — 15 meetings
Committee II/1— 15 meetings	Committee III/3 — 22 meetings
Committee II/2— 25 meetings	Committee III/4 — 6 meetings
Committee II/3— 20 meetings	Committee IV/1 — 22 meetings
Committee II/4— 15 meetings	Committee IV/2 — 16 meetings

These figures do not, however, accurately indicate the amount of work done since they fail to take into account subcommittee meetings which constituted an important part of the total work of the Committees. In the case of certain Committees, subcommittee meetings were nearly as numerous as, if not more numerous than, meetings of the full Committee. Because of the composition and size of the Committees, it was often found desirable, even necessary, to refer to subcommittees questions of a highly technical or specially difficult nature. Besides, the device of a joint subcommittee was often resorted to in order to find the solution of a problem of concern to two or more Committees.

The recommendations of the Committees, in the form of texts for inclusion in the Charter, were submitted to the Commissions for approval. In meetings of the Commissions, it was possible for decisions to be reopened and for further discussion to take place. This was not commonly done, however. In contrast with the Committee meetings which were not open to the public, the Commission meetings were public and were reported in full. The Commissions in turn reported to the Conference in plenary session.

The recommendations of the Committees were also referred to the Coordination Committee which, with the assistance of the Advisory Committee of Jurists, reviewed texts with an eye to improving their phraseology, securing uniformity of terminology, eliminating contradictions and inconsistencies, and obtaining the best arrangement of the substance of the proposed charter. The Coordination Committee could, on its own responsibility, make no change of a substantive nature, though it might ask a Committee to consider a proposal involving a change of substance which originated with it. In general, the function of the Coordination Committee, as suggested by its name, was to combine the Committee texts together into one document which would be clear and logical in its arrangement, all the while conforming to the substantive recommendations of the Committees as approved by the Commissions. The final draft of the Charter as thus prepared was then submitted to the Steering Committee for its approval, and finally to the Conference in plenary session. The signing of the Charter by the delegates on June 26, 1945 followed final approval by the Conference on the previous day.[1]

It thus becomes clear that the process which the Conference followed in the making of the Charter was one which gave ample opportunity for discussion, and more particularly afforded the opportunity to the delegates of those states not represented at the Dumbarton Oaks Conversations to express their points of view and support their proposals for amendment. Furthermore, decisions could be taken by a two-thirds vote of those present and voting. This process of necessity operated within the framework of a political situation which gave the Sponsoring Governments, because of their leading role in the conduct of the war and their indispensability to the new Organization, a measure of influence on the decisions taken which the smaller powers could not hope to have. Thus freedom of discussion, equality of voting power and the possibility of taking decisions by a special majority did not in fact deprive the great powers of an effective veto since the members of the Conference, when faced with the possibility that a particular decision would be unacceptable to one of the Sponsoring Governments and might for that

[1] UNCIO, *Verbatim Minutes of the Ninth Plenary Session*, Doc. 1210, P/20.

reason prevent it from joining the Organization, did not find it expedient to force the issue and accept the consequences.

In spite, however, of this effective "veto power" which a great power possessed, there were in practice fairly important questions on which the smaller nations were able to press their points of view successfully in the face of considerable great power resistance. While it can be argued that these matters were not usually of first importance and that, if they were, the concessions made by the great powers were more apparent than real, it would seem to be a justifiable view of the work of the Conference that the smaller powers did succeed in many instances in introducing important changes in the Dumbarton Oaks Proposals, even as modified by the amendments proposed by the Sponsoring Governments. It should be added that many of these amendments incorporated proposals of the smaller powers.

While the organization and procedures of the Conference were reasonably successful in achieving full discussion and fair consideration of the numerous proposals and points of view presented, they were not equally successful in producing a technically well-drafted document. The fact that different sections of the Dumbarton Oaks Proposals were referred to different technical committees, the assignments often being rather arbitrarily made, resulted in particular subjects falling within the competence of two or more technical committees. Thus, on the question of method of electing the Secretary-General, there were three technical committees which were concerned (Committees I/2, II/1, and III/1). The result was that in the absence of provision for proper coordination considerable confusion resulted in the closing days of the Conference because of conflicting conclusions reached. Furthermore, there were variations in the form in which Committee recommendations were submitted, and considerable lack of uniformity in the use of terms. Finally, the considerable pressure brought to bear on the Conference in its later stages to make particular deadlines had the result of placing on the Coordination Committee a superhuman responsibility which, with the greatest effort, could not possibly be performed in a wholly satisfactory manner. The result is that from a technical point of view the Charter undoubtedly leaves much to be desired. A simpler organization of the Conference, and more flexible procedures, combined with less pressure to make deadlines, would undoubtedly have made possible a clearer and more concise document.

CONFERENCE DOCUMENTATION AND RECORDS

Any international conference which undertakes a task of the dimensions of that facing UNCIO is bound to produce a vast volume of documentation. The Conference at San Francisco was no exception. The average daily output of documents was about half a million sheets of paper and on one day 1,700,000 sheets were issued and distributed. Seventy-eight tons of paper were used for the documentation of the Conference.[1] Much of this documentation was restricted as to circulation while the Conference was in session. This of course was in line with the general policy of only opening to the public meetings of the Conference in plenary session and of the Commissions, and limiting attendance at meetings of the Committees where the real work of the Conference was done to those with proper credentials. In general, the Committee documents, including specially designated working documents, were thus restricted, together with secretarial notices and communications. Many of the documents containing comments and proposals of the participating governments were at first restricted but in the course of the Conference most of these restrictions were removed. At the final plenary session of the Conference on June 25, 1945, the Conference accepted the recommendation of the Secretariat that all restrictions on the publication of documents classified as "Restricted" be lifted, with the exception of the working documents of the Coordination Committee, decision with respect to them being left to the Preparatory Commission.[2]

All the documents were published in the working languages of the Conference: English and French. Some were also published in Chinese, Russian and Spanish, which together with English and French, were the official languages of the Conference. With the exception of the *Journal* and the *Précis of Committee Proceedings*, which carried serial numbers and dates, and of forms and secretariat notices on blue paper (symbol SEC), all documents carried the designation Doc. or WD. in the upper right hand corner and a documents number which was assigned in sequence (Doc. 5 or WD. 5). Such documents in addition carried symbols which indicated the subject-matter of the document in question. The following system of classification by symbols was used:

G — general material, including Orders of the Day, Dumbarton Oaks Proposals, comments and proposed amendments, etc.

EX–SEC — Notices from the Executive Secretary (some overlapping with SEC).

P — agenda, verbatim minutes and other documents of plenary sessions.

DC — agenda, summary reports and other documents of meetings of Delegation Chairmen (later Steering Committee).

ST — same for Steering Committee.

[1] Eagleton, Clyde, "The Charter Adopted at San Francisco," *The American Political Science Review*, XXXIX (October 1945), p. 935.

[2] UNCIO, *Memorandum on Recommendation by the Secretariat as to Removal of Conference Documents from Restricted Category, June 24, 1945*, Doc. 1189, EX–SEC/20; *Verbatim Minutes of the Ninth Plenary Session*, Doc. 1210, P/20, p. 1.

ST/C — same for Credentials Committee.

EX — same for Executive Committee.

CO — same for Coordination Committee, including Advisory Committee of Jurists

Roman numeral, for example, I — same for Commission designated by number used.

Roman numeral followed by Arabic numeral, for example, I/1 — same for technical committee designated by numbers used.

Roman numeral, followed by Arabic numeral and capital letter, for example, I/1/A — same for subcommittee.

Documents thus designated by symbol carried a number indicating its order of issue within the series. Thus a document carrying the symbol and number III/2/5 was the fifth document to come from Committee III/2. If a document was amended, this was indicated by adding a number in parentheses, beginning with 1, to the symbol and number, and if an addition was made to the document, i.e. another document appended, this was indicated by adding a small letter in parentheses, beginning with a.

The records of the plenary sessions of the Conference and of the Commissions were published in the form of verbatim minutes. In the case of meetings of the technical committees, only summary reports of the discussions and decisions were prepared and distributed. These in many cases, and particularly in the early days of the Conference, were quite abbreviated in form. Under pressure from certain delegations, these became more complete in the case of some committees. Verbatim records of committee discussions were made and were available for use by the secretariat and delegates, but since they were not edited they have little value as records of the discussions. In fact, in some cases, they may be actually misleading because of their incompleteness and inaccuracies. Generally speaking, there were no records made of the discussions and decisions of subcommittees, with the exception of the reports to committees, and in some cases, apart from actual texts proposed, these were not presented in written form.

Except for the *Journal*, which was printed, the documents of the Conference were distributed in the first instance in mimeographed form. Some of the more important documents were subsequently distributed at the Conference in photolithographed form. During the concluding days of the Conference arrangements were made between the Secretary-General of the Conference and the Chairman and Associate Chairman of the United Nations Information Board for the reproduction photolithographically and publication in bound volumes of the documents of the Conference in so far as restrictions on publications had been removed.[1]

[1] The volumes are now in process of publication by the United Nations Information Organizations, in cooperation with the Library of Congress.

The treaty character of the Charter is further emphasized by the considerations which led another technical committee (Committee IV/2, Legal Problems) to recommend the omission of any provision governing the interpretation of the Charter. After pointing out that "under unitary forms of national government the final determination of such a question may be vested in the highest court or in some other national authority," the Committee's report went on to say:

However, the nature of the Organization and of its operation would not seem to be such as to invite the inclusion in the Charter of any provision of this nature. If two Member States are at variance concerning the correct interpretation of the Charter, they are of course free to submit the dispute to the International Court of Justice as in the case of any other treaty.[1]

THE CONTENT OF THE CHARTER

The Charter as finally adopted contained important modifications of the Dumbarton Oaks Proposals. Entirely new material was introduced, and provisions of the Dumbarton Oaks plan were changed, in major as well as minor respects. And yet the essential character of the Dumbarton Oaks plan remains. The Organization which the Charter provides is fundamentally in line with the League of Nations and Dumbarton Oaks ideas. It is based on the principle of voluntary cooperation between states in the promotion of common objectives. Like the Covenant and the Proposals, it recognizes the important inequalities of states and erects a structure which takes into account these inequalities. Following the line of the Dumbarton Oaks Proposals, it recognizes the larger powers as having special rights not accorded to the smaller, and it places on them correspondingly larger responsibilities. In this respect it departs from the express pattern of the League system though not departing as widely from its plain implications.

Largely for reasons of political expediency and because of certain adverse attitudes and prejudices that had developed, the revision of the League system was never seriously considered as a means of providing for the desired international organization. Rather it was decided to start from scratch and set up an organization which would not have to combat the unfavorable psychological attitudes which a revised League would very likely have to face in some quarters. It was of course soon discovered that it was as impossible as it was unwise to disregard the experience of the League of Nations. Those who carried out the preliminary studies leading up to the exchanges of views between governments found it indispensable to the successful accomplishment of their tasks to concern themselves with this experience. But in any case it was possible in a formal sense to start anew, to give the organization a

[1] *Ibid.*, *Report of the Rapporteur of Committee IV/2, as Approved by the Committee*, Doc. 933, IV/2/43 (2), p. 7.

DEVELOPMENT AND GENERAL PLAN

GENERAL FORM AND CHARACTER OF THE CHARTER

As compared with the Covenant of the League of Nations, the Charter is a lengthy document. It is also long as compared with the Dumbarton Oaks Proposals, though such a comparison is unfair since the Proposals gained their greater brevity in large part from their incompleteness. The Charter (apart from the Statute of the Court) contains 111 Articles, in addition to the Preamble and concluding provisions. Since the Covenant contained only 26, one might jump to the erroneous conclusion that the Charter is approximately four times as long. The greater number of Articles in the Charter is in large part due to the deliberate decision to keep the Articles of the Charter short. In a sense the Chapters of the Charter correspond more closely to the Articles of the Covenant, so far as length and content are concerned.

Nor does the Charter follow closely the structural pattern of the Dumbarton Oaks Proposals. Whereas the Proposals were divided into chapters, sections and paragraphs, each numbered consecutively within the next larger division, the architects of the Charter decided, while retaining the division into chapters, to put all the material of the Charter, apart from the Preamble and concluding provisions, into articles consecutively numbered from beginning to end. Subtitles within chapters are retained but without being given the position of numbered sections.

While the Preamble to the Charter opens with the words "We the peoples of the United Nations," the concluding words of the Preamble, "Accordingly our respective Governments, through representatives assembled in the city of San Francisco," etc., make it clear that the Charter is not a constituent act of the peoples of the United Nations, but rather an agreement freely entered into between governments. In this respect it does not differ from the Covenant of the League of Nations. The contractual character of the Charter is further emphasized by the recognition given in Article 2 to "the principle of the sovereign equality" of all Members of the Organization and by the provision that an amendment to the Charter shall come into force only when it has been ratified "in accordance with their respective constitutional processes by two-thirds of the Members of the Organization, including all the permanent members of the Security Council."[1] It is also to be noted that while the Charter contains no provision for withdrawal, the technical committee concerned with the matter (Committee I/2), in its report to Commission I, stated that in its opinion a Member would not be bound to remain in the Organization "if its rights and obligations as such were changed by Charter amendment in which it has not concurred and which it finds itself unable to accept."[2]

[1] *Charter of the United Nations*, Article 108.
[2] UNCIO, *Report of the Rapporteur of Committee I/2 on Chapter* (Membership), Doc. 1178, 1/2/76 (2), p. 5–6.

different name, and to provide it with what was in form at least, and to a considerable extent in substance, a new constitution.

1. *Purposes and Principles*

The original Dumbarton Oaks Proposals contained no preamble. In a sense the chapter containing the statement of purposes served that end. At San Francisco, however, it was decided to introduce a preamble. Of necessity this presented a drafting difficulty, since with the substance of the original chapters on purposes and principles retained, considerable duplication of ideas was inevitable.

The purposes of the Organization are stated in Article 1. These indicate the direction which the activities of the Organization are to take and the common ends of its members. They are stated in general and inclusive terms to make it clear that the Organization is not set up with any narrow end in view but rather for the purpose of promoting the common interests of states in peace, security and general well-being. The Organization is not to be exclusively concerned with the settlement of disputes that have arisen between states and with the taking of action to maintain or restore peace in the face of a threat or an actual use of force. To be sure, the first purpose is stated to be "to maintain international peace and security" by taking measures to remove threats to the peace and suppress acts of aggression, and by adjusting or settling disputes and situations which might lead to a breach of the peace. But there are also included among the purposes of the Organization the following: "to develop friendly relations among nations based on respect for the principle of equal rights and self-determination of peoples, and to take other appropriate measures to strengthen universal peace"; "to achieve international cooperation in solving international problems of an economic, social, cultural or humanitarian character, and in promoting and encouraging respect for human rights and for fundamental freedoms for all without distinction as to race, sex, language, or religion"; and "to be a center for harmonizing the actions of nations in the attainment of these common ends." It is difficult to think of a single matter within the sphere of international relations or affecting relations between states which cannot be brought within the scope of the Organization's activities in the achievement of these comprehensive purposes. Of course it must be borne in mind that this statement of ends is not in itself a grant of authority and that furthermore, certain restrictive provisions of the Charter do limit the activities in which the Organization may engage for these declared purposes.

Following the statement of purposes in Article 1, we have in Article 2 of the Charter an enumeration of the principles in accordance with which the Organization and its Members are to act in pursuit of the declared purposes of the Organization. These principles include the following: the sovereign equality of Members, the loyal fulfillment of obligations under the Charter, the peaceful settlement of international disputes "in such a manner that international peace and security, and justice, are not endangered," abstention from any threat or use of force "against the territorial integrity or political independence of any state," full assistance to the Organization in any action that it takes under the Charter, no assistance to any state against which such action is being taken, enforcement of respect for these principles by non-members in so far as it may be necessary to the maintenance of international peace and security, and no intervention in matters which are essentially within the domestic jurisdiction of a state.

For the most part these principles are in the nature of basic directives which clearly must guide the conduct of Organization and Members alike if the declared purposes of the Organization are to be attained. Nor is the application of these principles limited to Members, for in a paragraph somewhat reminiscent of Article XVII of the Covenant the general principle is laid down, binding on the Members of the Organization, that the conduct of states not Members of the Organization is to be made to conform to these principles "so far as may be necessary for the maintenance of international peace and security."

One of the principles enumerated in this Article, however, appears to strike a somewhat negative note. The new paragraph 7, a revised version of a paragraph of the Dumbarton Oaks Proposals which applied only to the pacific settlement of disputes,[1] denies to the Organization any authority "to intervene in matters which are essentially within the domestic jurisdiction of any state" or to "require the Members to submit such matters to settlement under the present Charter." It is stated, however, that this principle shall not prejudice the application of enforcement measures under Chapter VII. This paragraph constitutes perhaps the most substantial limitation that is to be found anywhere in the whole Charter upon the activity of the Organization.

2. *Membership and Organs*

The Charter contains much more detailed provisions on the question of membership than were to be found in the Dumbarton Oaks Proposals. The distinction between original and elected Members, contained in the Covenant of the League,[2] but which was not made, at least expressly, in the Dumbarton Oaks Proposals, is clearly stated. The original Members are to be those states which, having participated in the United Nations Conference at San Francisco or having previously signed the Declaration by United Nations of January 1, 1942, sign the present

[1] Chapter VIII, Section A, paragraph 7, see this volume, p. 314.
[2] Article 1.

Charter and ratify it in accordance with Article 110.[1] Elected Members are to be those states admitted to membership by decision of the General Assembly upon recommendation of the Security Council. The criterion laid down in the Dumbarton Oaks Proposals for membership has been supplemented so far as elected Members are concerned by the requirements that applicants for membership must "accept the obligations contained in the present Charter" and be judged by the Organization "able and willing to carry out these obligations." [2]

A Member of the United Nations against which preventive or enforcement action has been taken by the Security Council may be suspended from the exercise of the rights of membership by the General Assembly upon the recommendation of the Security Council.[3] In like manner a Member "which has persistently violated the Principles contained in the present Charter" may be expelled.[4] There is, however, in the Charter no express provision regarding voluntary withdrawal. This matter was discussed at length in technical committee, and while it was the decision that no express provision regarding withdrawal should be made, the Committee decided to include in its report an expression of its view that the right of withdrawal could be exercised.[5]

While the Charter does not provide for universal membership as was advocated by many delegations at the Conference, it does, by its specific provisions, make possible the eventual attainment of that goal. The criteria of membership laid down in the Charter are no more inherently restrictive than were the corresponding provisions of the Covenant of the League of Nations. Only in one respect do the Charter provisions present an opportunity for the limitation of membership that was not present under the Covenant. In order for the General Assembly to admit a state to membership, it must have before it a recommendation to that effect by the Security Council. Since such a recommendation can only be made with the concurrence of all the permanent members of that body, one permanent member of the Security Council can prevent the admission of any state which it desires to exclude. This possibility did not exist under the Covenant.

The Charter adds to the list of organs recognized by the Dumbarton Oaks Proposals as being the "principal organs" [6] of the Organization the Economic and Social Council and the Trusteeship Council.[7] The first was provided for in the Proposals, but was not given the recognition

---

[1] *Charter of the United Nations*, Article 3.
[2] *Ibid.*, Article 4.
[3] *Ibid.*, Article 5.
[4] *Ibid.*, Article 6.
[5] See comment on Article 6, this volume, p. 84.
[6] These were a General Assembly, a Security Council, an international court of justice and a Secretariat.
[7] *Charter of the United Nations*, Article 7.

in question, presumably because it was felt to be in a more subordinate position than the organs included in the list. It was included at San Francisco because of the increased importance that came to be attached to it in connection with the further development of the powers of the Organization in the economic and social field. The second was not provided for in the Proposals, and so the question of its inclusion first came up at the Conference when the decision was finally taken to set up an international trusteeship system.

3. *The General Assembly*

The first-named of the principal organs of the United Nations and the first to be treated in the Charter as to its composition, functions, powers and procedure is the General Assembly. This is logical in view of the fact that the Assembly is the most representative organ of the United Nations, and the one from which the authority of certain of the other organs is largely derived. It is also the organ which is chiefly responsible for the performance of the broad functions of discussion, recommendation, review, election, financial control and initiation of Charter amendments which will be so important to the successful functioning of the Organization. If the organization of the United Nations were to be likened to that of a state, the General Assembly might be called the Parliament or Congress of the United Nations. This analogy should not be pressed too far, however, because, since the United Nations is not a world state having independent powers of its own, the General Assembly is not a legislative body in the sense in which that term is commonly used. It can initiate studies, discuss and recommend, but it cannot adopt legislation binding upon the Member States or their individual citizens.

The General Assembly consists of the "Members of the United Nations," each of which is to have "not more than five representatives."[1] Each has one vote.[2] Decisions on "important questions," such as recommendations with respect to the maintenance of international peace and security, the election of non-permanent members of the Security Council, the admission of new Members, and budgetary questions, are to be taken by two-thirds majority of those present and voting.[3] Decisions on other questions, including the determination of additional categories of "important questions," are to be made by a majority of those present and voting.[4] The General Assembly is to meet in regular annual sessions and in such special sessions as occasion may require. It adopts its own rules of procedure, including rules governing the public character of its proceedings.[5]

[1] *Ibid.*, Article 9.   [2] *Ibid.*, Article 18, paragraph 1.
[3] *Ibid.*, paragraph 2.   [4] *Ibid.*, paragraph 3.
[5] *Ibid.*, Article 21.

The functions and powers of the General Assembly cover a wide range. In general, they are of the character usually associated with a legislative body, though as has been stated the Assembly does not have the power to legislate in the ordinary sense. The functions of the General Assembly may be broadly described as *deliberative, supervisory, financial, elective* and *constituent*.

The *deliberative* function is performed by virtue of extensive powers of discussion and recommendation which the Charter vests in the General Assembly. Under the Proposals the General Assembly was to have "the right to consider the general principles of cooperation in the maintenance of international peace and security," "to discuss any questions relating to the maintenance of international peace and security," and to make recommendations with regard to any such principles or questions.[1] The technical committee of the Conference concerned with the powers of the General Assembly (Committee II/2) at first recommended that this power of discussion and recommendation be extended to "any matter within the sphere of international relations." [2] Subsequently, following an appeal by the Soviet Delegation to the Steering Committee of the Conference, and at the request of that body, the Committee reconsidered the matter and adopted the formula which was finally approved by the Conference.[3] Under the new phraseology, the General Assembly may discuss "any questions or any matters within the scope of the present Charter or relating to the powers and functions of any organs provided for in the present Charter." [4] Furthermore, it may make recommendations thereon to the members of the Organization or to the Security Council, subject to the provision, taken over in substance from the Dumbarton Oaks Proposals, that the General Assembly is not to make a recommendation regarding any dispute or situation while the Security Council is exercising in respect thereof the functions assigned to it in the present Charter, unless the Council so requests.[5] Furthermore, by another provision added by the Conference, a procedure is laid down by which the General Assembly will be informed when a matter is being dealt with by the Security Council under the Charter and when the Security Council has ceased to deal with the matter.[6]

The Charter also gives the Assembly the power to initiate studies and make recommendations for purposes of "promoting international cooperation in the political field and encouraging the progressive development of international law and its codification," and "promoting inter-

[1] *Dumbarton Oaks Proposals*, Chapter V, Section B, paragraph 1, see this volume, p. 309.

[2] UNCIO, *Report of the Rapporteur of Committee II/2*, Doc. 1122, II/2/52 (1), p. 4.   [3] *Ibid.*

[4] *Charter of the United Nations*, Article 10.

[5] *Ibid.*, Article 12, paragraph 1.

[6] *Ibid.*, paragraph 2.

national cooperation in the economic, social, cultural, educational, and health fields, and assisting in the realization of human rights and fundamental freedoms for all without distinction as to race, sex, language, or religion." [1] Under a new Article adopted by the Conference upon the recommendation of the Sponsoring Governments the General Assembly is given broad authority to "recommend measures for the peaceful adjustment of any situation, regardless of origin, which it deems likely to impair the general welfare or friendly relations among nations." [2] While this power is limited to that of recommendation, it may conceivably in the course of time very closely approximate an international legislative authority, in that recommendations made by a representative body with the moral authority the Assembly is likely to acquire should have great weight.

The *supervisory* function of the General Assembly is based on numerous grants of power to control and regulate the activities of other organs and agencies. While the Security Council is made independently responsible for the maintenance of international peace and security, it is to some extent subject to Assembly influence. Not only is it stated in the Charter that the General Assembly "shall receive and consider annual and special reports from the Security Council," as was envisaged in the Dumbarton Oaks Proposals, but it is also specified that these reports "shall include an account of the measures that the Security Council has decided upon or taken to maintain international peace and security." [3] These may then be discussed by the General Assembly and may lead to recommendations by that body to the Council or to Member States. The General Assembly is also to receive reports from other organs of the United Nations. [4]

Both the Trusteeship Council and the Economic and Social Council are to act under the authority and close supervision of the General Assembly. [5] The General Assembly is given specific supervisory powers in connection with the administration of trust territories. [6] The staff of the Secretariat is to be appointed under regulations established by the General Assembly. [7] The General Assembly is also empowered to make recommendations for the coordination of the policies and activities of the various specialized agencies which either operate directly under its authority or are brought into relation with the Organization by agreements which the General Assembly approves. [8]

The *financial* function of the General Assembly is closely related to the supervisory. In the performance of this function the Assembly is directed to "consider and approve the budget of the Organization," [9]

[1] *Ibid.*, Article 13.
[2] *Ibid.*, Article 14.
[3] *Ibid.*, Article 15, paragraph 1.
[4] *Ibid.*, paragraph 2.
[5] *Ibid.*, Articles 60 and 85.
[6] *Ibid.*, Articles 85 and 87.
[7] *Ibid.*, Article 101.
[8] *Ibid.*, Articles 57, 58, 60, 63.
[9] *Ibid.*, Article 17, paragraph 1.

and to apportion expenses among the Members.[1] The General Assembly is also made responsible for approving financial and budgetary arrangements with specialized agencies and examining the administrative budgets of such agencies "with a view to making recommendations to the agencies concerned." [2]

The *elective* function of the General Assembly places it in a central position in the Organization since most of the other organs are dependent upon the Assembly for the choice of their members. Thus the General Assembly elects the non-permanent members of the Security Council,[3] all the members of the Economic and Social Council,[4] and a part of the members of the Trusteeship Council.[5] Acting concurrently with the Security Council, it participates in the election of judges of the International Court of Justice.[6] The Secretary-General is "appointed" by the General Assembly upon the recommendation of the Security Council.[7]

The *constituent* function of the General Assembly finds expression in the provision that amendments shall in the first instance be adopted by two-thirds vote of the Assembly.[8] It is also provided that the decision to call a General Conference to review the Charter shall be taken by the General Assembly, with the concurrence of the Security Council.[9] As we have already seen, it is the General Assembly which, upon the recommendation of the Security Council, admits new members to the Organization.[10]

This survey of the functions and powers of the General Assembly under the provisions of the Charter makes it appear as fairly certain that the role of the Assembly in the United Nations Organization will be important. In one respect, the General Assembly's position in the United Nations Organization differs from that of the Assembly under the Covenant. The provisions of the Covenant did not differentiate clearly the functions and powers of the Assembly and Council, particularly in connection with the maintenance of peace. In practice a differentiation of function did emerge, but it was continually being modified by changes that occurred in the prestige and influence of the two bodies. A certain amount of confusion and uncertainty necessarily resulted. The Charter attempts to make it clear that as regards *action* for the maintenance of international peace and security the Security Council is primarily responsible. The General Assembly has extensive powers

[1] *Ibid.*, paragraph 2.
[2] *Ibid.*, paragraph 3.
[3] *Ibid.*, Article 23, paragraph 1.
[4] *Ibid.*, Article 61, paragraph 1.
[5] *Ibid.*, Article 86, paragraph 1.
[6] *Statute of the International Court of Justice*, Article 4, paragraph 1.
[7] *Charter of the United Nations*, Article 97.
[8] *Ibid.*, Article 108.
[9] *Ibid.*, Article 109.
[10] *Ibid.*, Article 4.

of discussion and recommendation outside the sphere reserved to the Council. But it will be primarily concerned, one may with some confidence prophesy, "with the promotion of constructive solutions of international problems in the widest range of human relationships, economic, social, cultural and humanitarian." [1] It should become the international forum for the discussion of matters of common concern where, by methods of reason and persuasion, action in support of common objectives can be furthered.

4. *The Security Council*

If we continue our analogy of the Organization of the United Nations under the Charter to the government of a state, it becomes somewhat difficult to find an institution of national government which corresponds closely to the Security Council. This is largely due to the fact that under the plan of the Charter, provision is made for a decentralized arrangement for the discharge of those duties which we ordinarily think of as executive in character. The result is that the functions ordinarily associated under modern conditions with the chief executive of a state, in so far as provision is made for them in the Charter, are divided between three organs — the Security Council, the Economic and Social Council and the Trusteeship Council. In this respect the Charter plan differs markedly from the plan of the League Covenant which centralized functions of an executive character in the Council. Under the Charter, however, the Security Council is charged with the primary responsibility for the maintenance of peace and security, the function which historically is most closely associated with the executive branch of government. At least until the maintenance of international peace and security becomes more assured than it is at the present, the Security Council is likely to occupy a dominant position in the field of executive action.

The Council is to be composed of five permanent members (China, France, the Soviet Union, the United Kingdom and the United States) and six non-permanent members elected for two year terms by the General Assembly. In the election of non-permanent members, the General Assembly is to pay due regard to the contribution of Members of the United Nations to the maintenance of international peace and the other purposes of the Organization, and also "to equitable geographical distribution." [2] The Security Council is to be so organized "as to be able to function continuously," and to this end each Member of

---

[1] *Charter of the United Nations, Report to the President on the Results of the San Francisco Conference by the Chairman of the United States Delegation, the Secretary of State, June 26, 1945*, Washington, D. C., Department of State Publication 2349 (Conference Series 71), p. 65.

[2] *Charter of the United Nations*, Article 23, paragraph 1.

the Organization is to be represented at all times at the seat of the Organization.[1]

The powers of the Security Council are defined in sufficiently generous terms to permit it to fulfill its "primary responsibility." These powers will be described in greater detail later. For the present it is sufficient to say that the Security Council can intervene in any situation or dispute whose continuance is likely to endanger the maintenance of international peace and security for the purpose of bringing about a peaceful settlement, and in case it determines the existence of "any threat to the peace, breach of the peace, or act of aggression," it can decide what measures are to be taken "to maintain or restore international peace and security."[2] All functions of the United Nations with regard to trusteeship agreements for areas designated as strategic are to be exercised by the Security Council.[3] The Members of the Organization agree "to accept and carry out the decisions of the Security Council in accordance with the present Charter."[4] In discharging its duties the Security Council is bound to act in accordance with the purposes and principles of the Organization.[5] The Security Council is also made responsible for formulating plans to be submitted to the Members of the Organization "for the establishment of a system for the regulation of armaments."[6]

The question of Security Council voting procedure was one which the Sponsoring Governments had the greatest difficulty in answering and which caused the most extended and heated discussion at San Francisco. The rule finally adopted[7] frankly recognizes the larger responsibility of the greater powers for the maintenance of peace and makes any effective action by the Security Council dependent upon great power agreement. Decisions on procedural questions can be taken by the affirmative vote of any seven members of the Council. Decisions on all other matters, however, require in addition the concurrence of all the permanent members of the Security Council, with the proviso, however, "that in decisions under Chapter VI, and under paragraph 3 of Article 52, a party to a dispute shall abstain from voting."[8]

This requirement obviously places the permanent members of the Security Council in a highly privileged position, and means that the extensive powers vested in the Council may not in fact be exercised because of the inability of the permanent members to agree. It also means that in practice enforcement action will not be taken against a permanent member of the Council or against a state which has the support of a permanent member. It may also mean that the conciliatory functions of the Council will be considerably restricted since even a

---

[1] *Ibid.*, Article 28.
[3] *Ibid.*, Article 83, paragraph 1.
[5] *Ibid.*, Article 24, paragraph 2.
[7] *Ibid.*, Article 27.
[2] *Ibid.*, Article 39.
[4] *Ibid.*, Article 25.
[6] *Ibid.*, Article 26.
[8] *Ibid.*, paragraph 3.

decision to investigate a dispute with a view to determining whether its continuance is likely to endanger the maintenance of international peace and security can, according to the interpretation given by the four Sponsoring Governments and France, be blocked by the opposition of a permanent member which is not a party to the dispute.[1]

The idea back of the voting rule appears to be that the success of the Organization is wholly dependent upon the continuing agreement of the great powers, upon the ability of the principal members of the war-time coalition to continue in peace the cooperation which enabled them to prosecute the war to a successful conclusion. This conception was based on the premise that with the distribution of power that would in all probability exist at the conclusion of the war, there would be no real possibility of taking enforcement action against certain at least of these great powers, and very little chance, judging by League experience, of making the Organization operate successfully without their full participation and support. So, in effect, the Organization proposed is a league of peace-loving nations with an alliance of great powers for keeping the peace as its hard core of military strength and political reality. This of course involves a discrimination against the smaller nations which did not exist, at least on paper, under the League system, since under the Covenant unanimity was required for important Council decisions and any state, great or small, had an equal opportunity to protect its interests by an adverse vote.[2] On the other hand, if the new system works effectively in producing the desired result of peace and security, the smaller states may find in this result acceptable compensation for the sacrifices they are called upon to make.

5. The International Court of Justice

Continuing our analogy, we can have little difficulty in identifying the Court as the judicial branch of the United Nations Organization. In the course of the Dumbarton Oaks Conversations, the question of a court was discussed and agreement was reached that an international court of justice should be established as one of the principal organs of the proposed Organization. It was also agreed that the Statute of the Court should be a part of the Charter of the United Nations Organization. These conclusions were later adopted at San Francisco. It was impossible, however, at the time of the Dumbarton Oaks Conversations, to conclude an agreement upon the constitution and powers of the proposed court. Two views were in conflict: one which held that the pro-

[1] See *Statement by the Delegations of the Four Sponsoring Governments on the Voting Procedure in the Security Council*, this volume, p. 330.

[2] *Covenant*, Article V, paragraph 1. The text has been printed as an Appendix in *The United Nations in the Making: Basic Documents*, Boston, World Peace Foundation, 1945.

posed court should be a continuation of the Permanent Court of International Justice, brought into being under the Covenant of the League of Nations, and the other which held that this should be an entirely new court even though its statute might be based largely on the Statute of the Permanent Court.[1] There was also a difference of opinion as to whether or not the court should have compulsory jurisdiction.

At San Francisco it was decided that there should be a new court, not a continuance of the Permanent Court.

On the question of the Court's jurisdiction, there was strong support for the establishment of a general system of compulsory jurisdiction, but the view that finally prevailed took account of the fact that some states were apparently not ready to accept it. Thus a system was adopted under which each Member may by a declaration accept the compulsory jurisdiction of the Court, conditionally or unconditionally.[2] As a concession to the proponents of a general system, it is provided that declarations made under Article 36 of the Statute of the Permanent Court of International Justice which are still in force "shall be deemed, as between the parties to the present Statute, to be acceptances of the compulsory jurisdiction of the International Court of Justice for the period which they still have to run and in accordance with their terms."[3]

The Statute as finally approved[4] follows very closely that of the Permanent Court of International Justice. The Court is to be composed of a body of independent judges, 15 in number, elected for nine-year terms.[5] Judges are to be elected by the General Assembly and the Security Council, voting concurrently, from a list of nominations submitted by national groups.[6] The Court is to remain permanently in session.[7] Only states may be parties before the Court.[8] The conditions under which states not members of the United Nations shall have access to the Court are to be laid down by the Security Council.[9] Jurisdiction comprises "all cases which the parties refer to it" and all matters "specially provided for in the Charter" or "in treaties and conventions in force." Compulsory jurisdiction in enumerated categories of legal disputes may be accepted by special declaration, conditionally or unconditionally.[10] The Court is to decide cases generally on the basis of law.[11] The Charter provides that either the General Assembly or the Security

---

[1] *Revised Statute of the Permanent Court of International Justice*, The Hague, Sitjhoff, Publications of the Court Series D, No. 1 (4th ed.), p. 13–28; Hudson, Manley O., *The Permanent Court of International Justice, 1920–1942*, N. Y., Macmillan, 1943, p. 669–81.

[2] *Statute of the International Court of Justice*, Article 36.

[3] *Ibid.*, paragraph 5.

[4] See this volume, p. 365.

[5] *Statute of the International Court of Justice*, Articles 2, 3 and 13.

[6] *Ibid.*, Article 4. [7] *Ibid.*, Article 23.

[8] *Ibid.*, Article 34, paragraph 1. [9] *Ibid.*, Article 35, paragraph 2.

[10] *Ibid.*, Article 36. [11] *Ibid.*, Article 38.

Council may request the Court to give an advisory opinion on any legal question.[1] Other organs of the United Nations and specialized agencies may similarly request advisory opinions, if so authorized by the General Assembly.

While the Court which is provided for under the terms of the Charter and Statute is essentially the same as the Permanent Court of International Justice, there is one respect in which progress of some importance has been made. Whereas the Permanent Court's position was somewhat anomalous, being neither fully independent nor a recognized part of the League system, the new Court is to be the recognized judicial organ of the United Nations.[2]

6. The Secretariat

The Secretariat is the principal administrative agency of the United Nations. Every organization requires an administrative staff which will perform the numerous detailed day-to-day tasks which are necessary to the efficient performance of the organization's functions. The recruiting and directing of such a staff for an international organization present special problems. The experience of the League of Nations demonstrated the importance of the work of such a staff and that the special problems arising in connection with the organization and direction of an international administrative service are capable of reasonably satisfactory solutions. The provisions of the Charter dealing with the Secretariat are based upon careful study and evaluation of this experience.

The Secretariat is to be headed by a Secretary-General "appointed" by the General Assembly upon the recommendation of the Security Council.[3] The proposal of the Sponsoring Governments that express provision should be made in the Charter for four deputy secretaries-general was not accepted for the declared reason that it was judged better not to attempt to anticipate too far in advance the administrative requirements of the Secretariat.[4] The staff is to be appointed under regulations established by the General Assembly. Appropriate staffs are to be "permanently assigned" to the Economic and Social Council, the Trusteeship Council, and, as required, other organs of the United Nations. These staffs are to form a part, however, of the Secretariat,[5] and presumably remain subject to the Secretary-General's direction.

The functions of the Secretary-General are largely suggested by what had already been said. He is required to make an annual report to the

---

[1] *Charter of the United Nations*, Article 96.
[2] *Ibid.*, Article 92.
[3] *Ibid.*, Article 97.
[4] UNCIO, *Report of Rapporteur of Committee I/2 on Chapter X (The Secretariat)*, Doc. 1155, I/2/74 (2), p. 4.
[5] *Charter of the United Nations*, Article 101, paragraphs 1 and 2.

General Assembly on the work of the Organization.[1] Under the League system, the consideration of such an annual report afforded the Assembly the opportunity for an over-all survey and criticism of the work of the League. This Charter requirement therefore has great possibilities. The Secretary-General "may bring to the attention of the Security Council any matter which in his opinion may threaten the maintenance of international peace and security." [2] This too can become an important source of influence for the Secretary-General. At San Francisco, certain provisions were put into the Charter with a view to assuring the independence and efficiency of the Secretariat. The Secretary-General and his staff are not to seek or receive, in the course of the performance of their duties, instructions "from any government or from any other authority external to the Organization."[3] The Members of the Organization undertake "to respect the exclusively international character of the responsibilities of the Secretary-General and the staff" and "not to seek to influence them in the discharge of their responsibilities." [4] Furthermore it is stated that the "paramount consideration in the employment of the staff and in the determination of the conditions of service shall be the necessity of securing the highest standards of efficiency, competence, and integrity." [5]

7. Pacific Settlement of Disputes

The Charter system for the pacific settlement of disputes is in essence that of placing upon the parties themselves the responsibility for using means of peaceful settlement, while according to the Council authority to intervene at any time that the continuance of a particular dispute or situation is considered likely to endanger the maintenance of international peace and security. The Council cannot, however, impose an obligatory settlement upon the parties against their will; it can only act as an agency of conciliation.[6]

The basic obligation of Members, as stated in Article 2, is to "settle their international disputes by peaceful means in such a manner that international peace and security, and justice, are not endangered." Other provisions of the Charter, notably those of Chapter VI, provide for the implementation of this general principle. The parties to any dispute "the continuance of which is likely to endanger the maintenance of international peace and security" are obligated first of all to "seek a solution by negotiation, enquiry, mediation, conciliation, arbitration, judicial settlement, resort to regional agencies or arrangements, or other

[1] Ibid., Article 98.   [2] Ibid., Article 99.
[3] Ibid., Article 100.   [4] Ibid., paragraph 2.
[5] Ibid., Article 101.
[6] UNCIO, Report of the Rapporteur of Committee III/2, Doc. 1027, III/2/31 (1), p. 4.

peaceful means of their own choice."[1] The Security Council shall, if necessary, invite the parties to settle their disputes by such means.[2] If Members of the United Nations have entered into regional arrangements or instituted regional agencies for the settlement of their disputes, they "shall make every effort" to achieve peaceful settlement by such means before referring their disputes to the Security Council.[3] Furthermore, the Security Council is to encourage this. If, however, the parties fail to settle their dispute by such means, "they shall refer it to the Security Council" which, if it finds that the continuance of the dispute is likely to endanger the maintenance of international peace and security, may either recommend appropriate procedures or methods of adjustment, or such terms of settlement as it may consider appropriate.[4]

The Security Council may investigate any dispute, or any situation which might lead to international friction or give rise to a dispute, to determine whether its continuance is likely to endanger the maintenance of international peace and security.[5] Any Member of the United Nations may bring any such dispute or any such situation to the attention of the General Assembly or of the Security Council.[6] This may also be done by the Secretary-General on his own initiative.[7] A non-member may also do this with respect to a dispute to which it is a party if it accepts in advance the Charter obligations of pacific settlement.[8] The Council may, at any stage of a dispute or situation whose continuance it finds is likely to endanger the maintenance of international peace and security, "recommend appropriate procedures or methods of adjustments."[9] In making such recommendations the Security Council will naturally take into account, as it is expected to do, any procedures which have already been adopted by the parties. As an exception to the general view of the role of the Security Council which prevails in the Charter, if the parties so agree, any dispute of any kind whatsoever may be submitted to the Security Council for recommendations with a view to peaceful settlement.[10]

Two or three points should be specially noted which apply to the overall scheme of the Charter. While the principle of the obligatory submission to the Court of all legal disputes is not adopted, there is nevertheless recognition of the principle that "legal disputes should as a general rule be referred by the parties to the International Court of Justice."[11] Furthermore, while it is possible for disputes to be brought to the attention of the General Assembly, the assumption certainly is that in most cases it is the Security Council that will take action with

---

[1] *Charter of the United Nations*, Article 33, paragraph 1.
[2] *Ibid.*, paragraph 2.
[3] *Ibid.*, Article 52, paragraph 2.
[4] *Ibid.*, Article 37.
[5] *Ibid.*, Article 34.
[6] *Ibid.*, Article 35, paragraph 1.
[7] *Ibid.*, Article 99.
[8] *Ibid.*, Article 35, paragraph 2.
[9] *Ibid.*, Article 36.
[10] *Ibid.*, Article 38.
[11] *Ibid.*, Article 36, paragraph 3.

a view to settlement, since the General Assembly cannot make a recommendation with regard to a dispute or situation which is before the Security Council for action under the terms of the Charter. Furthermore, the General Assembly is required to refer any question on which action is necessary to the Security Council, either before or after discussion. Finally, the rule governing Council voting procedure, while it requires unanimity of the permanent members, except for the parties to a dispute, for a decision to investigate or make a recommendation to the parties, cannot prevent consideration and discussion by the Council of a dispute or situation brought before it under the provisions of the Charter.[1]

8. *Enforcement Action*

One of the notable features of the Charter adopted at San Francisco, and one of the respects in which it represents in the opinion of some the greatest advance over the Covenant of the League of Nations, is the provision made for enforcement action in the presence of a threat to the peace, breach of the peace or act of aggression. As has already been stated, the Security Council is made the responsible organ for seeing to it that in the face of such contingency effective action is taken.

The initial responsibility is placed on the Security Council to determine "the existence of any threat to the peace, breach of the peace, or act of aggression." [2] Once it decides that one of these situations exists, it is required to recommend or decide what measures shall be taken "in accordance with Articles 41 and 42" to maintain or restore international peace and security.

At the San Francisco Conference it was recognized that there was an intermediate situation which had not been adequately covered by the provisions of the Dumbarton Oaks Proposals. The Security Council might be faced with a situation which constituted a threat to the peace which could not be effectively handled by the immediate application of force. To cover this type of situation, the Security Council is now empowered "to call upon the parties concerned to comply with such provisional measures as it deems necessary or desirable." [3] These provisional measures are not to prejudice the rights or claims of the parties, but any failure to comply with them is to be taken into account by the Council in its subsequent action.

If the situation calls for the use of methods of coercion, the Security Council may first of all decide that "measures not involving the use of armed force" are to be employed, measures such as the interruption of economic relations or the severance of diplomatic relations.[4] If these means are considered or found to be inadequate, the Security Council

---

[1] See this volume, p. 125.
[2] *Charter of the United Nations*, Article 39.
[3] *Ibid.*, Article 40.
[4] *Ibid.*, Article 41.

"may take such action by air, sea, or land forces as may be necessary to maintain or restore international peace and security."[1]

To give assurance that effective forces will be at the disposal of the Security Council, all Members undertake "to make available to the Security Council, on its call and in accordance with a special agreement or agreements, armed forces, assistance, and facilities, including rights of passage, necessary for the purpose of maintaining international peace and security."[2] At San Francisco, the content of these agreements was defined in greater detail than in the Dumbarton Oaks Proposals, and furthermore it was specified, which it had not been in the Proposals, that the "agreement or agreements" should be negotiated "as soon as possible on the initiative of the Security Council" and should be concluded "between the Security Council and Members or between the Security Council and groups of Members."[3] To meet any urgent situation, Members are required to hold "immediately available national air force contingents for combined international enforcement action."[4]

To assist the Security Council in the preparation of plans for the use of armed force and in the strategic direction of the armed forces placed at the Council's disposal, provision is made for a Military Staff Committee consisting of the Chiefs of Staff of the permanent members of the Council.[5] This Committee is also to advise the Council on all questions relating to military requirements for the maintenance of peace and security, the regulation of armaments and possible disarmament. The Military Staff Committee, with the authorization of the Security Council and after consultation with the appropriate regional agencies, may establish regional subcommittees.

The Charter provides further guarantees of the effectiveness of such enforcement measures as may be undertaken. Members of the Organization are obligated to join in affording mutual assistance in carrying out the measures decided upon by the Security Council.[6] Furthermore, it is made clear that action required by the decisions of the Security Council are to be carried out by all the Members of the Organization, or by some, as the Council may decide.[7] Also the decisions are to be carried out by Member States both directly and in their capacities as members of appropriate international agencies.[8]

9. *Regional Arrangements*

Under the Dumbarton Oaks Proposals the general principle was laid down that regional arrangements or agencies were permitted for dealing with such matters relating to the maintenance of international peace

[1] *Ibid.*, Article 42.
[3] *Ibid.*, paragraph 3.
[5] *Ibid.*, Articles 46 and 47.
[7] *Ibid.*, Article 48, paragraph 1.
[2] *Ibid.*, Article 43, paragraph 1.
[4] *Ibid.*, Article 45.
[6] *Ibid.*, Article 49.
[8] *Ibid.*, paragraph 2.

and security as were appropriate for regional action, provided such arrangements or agencies and their activities were consistent with the purposes and principles of the Organization.[1] The Security Council was to encourage the settlement of disputes by such arrangements or agencies, and was to utilize such arrangements or agencies "for enforcement action under its authority," but no enforcement action was to be undertaken under regional arrangements or by regional agencies "without the authorization of the Security Council."[2]

The question of the relation of regional arrangements and agencies to the arrangements and agencies of the general international organization was one which concerned many states with limited or special interests and commitments or which were or expected to be parties to special or limited arrangements for the maintenance of peace and security. No group of states was more concerned than the American Republics, which, over a period of years, had developed a set of special commitments and agencies for the preservation of peace in the Western Hemisphere. By the Act of Chapultepec, adopted at the Mexico City Conference, March 3, 1945, the American Republics declared that for the duration of the war they would take common measures to deal with any threat or act of aggression against any one of them, and recommended that a treaty be concluded for the same purpose following the establishment of peace.[3] Though it was declared that the arrangements and activities referred to should be consistent with the purposes and principles of the general international organization, when established, it was clear that there were certain difficulties in harmonizing such a system of regional obligations with the provisions of the Dumbarton Oaks plan, particularly in view of the fact that a non-American permanent member of the Security Council might prevent any decision of the Council authorizing action under such arrangements.

The pressure for greater recognition of regional and other limited arrangements for the maintenance of peace came not alone from the American Republics. On March 22, 1945, the League of Arab States was formed,[4] and its members became anxious to have full recognition accorded to it. France had negotiated a treaty of mutual assistance with the Soviet Union, directed against Germany, and was particularly anxious to preserve her freedom of action under this arrangement.

At the San Francisco Conference these demands for greater recognition of regional and limited arrangements and agencies received full consideration. While the general principle of subordination of regional

[1] *Dumbarton Oaks Proposals*, Chapter VIII, Section C, paragraph 1, p. 315.

[2] *Ibid.*, paragraph 2.

[3] Department of State, *Bulletin*, XII, p. 339. Argentina was not represented at the Conference but adhered later.

[4] UNCIO, *The Pact of the League of Arab States, signed in Cairo, March 22, 1945*, Doc. 72, III/4/1.

arrangements and agencies to the purposes and principles of the Charter is retained in the final text, certain amendments were introduced which considerably strengthened the position of such regional arrangements and agencies. Under the provisions of Article 52 of the Charter, Members of the United Nations which enter into such arrangements or constitute such agencies "shall make every effort to achieve pacific settlement of local disputes through such regional arrangements or by such regional agencies before referring them to the Security Council." [1] The Security Council is also required to encourage "the development of pacific settlement of local disputes through such regional arrangements or by such regional agencies." [2]

The possibility of using regional arrangements and agencies as the basis for common action against acts of aggression without the requirement of Security Council authorization was attained by the insertion in Chapter VII of a new Article [3] safeguarding the "inherent right of individual or collective self-defense." By the provisions of this Article nothing in the Charter shall impair "the inherent right of individual or collective self-defense if an armed attack occurs against a Member of the United Nations, until the Security Council has taken the measures necessary to maintain international peace and security." Measures that are taken under this Article are to be immediately reported to the Security Council and are not in any way to "affect the authority and responsibility" of that body.

Finally, while the Charter provides that no enforcement action shall be taken under regional arrangements or by regional agencies without Security Council authorization, it makes an exception of "measures against any enemy state . . . provided for pursuant to Article 107 or in regional arrangements directed against renewal of aggressive policy on the part of any such state, until such time as the Organization may, on request of the Governments concerned, be charged with the responsibility for preventing further aggression by such a state." [4]

Under the Charter, as finally adopted, there can be little doubt that greater freedom is given to states to take action under regional and limited arrangements without strict control by the Security Council. Whether this operates in the long run to weaken or to strengthen the general system of the Charter for the maintenance of international peace and security remains for the future to determine.

10. *Economic and Social Cooperation*

Of all the provisions of the Dumbarton Oaks plan, those relating to *Arrangements for International Economic and Social Cooperation* were subjected to the most extensive and significant modification at the

---

[1] *Charter of the United Nations*, Article 52, paragraph 2.
[2] *Ibid.*, paragraph 3.   [3] *Ibid.*, Article 51.   [4] *Ibid.*, Article 53, paragraph 1.

United Nations Conference. In part this was due to the nature of the problems involved which excluded them largely from the area of political maneuver, but it was also the result of strong and persistent pressures that were brought to bear by certain delegations and by groups and organizations largely unofficial in character.[1] While the basic approach and plan of the Dumbarton Oaks Proposals were retained, the changes that were introduced went far in making precise and definite a plan which was nebulous in certain respects and which imposed on Members few specific commitments.

The provisions of the Charter are based on the premise that a necessary condition of the maintenance of international peace and security is the creation generally throughout the world of "conditions of stability and well-being."[2] It is only under such conditions that "peaceful and friendly relations among nations based on respect for the principle of equal rights and self-determination of peoples" can exist. With a view to the creation of such conditions, the United Nations undertake to promote "higher standards of living," "full employment," "conditions of economic and social progress and development," "solutions of international economic, social, health, and related problems," "international cultural and educational cooperation," and "universal respect for, and observance of, human rights and fundamental freedoms for all without distinction as to race, sex, language, or religion."[3] Also, Members of the Organization "pledge themselves to take joint and separate action in cooperation with the Organization" for the achievement of these purposes.[4]

While the Charter in principle accepts the idea that specialized organizations enjoying a large measure of autonomy will continue to exist or come into being for the purpose of facilitating international cooperation in the fields of economic, social and cultural relations, it nevertheless clearly and explicitly defines the authority of the Organization with respect to the establishment of such specialized organizations and the coordination of their activities. Thus it is provided that the Organization "shall, where appropriate, initiate negotiations among the states concerned for the creation of any new specialized agencies required for the accomplishment of the purposes" of the Organization.[5] Furthermore,

---

[1] Forty-two private national organizations were invited to send representatives to San Francisco to serve as Consultants to the United States Delegation. Regular meetings were held by the Consultants with the Chairman and members of the United States Delegation and a liaison staff kept the Consultants in continuous contact with the work of the Conference. Through these contacts the Consultants were largely instrumental in the introduction into the final Charter of certain important provisions, particularly relating to economic and social cooperation. See *Charter of the United Nations, Report to the President on the Results of the San Francisco Conference*, etc., cited above, p. 27.

[2] *Charter of the United Nations*, Article 55. [3] *Ibid.*

[4] *Ibid.*, Article 56. [5] *Ibid.*, Article 59.

it is provided that the various specialized agencies "established by inter-governmental agreement and having wide international responsibilities, as defined in their basic instruments" shall be brought into relationship with the United Nations Organization,[1] and the Organization "shall make recommendations for the coordination of the policies and activities of the specialized agencies." [2] Responsibility for the discharge of these functions is vested in the General Assembly, and under the authority of the General Assembly, in the Economic and Social Council.[3]

The Economic and Social Council consists of eighteen Members of the United Nations elected by the General Assembly.[4] Each member has one vote.[5] All decisions are taken by a majority vote of those present and voting.[6] The Council "shall set up" commissions in the economic and social fields and for the promotion of human rights and such other commissions as may be required.[7] It may make arrangements for repre-sentatives of specialized agencies to participate in its deliberations, with-out vote, and for its representatives to participate in the deliberations of the specialized agencies.[8]

The functions and powers of the Economic and Social Council are defined in the Charter in considerable detail, in fact more precisely than in the Dumbarton Oaks Proposals. The Council, along with the General Assembly and under its authority, is made responsible for the discharge of the functions of the Organization in the economic and social fields.[9] In order that it may discharge these functions, the Council is specifically empowered [10] to:

(1) "make or initiate studies and reports with respect to inter-national economic, social, cultural, educational, health, and related matters";

(2) "make recommendations with respect to any such matters to the General Assembly, to the Members of the United Nations, and to the specialized agencies concerned";

(3) "make recommendations for the purpose of promoting respect for, and observance of, human rights and fundamental freedoms for all";

(4) "prepare draft conventions for submission to the General Assembly, with respect to matters falling within its competence";

(5) call international conferences on matters coming within its competence;

(6) enter into agreements with specialized agencies defining the terms on which each agency shall be brought into relationship with the Organization, subject to approval by the General Assembly;

[1] Ibid., Article 57.   [2] Ibid., Article 58.
[3] Ibid., Article 60.   [4] Ibid., Article 61, paragraph 1.
[5] Ibid., Article 67, paragraph 1.   [6] Ibid., paragraph 2.
[7] Ibid., Article 68.   [8] Ibid., Article 70.
[9] Ibid., Article 60.   [10] Ibid., Articles 62–66.

(7) "coordinate the activities of the specialized agencies through consultation with and recommendations to such agencies and through recommendations to the General Assembly and to the Members of the United Nations";

(8) take appropriate steps to obtain reports from the specialized agencies and communicate its observations on these reports to the General Assembly;

(9) furnish information to the Security Council;

(10) perform services at the request of Members of the Organization and at the request of specialized agencies, subject to the approval of the General Assembly.

The Council is to perform such functions as fall within its competence in connection with the carrying out of Assembly recommendations.[1] It is also to "assist the Security Council upon its request." [2] Furthermore, it "shall perform such other functions . . . as may be assigned to it by the General Assembly." [3]

A comparison of the provisions of the Charter bearing on economic and social cooperation with the relevant provisions of the Covenant of the League of Nations indicates the great advance that has been made in the conception of organized international cooperation in this field. In large part, this advance is the result of the substantial achievements of the League of Nations which far surpassed the modest promise of the provisions of the Covenant. A more important consideration, however, is probably the general recognition that has come to exist of the close interrelation of political and economic and social problems, and of the opportunities for achieving substantial results through international cooperation in dealing with economic and social problems where the need is obvious and political considerations do not necessarily stand in the way of agreement.

11. *Administration of Non-Self-Governing Territories*

The provisions of the Charter with respect to non-self-governing territories are new, the Dumbarton Oaks Proposals having contained nothing on this matter. The Conference at the beginning had no specific proposals before it. Proposals however were subsequently submitted by the Delegations of Australia, China, France, the Soviet Union, the United Kingdom and the United States. On the basis of these proposals and after careful study and consultation a working paper was prepared and adopted by Committee II/4 as the basis of its subsequent discussions.[4] The plan which was finally adopted by the technical committee,

---

[1] *Ibid.*, Article 66, paragraph 1.   [2] *Ibid.*, Article 65.
[3] *Ibid.*, Article 66, paragraph 3.
[4] UNCIO, *Proposed Working Paper for Chapter on Dependent Territories and Arrangements for International Trusteeship*, Doc. 323, II/4/12; see this volume, p. 328.

and, with some changes of form, by the Coordination Committee and the Conference, represented a fusion of different plans and points of view. In a real sense, it was a compromise, or perhaps better, a series of compromises.

The provisions of the Charter bearing on the subject of non-self-governing territories are contained in three separate chapters: XI (*Declaration Regarding Non-Self-Governing Territories*); XII (*International Trusteeship System*); and XIII (*The Trusteeship Council*). The *Declaration Regarding Non-Self-Governing Territories* represents a definite advance over anything hitherto attempted, even under the mandates system of the League of Nations. It provides that all Members of the United Nations which "have or assume responsibilities for the administration of territories whose peoples have not yet attained a full measure of self-government" recognize the principle that "the interests of the inhabitants of these territories are paramount" and accept the obligation "to promote to the utmost . . . the well-being of the inhabitants of these territories." [1] To this end, they accept the specific obligations "to ensure . . . their political, economic, social, and educational advancement, their just treatment, and their protection against abuses"; "to develop self-government, to take due account of the political aspirations of the peoples, and to assist them in the progressive development of their free political institutions"; "to further international peace and security"; "to promote constructive measures of development"; and to transmit regularly to the Secretary-General "statistical and other information of a technical nature relating to economic, social, and educational conditions." [2] It is to be noted that these commitments, except the last, apply to all non-self-governing territories whether or not they are brought under the international trusteeship system provided in the Charter.

In addition, the Charter provides for the establishment of "an international trusteeship system for the administration and supervision of such territories as may be placed thereunder by subsequent individual agreements." [3] The basic objectives of this system are defined in detail as follows: [4]

a. to further international peace and security;

b. to promote the political, economic, social and educational advancement of the inhabitants of the trust territories, and their progressive development towards self-government or independence . . .;

c. to encourage respect for human rights and for fundamental freedoms for all without distinction as to race, sex, language, or religion, and to encourage recognition of the interdependence of the peoples of the world; and

d. to ensure equal treatment in social, economic, and commercial matters for all Members of the United Nations and their nationals, and also equal treatment for the latter in the administration of justice. . . .

---

[1] *Charter of the United Nations*, Article 73.   [2] *Ibid.*
[3] *Ibid.*, Article 75.   [4] *Ibid.*, Article 76.

It is stated that the system shall apply to such territories in the following categories "as may be placed thereunder by means of trusteeship agreements:[1]

a. territories now held under mandate;
b. territories which may be detached from enemy states as a result of the Second World War; and
c. territories voluntarily placed under the system by states responsible for their administration.

It is to be especially noted that there is no commitment for specific areas. Unlike the provisions of the League Covenant which at least created a moral obligation that certain areas would be brought under the mandates system provided for under Article 22, the provisions of the Charter place no express obligation of any kind on Members of the United Nations to place territories under their control under the trusteeship system. Whether the territories referred to are to be placed in the category of trust territories, and on what terms, is made to depend entirely upon individual agreements, subsequently approved by the General Assembly.[2]

Provision is also made that in any trusteeship agreement an area or areas of special strategic importance may be designated "a strategic area or areas."[3] The result of such designation will be to make the Security Council, instead of the General Assembly, responsible for the exercise of all functions of the United Nations with regard to trusteeship agreements relating thereto.[4] The basic objectives of the trusteeship system are to apply, however, and the Security Council is expected to avail itself of the services of the Trusteeship Council in the performance of its functions.

The functions of the United Nations with respect to trusteeship agreements for all areas not designated as strategic areas are to be exercised by the General Assembly.[5] The Trusteeship Council, acting under the authority of the General Assembly, is to assist that body in carrying out its functions.[6] The Council is to consist of those Members administering trust territories, permanent members of the Security Council which are not administering trust territories, and as many other Members of the Organization elected by the General Assembly as may be necessary to ensure that the total number is equally divided between those administering trust territories and those who are not.[7]

The General Assembly "and, under its authority, the Trusteeship Council" are given certain specific powers to enable them to carry out their functions. They may consider reports submitted by the adminis-

[1] *Ibid.*, Article 77.
[2] *Ibid.*, Article 79.
[3] *Ibid.*, Article 82.
[4] *Ibid.*, Article 83.
[5] *Ibid.*, Article 85, paragraph 1.
[6] *Ibid.*, paragraph 2.
[7] *Ibid.*, Article 86, paragraph 1.

tering authority which that authority is required to make,[1] accept petitions and examine them in consultation with the administering authority, "provide for periodic visits to the respective trust territories at times agreed upon with the administering authority," and do such other things as the trusteeship agreements may permit.[2]

As compared with the League of Nations Covenant, the Charter system is clearly a step forward in so far as it establishes a set of principles binding upon all Members which govern non-self-governing territories. On the other hand, in so far as the trusteeship system itself is concerned, there is less advance assurance under the Charter than there was under the mandates system that trust territories (or mandated territories as they were called under the Covenant) will actually be established. Furthermore, much greater freedom is accorded to interested states not only to determine whether given territories will be set up as trust territories but also to determine the conditions under which the trusteeship system is to operate. Vesting responsibility for the exercise of the functions of the United Nations in the General Assembly, and under its authority, in a Trusteeship Council, is clearly a step in advance, as it gives assurance of a more effective supervision by the international authority. Certainly it represents a useful advance over the League system that the power of inspection on the spot is granted, even though the exercise of this power is hedged about by a restriction in the interest of the administering territory. Placing strategic areas under a special regime, with the Security Council exercising the functions otherwise vested in the General Assembly, was probably a necessary concession to political expediency and the over-all requirements of security. In any case, it does not represent a retrogressive step in comparison with the provisions of the Covenant since under the mandates system the Council was responsible for exercising the functions of the League in all cases.

12. *Miscellaneous Provisions*

There were a number of matters which, it had been recognized, needed to be covered in the Charter that had not received attention in the Dumbarton Oaks Proposals. Thus there was nothing in the Proposals regarding the registration of treaties though this matter had been judged sufficiently important by the framers of the League Covenant to justify the giving of one whole article to it.[3] Four articles of the Charter are devoted to matters of this kind. They provide for the registration of treaties, it being prescribed that a treaty which is not so registered cannot be invoked before an organ of the United Nations,[4] the superiority

---

[1] *Ibid.*, Article 88.   [2] *Ibid.*, Article 87.
[3] *Covenant*, Article 18.
[4] *Charter of the United Nations*, Article 102.

of obligations under the Charter over obligations under other international agreements,[1] the enjoyment by the Organization of such legal capacity in the territory of each of its Members as is necessary to the performance of its functions,[2] and the enjoyment by the Organization, its officials and the representatives of its Members in the territory of each Member of such privileges and immunities as are necessary to the performance of the purposes and functions of the Organization.[3]

The Charter repeats in modified phraseology the provision of the Dumbarton Oaks Proposals under which, during the transitional period, the signatories of the Moscow Four-Power Declaration assume special responsibilities for the maintenance of international peace and security. The changes in phraseology which have been made are intended to clarify the meaning of these provisions, particularly by making clear the procedure by which this transitional period is to be terminated, and by defining the meaning of "enemy states" as used in the second paragraph of Article XII of the Dumbarton Oaks Proposals. Under the Charter it is explicitly stated that the special responsibility of the signatories of the Moscow Declaration will continue only "pending the coming into force of such special agreements referred to in Article 43 as in the opinion of the Security Council enable it to begin the exercise of its responsibilities under Article 42."[4]

13. *Entrance into Force and Revision of Charter*

The original Dumbarton Oaks Proposals contained no provision governing the entrance into force of the Charter when adopted. One of the amendments proposed by the Sponsoring Governments provided that the Charter should come into force "after its ratification in accordance with their respective constitutional processes by the Members of the Organization having permanent seats on the Security Council and by a majority of the other Members of the Organization." This was in substance accepted by the Conference.[5] In accordance with this provision, the Charter entered into force on October 24, 1945, following the deposit of ratifications by the permanent members of the Security Council and twenty-four other signatories.[6]

The Dumbarton Oaks Proposals contained a chapter [7] describing the procedure by which the Charter might be amended, but contained no provision with regard to the holding of a special conference to review and recommend the extensive revision of the Charter. One of the amendments proposed by the Sponsoring Governments made provision, how-

---

[1] *Ibid.*, Article 103.
[2] *Ibid.*, Article 104.
[3] *Ibid.*, Article 105.
[4] *Ibid.*, Article 106.
[5] *Ibid.*, Article 110.
[6] Department of State, *Bulletin*, XIII, p. 679; see this volume, p. 385.
[7] Chapter XI, see this volume, p. 317.

ever, for the holding of such a constitutional conference, upon decision by three-fourths vote of the General Assembly concurred in by vote of any seven members of the Security Council.

At the Conference, the provision of the Dumbarton Oaks Proposals regarding amendments was accepted with one modification. In order somewhat to equalize the position of the smaller powers, the original text was changed so that ratification by two-thirds of the Members of the Organization, including all permanent members of the Security Council, is necessary in order for an amendment to enter into force.[1] This makes it necessary for a larger number of the smaller states to ratify the amendment than was required by the Dumbarton Oaks Proposals, and thereby increases their relative power.

The idea of making special provision for a constitutional conference to review the Charter and recommend changes therein was generally accepted. There was disagreement, however, with regard to the procedure to be followed, and, more particularly, with regard to the desirability of setting a time limit at the conclusion of which such a conference would automatically be held. After extensive discussion and after various proposals had failed of adoption by the necessary two-thirds vote, a compromise formula was proposed by the American Delegation and adopted. Under the arrangement finally approved, such a conference may be called by a two-thirds vote of the General Assembly with the Security Council concurring by vote of any seven of its members. If such a conference is not called before the tenth annual session of the General Assembly, the proposal to call such a conference is to be placed on the agenda of that session of the General Assembly, and may be adopted by a majority vote of that body and a vote of seven members of the Security Council.[2] Thus, while there is no guarantee that a General Conference will be held at any specified time or within any defined period, there is an assurance that the proposal to hold such a conference will be considered and furthermore favorable action is facilitated by the requirement that only a majority vote of the General Assembly is necessary to the adoption of the proposal by that body.

SETTING UP THE ORGANIZATION

Consideration was also given at the Conference to the question of the initial setting-up of the United Nations Organization. It was recognized that with the successful conclusion of its work the Conference would terminate its existence. On the other hand, the Organization envisaged in the Charter could not come into existence until the Charter had been ratified by the requisite number of states and these ratifications had been deposited. It was also recognized that before the Organization

---

[1] *Charter of the United Nations*, Article 108.   [2] *Ibid.*, Article 109.

could be established there was a vast amount of preparatory work to be done. If this work could be undertaken immediately, the United Nations could be set up as a working organization with a minimum of delay once the necessary number of ratifications were deposited.

It was consequently decided at the United Nations Conference to conclude certain interim arrangements so that this preliminary work could be undertaken immediately. By an agreement signed on June 26, 1945,[1] a Preparatory Commission was established "for the purpose of making provisional arrangements for the first sessions of the General Assembly, the Security Council, the Economic and Social Council, and the Trusteeship Council, for the establishment of the Secretariat, and for the convening of the International Court of Justice." [2]

The Commission was to consist of one representative of each government signatory of the Charter.[3] When not in session, its functions and powers were to be exercised by an Executive Committee composed of the representatives of those governments represented on the Executive Committee of the Conference. The Commission was to be assisted by an Executive Secretary "who shall exercise such powers and perform such duties as the Commission may determine," and by such staff as might be required.[4] The specific functions of the Commission included the following: [5]

1. Convocation of General Assembly in its first session.

2. Preparation of provisional agenda for the first sessions of the principal organs of the Organization, and preparation of documents and recommendations relating to all matters on these agenda.

3. Formulation of recommendations regarding the possible transfer of certain functions, activities, and assets of the League of Nations to the United Nations on terms to be arranged.

4. Examination of problems involved in the establishment of relationships between the specialized intergovernmental organizations and agencies and the Organization.

5. Issuance of invitations for the nomination of candidates for the International Court of Justice in accordance with the provisions of the Statute.

6. Preparation of recommendations concerning arrangements for the Secretariat.

7. Preparation of recommendations concerning the location of the permanent headquarters of the Organization.

The agreement provided that the seat of the Commission should be in London. The first meeting of the Commission was held in San Fran-

---

[1] For text, see this volume, p. 379.
[2] *Interim Arrangements*, etc., Article 1.
[3] *Ibid.*, Article 2.
[4] *Ibid.*, Article 3.
[5] *Ibid.*, Article 4.

cisco on June 27, the day following the date of the signing of the Charter. It was provided that the next meeting should be held upon the call of the Executive Committee "as soon as possible after the Charter of the Organization comes into effect and whenever subsequently it considers such a session desirable." [1] The agreement further provided that the Commission should cease to exist upon the election of the Secretary-General of the Organization, at which time its property and records would be transferred to the Organization.[2]

THE INTERPRETATION OF THE CHARTER

As has already been pointed out, the Charter is an agreement between states, not a constituent act of the peoples of the world. It is an instrument of cooperation between the Members of the United Nations Organization who, according to the first principle of Article 2, retain their "sovereign equality." In our endeavor to understand the meaning of the Charter — what its purposes are, what are the obligations of Members of the United Nations Organization, what are the functions and powers of its organs — it is important to bear in mind this basic character of the document. Chief Justice Marshall, in interpreting the Constitution of the United States, justified the doctrine of liberal interpretation on the ground that it was a constitution that the Court was interpreting. In a sense the Charter is also a constitution. However, it would be disregarding the plain intent and purpose of some of the more powerful and influential governments represented at San Francisco, governments whose cooperation is necessary to the success of the Organization, if we assumed that the Charter was not also a treaty between states to be interpreted according to the principles of treaty interpretation.

This conclusion, however, does not exclude the possibility of applying a rule of liberal interpretation to the Charter's provisions. While the basic principle of interpretation is that "words must be interpreted in the sense which they normally would have in their context," [3] in the case where the words used are not clear, there is the opportunity to apply principles of liberal construction. Formerly the rule rather commonly applied was that words should be interpreted strictly in favor of national sovereign rights. Today the better view would seem

[1] *Ibid.*, Article 6. The first meeting of the Executive Committee was held in London on August 16, 1945. The Charter entered into force on October 24, following the deposit of ratifications by the five permanent members of the Security Council and a majority of the other 46 signatories of the Charter. Department of State, Press Release no. 798, October 24, 1945. The Preparatory Commission met on November 23 to act on the recommendations of the Executive Committee, and concluded its work on December 23. The General Assembly had its first meeting in London on January 10, 1946.

[2] *Ibid.*, Article 7.

[3] Advisory Opinion of the P.C.I.J. in Polish Postal Service in Danzig Case, Publications of P.C.I.J., Series B, no. 11, p. 39.

to be that consideration should be given to the general purposes of the parties on the assumption that parties intend to achieve the purposes they declare within the limits of the permissible interpretation of the words used.[1] Furthermore, the effect of such liberal interpretation of the provisions of the Charter relating to the powers and functions of the organs of the UNO will not be seriously to restrict the sovereignty of Members since in most cases the organs only have powers of recommendation.

In interpreting the Charter, we encounter one very special problem of treaty interpretation, namely, that of the weight to be attached to preparatory work (travaux préparatoires). The general principle to be followed seems reasonably clear. In the words of the Permanent Court of International Justice "there is no occasion to have regard to preparatory work if the text of a convention is sufficiently clear in itself."[2] But the practice of the Permanent Court seems clearly to support the view that preparatory work should be consulted with a view to determining the true intent of the parties where there is any doubt as to the meaning of the words used.[3] We would thus seem to be justified in making extensive and fairly detailed reference to the discussions that took place in UNCIO, not only to give some understanding of the play of forces that occurred, but also to throw light on the actual meaning of the Charter. However, a word of caution must be introduced. It must be remembered that the Charter is an agreement between all the states that ratify it, and consequently statements of interpretation cannot be accepted as conclusive unless there is clear evidence that they have been generally accepted. The statement of interpretation of the Yalta voting formula submitted by the Delegations of the Sponsoring Governments and France[4] threw important light on the intentions of these governments and the conflict of views that prevailed in the Conference, and gives an important clue to the manner in which Article 27 is likely to be interpreted in practice, but it was made very clear in the course of discussions that the interpretation was not necessarily accepted by the Conference. On the other hand, the statement with regard to the right of withdrawal[5] recommended by Committee I/2 and approved by the Commission and the Conference, with a relatively minor reservation by the Delegation of the Soviet Union, clearly stands as an authoritative indication of the intent of the parties and must govern the interpretation of the provisions of the Charter.

[1] See Hyde, C. C., *International Law, Chiefly as Interpreted and Applied by the United States*, Boston, Little, Brown, 3 vols., 1945, 2nd rev. ed., II, p. 1494.

[2] Judgment of the P.C.I.J. in the Case of the S. S. *Lotus*, Publications of the P.C.I.J., Series A, no. 10, p. 16.

[3] Hyde, *op. cit.*, II, p. 1492; Hudson, Manley O., *The Permanent Court of International Justice, 1920–1942: A Treatise*, N. Y., Macmillan, 1943, p. 652.

[4] See this volume, p. 330.   [5] *Ibid.*, p. 87.

The Future of UNO

The Charter which was written at San Francisco has been received with general approval. There has also been a healthy realization that while agreement on the Charter is the necessary first step to the organization of international peace and security, there is a lot of important work which remains to be done. The Charter at most provides a means of cooperation for the adjustment of differences and the achievement of common purposes. Its success will depend wholly upon the use that is made of it. That in turn will depend upon the policies of governments, and more fundamentally, upon the understanding which peoples come to have of the nature of the Organization and the conditions necessary to its success. The creation of such an understanding is the big educational task which we face in the months and years ahead.

It is easy enough to criticize the provisions of the Charter, and to point out its weaknesses and defects. While undoubtedly there are important advances that have been made in it, the case for the superiority of the Charter to the Covenant as an international constitutional document is not easy to establish. That however does not mean that the United Nations, like the League of Nations, must fail. The League failed largely because it did not succeed in getting sufficiently broad support from peoples and governments. The United States never joined; the Soviet Union did not join until very late; other states though members failed to give it full support. The Charter of the United Nations has received wider acceptance. All the nations which were associated together in World War II have become Members and we can hope that with the war experience fresh in their minds they will cooperate in good faith and strong purpose for the maintenance of a long period of peace. But, again, this will not come to the world as manna from heaven. Such successes as come to the United Nations as an organized effort to keep the peace and promote the general well-being of peoples will be entirely due to the steady and intelligent efforts of peoples and their governments.

PART II

COMMENTARY ON ARTICLES

CHARTER
OF THE UNITED NATIONS

WE THE PEOPLES OF THE UNITED NATIONS DETERMINED

to save succeeding generations from the scourge of war, which twice in our lifetime has brought untold sorrow to mankind, and

to reaffirm faith in fundamental human rights, in the dignity and worth of the human person, in the equal rights of men and women and of nations large and small, and

to establish conditions under which justice and respect for the obligations arising from treaties and other sources of international law can be maintained, and

to promote social progress and better standards of life in larger freedom,

AND FOR THESE ENDS

to practice tolerance and live together in peace with one another as good neighbors, and

to unite our strength to maintain international peace and security, and

to ensure, by the acceptance of principles and the institution of methods, that armed force shall not be used, save in the common interest, and

to employ international machinery for the promotion of the economic and social advancement of all peoples,

HAVE RESOLVED TO COMBINE OUR EFFORTS TO ACCOMPLISH THESE AIMS.

Accordingly, our respective Governments, through representatives assembled in the city of San Francisco, who have exhibited their full powers found to be in good and due form, have agreed to the present Charter of the United Nations and do hereby establish an international organization to be known as the United Nations.

Origin of Preamble. The Dumbarton Oaks Proposals did not contain any preamble. Those provisions relating to motives and intent which are customarily placed in the preamble were contained in the first two chapters of the Proposals, dealing with "Purposes" and "Principles." However, several delegations at the United Nations Conference on International Organization [1] proposed that there should be a preamble to the Charter. The most important of these proposals was that made by Field Marshal Smuts, the chairman of the Delegation of the Union of South Africa.

---

[1] Subsequently referred to as UNCIO.

On the basis of this and other proposals, this Preamble was drafted and inserted in the Charter. The process by which it was drafted was not conducive to the production of a literary and inspiring text. The Smuts draft was revised and put into tentative form by a technical committee on which each of the fifty governments participating in the work of the Conference was represented. The committee draft was subsequently reviewed by the Coordination Committee and apparently approved only because time did not permit a fresh approach to the problem. Last minute changes, deemed necessary to put the text into grammatical form, were made by the Steering Committee.

It was recognized in the technical committee discussions that it was difficult, practically impossible, to draw a sharp and clear-cut distinction between the Preamble, the statement of "Purposes" (Article 1) and the enumeration of governing "Principles" (Article 2). Such a differentiation was, however, attempted in these words:

(a) The "Preamble" introduces the Charter and sets forth the declared common intentions which brought us together in this Conference and moved us to unite our will and efforts, and made us harmonize, regulate, and organize our international action to achieve our common ends.

(b) The "Purposes" constitute the *raison d'être* of the Organization. They are the aggregation of the common ends on which our minds met; hence, the cause and object of the Charter to which member states collectively and severally subscribe.

(c) The chapter on "Principles" sets, in the same order of ideas, the methods and regulating norms according to which the Organization and its members shall do their duty and endeavor to achieve the common ends. Their understandings should serve as actual standards of international conduct.[1]

The committee was forced to admit however that the distinction between the three parts was "not particularly profound."

Legal Force. The legal force of a preamble is a matter concerning which different views are held. There are authorities who claim that the preamble is just as binding as any other part of an international instrument, that it is part and parcel of the agreement. Others, however, claim that a preamble does not have exactly the same effect as other provisions of a treaty. They hold that the legally binding provisions are to be found in subsequent articles and that the preamble only has legal value in so far as it throws light on the intentions of the parties. According to this point of view, the preamble is an ideological and political introduction where the parties state their aims and views. The preamble will under these conditions only be of legal importance if and when there are doubts about the interpretation of other stipulations. In such cases one may refer to the preamble for guidance.

The view of the technical committee of the Conference was that all

---

[1] UNCIO, *Report of Rapporteur of Committee 1 to Commission I*, Doc. 944, I/1/34 (1), p. 1–2.

provisions of the Charter, "being in this case indivisible as in any other legal instrument, are equally valid and operative." Each is to be construed and applied "in function of the others." [1]

It is clear of course that while the Preamble is an integral part of the Charter, it does not set forth the basic obligations of the Members. Nevertheless, the Preamble has significance as a statement of the basic motivating ideas of the Charter and of the purposes which the framers had in view. There can be little doubt that its words can be used as evidence of these ideas and purposes in any interpretation of the provisions of the Articles that follow. Thus within the limits of its purpose and character, it has the same legal value as other parts of the Charter.[2]

"We the peoples of the United Nations." The insertion of these words was proposed by the Delegation of the United States. The purpose was to emphasize that the Charter is an expression of the will of the peoples of the world and is primarily concerned with their welfare. The proposal was inspired by the opening words of the Constitution of the United States. Its adoption constituted an important departure from past practice which had been, as in the case of the Covenant of the League of Nations, to regard states or their governments as parties to such international instruments. It was necessary, however, in drafting the Charter to recognize that, even though the Charter reflected the resolution of peoples, the actual agreement must, of necessity, be between governments. Consequently, the preamble concludes with the words: "Accordingly our respective Governments, through representatives assembled in the city of San Francisco, . . . have agreed to the present Charter of the United Nations."

Purposes and Principles Set Forth in Preamble. The Preamble consists of a solemn affirmation of purposes in the name of "We the peoples of the United Nations" and a statement of principles of policy to be followed in the pursuit of these purposes. Inevitably, as we have seen, its terms to a large extent duplicate the more detailed enumeration of purposes and principles contained in Articles 1 and 2.

The first purpose stated is to save coming generations from the scourge of war. Here the word "war" is used instead of the word "force." It is quite clear that this is not meant in any way to limit the obligations of Article 2, paragraph 4, which applies to the threat or use of "force." War is here used not in its strict legal sense but as a popular expression describing the use of armed force in international relations.

The reaffirmation of "faith in fundamental human rights, in the dignity and worth of the human person, in the equal rights of men and

[1] *Ibid.*, p. 2.
[2] *Ibid.*, p. 2–3; *Charter of the United Nations, Report to the President on the Results of the San Francisco Conference*, etc., cited above, p. 34–5.

women" is a purpose which commands wide and earnest support among the peoples of the United Nations. In the Declaration by United Nations of January 1, 1942, they had recognized that victory in the war against the Axis powers was necessary "to defend life, liberty, independence and religious freedom, and to preserve human rights and justice in their own lands as well as in other lands." To many this represents the essence of the way of life which the United Nations have been engaged in defending against Axis aggression. Many at the Conference desired to incorporate in the Charter an international bill of rights further implementing this basic objective. Although this was not done, numerous Articles of the Charter are specifically intended to promote action in the direction indicated by this reaffirmation.[1] The phrase "and of nations large and small" appears to introduce the idea of equal rights of states [2] which is again affirmed in paragraph 2 of Article 1 and paragraph 1 of Article 2.

The third of the general purposes set forth in the Preamble is the establishment of "conditions under which justice and respect for the obligations arising from treaties and other sources of international law can be maintained." The "other sources of international law" referred to are apparently those enumerated in Article 38 of the Statute of the International Court of Justice.[3] Obviously the "conditions" which are here referred to include the existence of organized procedures for settling disputes peacefully and suitable arrangements for keeping recalcitrant states from disturbing the peace. Broadly conceived, however, these conditions would seem to include such economic and social relations between states as will make it possible for all peoples to enjoy decent standards of living and general well-being and will thereby make easier the task of maintaining an order based on respect for law.

The promotion of "social progress and better standards of life in larger freedom" is given as a separate and final general purpose. This purpose finds more detailed exposition in Article 1, paragraph 3. Its implementation is provided for particularly in Chapters IX and X.

[1] See particularly Articles 1, paragraphs 2 and 3; 8; 13; 55; 62; 68; and 76.

[2] The Charter employs the words "state," "nation," "people," and "Member," with the following meanings:

State — a people occupying a definite territory under a government that has reached such a stage in its development as to permit the admission of the political entity in question as a Member of the United Nations.

Nation — used in the Charter as synonymous with *state*, and not as referring to a people with a common culture irrespective of form of political organization.

People — the inhabitants of a state or of a territory which has not yet reached the degree of political development and stability necessary to statehood.

Member — a state which has deposited its ratification of the Charter under the terms of Article 110 or which has been admitted to membership under the terms of Article 4, and which has not been expelled or voluntarily withdrawn from membership. The word is used without capitalization to refer to a Member in its capacity as member of an organ of the United Nations.

[3] For text of *The Statute of the International Court of Justice*, see this volume, p. 365.

The phrase "in larger freedom" suggests a conception of freedom akin to that developed in President Roosevelt's annual message to Congress of January 6, 1941 in which he listed "four essential human freedoms": "freedom of speech and expression — everywhere in the world," "freedom of every person to worship God in his own way — everywhere in the world," "freedom from want — . . . — everywhere in the world," and "freedom from fear — . . . — anywhere in the world." [1]

The second part of the Preamble contains an enumeration of the specific policies which the peoples of the United Nations announce their determination to pursue in achieving the above ends. The present form of this part of the Preamble differs materially both from that of Marshal Smuts' original draft [2] and from that approved by Committee I/1.[3] In Marshal Smuts' draft the first policy was treated as fundamental to the others. It was accepted that nations might "work together to maintain international peace and security" by the specific means which followed, four in number. The Committee text raised the second policy to the level of a fundamental commitment with the third and fourth treated as specific means for carrying it out. Considerable dissatisfaction with the Committee draft was expressed, but in the closing days of the Conference time did not permit the thorough revision or even rewriting of the Preamble which some would like to have seen. However, when the Draft Charter was submitted to the Steering Committee of the Conference for its approval preliminary to adoption by the Conference in plenary session serious exception was taken to the phraseology of the second part of the Preamble and it was adopted with the understanding that certain improvements in form were to be made. The present text was the final result.

The policy enunciated in the first clause is of a fundamental nature, and as we have seen, was originally intended by General Smuts to be the basic guiding principle of which the remainder would be an elaboration. It would appear to be the affirmation of "the policy of the good neighbor" as stated by President Franklin D. Roosevelt in his inaugural address, March 4, 1933, in these words:

"In the field of world policy I would dedicate this nation to the policy of the good neighbor — the neighbor who resolutely respects himself and, because he does so, respects the rights of others — the neighbor who respects his obligations and respects the sanctity of his agreements in and with a world of neighbors." [4]

[1] *Documents on American Foreign Relations, III, 1940–41*, Boston, World Peace Foundation, 1941, p. 33.

[2] UNCIO, *Documentation for Meetings of Committee I/1*, Doc. 215, I/1/10, p. 3.

[3] *Ibid., Appendix to Rapporteur's Report, Committee I/1*, Doc. 945, I/1/34 (1) (a), p. 1.

[4] *Roosevelt's Foreign Policy, 1933–1941*, N. Y., Wilfred Funk, Inc., 1942, p. 3.

The policies contained in the second and third clauses are reaffirmed in Article 1, paragraph 1 and Article 2, and detailed provision is made for their implementation in other parts of the Charter, especially Chapters VI and VII.

The policy set forth in the fourth and final clause is reaffirmed in Article 1, paragraph 3, and detailed provisions for its implementation are to be found in other parts of the Charter, especially Chapters IX to XIII.

Name of the Organization. In the Dumbarton Oaks Proposals it had been suggested that the new Organization should be given the name "The United Nations." This title had been suggested by President Roosevelt, and by Field Marshal Smuts of the Union of South Africa in an address before the two Houses of the British Parliament on October 21, 1942.[1] The idea back of this suggestion was, first of all, that this name accurately described the kind of organization necessary to the achievement of common purposes, and, secondly, that it had already been given recognition in the Declaration by United Nations of January 1, 1942. The official British position was that the name was intended to affirm both the fact that the Organization "is a result of the common effort which has saved civilization from the Nazi and Fascist attacks and the belief that such a close union will continue in the future." [2]

There were, however, delegations at UNCIO who felt that the name was unwise because it tended to perpetuate the idea of a military coalition formed for limited purposes under given historical circumstances. They felt that the name was too exclusive, that it had implied action against certain states, and that it might impede progress towards universality. Certain difficulties of translation into other languages were also pointed out. Most of the delegates, however, felt that the proposed name was fitting. It was unanimously adopted by the technical committee as a tribute to President Franklin D. Roosevelt,[3] and the Committee's recommendation was accepted without dissent by Commission I and by the Conference.

There was consideration at the Conference of the question whether the definite article "the" should be considered part of the title, and, if so, whether it must always be capitalized. It was decided that the definite article should be included in the title, but that it should not for that reason be generally capitalized.

[1] Holborn, Louise W., Ed., *War and Peace Aims of the United Nations*, I, 1939–42, Boston, World Peace Foundation, 1943, p. 347.

[2] *British Parliamentary Papers*, Miscellaneous No. 6 (1944), Cmd. 6571, par. 1.

[3] UNCIO, *Report of Rapporteur of Committee 1 to Commission I*, Doc. 944, I/1/34 (1), p. 5.

CHAPTER I

PURPOSES AND PRINCIPLES

ARTICLE 1

The Purposes of the United Nations are:

1. To maintain international peace and security, and to that end: to take effective collective measures for the prevention and removal of threats to the peace, and for the suppression of acts of aggression or other breaches of the peace, and to bring about by peaceful means, and in conformity with the principles of justice and international law, adjustment or settlement of international disputes or situations which might lead to a breach of the peace;

Maintenance of Peace and Security as an Objective. The present Charter, like the Dumbarton Oaks Proposals, places the maintenance of peace and security as the very first purpose of the Organization. It should be noticed that the peace to be maintained is "international" peace. It is not the purpose, except incidentally and on account of international implications, to keep internal peace or to intervene in a civil war.[1] None of the other purposes of the Organization can be achieved without peace and security. Formal peace alone, however, is not enough. Armed peace with the fear of war as the recurrent theme is not sufficient for the achievement of the purposes of the new Organization. Peace must be accompanied by a feeling of security, security from war in particular.[2]

Some would hold that there must also be a guarantee of justice as an assurance of peace. There is no real peace and security, it is argued, if they are achieved only at the sacrifice of justice.[3] It was proposed, both in Committee I/1 and in Commission I, to make this principle explicit by inserting the words "in conformity with the principles of justice and international law" immediately after the words "maintain international peace and security." The purpose of this amendment was to rule out any possibility of "appeasement" or "a new Munich." The proposal was, however, defeated since it was not approved by the necessary two-thirds vote.

[1] See comment on Article 2, paragraph 7, this volume, p. 72.
[2] See Point 6 of the Atlantic Charter, *ibid.*, p. 305.
[3] See the statement about withdrawal in comment on Article 6, *ibid.*, p. 87.

The reasons for maintaining the text were very clearly given by the delegates who opposed the change. They were all in favor of justice, they were all against appeasement, but they did not want to tie the hands of the Security Council. Their view was that the chief role of the Council must be to prevent or to suppress the use of armed force. It must be able to do this without asking in each case which of the parties is wrong. Its first duty is to act as a policeman. After that, when the disorder is suppressed, it may act as an organ of conciliation. But no state which has taken the law into its own hands should be allowed to stop the Council from acting by saying that it is right and that its adversary is wrong. That claim can only be made at a later stage.[1]

Means for Maintaining International Peace and Security. To maintain international peace and security "effective collective measures for the prevention and removal of threats to the peace, and for the suppression of acts of aggression or other breaches of the peace" are to be taken. These words establish the principle of so-called collective security. The detailed implementation of this principle is left to Chapter VII. It is to be noted here, however, that the Charter does not attempt any definition of aggression. It was not considered desirable to attempt any such definition for fear that it would unduly limit the power of the Security Council and would play into the hands of the would-be aggressor.[2]

The Charter also proposes to achieve the maintenance of international peace and security by bringing about "by peaceful means, and in conformity with the principles of justice and international law, adjustment or settlement of international disputes or situations which might lead to a breach of the peace." These principles are implemented by Chapters VI and XIV in particular. It is to be noted that it is not intended that the Organization shall undertake the "adjustment or settlement" of all disputes or situations, only those "which might lead to a breach of the peace." The Charter thus by implication makes a distinction between disputes or situations of minor importance and those whose continuance " might lead to a breach of the peace."

The use of the words "by peaceful means" calls for a word of comment. "Peaceful" and "pacific" are used interchangeably in the Charter.[3] "Peaceful means" appears to have a more restricted meaning than "means short of war." The use of so-called armed reprisals is presumably not regarded as a peaceful means for the settlement of disputes.

"*In conformity with the principles of justice and international law.*" This phrase was not contained in the Dumbarton Oaks text but was inserted

[1] UNCIO, *Report of the Rapporteur of Committee 1 to Commission I*, Doc. 944, I/1/34 (1), p. 8.

[2] See comment on Article 39, this volume, p. 155.

[3] "Peaceful" is used in Article 1, paragraph 1; Article 2, paragraph 3; Article 33, paragraph 1. "Pacific" is used in the title of Chapter VI; in Article 35, paragraph 2; and in Article 38.

at San Francisco on the recommendation of several governments, including the four Sponsoring Governments. The insertion of these words was intended to provide a safeguard against the settlement of international questions on the basis of political expediency. It was intended to avoid such a sacrifice of the rights of small nations in the interest of a doubtful peace as was made at Munich. It must be admitted that the word "justice" is a fairly vague concept which leaves considerable discretion to the organ which is called upon to apply it.[1] The meaning of "international law" is more definite.[2]

For explanation of distinction between "disputes" and "situations," see comment on Article 32, p. 140.

2. To develop friendly relations among nations based on respect for the principle of equal rights and self-determination of peoples, and to take other appropriate measures to strengthen universal peace;

The Preamble, as we have seen, makes use of the words "good neighbors" in expressing much the same idea.[3]

In the Dumbarton Oaks Proposals, the words "to develop friendly relations among nations" alone were used. At UNCIO two new ideas were introduced. First of all the Charter says that friendly relations shall be based "on respect for the principle of equal rights . . . of peoples." It is rather difficult to define this phrase. The expression as it stands is really a mixture of two distinct ideas. The one is a legal concept, that all states are equal.[4] The other idea is the moral concept, expressed in Point 2 of the Atlantic Charter and recognized more specifically in the phrase "self-determination of peoples," that all peoples have the right to choose the form of government under which they shall live. While international practice affords only limited support for either idea, even the more conservative one of the equal legal rights of states, it clearly was the intention of the framers of the Charter at San Francisco that the Organization should actively seek to realize this ideal of equal rights, both of states and of peoples, as an important basis of "friendly relations among nations."

The Conference also introduced the principle of "self-determination of peoples." The principle of self-determination is of great historical importance. It played an important role after the First World War and was in substance affirmed in the Atlantic Charter.[5] It presumably has a two-fold meaning: respect for the wishes of the people concerned in

[1] See comment on Article 2, paragraph 3, this volume, p. 66.

[2] International public law may be defined as a body of rules governing the conduct of states in their mutual relations and generally obeyed by them on the assumption that they are thereby fulfilling a legal obligation. The sources of this international law are indicated in Article 38 of the *Statute of the International Court of Justice*.

[3] For definition of President Roosevelt's good neighbor policy, see this volume, p. 57.

[4] See comments on Article 2, paragraph 1, *ibid.*, p. 64.

[5] See Points 2 and 3, *ibid.*, p. 305.

determining territorial changes; and the right of peoples to choose the form of government under which they are to live. In committee discussion at UNCIO it was made clear that an essential element of the principle of self-determination "is a free and genuine expression of the will of the people."[1] It would seem that the delegations at San Francisco did not mean by using these words to encourage the peoples of dependent territories to demand their immediate independence, or members of a federated state of one kind or another to exercise the right of secession. This seems to follow clearly from Article 2, paragraph 7, and from the Chapters dealing with non-self-governing peoples (XI, XII and XIII).

The second part of this paragraph states that it is a purpose of the Organization "to take other appropriate measures to strengthen universal peace." This in effect authorizes the Organization to take any measures consistent with the basic principles of the Organization which are appropriate for strengthening "universal peace." We have here an example of lack of uniformity in the use of words. The first paragraph in Article 1 uses the expression "international peace and security" and the second paragraph speaks of "universal peace." It is fairly safe to assume that these two expressions should be interpreted in the same sense.

3. To achieve international cooperation in solving international problems of an economic, social, cultural, or humanitarian character, and in promoting and encouraging respect for human rights and for fundamental freedoms for all without distinction as to race, sex, language, or religion; and

The corresponding phrase in the Dumbarton Oaks Proposals was much briefer. It read as follows: "To achieve international cooperation in the solution of international economic, social and other humanitarian problems." Chapter IX (*Arrangements for International Economic and Social Cooperation*) declared it to be a purpose of the Organization to "promote respect for human rights and fundamental freedoms." At San Francisco it was decided, on the proposal of the four Sponsoring Governments, to transfer this phrase to the Chapter dealing with the purposes of the Organization and to add the qualifying words which appear in the present text. It was also agreed, likewise upon the proposal of the Sponsoring Governments, to spell out in somewhat greater detail the first part of the paragraph by inserting the word "cultural."

This paragraph affords clear evidence that the framers of the Charter recognized that the maintenance of peace and security is not solely a matter of settling disputes or dealing with threats to the peace or cases of actual aggression. There is also the need of creating conditions, other than purely political ones, favorable to the existence of peace. In this

[1] UNCIO, *Report of the Rapporteur of Committee 1 to Commission I*, Doc. 944, I/1/34 (1), p. 10.

paragraph the Charter recognizes that an Organization set up primarily to provide peace and security must also actively concern itself with the improvement of the economic and social conditions of peoples and the widening of the area of human freedom.

There is no attempt made to define the "human rights" and "fundamental freedoms" to which reference is made. President Roosevelt in his "Four Freedoms" address listed freedom of speech, freedom of religion, freedom from fear, and freedom from want. In the Atlantic Charter, freedom from fear and freedom from want were given express recognition as objectives. By the Declaration by United Nations, the signatories subscribed to the objectives of the Atlantic Charter, and, in addition, recognized the defense of religious freedom as one goal of their common war effort. At the San Francisco Conference, the United States Delegation made it clear that, in their understanding, the "fundamental freedoms" included freedom of speech, and that freedom of speech involved, in international relationships, freedom of exchange of information.[1] A proposal was made at the Conference that a declaration of human rights should be included in the Charter. This proposal was not accepted, chiefly for the reason that it was felt that the Organization, once formed, could best act upon this suggestion either through the commission provided for in Article 68 or by some other means.

4. To be a center for harmonizing the actions of nations in the attainment of these common ends.

The wording of this paragraph does not indicate any preference for a strict centralization of international activities. It is not the intention that all organizations established for these common ends should necessarily have their administrative offices and other organs located at the headquarters of the United Nations. They may, as before, be seated where it is most practical, Singapore, Rome, Paris, The Hague, etc. The proper interpretation of this phrase would seem to be that the Organization is to be a central focal and coordinating agency for carrying out common purposes. Functions such as those envisaged in Articles 57 and 63 would be in line with such an interpretation.

ARTICLE 2

The Organization and its Members, in pursuit of the Purposes stated in Article 1, shall act in accordance with the following Principles.

This Article is of fundamental importance in the total economy of the Charter. It lays down certain fundamental principles which the Organization operating through its various organs must respect. These same principles are also binding upon Members. Since the General Assembly,

[1] *Charter of the United Nations, Report to the President on the Results of the San Francisco Conference*, etc., cited above, p. 38.

the Security Council, the Economic and Social Council, and the Trustee-ship Council are composed of Member States, it might be thought that with respect, at least to the activities of these organs, the use of the word "Organization" is superfluous. This, however, is clearly not true of the Secretariat and the International Court of Justice. The Charter clearly distinguishes between the Organization and its Members. Both, by this Article, are to respect certain basic principles.

1. The Organization is based on the principle of the sovereign equality of all its Members.

The Dumbarton Oaks Proposals used the expression "the sovereign equality of all peace-loving states." This was modified at UNCIO so as to make the principle applicable only to Member States since it was not considered appropriate or desirable to give non-member states the benefits conferred by the Charter. The principle contains two parts. It includes the recognition of the sovereignty of Members and also of their equality. These two concepts will be examined separately.

The Concept of National Sovereignty. It is unnecessary here to engage in an extensive discussion of the meaning of sovereignty. It may be useful, however, to present certain basic ideas. According to one school of thought, sovereignty is a principle according to which the state is supreme and does not accept orders from any other authority. This in general harmonizes with the historical origin of the concept. Under-stood in this sense, there is an apparent contradiction between national sovereignty and international law. Absolute sovereignty and interna-tional law seem to become mutually exclusive terms.

The Charter, however, provides for an international organization. It creates a new legal order. Therefore, sovereignty in the Charter must obviously mean sovereignty subject to the provisions of the Charter. This implies that the Member States are free and sovereign within the limitations imposed upon them by the Charter. It means that they are assumed to have accepted in good faith the obligations of member-ship and to have delegated to the Organization the powers that they have expressly delegated, but that the residue of the so-called sovereign powers of states still remains with the Member States themselves.

One of the most serious apparent limitations on the absolute sover-eignty of Members is that contained in the provisions of Article 109, by which Members are bound by amendments adopted and ratified in accordance with the provisions of the Charter even though they them-selves may have voted against and refused to ratify these amendments. This limitation has, however, been greatly weakened in effect by the admission, though not in express words, of the right of withdrawal.[1] Attention should also be called to the provisions of Article 25 under

---

[1] See this volume, p. 86.

which Members agree to accept and carry out the decisions of the Security Council.[1] This of course will mean in practice that some states will be bound by decisions to which they have not been parties. However, they will have agreed in advance to this limitation on their freedom of action, and as the Permanent Court of International Justice pointed out in a number of its decisions, part of the sovereignty of a state consists of the right to limit itself by entering into treaty obligations.[2]

The strongest safeguard of the sovereignty of Member States as defined above is to be found in the provisions of Article 2, paragraph 7, denying the authority of the Organization to intervene in matters essentially within the domestic jurisdiction of states.

The Concept of State Equality. This is really just an application of the concept of national sovereignty. States are sovereign, and for that reason they have an equal capacity for rights as members of the international community. Every state, irrespective of origin, size or form of government, has an equal right to order its own internal affairs and in general to direct its policy within the limits of international law. States are entitled to have the rules of international law applied equally and impartially in the settlement of disputes which they refer to an international court of justice.

This equality before the law does not of course mean that states are equally capable of getting their rights respected in a world which still permits individual states to rely primarily on their own power to secure respect for their rights. Nor does equality, thus conceived, mean political equality. Costa Rica is not the equal of the United States in political power and influence, nor is Finland the equal of the Soviet Union.

The above interpretation of the concept of equality is consistent with the provisions of the Charter. Thus under the Charter certain Members have the right to be permanent members of the Security Council, while the others can only be members of the Council when elected by the General Assembly, and then only for limited periods of time. Under Article 27, while the Security Council can take a decision by less than a unanimous vote, in the case of non-procedural matters unanimity of the permanent members is required. Thus the permanent members have a control over Security Council decisions which is denied to other Members of the Organization.[3]

Meaning of "Sovereign Equality." It is, therefore, quite clear that the "sovereign equality" of the Member States does not mean that they are absolutely sovereign or absolutely equal. Both parts of the principle

[1] For further comment, see *ibid.*, p. 122.

[2] See, for example, Judgment in the S. S. *Wimbledon* Case, Documents of the P.C.I.J., Series A, No. 1.

[3] For full discussion of the meaning of the concept of equality of states, see Dickinson, E. D., *The Equality of States in International Law*, Cambridge, Harvard Univ. Press, 1920.

suffer rather important exceptions. Some indication of the content of the term was given by Committee I/1 in its report to Commission I. This statement was approved by the Commission and by the Conference in plenary session. According to it, sovereign equality includes the following elements:

(1) that states are juridically equal;
(2) that each state enjoys the right inherent in full sovereignty;
(3) that the personality of the state is respected, as well as its territorial integrity and political independence;
(4) that the state should, under international order, comply faithfully with its international duties and obligations.[1]

2. All Members, in order to ensure to all of them the rights and benefits resulting from membership, shall fulfil in good faith the obligations assumed by them in accordance with the present Charter.

Though this principle would seem to be fairly obvious, and indeed fundamental to the establishment of any international legal order, it was considered desirable to state it explicitly as one of the basic principles of the Charter. It was contained in the Dumbarton Oaks Proposals. There is, apart from drafting changes, only one major change. The Charter has added the words "in good faith." This addition cannot be said to add much in substance. It was inserted by Commission I when the report of the technical committee was under consideration at the request of the Delegate of Colombia, who thought that it was appropriate to state the idea of good faith as "a *leit motif*" of the new Organization because good faith had so often been conspicuously lacking from international relations in the years immediately preceding. The amendment was adopted by a unanimous vote.[2]

The paragraph states the reason why Members are to fulfil in good faith their obligations under the Charter. It is because that is necessary if all Members are to be ensured the rights and benefits of membership. In other words, the advantages of membership are only to be had if the burdens of membership are loyally assumed. This principle finds specific application in Article 19.

3. All Members shall settle their international disputes by peaceful means in such a manner that international peace and security, and justice, are not endangered.

The principle laid down in this paragraph is basic to the provisions of the Charter for the pacific settlement of disputes, especially Chapters VI and XIV.

[1] UNCIO, *Report of Rapporteur of Committee 1 to Commission I*, Doc. 944, I/1/34 (1), p. 12; *Verbatim Minutes of Second Meeting of Commission I, June 15, 1945,* Doc. 1123, I/8, p. 5–7; *Verbatim Minutes of the Ninth Plenary Session, June 25, 1945,* Doc. 1210, P/20, p. 3.
[2] *Ibid., Verbatim Minutes of the Second Meeting of Commission I, June 15, 1945,* Doc. 1123, I/8, p. 7–16.

At the San Francisco Conference, the word "international" was inserted in the Dumbarton Oaks text to make it clear that the obligation does not apply to domestic disputes. This same result would, however, have been achieved by the provisions of paragraph 7 of this Article, but it was thought desirable to make the meaning clear beyond a doubt. The meaning of the phrase "by peaceful means" has already been the subject of comment.[1] It is obvious that this rules out recourse to certain measures short of war which involve the use of force, such as armed reprisals. A positive, though not an exhaustive, enumeration of peaceful means is given in Article 33, paragraph 1.

This paragraph does not obligate Members to settle all their international disputes. It does, however, create a positive duty to seek the settlement of their disputes by peaceful means.[2] Since they are to settle their international disputes "in such a manner that international peace and security" are not endangered, it can be assumed, as other provisions of the Charter expressly recognize, that generally speaking international disputes become matters of concern to the Organization only when their continuance threatens international peace and security. It is quite consistent with the principle laid down in this paragraph that minor disputes, that is, those whose continuance does not threaten international peace and security, should remain unsettled for extended periods of time, until they appear to the parties ripe for settlement. However, even "minor disputes" must in the end be settled "by peaceful means," if they are to be settled at all, since an attempt to settle them by other than peaceful means would give them the character of disputes whose continuance threatens international peace and security.

At San Francisco, on the proposal of the Delegation of Bolivia, it was decided to insert the words "and justice" in the Dumbarton Oaks text. The purpose of this clearly was to prevent a recurrence of appeasement at the expense of the smaller nations. It is not enough that peace and security should be safeguarded; the principles of justice must also be respected.[3]

4. All Members shall refrain in their international relations from the threat or use of force against the territorial integrity or political independence of any state, or in any other manner inconsistent with the Purposes of the United Nations.

This obligates Members to refrain from the threat or use of force in their international relations. This, of course, is the underlying and cardinal principle of the whole Organization.

First of all it is stated, although this is in the last part of the paragraph, that it is only *force used in a way inconsistent with the Purposes of the*

---

[1] See this volume, p. 60.
[2] See comment on Article 33, *ibid.*, p. 140.
[3] See comment on Article 1, paragraph 1, *ibid.*, p. 59.

Charter, which is forbidden. This means that the threat or use of force is permitted in connection with the application of measures of collective security.[1] It is also clear that self-defense is permitted, although this can be a dangerous principle.[2] The Delegation of New Zealand proposed that the right of self-defense should be more positively stated by making it an obligation of all Members collectively to resist any act of aggression against any Member. This amendment gained considerable support but failed to obtain the required two-thirds majority.[3]

The paragraph specifies that the threat or use of force *"against the territorial integrity or political independence of any state"* is forbidden. The words in quotes were inserted at UNCIO in response to the demand of the smaller states that there should be included in the Charter some more specific guarantee than was offered by the phraseology of the Dumbarton Oaks Proposals that force would not be used by the more powerful Members to violate the territorial integrity or political independence of smaller and weaker states. The paragraph as revised should be compared with Article 10 of the Covenant which President Wilson referred to as "the heart of the Covenant." The first sentence of Article 10 placed upon Members of the League the obligation "to respect and preserve as against external aggression the territorial integrity and existing political independence of all Members of the League." The Charter provision would appear to place upon Members of the United Nations the same obligation to "respect" the territorial integrity and political independence of Members, without however requiring them to take positive action to preserve these "against external aggression." It was the purpose of the New Zealand amendment, referred to above, to impose this obligation as well.

The interpretation of the expressions "territorial integrity" and "political independence" raises the same difficulties as under Article 10 of the Covenant.[4] Would the principle here laid down be violated if a Member sent its armed forces into the territory of another Member for "protective" purposes with the declared intention of withdrawing them as soon as the threat to the weaker state had been removed? In other words, is the territorial integrity of a state respected so long as its territory is left intact, i.e. so long as none of its territory is taken from it, or does respect for the territorial integrity of a state require respect for the territorial inviolability of a state, i.e., the right of a state to

---

[1] See Article 2, paragraph 5 and Chapters VII and VIII, as well as Articles 106 and 107.

[2] See Article 51 and comment thereon, this volume, p. 174.

[3] UNCIO, *Summary Report of Twelfth Meeting of Committee I/1, June 6, 1945,* Doc. 810, I/1/30, p. 1–5.

[4] Cf. Kelsen, Hans, *Legal Technique in International Law: A Textual Critique of the League Covenant,* Geneva Research Centre, Geneva Studies, X, No. 6 (December 1939), p. 66–81.

exercise exclusive jurisdiction within its own territory? Obviously, the consequences of the two interpretations might be radically different.

The expression "political independence" lends itself to easier interpretation. Clearly the "political independence" of a state is in fact violated if a state is coerced through the threat or use of force by a more powerful state into taking action which it would not otherwise take. On the other hand, we have seen that it is possible even here to use fictions which are intended to have the effect of concealing the real character of the action taken.

It would thus appear that these words, undoubtedly inserted to provide an added guarantee that force will not be used by any Member for its purely selfish purposes at the expense of another, will only serve their purpose to the extent that the Members of the Organization, and particularly the permanent members of the Security Council, loyally respect the spirit and intent of the words in question, and act through the Security Council to implement effectively the general principle here laid down.

The obligation not to use force is limited to *the use of force in "international relations."* This, of course, means that the Charter does not in this paragraph forbid use of force within the state itself, including its colonial possessions. This would also seem to follow from Article 2, paragraph 7. But even in this case, the use or threat of force can be dealt with by the Security Council if it is deemed to have dangerous international repercussions, which a civil war often will have. The question of the intervention of the Organization in such cases will be discussed in the comment on Article 2, paragraph 7.[1]

It should be borne in mind that whereas the Covenant of the League prohibited under certain conditions "resort to war" the Charter forbids *"the threat or use of force."* This expression covers a wider range of situations than "resort to war." War has in the past been regarded as a legal concept with certain effects depending on the entry into force of a so-called "state of war." [2] This state of war was not a necessary result of any use of force. It was generally accepted that no state of war existed if none of the parties involved so desired or if third states did not wish to enforce the laws of neutrality. In this way any limitation of the right to make war could be nullified. "Means short of war" have often been used in the past to coerce smaller or weaker states without going to the trouble of declaring war.[3] Peaceful blockade and other forms of "reprisals" have been resorted to without the formality of declaring war.

[1] See this volume, p. 72.

[2] See Wright, Quincy, "When Does War Exist?" *American Journal of International Law*, XXVI (April 1932), p. 362.

[3] See Hindmarsh, A. E., *Force in Peace*, Cambridge, Harvard Univ. Press, 249 p., 1933.

While it is not explicitly stated, it can be presumed that the word "force" as used in this paragraph means only "armed force." The Charter does not specifically forbid the use of economic force, although it tries to create such conditions in the world that even economic warfare will be rendered superfluous. Furthermore, under Chapter VII, the Security Council is given broad powers to determine the existence of any threat to the peace, and to take appropriate measures for dealing with the situation.

Not only the actual use of force, but even the threat of force is forbidden. This means among other things that even armed demonstrations are forbidden. It might, however, be rather difficult for the Organization to decide when an army maneuver in reality is meant as a threat. Under Article 39, the Organization is given the discretionary power to intervene when the peace of the world is threatened.

5. All Members shall give the United Nations every assistance in any action it takes in accordance with the present Charter, and shall refrain from giving assistance to any state against which the United Nations is taking preventive or enforcement action.

This paragraph combines paragraphs 5 and 6 of Chapter II of the Dumbarton Oaks Proposals. The two principles here stated are complementary, and are given detailed application in Chapter VII of the Charter. A question which is not expressly answered in the Charter is whether the obligations assumed by Members under this paragraph apply to action taken by the parties to the Moscow Four-Power Declaration and France "on behalf of the Organization" under the provisions of Article 106 of the Charter. On this point, see comment on Article 106.[1]

6. The Organization shall ensure that states which are not Members of the United Nations act in accordance with these Principles so far as may be necessary for the maintenance of international peace and security.

This paragraph corresponds to the last unnumbered paragraph of Chapter II of the Dumbarton Oaks Proposals. It represents a somewhat different approach to the problem of what to do with disputes and situations involving non-member states from that adopted in the Covenant of the League of Nations. Article 17 of the Covenant provided that in the event of a dispute involving a state not a Member of the League the state should be invited "to accept the obligations of membership" "for the purposes of such dispute" upon conditions deemed just by the Council. If the invitation were accepted, the provisions of Articles 12 to 16 inclusive would be applicable with such modifications as might be deemed necessary by the Council. If a non-member refused to accept

---

[1] See this volume, p. 286.

the obligations of membership and resorted to war against a Member, the sanctions provisions of the Covenant became applicable. If both parties, being non-members, refused to accept the obligations for the purposes of the dispute, the Council might take such measures and make such recommendations as would prevent hostilities and result in the settlement of the dispute. These provisions were never fully put into operation in a specific case. Consequently there is no basis of experience for judging their effectiveness.

The Charter places on the Organization the obligation to see that states which are not Members act in accordance with the principles of Article 2 "so far as may be necessary for the maintenance of international peace and security." It is clear that the Organization thereby actually assumes authority not based on the consent of the states affected. The Charter does not of course create any legal obligations for states not Members of the Organization.[1] They are therefore not obligated in a legal sense to act according to the Principles of the Charter for any purpose whatsoever. The Charter system therefore provides for the imposition, by force if necessary, of the prescribed conduct without any legal basis in contractual agreement. This means, more specifically, that the Security Council, upon which "primary responsibility for the maintenance of international peace and security" is placed, is required to enforce upon non-members conformity with the Charter Principles so far as may be necessary to the maintenance of international peace and security. Because of the recent experience with aggression by Japan and Germany when these states were not Members of the League of Nations, there was no question at San Francisco but what some provision of this nature for dealing with threats to or violations of the peace by states not Members of the Organization should be made. Otherwise the whole scheme of the Charter might be jeopardized.

The provisions of this paragraph should be considered in connection with the terms of Article 35, paragraph 2, which permits a state not a Member of the United Nations to bring to the attention of the Security Council or General Assembly any dispute to which it is a party "if it accepts in advance, for the purposes of the dispute, the obligations of pacific settlement provided in the present Charter," and of Article 106 which empowers the parties to the Moscow Four-Power Declaration and France to take such joint action on behalf of the Organization, pending the coming into force of the special agreements referred to in Article 43, as may be necessary for the purpose of maintaining international peace and security.

[1] This view is not accepted by all writers. Dr. Hans Kelsen, for example, holds that international treaties can impose legal obligations on states not parties to them. See his *Peace Through Law*, Chapel Hill, N. C., Univ. of North Carolina Press, 1944, p. 38.

7. Nothing contained in the present Charter shall authorize the United Nations to intervene in matters which are essentially within the domestic jurisdiction of any state or shall require the Members to submit such matters to settlement under the present Charter; but this principle shall not prejudice the application of enforcement measures under Chapter VII.

Origin of Paragraph. The exception of domestic jurisdiction was given a more modest place in the Dumbarton Oaks Proposals. There it figured as an exception to the provisions relating to the pacific settlement of disputes. At UNCIO the Sponsoring Governments proposed to take it out of this Chapter and insert it in modified form as one of the basic principles of the Organization. This proposal was unanimously adopted subject to one change which was made at the instance of the Australian Delegation.

The effect of transferring the provision to the Chapter establishing basic principles is to make it a limitation upon all the activities of the Organization rather than merely a limitation upon the action of the Organization under Chapter VI (the equivalent of Section A of Chapter VIII of the Dumbarton Oaks Proposals). This seemed desirable to some because of the considerable increase made at San Francisco in the power of the Organization to deal with economic, social and cultural matters. Without such a limitation it was argued by some that the Organization could intervene directly in the domestic economic, social and cultural arrangements of Member States.[1] On the other hand, it was strongly argued that this provision, particularly in the form in which it was proposed at San Francisco, would operate as a serious restriction upon the freedom of action of the Organization in dealing with the problems of a changing world. It was suggested that it embodied an antiquated idea wholly incompatible with the establishment of an organized international order.

Comparison with Provisions of League Covenant. All the questions involved in this paragraph were very warmly debated at San Francisco. It was felt by many that the present wording was too restrictive and actually represented a retrogression in international life. It was pointed out that the provisions of the League of Nations Covenant did not go nearly as far in limiting the scope of the League's activity. Article 15, paragraph 8, applying only to the submission of disputes to the Council for settlement, read: "If the dispute between the parties is claimed by one of them, and is found by the Council, to arise out of a matter which by international law is solely within the domestic jurisdiction of that party, the Council shall so report, and shall make no recommendation as to its settlement." However, the second paragraph of Article 11

---

[1] *Charter of the United Nations, Report to the President on the Results of the San Francisco Conference*, etc., cited above, p. 44; UNCIO, *Summary Report of the Seventeenth Meeting of Committee I/1, June 14, 1945*, Doc. 1019, I/1/42, p. 1.

which was more commonly used as the basis for League action in keeping the peace contained no such limitation.

It was considered quite possible for the Council or Assembly to exercise mediatory and conciliatory functions within the framework of the League even if the conflict should arise out of a matter within the domestic jurisdiction of one of the parties. It was understood as a matter of course that no recommendation made under Article 11 had any obligatory effect whatsoever. Article 5 of the celebrated but unratified Geneva Protocol of 1924[1] made this quite clear and stated it *expressis verbis*. This kind of conciliation now appears excluded due to the strict formulation of Article 2, paragraph 7.

Meaning of "Domestic Jurisdiction." An important question to be considered is the actual meaning of the term "domestic jurisdiction." This is not the place to go into all the intricacies of this question. It is enough to state that there are — even according to modern theories — certain matters that are outside the scope of international law. It is left to the states concerned to settle these if they are considered internal or domestic matters. Matters of immigration restriction, granting of citizenship, and import duties are usually considered purely domestic matters, unless regulated by the provisions of treaties. Many of these matters are of the greatest political importance and can give rise to the most serious international complications. They may, it should be understood, be of the most momentous importance for other states although they are left to the individual states to settle. It should also be understood that while the reservation regarding "domestic jurisdiction" has been common, as for example, in arbitration treaties and in the acceptance of the obligatory jurisdiction of the Permanent Court, the content of the term is highly flexible. A good example of this fluidity or elasticity is the treatment of aliens. At one time any state could treat aliens exactly as it wished. Today there are definite rules regarding the treatment of aliens. It may be difficult from time to time to determine whether a question is or is not a part of this reserved domain. It should be clear that a matter ceases to be a matter of domestic jurisdiction if it is regulated by an international treaty.[2]

In the discussion thus far it has been assumed that international law provides the standard by which it is to be determined whether a matter falls within the domestic jurisdiction of a state or not. The Dumbarton Oaks Proposals, following in this regard the Covenant of the League of Nations, made explicit provision to this effect. At San Francisco,

---

[1] *Protocol of Arbitration, Security and Disarmament*, Boston, World Peace Foundation Publications, VII, No. 7 (1924), p. 401.

[2] See Advisory Opinion of the Permanent Court of International Justice in the case of the *Nationality Decrees in Tunis and Morocco*, Publications of the P.C.I.J., Series B, No. 4.

following the proposal of the Sponsoring Governments, it was decided to omit all reference to international law as a measuring rod. It was argued that the provisions of international law on this subject are indefinite and inadequate and do not provide a reliable or acceptable guide. It was also stated that the proposal of the Sponsoring Governments dealt with domestic jurisdiction "as a basic principle," and not, as had been the case in the original Dumbarton Oaks Proposals and in Article 15 of the Covenant, "as a technical and legalistic formula designed to deal with the settlement of disputes by the Security Council." On the other hand, it was pointed out that by omitting all reference to an objective standard, the matter is left entirely to the discretion of the state or states concerned and will be decided on grounds of political interest and expediency.[1]

Use of Word "Essentially." The Dumbarton Oaks Proposals stated that the matter should be "solely" within the domestic jurisdiction in order for the reservation to operate. This was changed at San Francisco and the word "essentially" was substituted for the word "solely," thereby making it clear that the reservation should have a wider application. If a matter is on the borderline between international concern and domestic jurisdiction, it may be placed outside the authority of the Organization if one can claim that it is "essentially" within the domestic jurisdiction. In justification of the use of the word "essentially," it was argued that the word "solely" is inadequate as a test in view of the fact that under modern conditions what one nation does domestically almost always has at least some external repercussions.[2]

Who Decides Whether Paragraph Applies. Another question that is intimately linked up with the questions already considered is who is to decide whether or not a matter is "essentially within the domestic jurisdiction" of a state. Under the Covenant of the League the Council was empowered to decide this question. The Dumbarton Oaks Proposals contained no explicit provision. Certain delegations proposed at San Francisco that this question should be referred to the International Court of Justice. This proposal was rejected because it involved acceptance of the compulsory jurisdiction of the Court, which certain states were not prepared to do. It was consequently decided to omit any special provision, the assumption being that the paragraph will be interpreted in the same manner as other parts of the Charter, that is, by the organs concerned and by the Members themselves.[3] The possibility that the

[1] For Committee discussion of questions raised with respect to this paragraph, see UNCIO, *Summary Report of Sixteenth Meeting of Committee I/1, June 13, 1945,* Doc. 987, I/1/40, and *Summary Report of Seventeenth Meeting of Committee I/1, June 14, 1945,* Doc. 1019, I/1/42.

[2] *Charter of the United Nations, Report to the President on the Results of the San Francisco Conference,* etc., cited above, p. 45.

[3] See UNCIO, *Report of Committee IV/2,* Doc. 933, IV/2/42 (2).

question will be referred to the International Court either by agreement of the parties or by an organ of the United Nations is, of course, not excluded.

Effect of Denial of Authority. The first effect is that the Organization cannot intervene. The words could perhaps have been better chosen. The Organization never intervenes in the orthodox sense of that word. What the provision means is that the Organization shall not exercise any authority, not even make recommendations of any kind, with respect to any matter "essentially within the domestic jurisdiction" of a state. Nor shall it attempt to promote the solution of any conflict when it is found that the matter falls within the domestic jurisdiction of one of the parties to the dispute. In addition, and this is expressly stated, Members are not obligated to submit any such matters to settlement under the provisions of the Charter. They are not, however, free to use force or the threat of force to achieve the settlement of such disputes since the Security Council's authority to take necessary enforcement measures to keep the peace is safeguarded by the exception at the end of the paragraph.

Exception Regarding Application of Enforcement Measures. The sole limitation on the broad principle stated in the paragraph is that it shall not prejudice the application of enforcement measures under Chapter VII. Under Chapter VIII, Section B, of the Dumbarton Oaks Proposals the Organization had the right to "make recommendations or decide upon measures to be taken to maintain or restore peace and security." This provision was capable of being interpreted to mean that the Security Council could recommend or decide upon the terms of settlement of a dispute, as well as take enforcement measures. Since the "domestic jurisdiction" reservation in the Dumbarton Oaks Proposals applied only to the provisions of Chapter VIII, Section A, the fear was expressed that the result which it was desired to prevent could be achieved under Section B. The amendment proposed by the Sponsoring Governments at San Francisco did not give full satisfaction on this point since it stated that the principle laid down "shall not prejudice the application of Chapter VIII, Section B." Another amendment proposed by the Sponsoring Governments to Chapter VIII, Section B, paragraph 2, did make it clear, however, that the action to be taken under that paragraph was to be of the kind described in paragraphs 3 and 4, i.e., enforcement action.

These proposed changes did not, however, give full satisfaction to those, notably the Australian Delegates, who feared that the Security Council might, under its authority to deal with threats to the peace or violations of the peace, actually take action affecting matters within the domestic jurisdiction of states. Consequently, an amendment was proposed by the Australian Delegation and adopted by the technical committee and by the Conference which rephrased the exception at the end of the paragraph in its present form.[1] As the paragraph stands, the only authority that the Organization has to deal with a matter "essentially within the domestic jurisdiction" of a state is to take "enforcement measures" under Chapter VII to maintain or restore international peace and security.

Authority of Organization in Cases of Civil War. A civil war is eminently a domestic matter. Any intervention by an outside state or group of states with a view to influencing the course of the struggle constitutes a violation of the state's independence.[2] By the terms of this Article the United Nations Organization is denied authority to intervene in any such domestic struggle, even though the sole purpose is to restore peace. That peace would be domestic, not international. However, as the result of foreign intervention or because of the nature of the domestic conflict, a situation may be created which endangers the maintenance of international peace and security. Faced with such a situation, the Security Council would undoubtedly possess the authority to act, to make necessary investigations under Article 34, and, under Article 39, to make recommendations or take decisions deemed necessary to the maintenance of international peace and security. Such recommendations and decisions, however, would have to be limited to the protection of the legitimate United Nations interest in the maintenance of "international peace and security" and could not be directed to the purely domestic aspects of the situation, i.e., the settlement of the civil war.

[1] For text, see *ibid.*, *Amendment by the Australian Delegation to Proposed Paragraph 8 of Chapter II (Principles). Memorandum by Dr. H. V. Evatt on Behalf of the Australian Delegation*, Doc. 969, I/1/39; see, also, in opposition to amendment, *Statement by the Norwegian Delegation (Dr. Arnold Raestad) on Paragraph 8, Chapter II, June 12, 1945*, Doc. 929, I/1/37.

[2] See Wilson, G. G., *International Law*, 9th ed., N. Y., Silver, Burdett and Co., 1935, p. 96–7.

MEMBERSHIP

ARTICLE 3

The original Members of the United Nations shall be the states which, having participated in the United Nations Conference on International Organization at San Francisco, or having previously signed the Declaration by United Nations of January 1, 1942, sign the present Charter and ratify it in accordance with Article 110.

Universal vs. *Limited Membership.* The question of membership is of course of fundamental importance for an international organization of the kind contemplated at San Francisco. The Dumbarton Oaks Proposals had simply provided that membership should be open to all peace-loving states [1] and that the General Assembly should be empowered, upon the recommendation of the Security Council, to admit new members. The Charter as finally adopted follows the general lines of the League of Nations Covenant.[2]

Certain of the delegations at San Francisco, particularly those of the Latin American states, were of the opinion that the Organization should be completely universal from the beginning. This also was advocated by a number of groups and organizations which made proposals for an international organization before the Conference at San Francisco was convened. However, the prevailing view at the Conference was that it would be unwise to take in all states irrespective of their political views and prevailing ideologies. The majority of states represented at San Francisco felt that it was necessary to demand certain guarantees from the states that were admitted. On the other hand there seemed to be a general agreement to the effect that the new organization should tend towards universality, that is, should eventually include all states.[3]

This question of universal *vs.* limited membership is the permanent dilemma of an international organization. A closed organization can be strong and efficient but it may easily invite counter alliances and become wrecked on the shoals of power politics. On the other side, one may be forced to sacrifice so much in order to obtain a universal membership —

[1] Chapter III, this volume, p. 309.
[2] See *Covenant*, Article 1.
[3] For definition of "state," see note 2, p. 56.

or a close approach to it — that the organization becomes loose and its substance very thin.

Classes of Membership. The Charter divides Members into two classes, original Members and elected Members. This distinction, however, is of a purely formal nature and does not in any way imply that there is to be any difference in status between these two classes of Members.

Original Members. The original Members of the Organization consist of the states which, having participated in the San Francisco Conference or having been parties to the Declaration by United Nations of January 1, 1942, sign the Charter and ratify it in accordance with the provisions of Article 110.

The following states were original signatories of the Declaration by United Nations of January 1, 1942:

The United States of America	Greece
The United Kingdom of Great Britain and Northern Ireland	Guatemala
	Haiti
The Union of Soviet Socialist Republics	Honduras
	India
China	Luxembourg
Australia	Netherlands
Belgium	New Zealand
Canada	Nicaragua
Costa Rica	Norway
Cuba	Panama
Czechoslovakia	Poland
Dominican Republic	South Africa
El Salvador	Yugoslavia

The following states subsequently adhered to the Declaration:

Mexico	June 5, 1942	Peru	Feb. 11, 1945
Philippines	June 10, 1942	Chile	Feb. 12, 1945
Ethiopia	July 28, 1942	Paraguay	Feb. 12, 1945
Iraq	Jan. 16, 1943	Venezuela	Feb. 16, 1945
Brazil	Feb. 8, 1943	Uruguay	Feb. 23, 1945
Bolivia	Apr. 27, 1943	Turkey	Feb. 24, 1945
Iran	Sept. 10, 1943	Egypt	Feb. 27, 1945
Colombia	Dec. 22, 1943	Saudi Arabia	Mar. 1, 1945
Liberia	Feb. 26, 1944	Syria	Mar. 1, 1945
France	Dec. 26, 1944	Lebanon	Mar. 1, 1945
Ecuador	Feb. 7, 1945		

The following states participated in the United Nations Conference on International Organization, either from the beginning or following admission by vote of the Conference:

Argentina	Brazil
Australia	Byelorussian Soviet Socialist Republic
Belgium	Canada
Bolivia	Chile

China
Colombia
Costa Rica
Cuba
Czechoslovakia
Denmark
Dominican Republic
Ecuador
Egypt
El Salvador
Ethiopia
France
Greece
Guatemala
Haiti
Honduras
India
Iran
Iraq
Lebanon
Liberia

Luxembourg
Mexico
Netherlands
New Zealand
Nicaragua
Norway
Panama
Paraguay
Peru
Philippine Commonwealth
Saudi Arabia
Syria
Turkey
Ukrainian Soviet Socialist Republic
Union of South Africa
Union of Soviet Socialist Republics
United Kingdom
United States of America
Uruguay
Venezuela
Yugoslavia

The only signatory of the Declaration by United Nations that did not participate in the Conference was Poland, which did not at the time of the Conference have a government recognized by all the Sponsoring Governments. The so-called "Lublin Government" had been recognized by the Soviet Union on January 5, 1945. After agreement had been reached permitting recognition of a properly constituted Polish Government by the Governments of the United Kingdom and the United States, the Polish representative signed the Charter on October 15, 1945.[1]

Meaning of "States." A special question that requires consideration is the meaning of the word "states" as used in this Article. If the word is taken in its strict legal sense, as used in international law, it would exclude certain political bodies that participated in the Conference with full expectation of becoming Members of the Organization. It is very difficult to draw a firm line of distinction between "states," on the one hand, and colonies, protectorates, etc., on the other. The League of Nations Covenant in the second paragraph of Article I used the expression "any fully self-governing state, dominion or colony." The Charter of the United Nations has not used such an expression, but has simply used the word "state" or "states."

It is quite clear in view of the attendant circumstances that the word "state" is not to be understood in its usual legal sense. The participation of two constituent republics of the Soviet Union in the Conference indicates that parts of a union, highly centralized in many respects in fact, may be independent members of the new Organization. The inclusion

---

[1] Department of State, *Bulletin*, XIII, p. 627.

of India further indicated that the possession of full and generally recognized independence was not necessary, as did the inclusion of the Philippine Commonwealth, Lebanon and Syria.[1] The word "state" would
therefore appear to be used in this and following Articles to include any
Member of the Organization, and any political body which at any given
time is considered eligible for membership. Article 34 of the Statute of
the Court uses the word in the same sense.

ARTICLE 4

**1. Membership in the United Nations is open to all other peace-loving
states which accept the obligations contained in the present Charter and,
in the judgment of the Organization, are able and willing to carry out
these obligations.**

While membership in the Organization is to be limited at the beginning, the way is opened for the future attainment of universality. While
states which are not included among the original Members are not
allowed as a matter of right to become Members, the conditions of membership and the method of admitting new Members are such that universality becomes possible of attainment.

Requirement That States Be "Peace-Loving." The original phraseology
of the Dumbarton Oaks Proposals by which membership was declared
"open to all peace-loving states" is retained. The term "peace-loving"
is of course extremely vague and open to different interpretations. It
was used in the Moscow Four-Power Declaration of October 30, 1943.
The Declaration of Tehran of December 1, 1943 presumably expressed
the same idea when it stated that the signatory powers would collaborate
with all peoples who "in heart and mind are dedicated; as are our own
peoples, to the elimination of tyranny and slavery, oppression and intolerance." It has been suggested that the best definition of a "peace-
loving" state is one that declared war on one or more of the Axis powers.

The expression is quite obviously a political term without any generally recognized and accepted meaning. In practice it will be interpreted by the Members of the Organization acting through the General
Assembly and the Security Council, and more particularly, by the great
powers, designated as permanent members of the Security Council,
who must be in agreement on the admission of any state before that
state can become a Member.

At the San Francisco Conference, an interpretative commentary submitted by the Delegation of Mexico was approved by Commission I
and subsequently by the Conference in plenary session which read as
follows:

[1] The French Government at the time of the Conference took the view that its
responsibilities under Article 22 of the *Covenant of the League of Nations* were not
yet terminated in Lebanon and Syria.

It is the understanding of the Delegation of Mexico that paragraph 2 of Chapter III cannot be applied to the states whose regimes have been established with the help of military forces belonging to the countries which have waged war against the United Nations, as long as those regimes are in power.[1]

By the Potsdam Declaration of August 2, 1945, the Governments of the United Kingdom, of the Union of Soviet Socialist Republics and of the United States announced their agreement that the conclusion of satisfactory peace treaties with recognized democratic governments of Italy, Bulgaria, Finland, Hungary and Rumania would make it possible for them to support applications from these states for membership in the United Nations. They furthermore made the following statement with respect to states which had remained neutral in the war:

The three governments, so far as they are concerned, will support applications for membership from those states which have remained neutral during the war and which fulfill the qualifications set out above [Article 4 of the Charter].

The three governments feel bound, however, to make it clear that they for their part would not favor any application for membership put forward by the present Spanish Government, which, having been founded with the support of the Axis powers, does not, in view of its origins, its nature, its record and its close association with the aggressor states, possess the qualifications necessary to justify such membership.[2]

Other Conditions of Membership. In addition to the general requirement that states must be peace-loving, the Charter requires that states in order to become Members must accept the obligations contained in the present Charter. It is not stated whether there is any possibility of limited acceptance of obligations or acceptance with reservations. It is, however, unlikely that the new Organization will permit membership of the kind that was given to Switzerland after the last war which permitted that country to combine membership with a status of neutrality. At San Francisco the French Delegation did make a formal proposal to the effect that a stipulation should be inserted in the Charter stating that membership was incompatible with the status of permanent neutrality. The French delegation withdrew this amendment when it was made clear that the same result was achieved by the generally accepted interpretation of Article 2, paragraph 5, and Article 4, paragraph 1.[3]

In addition the state must, in the judgment of the Organization, be able and willing to carry out the obligations of membership. This stipulation also allows the widest discretion to the Organization and is similar to the provision of Article 1, paragraph 2, of the Covenant of the League of Nations.

[1] UNCIO, *Verbatim Minutes of the Ninth Plenary Session, June 25, 1945*, Doc. 1210, P/20, p. 4–5.

[2] Department of State, *Bulletin*, XIII, p. 159–60; see this volume, p. 381.

[3] See UNCIO, *Report of the Rapporteur of Committee I/2 on Chapter III (Membership)*, Doc. 1178, I/2/76 (2), p. 4; and *Report of Rapporteur of Committee 1 to Commission I*, Doc. 944, I/1/34 (1), p. 14.

Incidental Effects of Admission to Membership. It might be asked whether admission of a state to membership has any other effect than to place it under the obligations and confer upon it the rights of membership. This question must, probably, from the point of view of positive law, be answered in the negative. On the other hand, it is undoubtedly true that the admission of any state to membership under the conditions laid down in the Charter practically and for most purposes will mean a kind of collective recognition by the international community. This effect of membership was also in fact foreshadowed in an amendment proposed by the Norwegian Delegation to the Dumbarton Oaks Proposals which aimed at giving the Organization the power of recommending collective recognition and withdrawal of recognition of new states and governments.[1] This might point the way to future solution of the difficult situation resulting from a state or government being recognized by one group of states and not by another.

2. The admission of any such state to membership in the United Nations will be effected by a decision of the General Assembly upon the recommendation of the Security Council.

The Covenant of the League permitted new Members to be admitted by two-thirds vote of the Assembly. Under the Charter there is the additional requirement that admission be recommended by the Security Council. This, in effect, means that any Member which is a permanent member of the Security Council will be able by its sole opposition to prevent a state from becoming a Member of the Organization, since a decision by the Security Council on the question of recommending a state for membership will not be a decision on a question of procedure, and will therefore require the concurrence of seven members of the Council, including all the permanent members.

ARTICLE 5

A Member of the United Nations against which preventive or enforcement action has been taken by the Security Council may be suspended from the exercise of the rights and privileges of membership by the General Assembly upon the recommendation of the Security Council. The exercise of these rights and privileges may be restored by the Security Council.

No provision was made for the suspension of Members in the League Covenant. The Dumbarton Oaks Proposals contained a provision in the section dealing with the functions and powers of the General Assembly for the suspension of Members. This provision was adopted at UNCIO

---

[1] *Ibid., Amendments and Observations on the Dumbarton Oaks Proposals, Submitted by the Norwegian Delegation, May 3, 1945*, Doc. 2, G/7 n(1), p. 2.

and was transferred, in modified form, to the chapter dealing with membership. The wording of the Article makes it clear that it is only the exercise of the rights and privileges of membership that is effected.

Conditions and Manner of Suspension. The only condition under which the exercise of the rights and privileges of a Member can be suspended is that "preventive or enforcement action" has already been taken by the Security Council against it. This refers to action by the Security Council under Chapter VII. The suspension of rights and privileges of membership is thus made to appear as not being of itself a part of "preventive or enforcement action" but the effect is bound to be that, and the purpose also is clearly that. While suspension requires a two-thirds vote of the General Assembly, the Assembly can only take this action on the recommendation of the Security Council. Thus the Security Council, upon which is placed primary responsibility for taking action to maintain international peace and security under the Charter,[1] can alone take the initial action, and the role of the General Assembly becomes that of approving or disapproving the recommendation made. Moreover, to emphasize further the importance of the Security Council's role, that body alone is empowered to restore the exercise of the rights and privileges in question. At UNCIO, certain delegations wished to give the General Assembly the same control over restoration as over the initial suspension, but the prevailing view was that here the Security Council should be allowed to act alone since the consequences of restoration were not as serious, and quick action might be necessary to attain the desired result.

Rights and Privileges Affected. The Charter does not specify in detail what are the rights and privileges which will be affected by suspension. It is quite clear that the rights of representation and of voting will be lost for the period of suspension. The general idea must be that such a state for all intents and purposes shall be treated as a non-member state. For that reason such a state cannot participate in the meetings of the General Assembly. Certainly it cannot be elected a member of the Security Council, the Economic and Social Council or the Trusteeship Council. If it is already a member of one of these Councils, it is quite clear that its representatives cannot attend meetings of these organs.

It is a more difficult question whether such a Member can continue as administrator of a trust territory. In League practice states which ceased to be Members were allowed to continue as mandatory powers under Article 22 of the Covenant. The answer to the question of the effect of suspension under the terms of the Charter would appear to depend upon whether the rights of the administering state are regarded as among the rights of membership or rather as rights flowing from the specific trusteeship agreement. However, such a state should not be

[1] *Charter of the United Nations*, Article 24.

in a more favored position than non-member states in respect to trust territories administered by other Member States or by the Organization.[1]

As far as positions in the Secretariat are concerned, the suspension of the rights and privileges of a Member State should not affect the nationals of that state. When a man or a woman has been appointed on the international secretariat, he or she is an international and not a national official. For that reason he or she must be permitted, so far as the provisions of the Charter are concerned, to continue serving the international community, regardless of the acts of the state of allegiance.

Since the International Court of Justice is an organ of the United Nations and its Statute is an integral part of the Charter, it would appear to follow that all rights and privileges relating to participation in the work of the Court which result from membership in the United Nations Organization are equally affected. Also, while it is undoubtedly in the general interest to have the procedures of pacific settlement utilized to the fullest extent possible, a Member whose privileges and immunities have been suspended would presumably have no greater right to bring disputes and situations to the attention of the Security Council and the General Assembly under Article 35 than a non-member.

ARTICLE 6

• A Member of the United Nations which has persistently violated the Principles contained in the present Charter may be expelled from the Organization by the General Assembly upon the recommendation of the Security Council.

The Covenant of the League provided for the expulsion of a member which had "violated any covenant of the League" by vote of the Council "concurred in by the Representatives of all the other Members of the League represented thereon." [2] The only action taken under this provision was when the Council, presented by the Assembly with a resolution condemning Soviet action and asking the Council to pronounce upon the question, voted the expulsion of the Soviet Union on December 14, 1939 [3] on the ground that the Soviet Union had violated its obligations under the Covenant by its action against Finland. The legality of this action has been doubted.[4]

Reasons for Provisions. The Dumbarton Oaks Proposals included among the functions and powers of the General Assembly a provision to the effect that the body "should be empowered, upon recommendation

[1] *Ibid.*, Article 76, paragraph *d*, with respect to rights of Member States.
[2] *Covenant*, Article 16, paragraph 4.
[3] See *The Appeal of the Finnish Government to the League of Nations. A Summary Based Upon the Official Documentation.* Special Supplement to the Monthly Summary of the League of Nations, December 1939, p. 60-9.
[4] See Gross, Leo, "Was the Soviet Union Expelled from the League of Nations?" *American Journal of International Law*, XXXIX (January 1945), p. 35.

of the Security Council, to expel from the Organization any member of the Organization which persistently violates the principles contained in the Charter." At UNCIO, there was considerable opposition to this proposal on the ground, among others, that expulsion would in effect weaken the position of the Organization since from the time expulsion became effective the expelled Member would no longer be bound by the obligations of the Charter. It was proposed instead to broaden the provisions regarding suspension of the rights and privileges of membership to cover the case of a Member which "persistently violates the principles" of the Charter. There was, however, strong opposition to this proposal, particularly on the part of the Delegation of the Soviet Union, which appealed from a decision of the technical committee in favor of the deletion of the provision for expulsion to the Steering Committee. As a result, the matter was reconsidered and the provision of the present Charter was finally adopted.[1]

The argument in favor of retaining the provision for expulsion was in essence that, in grave cases, it was desirable to have a stronger form of penalty and method of expressing disapprobation than the suspension of rights and privileges. It was argued that a Member engaged in persistently violating the Principles[2] of the Charter would have demonstrated that it did not satisfy the basic requirement of membership, and would be like a cancerous growth which it would be better to remove completely than to allow to remain in the body of the Organization and persist in its evil influence. As a non-member the expelled Member would be subject to such action as the Organization might consider necessary in order to maintain peace and security. It would not in all likelihood contribute materially to the achievement of this or other purposes of the Organization to be able to say that the state in question was legally subject to certain obligations of membership when by its action it showed an utter disregard for such obligations.

Conditions Governing Expulsion. A Member, in order to be expelled, must have violated "the Principles contained in the present Charter." The reference presumably is to the principles enumerated in Article 2. It is not stated whether all these principles are of equal importance in this connection. It is, however, stated that there must have been "persistent" violation of Charter principles, thereby showing that it is a question of a frame of mind on the part of the Member that is inconsistent with membership. The use of the word "persistent" suggests that expulsion will only be resorted to in the very gravest cases and as a last resort.

---

[1] For account of Committee discussion and action taken, see UNCIO, *Report of the Rapporteur of Committee I/2 on Chapter III (Membership)*, Doc. 1178, I/2/76 (2), p. 6–9.

[2] That is, the Principles set forth in Article 2.

Expulsion is obviously conceived of as a form of action going beyond the enforcement measures for the taking of which the Security Council is made responsible. In effect, it is a measure to be taken when all other measures have failed. In view of its gravity, and in view of the fact that its effect is conceivably to reverse an action in which the General Assembly and the Security Council have cooperated, namely, that of admitting a new member, a decision by each of these bodies is required. Article 18, paragraph 2, explicitly states that the decision of the General Assembly must be by "a two-thirds majority of the members present and voting." It is clear that the matter is of such a character as to require the affirmative vote of seven members with the concurrence of all permanent members of the Security Council, pursuant to the provisions of Article 27, paragraph 3.

WITHDRAWAL FROM MEMBERSHIP

The Dumbarton Oaks Proposals did not contain any provision with respect to withdrawal. The commentary published by the British Foreign Office expressed the view that "states would have no right of withdrawing voluntarily; the intention is that membership of the Organisation shall be permanent." [1] This interpretation seemed logical since other comparable international documents generally mention how withdrawal can be effected. The Covenant of the League of Nations stipulated in Article 1, paragraph 3, that a member might withdraw after a two-years' notice. The resolution of February 18, 1928 on the Organization of the Pan American Union states in its fifth point that the members may withdraw. Article XV of the Articles of Agreement of the International Monetary Fund gives the members complete freedom of withdrawal and Article VI of the Articles of Agreement of the International Bank for Reconstruction and Development contains a like provision. Article XIX of the Constitution of the Food and Agriculture Organization of the United Nations accords to any member the right to withdraw after a year's notice, given at any time after four years from the date of acceptance of the Constitution. Article X of the UNRRA Agreement permits withdrawal six months after its entry into force. Article 95 of the International Civil Aviation Convention permits denunciation after three years. It might, then, be assumed that the silence of the Dumbarton Oaks Proposals on this score had a certain significance.

Many delegations at UNCIO thought that silence must exclude withdrawal due to the fact that no multipartite treaty can be unilaterally denounced by one of the signatories. Others claimed, however, that Members clearly had the right to withdraw since such withdrawal was not expressly forbidden. Certain delegates were of the opinion that it

---

[1] *British Parliamentary Papers*, Cmd. 6571, 1944, point 22, cited above.

would weaken the permanent character of the Organization and the tendency towards universality if Members were free to withdraw. Other delegates claimed that membership was voluntary and that, consequently, termination of membership must be voluntary as well. The argument of universality was of little value, they claimed, since the Organization has already rejected universality as a principle. They claimed also that voluntary withdrawal was a natural consequence of the right to expel Members.

Certain delegations claimed also that it might be difficult, if not impossible, to obtain ratification of the Charter in their countries if membership were to be regarded as permanent. Attention was called to the provisions of Articles 108 and 109 relating to amendments. Certain delegations said that it was impossible for constitutional reasons for their states to accept membership if membership implied that they would be bound by amendments which they had voted against and had refused to ratify. They must, they stated, be free in such cases to leave the Organization since their constitutions made it impossible to accept unlimited and unknown obligations. Furthermore, this would be a violation of the principle of voluntary association which was the foundation stone of the Organization.

Thus, it became more and more clear that the principle of withdrawal must be accepted in one form or another. The question thus arose as to whether there should be an explicit provision permitting withdrawal or whether this right should be based on an agreed interpretation of the Charter. Most delegations took the view that an express stipulation would weaken the Organization by giving too much encouragement to Members to withdraw. The result of this discussion was the adoption of a declaration of interpretation which was incorporated in the Report of Committee I/2 and was subsequently approved by Commission I and the Conference in plenary session.

As approved by the Conference, the declaration reads as follows:

The Committee adopts the view that the Charter should not make express provision either to permit or to prohibit withdrawal from the Organization. The Committee deems that the highest duty of the nations which will become Members is to continue their cooperation within the Organization for the preservation of international peace and security. If, however, a Member because of exceptional circumstances feels constrained to withdraw, and leave the burden of maintaining international peace and security on the other Members, it is not the purpose of the Organization to compel that Member to continue its cooperation in the Organization.

It is obvious, however, that withdrawal or some other forms of dissolution of the Organization would become inevitable if, deceiving the hopes of humanity, the Organization was revealed to be unable to maintain peace or could do so only at the expense of law and justice.

Nor would it be the purpose of the Organization to compel a Member to remain in the Organization if its rights and obligations as such were changed by

Charter amendment in which it has not concurred and which it finds itself unable to accept, or if an amendment duly accepted by the necessary majority in the Assembly or in a general conference fails to secure the ratification necessary to bring such amendment into effect.

It is for these considerations that the Committee has decided to abstain from recommending insertion in the Charter of a formal clause specifically forbidding or permitting withdrawal.[1]

At the time of the submission of the declaration to the Conference for approval, the Soviet Delegation made a statement to the effect that it could not agree to the expression "and leave the burden of maintaining international peace and security on the other Members." It expressed the opinion that it is wrong to condemn beforehand the grounds on which any state might find it necessary to exercise the right of withdrawal from the Organization, since the right is an expression of state sovereignty.[2]

The declaration as approved by the Conference emphasizes that it is "the highest duty" of Members to continue their cooperation as Members for the achievement of the purposes of the Organization. This duty, however, is not conceived as strictly legal or as absolute, since the statement goes on to say that if a Member because of "exceptional circumstances" feels constrained to withdraw, it is not the purpose of the Organization to compel the Member to continue its membership. The declaration then proceeds to particularize these circumstances by specifying certain conditions, by way of illustration, under which withdrawal would be proper. These include the failure of the Organization to maintain peace or to do so without the sacrifice of law and justice, a change in the rights and obligations of a Member by amendment to the Charter without its specific concurrence, and failure of an amendment to secure the necessary number of ratifications after it has been adopted by the necessary majority of the General Assembly or by a General Conference called specially for the purpose. It is clear from the declaration that this particularization does not exhaust the "exceptional circumstances" which would provide justification for withdrawing.

The effect of this declaration, taken together with the absence of any express provision regarding withdrawal in the Charter, is to place upon each Member the duty to justify its withdrawal in the eyes of the Organization and its Members. Each Member retains the power to withdraw at will. It must, however, give its reasons, and these reasons must be such as to justify the action in the eyes of the Organization

[1] For discussion leading up to the adoption by the technical committee of this statement, see UNCIO, *Summary Report of Twenty-Eighth Meeting of Committee I/2*, June 17, 1945, Doc. 1086, I/2/77. Also, see *Report of the Rapporteur of Committee I/2 on Chapter III (Membership)*, Doc. 1178, I/2/76 (2), p. 4–6; *Verbatim Minutes of Fourth Meeting of Commission I*, Doc. 1186, I/12, p. 1–4; *Verbatim Minutes of the Ninth Plenary Session, June 25, 1945*, Doc. 1210, P/20, p. 5–6, 8–9.

[2] *Ibid., Verbatim Minutes*, etc., p. 8.

and its Members, or the Member State will incur the moral condemna-
tion of the Members of the Organization and of "the conscience of the
world." [1] If the action is thought to be unjustified by the remaining
Members of the Organization, no action will or can be taken to prevent
the Member from withdrawing. If the act is accompanied or followed
by other acts which constitute a threat to or violation of the peace, the
Organization is obligated and empowered to take the same measures
to maintain or restore peace which would be taken if the state in question
had remained a Member.

While the Charter, as interpreted by the declaration above quoted,
does not lay down any specific rules governing withdrawal, it can be
assumed, once the right of withdrawal has been admitted in principle,
that the general principles of international law governing the termination of multipartite agreements are applicable in this case. The
specific circumstances given in the declaration as justifying withdrawal
would appear to be covered by these principles. Thus, failure of other
Members to live up to their obligations under the Charter would afford
a justifiable reason for termination of the agreement under international
law. Modification of the Charter without the express consent of a
Member might properly be regarded as creating a situation covered by
the principle that the obligation of parties to an international agreement
is of a contractual nature and cannot be modified for one party without
the consent of that party. It is to be noted that the comparable provision of the League Covenant provided that no amendment should
bind a Member which signified its dissent therefrom, but in that case
the state in question would cease to be a Member of the League. [2] The
situation where amendments approved by the General Assembly or
General Conference fail to receive the number of ratifications necessary
to enter into force might also be regarded as covered by the principle
of *rebus sic stantibus* according to which all obligations are entered into
on the assumption that the conditions under which they were contracted
are not modified in any fundamental respect, since many states signed
the Charter and ratified it on the tacit assumption that certain changes
will be possible by process of amendment which were considered highly
desirable at San Francisco, but which were not then insisted upon in
the interest of harmony and in the belief that the opportunity would be
afforded for their later adoption.

[1] Phrase used by Senator Vandenberg in discussing this matter at hearings before
the Committee on Foreign Relations, United States Senate, July 9, 1945, *Hearings
before the Committee on Foreign Relations, United States Senate, 79th Cong., 1st sess., on
The Charter of the United Nations for the Maintenance of International Peace and
Security, Submitted by the President of the United States on July 2, 1945*, [Revised]
July 9, 10, 11, 12, and 13, 1945. Washington, D. C., Govt. Printing Office, 1945,
p. 237.

[2] *Covenant*, Article 26, paragraph 2

CHAPTER III

ORGANS

ARTICLE 7

1. There are established as the principal organs of the United Nations: a General Assembly, a Security Council, an Economic and Social Council, a Trusteeship Council, an International Court of Justice, and a Secretariat.

The Dumbarton Oaks Proposals named the General Assembly, the Security Council, the International Court of Justice and the Secretariat as the "principal organs" of the proposed Organization. At San Francisco, the increased importance given to the economic and social work of the Organization seemed to justify the inclusion of the Economic and Social Council. The Trusteeship Council, which was not provided for in the Dumbarton Oaks Proposals, was also included.

Except for the two additional councils, the organizational pattern of the United Nations parallels that of the League of Nations. The General Assembly, from the point of view of organization and functions, closely parallels the Assembly of the League of Nations; the International Court of Justice is very similar to the Permanent Court of International Justice which, while not technically an organ of the League, practically functioned in that capacity; and the Secretariat corresponds to the League Secretariat. The important difference arises from the fact that "executive" functions under the new Organization are divided between the Security Council, the Economic and Social Council and the Trusteeship Council, the latter two being in reality subordinated to the authority of the General Assembly. This last fact makes it somewhat illogical to include these two bodies in the category of "principal organs." From the point of view of the amount of independent authority vested in them, they might better perhaps be regarded as subsidiary organs of the United Nations. Considering, however, the anticipated importance of their activities, their inclusion in the category of "principal organs" appeared justified.

2. Such subsidiary organs as may be found necessary may be established in accordance with the present Charter.

This paragraph repeats the substance of Chapter IV, paragraph 2, of the Dumbarton Oaks Proposals. It repeats, in general terms, certain

other provisions of the Charter. Thus, Article 22 states that the Assembly
may establish such subsidiary organs as it deems necessary for the performance of its functions. Article 29 gives the same power to the Security
Council. Article 68 imposes upon the Economic and Social Council
the duty to set up specified commissions and such others as may be
needed. Finally Article 47, fourth paragraph, empowers the Military
Staff Committee, with the authorization of the Security Council, to
establish regional subcommittees. It might also be mentioned for the
sake of completeness that the International Court of Justice under
Article 26 of the Statute is empowered to set up chambers.

ARTICLE 8

**The United Nations shall place no restrictions on the eligibility of men
and women to participate in any capacity and under conditions of equality
in its principal and subsidiary organs.**

The Covenant of the League contained a provision of like nature
assuring that "all positions under or in connection with the League,
including the Secretariat, shall be open equally to men and women." [1]
This provision appeared in the Article dealing with "Seat, Qualifications of Officials, Immunities." The Dumbarton Oaks Proposals contained no comparable provision. At San Francisco, there was strong
support for including a provision of this nature with the broadest application, which explains why it was decided to include it in the Chapter
dealing with "Organs."

The proposal leading to this Article was discussed at some length in
the technical committee of the Conference. It was found to be necessary
to set up a subcommittee to prepare a draft. This was subsequently
changed several times. There was no open opposition to the principle of
complete equality between men and women. Certain delegates, however,
thought it superfluous to insert any such provision. They stated, first
of all, that it was absurd to put into the Charter anything that was self-
evident. Secondly, they pointed out the danger of antithetical interpretation in other international treaties if it was found necessary to state
the principle here. These arguments were overruled because of the very
great importance attributed by some delegates to having the principle
expressly stated. Thereafter there was a rather long discussion concerning the form.

The idea of the equality of men and women is expressed in other provisions of the Charter.[2] The present Article is only a concrete application
of this general principle. It is to be noted that Article 8 uses a negative
form. The reason for this is quite clear. It was decided to establish the

[1] *Covenant*, Article 7, paragraph 3.
[2] See Preamble; Article 1, paragraph 3; Article 55 *c*; and Article 76.

principle not only that women should be able to share the jobs of the Secretariat on an equal basis with men, but also that they should be able, as far as the Organization is concerned, to serve as delegates, substitute delegates, etc. This, however, could not be expressed by a positive provision in the Charter. It must be left to the Members themselves to decide whether they want to employ women, as they have often done in the past in international organizations. What the Article means is that the Organization will in no way prevent the Members from appointing women.

CHAPTER IV

THE GENERAL ASSEMBLY

Composition

ARTICLE 9

1. The General Assembly shall consist of all the Members of the United Nations.

It is customary in all international organizations that there should be one body in which all the members are represented directly.

2. Each Member shall have not more than five representatives in the General Assembly.

The size and composition of the representation of Members in the General Assembly was discussed at some length at UNCIO. Certain delegations felt rather strongly that nothing should be said in the Charter about the number of representatives which should be permitted. This would be left to the states themselves. Others felt that the number ought to be fixed in one way or another, following League practice. One of the reasons for this was the fear of certain small states that the great powers would have too large delegations. The number was eventually fixed at five.

The experience both of the League of Nations and of UNCIO shows that the delegations may be vastly enlarged by the use of "alternate delegates," "advisers," "technical advisers," and "experts." Such staff members often, to all intents and purposes, act as delegates by performing representative functions on committees and subcommittees. This practice becomes necessary and inevitable if the demands of committee work become so heavy that the regular delegates are unable to meet them. The only safeguard against abuse is well-drafted and observed rules of procedure.[1]

[1] The Provisional Rules of Procedure for the General Assembly recommended by the Executive Committee to the Preparatory Commission provided that each Delegation should consist of not more than five representatives and five alternate representatives, and "as many advisers, technical advisers, experts and persons of similar status as may be required by the Delegation" (Rule 14). It was also provided that an alternate representative might act as a representative upon designation by the Chairman of the Delegation (Rule 16) and that advisers, technical advisers, experts and other persons of similar status might act as members of Committees, upon designation by the Chairman of the Delegation. Persons of this status would not, however, unless designated as alternate representatives, be eligible for appointment as Chairman or Rapporteur of Committees or for seats in the General Assembly (Rule 17). *Report by the Executive Committee to the Preparatory Commission of the United Nations,* PC/EX/113/Rev. 1, 12 November, 1945, p. 19.

Functions and Powers

ARTICLE 10

The General Assembly may discuss any questions or any matters within the scope of the present Charter or relating to the powers and functions of any organs provided for in the present Charter, and, except as provided in Article 12, may make recommendations to the Members of the United Nations or to the Security Council or to both on any such questions or matters.

Discussion at San Francisco. The Dumbarton Oaks Proposals clearly and avowedly adopted the principle that a clear distinction should be made between the functions and powers of the General Assembly and those of the Security Council, in order to avoid the overlapping and alleged confusion that attended the granting of wide and undifferentiated powers to the Assembly and Council of the League of Nations. To this end Chapter V, Section B, of the Proposals sought to define with some definiteness the nature and scope of the General Assembly's powers. For one thing, it was to be a body to discuss, to consider and to recommend, but not to take action. The latter was to be the prerogative of the Security Council. Furthermore, while it was given broad powers of discussion and recommendation in respect to matters of general welfare, its powers were more narrowly defined with respect to political matters and it was expressly denied the right to make recommendations with respect to matters relating to the maintenance of peace and security being dealt with by the Security Council.

There was a fairly widely held view before and during the Conference at San Francisco, especially on the part of the delegates from the smaller countries, that it was necessary to strengthen the position of the General Assembly, particularly as a forum for discussion and criticism. Many of the amendments to the Dumbarton Oaks Proposals submitted by the smaller nations had this purpose in view. The matter was thoroughly and extensively discussed at UNCIO. The technical committee to which this matter was referred (Committee II/2) adopted a text which, while recognizing the Council's special responsibility, would have permitted the General Assembly to discuss any matter within the sphere of international relations.[1] The Delegation of the Soviet Union refused to accept this decision and appealed to the Steering Committee of the Conference. Its argument was that under the proposed text the General Assembly would be able to deal with matters exclusively within the domestic jurisdiction of Members and, by concerning itself with matters in an irresponsible fashion, would create tensions and misunderstandings.

[1] UNCIO, *Summary Report of Fifteenth Meeting of Committee II/2, May 30, 1945,* Doc. 686, II/2/34.

This question of the extent of the General Assembly's powers of discussion and recommendation produced the last serious "crisis" or "deadlock" of the Conference. It was finally settled on the basis of a proposal made by a subcommittee of the Executive Committee, consisting of Ambassador Gromyko of the U.S.S.R., Secretary of State Stettinius of the United States and Foreign Minister Evatt of Australia. The formula agreed upon and finally adopted by the technical committee,[1] Commission II and the Conference grants the General Assembly a wider power to discuss and make recommendations than that suggested in the Dumbarton Oaks Proposals. It allows the General Assembly about the same opportunities for discussion and for making recommendations as were accorded the League Assembly under the Covenant, with the important difference that the General Assembly is not to make any recommendation on any dispute or situation with respect to which the Security Council is exercising its functions under the Charter, unless the Council so requests.

Scope and Importance of Article. The very fact that the discussion clause has been put in the very forefront of the powers of the Assembly shows that it is considered to be very important indeed. It is in reality the key to the whole role of the Assembly in the United Nations Organization. The General Assembly has thereby been designated as the open conscience of the world. It is to be a world forum where all important questions within the scope of the Charter can be discussed. The Assembly is to be the criticizing, the reviewing and the overseeing organ, but not the executive. It is to be the ears and eyes and mouth of the Organization, but not the hands.

Delimitation of Powers of General Assembly and Security Council. The scope of the General Assembly's power of discussion and recommendation under this Article was well brought out in the course of the Commission discussion at UNCIO. Speaking on the report of Committee II/2, Dr. Evatt, the Australian Delegate, said:

It is not my purpose to trace the history of the matter because the text that is now put before the Commission means, in our view, the clear right of the Assembly to discuss any question or any matter within the scope of this Charter. That scope will include every aspect of the Charter, everything contained in it and everything covered by it. It will include the Preamble of the Charter, the great purposes and principles embodied in it, the activities of all its organs; and the right of discussion will be free and untrammelled and will range over that tremendous area.[2]

While this is the view of one delegate, considering Dr. Evatt's important part in the drafting of the text and the reasonableness of the interpre-

[1] See *ibid., Summary Report of Twenty-fifth Meeting of Committee II/2, June 20, 1945*, p. 2–4.

[2] *Ibid., Verbatim Minutes of the Fourth Meeting of Commission II, June 21, 1945*, Doc. 1151, II/17, p. 19.

tation in the light of the phraseology used, it would seem wholly justifiable to accept it. According to such an interpretation it would be very difficult indeed to find any matter touching upon international relations which would not fall within the scope of the Assembly's power of discussion under this Article. It is only necessary to mention some of the subjects that are covered through being referred to in the Charter as among the purposes and objectives of the Organization: "respect for the principle of equal rights and self-determination of peoples," "international cooperation in solving international problems of an economic, social, cultural, or humanitarian character," "promotion of and encouragement of respect for human rights and fundamental freedoms," and promotion of social progress and "better standards of life in larger freedom."

It should again be emphasized that the Organization in this respect is widely different from the League of Nations. The Council and the Assembly had in the League system the same all-embracing powers to deal "with any matter within the sphere of action of the League or affecting the peace of the world." [1] This, of course, made possible considerable overlapping since the two chief organs might be treating the same matter at the same time. The United Nations Organization has chosen another way and has specifically provided, as will be seen, particularly when Article 24, paragraph 1, is considered,[2] that the Security Council shall deal with matters regarding peace and security and shall be the executive organ for these matters whereas the Assembly, in regard to such matters, is to be a debating and criticizing organ. In matters regarding welfare, however, the Assembly comes into its own.

The General Assembly can make recommendations both to the Members of the Organization as such and to the Security Council. It should be kept in mind that "recommendations" are not the same as "decisions." They have no obligatory character whatsoever. However, the provisions of Article 18, paragraph 2, relative to voting procedure, apply, since, in the sense in which the word "decisions" is used in that paragraph, the General Assembly must take a decision before it can make a recommendation. The only limitation upon the Assembly's power of recommendation other than that implied in the general grant of power is contained in the reference to Article 12.

"*The present Charter.*" There is one point of a somewhat technical nature which arises in connection with the interpretation of this Article which deserves a word of comment. The Article refers to questions and matters within the scope of "the present Charter." The expression "the present Charter" is used consistently throughout the Charter as the method of referring to the Charter. It is not intended to be a reference

---

[1] *Covenant*, Article 3, paragraph 3 and Article 4.
[2] See this volume, p. 120.

to the Charter as it now stands in the year 1945. If the Charter is subsequently amended to extend its scope, the General Assembly's power of discussion will be extended by that much. "The present Charter" simply means, then, the Charter as it is at any given time.

ARTICLE 11

1. The General Assembly may consider the general principles of cooperation in the maintenance of international peace and security, including the principles governing disarmament and the regulation of armaments, and may make recommendations with regard to such principles to the Members or to the Security Council or to both.

This paragraph corresponds very closely to the first part of Chapter V, Section B, paragraph 1, of the Dumbarton Oaks Proposals. The provision with regard to the General Assembly's power to make recommendations is more explicit. Following as it does Article 10, it becomes a specific application of the more comprehensive provisions of that Article.

It should be noted that the provisions with respect to disarmament in the Charter are considerably weaker than the provisions contained in Articles 8 and 9 of the Covenant of the League of Nations. The Members of the League recognized the dangers of the private armament industry. A proposal to introduce a similar statement in the Charter was defeated. It is quite clear that disarmament takes a more modest place in the system of the United Nations than it did in the League system. Security is the foremost consideration. The League aimed to develop a system whereby "Security, Arbitration and Disarmament" would work hand in hand and on an equal basis. The United Nations has chosen another road. If one should attempt to define the three pillars of this system, they would be: "Security, Pacific Settlement and Welfare." Disarmament is given a very subordinate position.

Under the Covenant, while the Council was specifically empowered to formulate plans for the reduction of national armaments "for the consideration and action of the several governments," [1] the Assembly's general authority was sufficiently broad to permit it to do the same thing. The Charter, however, expressly grants to the General Assembly the power to consider "the principles governing disarmament and the regulation of armaments," and to make recommendations with respect to such principles, while the Security Council alone is made responsible, under the terms of Article 26, " for formulating . . . plans to be submitted to the Members of the United Nations for the establishment of a system for the regulation of armaments." This definition of authority of course governs any action taken by the United Nations Organization with a view to the control of the use of atomic power for military purposes.

[1] *Covenant*, Article 8, paragraph 2.

A special point to be noted in connection with this paragraph is the use of the word "consider" in place of the word "discuss" which we find used in Article 10 and in Article 11, paragraph 2. The distinction goes back to the Dumbarton Oaks Proposals. It has been suggested that there is a "shade of difference" between the two words, that "consider" is more comprehensive than the word "discuss," and may have the implication of leading to some form of action, as, for example, the making of a recommendation.[1] This distinction would seem, however, to lose much of its point in view of the fact that in paragraph 1 of Article 11, where the word "consider" is used, the General Assembly is expressly given the power to recommend, as in Article 10 and Article 11, paragraph 2, where the word "discuss" is employed.

2. The General Assembly may discuss any questions relating to the maintenance of international peace and security brought before it by any Member of the United Nations, or by the Security Council, or by a state which is not a Member of the United Nations in accordance with Article 35, paragraph 2, and, except as provided in Article 12, may make recommendations with regard to any such questions to the state or states concerned or to the Security Council or to both. Any such question on which action is necessary shall be referred to the Security Council by the General Assembly either before or after discussion.

This paragraph is also a special application of the general principle expressed in Article 10. It follows closely provisions contained in Chapter V, Section B, paragraph 1 of the Dumbarton Oaks Proposals. The one additional provision, permitting a state that is not a Member to bring a question of the nature indicated before the General Assembly, simply harmonizes this paragraph, dealing with the powers of the General Assembly, with the provisions of Article 35, paragraph 2, dealing with the pacific settlement of disputes.

This paragraph, with the limitation on the General Assembly's power contained in the reference to Article 12, gives definite application to the general principle upon which the peace and security system of the Charter is based, namely, that the General Assembly is primarily the organ for discussion while the Security Council is the organ for action. There are, however, two circumstances in which the General Assembly can make recommendations with respect to "questions relating to the maintenance of international peace and security." The first is when the Security Council is not exercising, in respect to such questions, its functions under the Charter. The second is when the Security Council requests the General Assembly to consider the question and to make recommendations. The first circumstance is limited, however, by the requirement of the last sentence of this paragraph that any question on

---

[1] Testimony of Leo Pasvolsky before Senate Committee on Foreign Relations, *Hearings . . . on The Charter of the United Nations,* etc., cited above, p. 242.

which action is necessary shall be referred to the Security Council, so that it is presumably only where the Security Council has failed to take action after a question has been referred to it, or where following unsuccessful action the Security Council voluntarily ceases to deal with the question, that the General Assembly can step in and make recommendations as well as discuss the subject matter.

A question might be raised with regard to the nature of the "action" referred to in the last sentence of this paragraph. Presumably, it is action of the kind that the Security Council is empowered to take under the provisions of Chapters V, VI, VII and VIII. This would seem to be a logical interpretation, considering that one main purpose of the Charter is to avoid the general overlapping of functions and powers which characterized relations between the League Assembly and Council.

The provisions of this paragraph make it possible for the Security Council to transfer a matter to the Assembly in the same way as the League Council could do under Article 15, paragraph 9 of the Covenant. The Security Council is not, however, required to do this at the request of one of the parties as was the rule under the Covenant. Furthermore, any decision by the Security Council to do this would presumably be taken in accordance with Article 27, paragraph 3, requiring the concurrence of the permanent members of the Council. On the scope and application of the exception contained in this paragraph, see comment on Article 12.[1]

3. The General Assembly may call the attention of the Security Council to situations which are likely to endanger international peace and security.

This paragraph is another of the additions made at San Francisco with a view to strengthening the position of the General Assembly. While recognizing by implication the primary responsibility of the Security Council for taking action to maintain international peace and security, it empowers the General Assembly to call the attention of the Security Council to situations which are likely to endanger peace and security. This enables the General Assembly to take a decision as to whether in its opinion such a situation exists and to place openly upon the Security Council responsibility for dealing with it. It is intended to reduce the likelihood that a particular situation in which one of the permanent members of the Council has a special interest will be permitted to continue and become aggravated because of the inaction of the Council and the dilatory tactics of its members.

4. The powers of the General Assembly set forth in this Article shall not limit the general scope of Article 10.

---

[1] See below, p. 100.

This paragraph is intended to make clear that the provisions of Article 11 are intended to particularize, but not restrict, the more general provisions of Article 10.

ARTICLE 12

1. While the Security Council is exercising in respect of any dispute or situation the functions assigned to it in the present Charter, the General Assembly shall not make any recommendation with regard to that dispute or situation unless the Security Council so requests.

This paragraph which has already been referred to under Articles 10 and 11 does not need much further comment. It is quite clear that the object is to ensure that the General Assembly shall not interfere with the exercise by the Security Council of its function to maintain peace and security by the exercise of the powers vested in it by Chapters V, VI, VII and VIII. The Council is given this function because it is the organ best constituted to work quickly and efficiently. It was felt at Dumbarton Oaks and at San Francisco that this speed and efficiency might be endangered if the General Assembly were permitted to make recommendations with respect to questions under treatment by the Council. For that reason it was deemed wise to introduce a special provision to prevent interference and overlapping of action. This reason obviously disappears if the Security Council should request the opinion of the Assembly. This is expressly recognized in the latter part of the paragraph.

It is stated in this paragraph that the Assembly shall not make any recommendation under the circumstances indicated. This does not mean that the Assembly cannot discuss such disputes or situations. The wording of Articles 10 and 12 makes it clear that discussion is permitted.

The Assembly may also at any time, it would seem, make recommendations regarding the general principles of cooperation in the maintenance of peace and security if these recommendations are not so specific that they have the character of being directed to a definite situation or conflict then before the Security Council.

2. The Secretary-General, with the consent of the Security Council, shall notify the General Assembly at each session of any matters relative to the maintenance of international peace and security which are being dealt with by the Security Council and shall similarly notify the General Assembly, or the Members of the United Nations if the General Assembly is not in session, immediately the Security Council ceases to deal with such matters.

There was no comparable provision in the Dumbarton Oaks Proposals. One of the major concerns of the smaller powers was that the Security Council might by one means or another keep a dispute or situation from coming before the General Assembly for consideration and recommendation, even though the Security Council was obviously not engaged in dealing with the matter in any active way. This paragraph was agreed upon at San Francisco, after lengthy discussion, for the purpose of giving some assurance that the principle of the first paragraph was not misused in practice. It was also felt that the Members of the United Nations should be kept informed regarding matters before the Security Council for consideration and action.

The first part of this paragraph places upon the Secretary-General the obligation to notify the General Assembly at each session of any matters relative to the maintenance of international peace and security which are being dealt with by the Security Council. This obligation does not extend to reporting action taken since the purpose of the report is to assist the Assembly in determining its agenda. The one condition imposed is that the Secretary-General must act "with the consent of the Security Council." And this consent presumably requires the concurrence of all permanent members.

The second part of the paragraph requires the Secretary-General to notify the General Assembly immediately, if it is in session, and the Members of the United Nations, if the General Assembly is not in session, when the Security Council has ceased to deal with such matters. The word "similarly" would appear to refer to the requirement of Security Council consent. The action of the Secretary-General in this case is thus subject to the same condition as is expressly stated in the first part of the paragraph. Consequently, the Security Council decides itself when it has ceased to deal with a matter under paragraph 1, and the General Assembly cannot make a recommendation until it is in effect invited to do so.

ARTICLE 13

1. The General Assembly shall initiate studies and make recommendations for the purpose of:
   a. promoting international cooperation in the political field and encouraging the progressive development of international law and its codification;
   b. promoting international cooperation in the economic, social, cultural, educational, and health fields, and assisting in the realization of human rights and fundamental freedoms for all without distinction as to race, sex, language, or religion.

The obligation placed upon the General Assembly by this paragraph, i.e. to "initiate studies and make recommendations," should provide the basis for important constructive work by that body. It directs the General Assembly to initiate the organization of studies within the wide range of subjects covered by sections a and b, to discuss the results of these studies, and to make recommendations, presumably either to

Members or to the appropriate organs of the United Nations or to both, with respect to action which should be taken. It opens up the possibility of the continuation of a form of international activity which proved to be very useful under the League system.

International cooperation in the fields specified will commonly take the form of the drafting and putting into force of international agreements dealing with specific aspects of the matters under consideration. At UNCIO, a proposal was submitted that the General Assembly be empowered to "submit general conventions for the consideration" of states both Members and non-members. This proposal was defeated. One cannot, however, draw the conclusion that the General Assembly will therefore lack the power to submit general conventions. The Assembly of the League of Nations, without specific authority, undertook the drafting of international agreements, as in the case of the Geneva Protocol of 1924. There is nothing in the Charter to prevent a recommendation of the General Assembly from taking this form.

The words of the paragraph down to a were taken verbatim from the Dumbarton Oaks Proposals, with the sole exception of the substitution of "shall" for "should." Sections a and b of the paragraph, defining the specific purposes of the General Assembly action, represent a considerable elaboration of the Dumbarton Oaks text. The effects of this are twofold: first, the matters with regard to which the Assembly is to initiate studies and make recommendations are stated more specifically and concretely; and second, the field of the Assembly's activity is undoubtedly to some extent broadened, though probably not to any great extent if we take into account other provisions of the Dumbarton Oaks Proposals, notably Chapter IX, Section A, paragraph 1.

"*Promoting international cooperation in the political field.*" This is a phrase rather difficult to define. All interstate relations are in a sense political. However, when section a is compared with section b it becomes clear that the words "the political field" are used to distinguish a particular area of international relations from "the economic, social, cultural, educational, and health fields." Besides "political" is apparently used in contradistinction to "legal" since section a goes on to speak of the development and codification of international law as distinct from the promotion of international political cooperation. This first phrase in section a would appear, then, to be little more than a repetition of the idea contained in the first paragraph of Article 11.

"*Encouraging the progressive development of international law and its codification.*" The inclusion of this phrase was due in large part to the insistence at San Francisco that more emphasis be placed on law as the basis of the Organization. It was in line with the inclusion in the Articles dealing with Purposes and Principles of references to international law and justice. Since international law includes all treaties and other agreements between states,[1] an international agreement which is entered into as the result of recommendations made by the General Assembly will be a step in the "progressive development of international law." Furthermore, international law may be developed through the practice of states in response to Assembly recommendations, and by the practice of the Organization itself.

Codification of international law is a more ambitious goal. Here we have in play two conflicting legal ideas. According to one school of thought it is desirable to draft a code, comparable to the Napoleonic Codes, which will give certainty and definiteness to the rules of international law. According to another school of thought, to attempt at this time to codify international law would not only end in failure but would be harmful to the development of international law, due to the fact that it would be forced into a strait jacket and be denied the opportunity for natural growth. Judging from League experience and the proposals of the more moderate advocates of codification, the application of this particular provision of the Charter will result in the drafting of multipartite treaties such as the Hague Nationality Convention of 1930 [2] and the Hague Conventions of 1899 and 1907, which put into agreed form the rules relating to certain specific subjects of international relations. Thus, in a sense, these so-called "codes" are little more than international statutes.

Economic and Social Cooperation. Section *b* of this paragraph represents a considerable proliferation and amplification of the comparable provisions of the Dumbarton Oaks Proposals. The scope of "economic" and "social" is clarified, if not extended, by the introduction of the words "cultural, educational, and health." Furthermore, "assisting in the realization of human rights and fundamental freedoms" is made a specific obligation of the General Assembly, and the exact meaning of these goals is further clarified by the addition of the words "for all without distinction as to race, sex, language, or religion." It is, of course, necessary to bear particularly in mind in connection with this paragraph the limitation imposed by Article 2, paragraph 7. Further discussion of Assembly action in this "non-political" field will be necessary in connection with Chapters IX and X.

2. The further responsibilities, functions, and powers of the General Assembly with respect to matters mentioned in paragraph 1 (*b*) above are set forth in Chapters IX and X.

See comment on Articles of Chapters IX and X.

[1] See *Statute of the International Court of Justice*, Article 38.
[2] For *Final Act of Conference*, see League of Nations Document 1930. V. 7. N. Y., Columbia Univ. Press, agents. For official documents relating to preparation and work of Conference, see *American Journal of International Law*, XXIV (1930), Supplement, p. 1, 169. See also Hudson, Manley O., "The First Conference for the Codification of International Law," *ibid.*, XXIV (1930), p. 447.

ARTICLE 14

Subject to the provisions of Article 12, the General Assembly may recommend measures for the peaceful adjustment of any situation, regardless of origin, which it deems likely to impair the general welfare or friendly relations among nations, including situations resulting from a violation of the provisions of the present Charter setting forth the Purposes and Principles of the United Nations.

Origin of Article. This Article had no counterpart in the Dumbarton Oaks Proposals except for the provision of Article V, Section B, paragraph 6 which said that the General Assembly should initiate studies and make recommendations for the purpose of "adjusting situations likely to impair the general welfare." The scope and purpose of this provision were obviously more limited than the scope and purpose of the Article under consideration. Article 19 of the Covenant of the League provides a closer parallel.

This Article was one of the amendments proposed by the Sponsoring Governments at San Francisco. It was intended to provide a means by which situations which threaten the general welfare or friendly relations between states may be considered and recommendations made with respect to them. It represents a modest approach to the problem of "peaceful change" in a dynamic world. The approach is modest, since no recommendation made by the General Assembly has any binding force. Like advice given by the Assembly under Article 19 of the Covenant, any recommendations made by the General Assembly under this Article may be disregarded, and the Member or Members so disregarding them, suffer no specifically prescribed penalties. There is no provision for enforcement action. The only forces behind a recommendation are the power of public opinion and the moral force of the General Assembly.

Revision of Treaties. In the early stages of the discussions leading up to the formulation of this Article, the revision of treaties was the aspect of the problem chiefly in mind. In fact in the original draft of the Article and in other amendments proposed at San Francisco there was specific reference to revision of treaties. There was strong objection, however, to the inclusion of any reference to the revision of treaties on the ground that it would weaken the structure of international contractual obligations which provides the basis for orderly relations among the nations of the world, and in particular would be an invitation to the enemy states in World War II to seek revision of the peace treaties.[1] Since the objective was not solely the revision of treaties, but rather the consideration of any situation or condition which might impair the general welfare

---

[1] For discussion of question of treaty revision by the technical committee see UNCIO, *Summary Report of Seventeenth Meeting of Committee II/2, June 1, 1945,* Doc. 748, II/2/39; *Summary Report of Eighteenth Meeting, June 2, 1945,* Doc. 771, II/2/41; and *Summary Report of Nineteenth Meeting, June 4, 1945,* Doc. 790, II/2/42.

or friendly relations among nations, without regard to whether it has relation to a treaty or not, the more general phraseology was introduced.

In support of this view of the scope of the Article, we may quote the summary report of the statement of the Delegate of the United States (Senator Arthur H. Vandenberg), who played a very conspicuous part in the drafting of the Article. He explained that

although he had originally contemplated a specific allusion in the Charter to the question of revision of treaties, he had foregone this in favor of the broad version . . . put forward by the four sponsoring governments and France. It was inconsistent to launch an international Organization based on international integrity and at the same time to intimate any lack of respect for the instruments through which international integrity functions, namely, treaties. He recognized the objections to identifying treaties as such with this paragraph and held that the concern of the Assembly was not with treaties *per se*, but with adjusting conditions which might impair peace and good relations between nations. Considerations of the general welfare may call for a recommendation that a treaty be respected rather than revised. He submitted that it was wiser not to connect the broad version (of the paragraph) with any specific definition regarding treaty revision. The phrase "the peaceful adjustment of any situation, regardless of origin," in his view, should not be interpreted to mean that the subject of treaty revision was foreclosed to the Assembly. If treaties gave rise to situations which the Assembly deemed likely to impair the general welfare or friendly relations among nations, it could make recommendations in respect of these situations.[1]

Scope of Article. The General Assembly is empowered under this Article to recommend measures for the peaceful adjustment of "any situation, regardless of origin, which it deems likely to impair the general welfare or friendly relations among nations." The words "regardless of origin" are important since they make it clear that the situation in question may result from dissatisfaction with a treaty, or from a conflict of political interests that does not necessarily involve any challenge to existing treaties.

The specific reference to the provisions of the Charter setting forth the "Purposes and Principles of the United Nations" makes it clear that under this Article the General Assembly can deal with any alleged violation of principles such as that "of equal rights and self-determination of peoples."

There are two important limitations upon the authority conferred in this Article. The one is contained in the text in the express reference to Article 12. It is there stated that the Assembly shall not make recommendations regarding any question that is already being dealt with by the Security Council in the exercise of its functions under the Charter.

[1] *Ibid., Summary Report of Seventeenth Meeting of Committee II/2, June 1, 1945,* Doc. 748, II/2/39, p. 2. See also statement of Senator Arthur H. Vandenberg, who was chiefly instrumental in the formulation of this Article, before the Senate Foreign Relations Committee, *Hearings . . . on The Charter of the United Nations,* etc., cited above, p. 251.

The other important limitation is not mentioned in the text of the present Article. That is the all-embracing exception of Article 2, paragraph 7, which makes it impossible for the Assembly to make any recommendation if the situation should rise from any matter that is essentially within the domestic jurisdiction of any state.

In spite of the potential importance of this Article which has led to the observation that by its terms the General Assembly becomes "the town-meeting of the world," it must be stated that in effect its provisions are implicit in the more comprehensive terms of Article 10. In fact, Articles 11, 12, 13 and 14 can properly be regarded as elaborations and detailed applications of the comprehensive terms of that Article.

ARTICLE 15

1. The General Assembly shall receive and consider annual and special reports from the Security Council; these reports shall include an account of the measures that the Security Council has decided upon or taken to maintain international peace and security.

The first part of this paragraph was contained in the Dumbarton Oaks Proposals. Taken in conjunction with Article 24, paragraph 3, it places upon the Security Council the obligation to make annual and special reports to the General Assembly. The annual reports presumably will be submitted at the regular sessions of the General Assembly. The special reports will presumably deal with specific matters, such as measures that have been taken to deal with specific disputes or situations. It is not made clear who decides when these special reports shall be submitted. Article 24, paragraph 3, says this is to be done "when necessary" but also leaves open the question as to who is to decide. The General Assembly presumably can ask that a special report be made, but the Security Council appears to retain considerable freedom of action.

It is stated that the General Assembly shall "receive and consider" annual and special reports from the Security Council. The meaning of the word "consider" is of great importance. At UNCIO this Article was discussed extensively. Opinions were at times sharply divided between the adherents of the supremacy of the Assembly on the one hand and the supporters of the authority of the Security Council on the other. It is clear that the General Assembly has the right to examine and discuss the reports very carefully. It would appear equally clear that if the action of the General Assembly is to have any effect, it must be able to come to conclusions regarding the substance of the reports and give expression to them. This would clearly imply the power to make recommendations on matters covered.[1]

[1] On meaning of the word "consider," see comment on Article 11, paragraph 1, this volume, p. 97.

This interpretation is supported by the discussions and decisions of UNCIO and of the committees and commissions concerned with this matter. The matter came up before two of the Conference's technical committees (II/2 and III/1) and these Committees arrived at conflicting results. The text adopted by Committee II/2 went further than that of Committee III/1 in empowering the General Assembly to discuss and take action on reports of the Security Council. Because of this conflict and because of the belief entertained by certain delegates that the Committee II/2 text, if adopted, would improperly encroach upon the authority of the Security Council, an appeal was taken to the Steering Committee which referred the matter back to Committee II/2 for consultation with Committee III/1, and if necessary or desirable with Committee III/3, in order that there be prepared "a jointly agreed upon redraft of the paragraph." This consultation took the form of a special joint meeting of subcommittees II/2/B and III/1/C which, after full discussion of the matter, adopted a text substantially like the one contained in the Charter.[1] The original Committee II/2 text was substantially revised. The paragraph specifically empowering the General Assembly to approve or disapprove in whole or in part any report of the Security Council and to submit recommendations to the Security Council was dropped. In the course of the discussion in Committee II/2, it was made clear by the Delegates of the United States and of the Soviet Union (which had been the author of the revised text in the joint subcommittee meeting) that the new text did not derogate in any way from the General Assembly's powers under other provisions of the Charter. The General Assembly would have at all times the right to discuss any questions arising from matters contained in the Security Council's reports and, subject to the limitation contained in Article 12, make recommendations thereon. The Delegate of the Soviet Union added that in his opinion the Assembly should not have the right to make recommendations on the reports themselves, as distinct from the matters reported, since this would amount to approving or disapproving the reports and would violate the principle governing the respective positions of the General Assembly and the Security Council.[2]

This view was formally accepted by the two committees and incorporated in resolutions of interpretation adopted by them. That adopted by Committee III/1 reads as follows:

That paragraph 8 does not limit in any way the powers of the Assembly set forth in paragraphs 1 and 6, and consequently when the General Assembly is

[1] UNCIO, *Summary Report of Special Joint Meeting of Subcommittees II/2/B and III/1/C, June 11, 1945.* Doc. 921, II/2/B/13, III/1/C/2. It is to be noted that the final vote was taken by the two subcommittees separately. In Subcommittee II/2/B the vote was 4–4; in III/1/C, 8–0 for adoption.

[2] *Ibid., Summary Report of Twenty-second Meeting of Committee II/2, June 13, 1945,* Doc. 971, II/2/50, p. 1.

considering reports from the Security Council it may exercise the powers of discussion and recommendation stated in those paragraphs.[1]

This interpretation was adopted also by Commission II and submitted to the Conference, by which it was accepted, in these words:

Commission II calls particular attention to the word "consider" as used in the Charter in connection with reports of the Security Council and other organs. It is the intention of Commission II that this word shall be interpreted to encompass the right to discuss, and that the power of the Assembly to discuss and make recommendations as defined in Articles 10, 11, 12 and 14 is not limited in any way with respect to its consideration of reports from the Security Council.[2]

This paragraph specifies that the reports of the Security Council to the General Assembly shall give an account of the measures it has taken for the maintenance of peace and security. It is thereby established that the Security Council, although primarily responsible for the maintenance of peace and security, still owes the public opinion of the world, through the General Assembly, an account of how it has performed this important task. The position of the General Assembly as the conscience of mankind is thereby safeguarded.

2. The General Assembly shall receive and consider reports from the other organs of the United Nations.

Article 98 provides for an annual report by the Secretary-General. It is clearly within the power of the General Assembly to require such reports from the Economic and Social Council and the Trusteeship Council as it may desire since these organs function under its authority. There is no special provision concerning reports from the International Court of Justice. However, the Permanent Court of International Justice did publish annual reports; and it seems obvious that such reports must be made to the General Assembly under this paragraph.

ARTICLE 16

The General Assembly shall perform such functions with respect to the international trusteeship system as are assigned to it under Chapters XII and XIII, including the approval of the trusteeship agreements for areas not designated as strategic.

See comment on Articles of Chapters XII and XIII, especially Article 85.

---

[1] *Ibid., Report of the Rapporteur of Committee III/1*, Doc. 1050, III/1/58, p. 17; see also *Report of the Rapporteur of Committee II/2*, Doc. 1122, II/2/52 (1), p. 4.
[2] *Ibid., Revised Report of the Rapporteur of Commission II to the Plenary Session*, Doc. 1180, II/18 (1), p. 3.

ARTICLE 17

1. The General Assembly shall consider and approve the budget of the Organization.

This Article gives the Assembly the important power to pass upon the budget of the Organization. This was the practice of the League of Nations decided upon after long discussions between the adherents of giving this right to the Council and the adherents of giving it to the Assembly. The Covenant contained no specific provision. The power to approve the budget carries with it of course the important power of reviewing the work of the Organization and of controlling its activities.

There was some discussion at San Francisco of the possible inclusion of details of budgetary procedure in the Charter. It was decided that it was more appropriate to leave these matters to be covered by subsequent regulations.[1]

2. The expenses of the Organization shall be borne by the Members as apportioned by the General Assembly.

It was considered unwise to attempt at San Francisco to lay down the rules for the apportionment of the expenses of the Organization. It is a question of considerable difficulty and complexity, and can best be left to the General Assembly for decision.

It is interesting to note in this regard that the Covenant of the League originally provided that the expenses of "the Secretariat" should be borne by the Members of the League in accordance with the apportionment of expenses of the International Bureau of the Universal Postal Union. In the light of experience, this was amended to provide that the expenses of the League should be borne by Members "in the proportion decided by the Assembly." This permitted greater flexibility and provided the precedent for the method adopted at San Francisco.

Expenses referred to in this paragraph do not include the cost of enforcement action. See Article 49 and comment.[2]

3. The General Assembly shall consider and approve any financial and budgetary arrangements with specialized agencies referred to in Article 57 and shall examine the administrative budgets of such specialized agencies with a view to making recommendations to the agencies concerned.

This paragraph lays down the rule that the Assembly shall also consider and approve financial engagements with the special agencies referred to in Article 57. It shall also examine the administrative budgets

---

[1] For *Regulations for the Financial Administration of the League of Nations,* see League of Nations Document C. 81. M. 81. 1945. X (issued September 15, 1945).

[2] See this volume, p. 174.

of the agencies and make recommendations with regard to them to the agencies concerned. Presumably these recommendations may take a variety of forms, including the submission of alternative budgets.

It should be noted in this connection that the League budget included the budgets of such technical organizations as the Economic and Financial Organization, the Health Organization, the Communications and Transit Organization, and the Intellectual Cooperation Organization, as well as the budgets of the two autonomous organizations, the Permanent Court of International Justice and the International Labor Organization. The League system, however, was based on the principle that all international bureaus already established and all commissions for the regulation of matters of international interest "hereafter constituted" should "be placed under the direction of the League." [1] This goal was only attained in part. It was consistent, however, with this principle of unified control and direction that the budgets of the technical organizations, commissions and committees developed within the League system, or brought within it, should be included in the League budget and subjected to Assembly control.

The principle of the United Nations as applied to the structure of the Organization is a different one. It proceeds on the assumption that the numerous specialized technical organizations established to meet highly specialized needs should be autonomous.[2] While the United Nations Organization is given certain functions of initiation, coordination and assistance, relations between the United Nations Organization and the specialized agencies are to be determined by agreement. The provisions of this paragraph recognize on the one hand the essentially autonomous status of the specialized agencies, while making it possible for the General Assembly as the representative organ of the United Nations Organization to discuss and give full publicity to the administrative practices of these agencies and to make constructive recommendations for their improvement.

The purpose of this paragraph was carefully considered by a subcommittee of the Executive Committee of the Preparatory Commission, and its views were set forth in some detail in a report which it prepared.[3] The primary object of this paragraph was stated to be "to encourage and develop a large measure of fiscal and administrative co-ordination in the interest of greater operating efficiency and economy for the entire structure of the Organization and the specialised agencies related to it." It was not considered that there was any intention to confer on the General Assembly " a financial power which could be used by it to con-

[1] *Covenant*, Article 24.
[2] See Article 57 and comment, this volume, p. 194.
[3] *Report by the Executive Committee to the Preparatory Commission of the United Nations*, cited above, p. 102, 105.

trol the policies of the specialised agencies." Relationship on policy matters, it was pointed out, are dealt with in other articles of the Charter.

The subcommittee recognized that the paragraph deals with two distinct matters: the consideration and approval of financial and budgetary arrangements made with the specialized agencies referred to in Article 57, and the examination of the administrative budgets of such agencies followed by the making of suitable recommendations. The meaning of the term "administrative budget," as used in the second part of the paragraph, gave rise to some discussion. It was suggested that the term might have been used to underline the point that the budget was to be examined "from the angle of good administration and not of policy." It was also pointed out that there is clearly an area of possible expenditure — such as the relief operations of UNRRA — which would not be subject to this kind of examination. "Even in such cases, however, the administrative costs of salary, office expenses and general expenditure of a recurring character, are comparable to those of other agencies, and their examination may lead to fruitful comparisons and contrasts." The subcommittee expressed the view "that the term ought not to be given a restrictive interpretation."

The first part of paragraph 3 envisages varying degrees of financial and budgetary relationship between the Organization and the specialized agencies. The subcommittee, above referred to, assumed that under the arrangements concluded with some of the agencies the responsibility might be placed on the General Assembly to approve their budgets. The term "consolidated budget" was used to describe such an arrangement, which of course would be in line with League practice as described above. One advantage of such a consolidated arrangement would be the simplification of the process of preparation, examination and approval of Organization and agency budgets. It was recognized, however, that in spite of the advantages of such an arrangement, there will be certain practical difficulties, such as the need of amending the constitutions of certain of the specialized agencies and the fact of differing memberships, in the way of its realization. The view, nevertheless, was expressed that "the establishment of a consolidated system to cover as many as possible of the specialised agencies is to be regarded as a desirable objective."

Voting

ARTICLE 18

1. Each member of the General Assembly shall have one vote.

There was one obvious alternative to this rule, namely, the establishment of a system of weighted voting. Such a system of weighted voting has been found more feasible for organizations of a technical nature.[1]

This alternative had, of course, strong theoretical arguments in its support, but the practical difficulties in the way of getting agreement on any formula which would give proper weight to the many criteria that needed to be taken into account were so great that no serious consideration was given to it either at Dumbarton Oaks or at San Francisco.

2. Decisions of the General Assembly on important questions shall be made by a two-thirds majority of the members present and voting. These questions shall include: recommendations with respect to the maintenance of international peace and security, the election of the non-permanent members of the Security Council, the election of the members of the Economic and Social Council, the election of members of the Trusteeship Council in accordance with paragraph 1 (c) of Article 86, the admission of new Members to the United Nations, the suspension of the rights and privileges of membership, the expulsion of Members, questions relating to the operation of the trusteeship system, and budgetary questions.

The general rule in international organizations and conferences of a political nature has been until now the rule of unanimity. This was the rule of the League of Nations consecrated in Article V of the Covenant.[2] It has been completely discarded in the Charter, except for the requirement of unanimity of the permanent members of the Security Council for certain decisions. This paragraph enumerates certain questions which shall be settled by a two-thirds majority. They include the following:

(*a*) Recommendations concerning the maintenance of peace and security.

(*b*) Election of non-permanent members of the Security Council (Article 23).

(*c*) Election of the members of the Economic and Social Council (Article 61).

(*d*) Election of the members of the Trusteeship Council (Article 86, paragraph 1 (*c*)).

(*e*) Admission of new Members (Article 4, paragraph 2).

(*f*) Suspension of Members from the exercise of their rights and privileges of membership (Article 5).

(*g*) Expulsion of Members (Article 6).

[1] See, for example, Article XI, Section 5, of the *Articles of Agreement for the International Monetary Fund* and Article V, Section 3, of the *Articles of Agreement for the International Bank for Reconstruction and Development.* See, also, Sohn, Louis B., "Weighting of Votes in an International Assembly," *American Political Science Review,* XXXVIII (December 1944), p. 1192.

[2] Many important exceptions were made in practice in addition to the specific exceptions contained in the Covenant. See Riches, Cromwell A., *Majority Rule in International Organization,* Baltimore, Johns Hopkins Press, 1940, 322 p.

(h) Questions relating to the operation of the trusteeship system (Chapters XII and XIII).

(i) Budgetary questions (Article 17).

The rule of two-thirds majority applies also to the adoption of amendments to the Charter by the General Assembly (Article 108) and to the decision fixing the date and place of a General Conference to review the Charter (Article 109). In these two Articles, however, the words "present and voting" do not appear, which raises the question whether or not their omission was deliberate. If so the actual vote required might be different in these two cases.[1]

"Recommendations with respect to the maintenance of international peace and security" presumably include all recommendations made under the provisions of Articles 10, 11 and 14 which relate to the general principles of cooperation in the maintenance of international peace and security (Article 11, paragraph 1) and to specific questions brought before the General Assembly under the terms of Article 11, paragraph 2. While the recommendations in question may be made under the terms of Articles 10 and 14, as well as under the more specific provisions of Article 11, it would appear that with respect to many matters with which the General Assembly can deal under Articles 10 and 14, a recommendation can be adopted by a majority vote.

3. Decisions on other questions, including the determination of additional categories of questions to be decided by a two-thirds majority, shall be made by a majority of the members present and voting.

All other questions shall be settled by simple majority. The Assembly can itself by simple majority decide to include other questions among those important questions which shall be decided by a two-thirds vote. However, it must be clear that the General Assembly cannot make such a decision if the Charter specifically provides that the decision shall be taken by simple majority, or in any other specified way. It is, for instance, stated in Article 10, paragraph 1, of the Statute of the Court that candidates, in order to be elected as judges, must obtain an absolute majority of votes in the General Assembly. Also, it is provided in Article 109, paragraph 3, of the Charter that if the General Conference for the review of the Charter is not held before a specified time, a proposal to call such a Conference is to be placed upon the agenda of the General Assembly and may be adopted by a majority vote of the members.

A question which the Charter does not expressly answer is whether the General Assembly, once it has determined by a majority vote additional categories of questions to be decided by a two-thirds vote, can reverse its action by a majority vote. It would seem the right interpre-

[1] See comment on Articles 108 and 109, this volume, p. 291-7.

tation that categories established by Article 18, paragraph 2, cannot be abolished except by the method specified for amending the Charter, but that "additional categories" established under paragraph 3 can be abolished or modified by the Assembly by majority vote of the members present and voting.

ARTICLE 19

A Member of the United Nations which is in arrears in the payment of its financial contributions to the Organization shall have no vote in the General Assembly if the amount of its arrears equals or exceeds the amount of the contributions due from it for the preceding two full years. The General Assembly may, nevertheless, permit such a Member to vote if it is satisfied that the failure to pay is due to conditions beyond the control of the Member.

It was thought desirable, on the basis of the experience of the League of Nations, to provide some penalty for a Member who is seriously in arrears in its financial contributions to the Organization. It was therefore decided that a Member shall have no vote in the Assembly if the amount of its arrears exceeds its contribution for the past two years. The Assembly is given discretionary power, however, to lift this penalty if it is satisfied that the failure is due to conditions beyond the control of the Member. Such conditions are not specified. They might conceivably include natural disasters such as earthquakes or great floods, revolutions and economic depressions.

It is to be noted that there is in the Charter no corresponding provision for denial of the voting privilege to a member of the Security Council, the Economic and Social Council or the Trusteeship Council. Since the elected members of these organs are chosen for terms of two to three years, the penalty would presumably be applicable in a one-year period at most. With regard to permanent members the situation obviously would be different and the fact that permanent members of the Security Council do not lose their voting privileges in that body through financial delinquency can be pointed to as another instance where the great powers enjoy special privileges.

Procedure

ARTICLE 20

The General Assembly shall meet in regular annual sessions and in such special sessions as occasion may require. Special sessions shall be convoked by the Secretary-General at the request of the Security Council or of a majority of the Members of the United Nations.

It is thus definitely settled in advance that the General Assembly shall meet in regular annual sessions. This was also the practice of the

League of Nations although it was not specifically required by the Covenant.[1] This ensures that the representative body of the Organization will have an opportunity at least once a year to review the work of the Organization. It gives assurance that world public opinion will have this opportunity to express itself. But if the public opinion of the world is to have this chance, it is clear that the meetings of the General Assembly must, for the most part, be open to the public. Such was the case with the League of Nations.

Rule no. 11 of the *Rules of Procedure of the Assembly* stated:

(1) The public shall be admitted to the plenary meetings of the Assembly, by cards distributed by the Secretary-General.

(2) The Assembly may decide that particular meetings shall be private.

(3) All decisions of the Assembly upon items on the agenda, which have been taken at a private meeting, shall be announced at a public meeting of the Assembly.[2]

Such also was the case with the plenary meetings and Commission meetings of UNCIO. The question whether sessions of the General Assembly should be open to the public was discussed at San Francisco, but it was decided not to insert any definite stipulation in the Charter. However, upon the recommendation of Committee II/2, the following statement was inserted in the report of Commission II, and was adopted by the Conference:

The Conference is of the opinion that regulations to be adopted at the first session of the General Assembly shall provide that, save in exceptional cases, the sessions of the General Assembly shall be open to the public and the press of the world.[3]

The Article also provides for special sessions as occasion may require. Such sessions are to be called by the Secretary-General at the request either of the Security Council or of the majority of the Members of the

[1] The first paragraph of Rule 1 of the *Rules of Procedure of the Assembly of the League* stated: "The Assembly shall meet in general session every year, at the seat of the League of Nations, commencing the second Monday in September, provided that the second Monday does not fall later than the 10th. If the second Monday falls later than the 10th, the session will begin on the first Monday."

[2] League of Nations, *Rules of Procedure of the Assembly*, Geneva, 1937, League of Nations Document 1937.1. N. Y., Columbia Univ. Press, agents.

[3] UNCIO, *Revised Report of the Rapporteur of Commission II to the Plenary Session*, Doc. 1180, II/18 (1), p. 2.

The Provisional Rules of Procedure for the General Assembly adopted by the Executive Committee and recommended to the Preparatory Commission contained the following rule relating to publicity of meetings of the Assembly and its Committees:

"Rule 67. The meetings of the General Assembly and its Main Committees shall be held in public unless the body concerned decides that exceptional circumstances require that the meeting be held in private. Meetings of other Committees and subsidiary organs shall be held in public unless the body concerned decides otherwise." (*Report by the Executive Committee to the Preparatory Commission of the United Nations*, cited above, p. 23.)

Organization. The League of Nations Covenant permitted special sessions to be called. Five extraordinary sessions, some for dealing with serious international conflicts and others to admit new Members to the League, were held. The Rules of Procedure for the Assembly provided that extraordinary sessions could be held when a previous meeting of the Assembly had so decided, when the Council demanded it by a majority vote, or when the majority of the Members of the League had so agreed upon a demand coming from one of the Members.

ARTICLE 21

The General Assembly shall adopt its own rules of procedure. It shall elect its President for each session.

This Article conforms to the general practice of international organizations, including the League of Nations.[1]

ARTICLE 22

The General Assembly may establish such subsidiary organs as it deems necessary for the performance of its functions.

The meaning of this Article is clear. The need of including such a specific grant of power might be questioned, particularly in view of the provision of Article 7, paragraph 2.

[1] For Provincial Rules recommended by the Executive Committee to the Preparatory Commission, see *Report by the Executive Committee to the Preparatory Commission of the United Nations*, cited above, p. 18.

CHAPTER V

THE SECURITY COUNCIL

Composition

ARTICLE 23

1. The Security Council shall consist of eleven Members of the United Nations. The Republic of China, France, the Union of Soviet Socialist Republics, the United Kingdom of Great Britain and Northern Ireland, and the United States of America shall be permanent members of the Security Council. The General Assembly shall elect six other Members of the United Nations to be non-permanent members of the Security Council, due regard being specially paid, in the first instance to the contribution of Members of the United Nations to the maintenance of international peace and security and to the other purposes of the Organization, and also to equitable geographical distribution.

Permanent Members. The first thing to be noted is that the Charter of the United Nations has kept the distinction between great powers and other states which was made in the Covenant of the League in its provisions relating to the composition of the Council. It was felt at San Francisco that there ought to be a definite relationship between the obligations imposed on certain states and their capacity to influence the decisions of the Organization. Power and responsibility should be joined together. This was the basis on which it was decided to accord a special position to certain states. These states are the ones which may be regarded as the most important guarantors of security, the countries who, upon the basis of their industrial resources and man power, are most likely to be called upon to furnish the necessary force to keep the peace of the world. They are, at the present time, the leaders of the military alliance that has conquered the Axis powers and is now engaged in determining and enforcing the terms of peace. They are the Republic of China, France, the Union of Soviet Socialist Republics, the United Kingdom of Great Britain and Northern Ireland and the United States of America.

There is a static element in this arrangement. It may be that these are the "great powers" today, but that does not of necessity mean that they will always continue to be such. That was one of the reasons for opposition to the present text. The opinion was expressed that the most powerful states would always be elected, and that it was, therefore, not only superfluous, but even harmful to mention them by name and thereby tie the hands of the Organization. Some thought it would have been wiser to state in the Charter that this permanent membership might be changed, taking into account the changing conditions of the world. This was in part done in the Covenant of the League of Nations which permitted the Council with the approval of the majority of the Assembly to create new permanent members.[1] This has not been done in the Charter. Consequently the number of permanent members and the names of states so designated can only be changed by the formal procedure of amending the Charter according to Articles 108 and 109.

Non-Permanent Members. In addition to the permanent members, there are to be six non-permanent members. This provision was in the Dumbarton Oaks Proposals and was kept in the Charter after considerable discussion and after several proposals to increase the membership had been defeated. It may be difficult enough to decide on the number of states to be represented on the Council, but it is still more difficult to find an equitable distribution of these seats.

The same problem arose in the League of Nations. The membership of the Council was enlarged from time to time so as to make it possible for additional groups of states to be represented. Furthermore, a special category of semi-permanent members was introduced, consisting of states which on the basis of their importance were declared eligible for re-election. It was recognized in the League that certain groups should always have representatives on the Council. Thus the Scandinavian States (Denmark, Finland, Norway and Sweden) had one representative. So had the Little Entente (Czechoslovakia, Rumania and Yugoslavia). Latin America had three members, the Far East one, the Near East one, and so on. Still there were some Members who were never represented on the League Council. This problem of equitable representation will be still more difficult in the United Nations with only six elective members on the Security Council.

Criteria Governing Choice of Non-Permanent Members. In the discussions of this problem in the technical committee (Committee III/1) at San Francisco, numerous possible criteria upon the basis of which the non-permanent members might be selected were considered as follows: [2]

full equality for all member nations, geographical distribution, rotation, contribution of the members of the Organization towards the maintenance of international peace and security and towards the other purposes of the Organization, guaranties concerning the active defense of international order and means to participate substantially in it, combinations of elements including population, industrial and economic capacity, future contributions in armed forces and assistance pledged by each Member state, contributions rendered in the second World War and so on; also special assignment of non-permanent seats to certain groups of nations.

[1] *Covenant,* Article 4, paragraph 2.
[2] UNCIO, *Report of the Rapporteur of Committee III/1,* Doc. 1050, III/1/58, p. 2–3.

The Dumbarton Oaks Proposals had set forth no special criteria to be taken into account in the election of non-permanent members. By so doing it had placed all Members of the Organization on an equal basis. At San Francisco, the claim was advanced by certain delegations, notably the Canadian, that there were states such as Australia, Brazil, Canada and the Netherlands which, because of their economic and military importance and more especially because of the contribution which they would be expected to make to the maintenance of peace and security, were entitled to special consideration. It was pointed out that from the point of view of power and influence there was less difference between these states and the so-called "great powers" than between these "middle powers" and many of the smaller nations.

As a concession to this point of view the Conference agreed to include as a first criterium to be taken into account by the General Assembly in the election of non-permanent members "the contribution of Members of the United Nations to the maintenance of international peace and security and to the other purposes of the Organization." Only a relatively small number of states stood to benefit, however, from the application of this criterium. There still remained the problem of fair distribution of seats among the smaller nations. As we have seen, this problem was met by the League by increasing the number of non-permanent seats and by following the practice of group representation which in most instances amounted to geographical distribution. The framers of the Charter decided to meet the problem by introducing as a second criterium "equitable geographic distribution."

These criteria will not operate automatically. Their inclusion does not mean that all the "middle powers" will have seats on the Security Council or that all geographical areas will necessarily be represented. First of all, it is left to the Assembly to decide which states satisfy these criteria. Secondly, it follows from the next paragraph that states chosen are not eligible for re-election. Thereby it is made quite clear that no state has a claim to more than occasional representation. Finally, there is no appeal in case the General Assembly disregards these criteria. One might, therefore, say that the criteria governing the distribution of non-permanent seats are nothing more than solemn exhortations to the General Assembly to act in a certain way. If the Assembly should disregard these exhortations, the political effects might be serious, but there would be no legal consequences. The elections would still be valid.

2. The non-permanent members of the Security Council shall be elected for a term of two years. In the first election of the non-permanent members, however, three shall be chosen for a term of one year. A retiring member shall not be eligible for immediate re-election.

Under the League Covenant the term of non-permanent members was three years. The members of the Economic and Social Council and the elected members of the Trusteeship Council are elected for three years. But it was deemed wiser in the case of the Security Council to have a shorter period in order to give more Members the opportunity of membership. It is furthermore provided that at the first elections three of the non-permanent members shall be elected for one year terms and three for two year terms so as to ensure a greater continuity in the non-permanent membership of the Council. A retiring member is declared not eligible for immediate re-election. The Economic and Social Council with its greater membership does not have this rule. There is no specified period that a state must wait before again becoming eligible for election to the Security Council.

The League of Nations developed a system under which certain members of the Council were virtually semi-permanent through being declared eligible for re-election. Under the Charter, the interests of the "middle powers" are taken care of in another way.[1]

This paragraph makes no provision for a special election in case a member of the Council ceases to be a member before its term has expired. This might happen if the member in question ceased to exist as a state or ceased to be a Member of the Organization, either because of expulsion or through voluntary withdrawal. It is not believed that a Member whose privileges have been suspended will cease to be a member of the Council. Presumably the matter of elections to fill vacancies will be covered by rules adopted by the General Assembly.

3. Each member of the Security Council shall have one representative.

This provision is to be contrasted with that of Article 9, paragraph 2, applying to the General Assembly, which permits each Member to have five representatives in that body. This rule has special significance in connection with the provisions of Article 28, paragraphs 1 and 2.

Functions and Powers

ARTICLE 24

1. In order to ensure prompt and effective action by the United Nations, its Members confer on the Security Council primary responsibility for the maintenance of international peace and security, and agree that in carrying out its duties under this responsibility the Security Council acts on their behalf.

This paragraph states the basic principle governing the role of the Security Council.[2] The Members of the Organization confer on the

---

[1] For comment on paragraph 1, see this volume, p. 117, above.

[2] For comment on Article 10 bearing on relations of General Assembly and Security Council, see *ibid.*, p. 94.

Security Council the primary responsibility for the maintenance of peace and security. They do not yield up all responsibility. The Assembly also has, according to the stipulations in Articles 10 to 15, certain powers and responsibilities in this sphere. But the Council has the chief responsibility.

The reason for placing this responsibility on the Security Council is that that organ by virtue of its size and composition is regarded as best suited to assure "prompt and effective action." This definite allocation of responsibility for the maintenance of international peace and security to a small body on which the great military powers are permanently represented is regarded by many as the great advance this Organization has made over the security system of the League of Nations.

The Members, furthermore, agree that the Security Council shall act on their behalf. This provision, taken in conjunction with the provision of Article 25, results in the relinquishment by certain Members of the Organization of a considerable amount of their freedom of action, since they agree in advance to be represented by and to be bound by the decisions of a body on which they are not necessarily represented and over whose decisions they have no effective control. This of course is not true of the permanent members of the Security Council.

2. In discharging these duties the Security Council shall act in accordance with the Purposes and Principles of the United Nations. The specific powers granted to the Security Council for the discharge of these duties are laid down in Chapters VI, VII, VIII, and XII.

This is a specific application of Article 2. It is intended to give assurance that the Security Council in the discharge of the duties conferred upon it by this Article and stated in greater detail in Chapters VI, VII, VIII and XII will not act arbitrarily but in accordance with the basic purposes and principles of the Organization. It must of course be admitted that this leaves considerable discretionary power to the Security Council since it alone is responsible for the interpretation of the Charter in so far as it determines its powers and functions, and prescribes limitations upon the exercise of the same.

At the United Nations Conference an attempt was made to establish a further limitation on the power of the Security Council by incorporating in the Charter a definition of aggression. This attempt was defeated. One argument that was made against such a definition of aggression was that it would weaken the power of the Security Council to an undesirable extent, that it would deprive the Council of the discretionary power that must be vested in it if it is to deal with unforeseeable situations in an effective manner.[1]

---

[1] See comment on Article 39, *ibid.*, p. 155.

There is, however, in the rule governing voting procedure laid down in Article 27 another guarantee against abuse of power. In order for the Security Council to take substantive decisions carrying out its responsibility under this Article, there must be concurrence among at least seven members of the Council, including all the permanent members (except that parties to a dispute cannot vote). This means that any permanent member, subject to the exception just noted, can prevent a decision from being taken. Furthermore, no decision can be taken by the permanent members without the concurrence of two other members. It is quite possible that the real difficulty will be, not that the Security Council will abuse its power, but rather that it will be unable to use its power.

The fact that the words "Purposes" and "Principles" are used in capitalized form suggests that the reference is to the specific provisions of Articles 1 and 2 respectively.[1]

3. The Security Council shall submit annual and, when necessary, special reports to the General Assembly for its consideration.

See comment on Article 15, paragraph 1.

ARTICLE 25

The Members of the United Nations agree to accept and carry out the decisions of the Security Council in accordance with the present Charter.

This Article logically follows Article 24 since it lays down a rule which is the logical consequence of the provisions of the previous Article. Members agree to "accept and carry out" the decisions of the Security Council taken in accordance with the terms of the Charter, since they have already agreed that the Council "acts on their behalf" in carrying out the "primary responsibility" conferred upon it to maintain international peace and security. The precise extent of this obligation of Members can be determined only by reference to other provisions of the Charter, particularly Chapters VI, VII, VIII and XII. Decisions of the Security Council take on a binding character only as they relate to the prevention or suppression of breaches of the peace.

The word "decisions" as used in this Article clearly does not include recommendations which the Security Council is empowered to make under Articles 36, 37 and 38. It was made clear in the discussions at San Francisco, as it should be apparent from the wording of the Charter, that such recommendations have no binding force.

It is, also, quite clear that this Article does not apply to measures taken by individual Members under Article 107. A certain doubt might

---

[1] See comment on these Articles, *ibid.*, p. 59–76.

arise concerning Article 106. However, it seems correct to say that "joint action on behalf of the Organization" by the five Great Powers in question does not have obligatory effect under this Article for the other Members. Such measures are taken on behalf of the Organization by the five Great Powers but not by the Council.

ARTICLE 26

In order to promote the establishment and maintenance of international peace and security with the least diversion for armaments of the world's human and economic resources, the Security Council shall be responsible for formulating, with the assistance of the Military Staff Committee referred to in Article 47, plans to be submitted to the Members of the United Nations for the establishment of a system for the regulation of armaments.

This Article, taken together with the first paragraph of Article 11,[1] provides the Charter system of international control of armaments. These two Articles correspond to Articles 8 and 9 of the League Covenant.

It is obvious that the League system was much more ambitious and detailed than that of the United Nations. Under the Covenant, Members recognized that the maintenance of peace required "the reduction of armaments"; there is no such explicit recognition of this principle in the Charter. Under the Covenant, Members recognized that the private manufacture of munitions and implements of war was open to grave objection, and should be controlled; there is no mention of this problem in the Charter. Under the Covenant, Members agreed to the interchange of "full and frank information as to the scale of their armaments, their military, naval and air programs and the conditions of such of their industries as are adaptable to warlike purposes"; there is no comparable obligation placed on Members of the United Nations. As the League system developed, "disarmament" came to be accepted as one of the three coordinate bases of a peace structure. There is no suggestion in the Charter that the reduction and limitation of armaments by international agreement will be seriously undertaken until peace and security have been assured.

The procedure for establishing "a system for the regulation of armaments" envisaged in this Article roughly parallels that provided for in the Covenant. The Security Council is made responsible for formulating plans. It is to have the assistance of the Military Staff Committee. These plans are to be submitted to the Members of the Organization for their consideration. Members will presumably take action on these plans in accordance with their constitutional procedures. No Member will be bound except following its specific acceptance of the plan or plans

[1] See comment, *ibid.*, p. 97.

submitted. A multilateral agreement, and not a series of bilateral agreements, is obviously intended.

This Article is to be understood in relation to Article 43 which provides for a special agreement or agreements specifying the armed forces, assistance and facilities which members undertake to place at the disposal of the Security Council for enforcement purposes. The "system for the regulation of armaments" envisaged in this Article is therefore one which provides minimum as well as maximum limits. In this respect it differs substantially from the League system as envisaged in Article 8 of the Covenant.

Voting

ARTICLE 27

1. Each member of the Security Council shall have one vote.

The fact that the Security Council was so constituted as to give special representation to certain members with special interests made any serious consideration of weighted voting unnecessary. This rule, following the international practice of the past, was accepted without question.

2. Decisions of the Security Council on procedural matters shall be made by an affirmative vote of seven members.

Questions of procedure are to be decided by the affirmative vote of any seven members of the Security Council, whether they are permanent members or not. It is not explained, however, what matters shall be considered procedural. It seems clear that matters arising under Articles 28 to 32 are procedural in character. It appears to be the proper interpretation that very few other matters are to be considered as procedural. According to the joint statement of the Sponsoring Governments at San Francisco, decisions under Chapters VI, VII and VIII which do not involve "taking direct measures in connection with settlement of disputes, adjustment of situations likely to lead to disputes, determination of threats to the peace, removal of threats to the peace, and suppression of breaches of the peace" [1] are governed by this paragraph. Thus it would appear that the Security Council may by an unqualified majority of seven decide to place a particular matter on its agenda or allow parties to a dispute or other states to be heard. While the joint statement of the Sponsoring Governments was not accepted by the San Francisco Conference as an official interpretation of the provisions regarding Council voting procedure, there is little doubt but what these specific interpretations, representing concessions by the

[1] UNCIO, *Statement by the Delegations of the Four Sponsoring Governments on Voting Procedure in the Security Council*, Doc. 852, III/1/37(1), p. 1, see *ibid.*, p. 128 below.

Great Powers, were accepted, without prejudice to the exact definition of the full scope of application of the paragraph.

It is not stated in this paragraph who is going to decide when a matter is procedural, or by what vote this decision is to be taken. This, obviously, must be settled by the Council itself and it is logical to assume that the question will be regarded as non-procedural, with the concurrence of all permanent members necessary to a decision. That was the view expressed by the Sponsoring Governments in their Statement of Interpretation.[1]

3. Decisions of the Security Council on all other matters shall be made by an affirmative vote of seven members including the concurring votes of the permanent members; provided that, in decisions under Chapter VI, and under paragraph 3 of Article 52, a party to a dispute shall abstain from voting.

Disagreement on Interpretation of Yalta Formula. No question which came up in connection with the drafting and adoption of the Charter caused so much disagreement and created so much difficulty as that relating to the scope of the application of the rule laid down in this paragraph. The Sponsoring Governments themselves were not able to reach agreement on this matter in the course of the Dumbarton Oaks Conversations. It was not until the Yalta Conference that an accord was reached. The agreed formula was submitted to the other United Nations at the time the invitation to the United Nations Conference was extended. It was submitted to the Conference as an integral part of the Dumbarton Oaks Proposals and was eventually adopted in the form in which it was submitted.

The proposals with regard to votes necessary to decisions were the controversial features of the Yalta formula. Numerous suggestions were made by governments participating in the San Francisco Conference for their amendment, all intended to remove or lessen the so-called "veto power" of a permanent member of the Security Council. When the question came up for consideration in the appropriate technical committee of the Conference (Committee III/1), representatives of the Sponsoring Governments were asked to interpret paragraphs 2 and 3, and particularly 3, by indicating how they would be applied in specific situations. It was soon clear that the Sponsoring Governments themselves were not in agreement as to the interpretation to be given.

A subcommittee of Committee III/1, consisting of the Delegates of Australia, China, Costa Rica (Rapporteur of the Committee), Cuba, Egypt, France, Greece, the Netherlands, the Union of Soviet Socialist Republics, the United Kingdom and the United States of America was created to seek a clarification of the meaning of the paragraphs. Under

[1] *Ibid.*

the procedure agreed upon by the subcommittee,[1] representatives of delegations other than those of the Sponsoring Governments proposed questions which were then collated by the Committee Secretariat and submitted on May 22 to the Delegates of the Sponsoring Governments who were members of the subcommittee for their answers. A list of twenty-three questions was prepared and submitted in this manner. The questions submitted were as follows:[2]

(1) If the parties to a dispute request the Security Council (under Article 38)[3] to make recommendations with a view to its settlement, would the veto be applicable to a decision of the Security Council *to exercise its power to investigate* the dispute for that purpose?

(2) If the Security Council has investigated a dispute under this paragraph (Article 38), would the veto be applicable to a decision of the Security Council *to recommend to the Parties certain terms*, with a view to the settlement of the dispute?

(3) If the attention of the Security Council is called to the existence of a dispute, or a situation which may give rise to a dispute (under Article 34), would the veto be applicable to a decision of the Security Council *to exercise its power to investigate* the dispute or situation?

(4) If the Security Council has investigated the dispute, would the veto be applicable to a decision by the Security Council that *the continuance of the dispute* is likely to endanger the maintenance of international peace and security?

(5) If the Security Council has decided that the continuance of a dispute is likely to endanger the maintenance of international peace and security, would the veto be applicable to a decision of the Security Council *to call upon* the parties to settle their dispute by the means indicated in paragraph 3 (Article 33)?

(6) If a dispute is referred to the Security Council by the parties under this paragraph (Article 37), would the veto be applicable to a decision by the Security Council under the second sentence of this paragraph that *it deems the continuance of the particular dispute is in fact likely to endanger* the maintenance of international peace and security?

(7) If the Security Council deems that the continuance of the particular dispute is in fact likely to endanger the maintenance of international peace and security, would the veto be applicable to a decision of the Security Council under the second sentence of this paragraph (Article 37) *to take action* under paragraph 5 (Article 36)?

(8) If the Security Council deems that the continuance of the particular dispute is in fact likely to endanger the maintenance of international peace and security, would the veto be applicable to a decision of the Security Council under the second sentence of this paragraph (Article 37) *to recommend to the parties such terms of settlement* as it considers appropriate?

(9) Would the veto be applicable to a decision of the Security Council (under Article 36), at any stage of a dispute, to recommend to the parties appropriate procedures or methods of adjustment?

[1] *Ibid., Summary Report of First Meeting of Subcommittee III/1/B, May 19, 1945*, Doc. 481, III/1/B/1.

[2] *Ibid., Questionnaire on Exercise of Veto in Security Council*, Doc. 855, III/1/B/2 (a).

[3] References in the original questionnaire to the provisions of the Dumbarton Oaks Proposals to which the questions related have for the most part been omitted. References to the corresponding Articles of the Charter have been inserted in parentheses. For complete text of Questionnaire, see this volume, p. 333.

(10) Would the veto be applicable to a decision of the Security Council under the first sentence of this paragraph (Article 36, paragraph 3) that a dispute *is of a justiciable* [i.e. legal] *character?*

(11) Would the veto be applicable to a decision of the Security Council under the first sentence of this paragraph to *refer a justiciable dispute* [1] to the International Court of Justice?

(12) Would the veto be applicable to a decision of the Security Council to *deal with a justiciable dispute by some other means of adjustment?*

(13) Would the veto be applicable to a decision of the Security Council (under Article 96, paragraph 1) to refer to the International Court of Justice a legal question connected with a *non-justiciable dispute?*

(14) Would the veto be applicable to a decision of the Security Council [2] that it *deemed* that a failure would constitute a threat to the maintenance of peace and security?

(15) Would the veto be applicable to a decision of the Security Council [2] that *it should take any measures* necessary for the maintenance of international peace and security?

(16) Would the veto be applicable to a decision of the Security Council (under Article 39) that it *determined* the existence of any threat to the peace, etc.?

(17) Would the veto be applicable to a decision of the Security Council (under Article 40) that it *may call* upon the parties, etc.?

(18) Would the veto be applicable to a decision of the Security Council (under Article 40) that failure to comply *should be duly taken account of*, etc.?

(19) In case a decision has to be taken as to whether a certain point is a procedural matter (Article 27, paragraph 2), is that preliminary question to be considered in itself as a procedural matter or is the veto applicable to such preliminary question?

(20) If a motion is moved in the Security Council on a matter, other than a matter of procedure, under the general words in paragraph 3 (of Article 27), would the *abstention from voting* of any one of the permanent members of the Security Council *have the same effect* as a negative vote by that member in preventing the Security Council from reaching a decision on the matter?

(21) If one of the permanent members of the Security Council is a party to a dispute, and in conformity with the proviso to paragraph 3 (of Article 27) has abstained from voting on a motion on a matter, other than a matter of procedure, *would its mere abstention prevent* the Security Council from reaching a decision on the matter?

(22) In case a decision has to be made under Chapter VIII, Section A,[3] (Chapter VI of the Charter), or under the second sentence of Chapter VIII, Section C, paragraph 1 (Article 52), will a permanent member of the Council be entitled to participate in a vote on the question whether that permanent member is itself a party to the dispute or not?

(23) In view of questions raised by several delegations, the Greek Delegation would like to be informed whether, under Chapter 10, paragraph 1, of the Dumbarton Oaks Proposals as amended by the Four Governments (Article 97), the recommendation of the Security Council to the Assembly in respect of the election of the Secretary General and his deputies is subject to veto.

[1] Refers to Chapter VIII, Section A, paragraph 6, of the Dumbarton Oaks Proposals which was revised at San Francisco so as to eliminate this particular phraseology.

[2] Under Chapter VIII, Section B, paragraph 1, of the Dumbarton Oaks Proposals. There is no corresponding Article in the Charter.

[3] Of the Dumbarton Oaks Proposals.

Interpretation of Sponsoring Governments. After exchanges of views during a period of over two weeks, the Delegations of the Sponsoring Governments were able to announce on June 7 their agreement on a joint Statement of Interpretation. This Statement was subscribed to by the French Delegation. It was as follows:[1]

STATEMENT BY THE DELEGATIONS OF THE FOUR
SPONSORING GOVERNMENTS ON VOTING PROCEDURE
IN THE SECURITY COUNCIL

Specific questions covering the voting procedure in the Security Council have been submitted by a Sub-Committee of the Conference Committee on Structure and Procedures of the Security Council to the Delegations of the four Governments sponsoring the Conference — The United States of America, the United Kingdom of Great Britain and Northern Ireland, the Union of Soviet Socialist Republics, and the Republic of China. In dealing with these questions, the four Delegations desire to make the following statement of their general attitude towards the whole question of unanimity of permanent members in the decisions of the Security Council.

I

1. The Yalta voting formula recognizes that the Security Council, in discharging its responsibilities for the maintenance of international peace and security, will have two broad groups of functions. Under Chapter VIII, the Council will have to make decisions which involve its taking direct measures in connection with settlement of disputes, adjustment of situations likely to lead to disputes, determination of threats to the peace, removal of threats to the peace, and suppression of breaches of the peace. It will also have to make decisions which do not involve the taking of such measures. The Yalta formula provides that the second of these two groups of decisions will be governed by a procedural vote — that is, the vote of any seven members. The first group of decisions will be governed by a qualified vote — that is, the vote of seven members, including the concurring votes of the five permanent members, subject to the proviso that in decisions under Section A and a part of Section C of Chapter VIII parties to a dispute shall abstain from voting.

2. For example, under the Yalta formula a procedural vote will govern the decisions made under the entire Section D of Chapter VI. This means that the Council will, by a vote of any seven of its members, adopt or alter its rules of procedure; determine the method of selecting its President; organize itself in such a way as to be able to function continuously; select the times and places of its regular and special meetings; establish such bodies or agencies as it may deem necessary for the performance of its functions; invite a Member of the Organization not represented on the Council to participate in its discussions when that Member's interests are specially affected; and invite any state when it is a party to a dispute being considered by the Council to participate in the discussion relating to that dispute.

3. Further, no individual member of the Council can alone prevent consideration and discussion by the Council of a dispute or situation brought to its attention under paragraph 2, Section A, Chapter VIII. Nor can parties to such

[1] UNCIO, Doc. 852, III/1/37(1).

dispute be prevented by these means from being heard by the Council. Likewise, the requirement for unanimity of the permanent members cannot prevent any member of the Council from reminding the Members of the Organization of their general obligations assumed under the Charter as regards peaceful settlement of international disputes.

4. Beyond this point, decisions and actions by the Security Council may well have major political consequences and may even initiate a chain of events which might, in the end, require the Council under its responsibilities to invoke measures of enforcement under Section B, Chapter VIII. This chain of events begins when the Council decides to make an investigation, or determines that the time has come to call upon states to settle their differences, or makes recommendations to the parties. It is to such decisions and actions that unanimity of the permanent members applies, with the important proviso, referred to above, for abstention from voting by parties to a dispute.

5. To illustrate: in ordering an investigation, the Council has to consider whether the investigation — which may involve calling for reports, hearing witnesses, dispatching a commission of inquiry, or other means — might not further aggravate the situation. After investigation, the Council must determine whether the continuance of the situation or dispute would be likely to endanger international peace and security. If it so determines, the Council would be under obligation to take further steps. Similarly, the decision to make recommendations, even when all parties request it to do so, or to call upon parties to a dispute to fulfill their obligations under the Charter, might be the first step on a course of action from which the Security Council could withdraw only at the risk of failing to discharge its responsibilities.

6. In appraising the significance of the vote required to take such decisions or actions, it is useful to make comparison with the requirements of the League Covenant with reference to decisions of the League Council. Substantive decisions of the League of Nations Council could be taken only by the unanimous vote of all its members, whether permanent or not, with the exception of parties to a dispute under Article XV of the League Covenant. Under Article XI, under which most of the disputes brought before the League were dealt with and decisions to make investigations taken, the unanimity rule was invariably interpreted to include even the votes of the parties to a dispute.

7. The Yalta voting formula substitutes for the rule of complete unanimity of the League Council a system of qualified majority voting in the Security Council. Under this system non-permanent members of the Security Council individually would have no "veto." As regards the permanent members, there is no question under the Yalta formula of investing them with a new right, namely, the right to veto, a right which the permanent members of the League Council always had. The formula proposed for the taking of action in the Security Council by a majority of seven would make the operation of the Council less subject to obstruction than was the case under the League of Nations rule of complete unanimity.

8. It should also be remembered that under the Yalta formula the five major powers could not act by themselves, since even under the unanimity requirement any decisions of the Council would have to include the concurring votes of at least two of the non-permanent members. In other words, it would be possible for five non-permanent members as a group to exercise a "veto." It is not to be assumed, however, that the permanent members, any more than the non-permanent members, would use their "veto" power wilfully to obstruct the operation of the Council.

9. In view of the primary responsibilities of the permanent members, they could not be expected, in the present condition of the world, to assume the obligation to act in so serious a matter as the maintenance of international peace and security in consequence of a decision in which they had not concurred. Therefore, if a majority voting in the Security Council is to be made possible, the only practicable method is to provide, in respect of non-procedural decisions, for unanimity of the permanent members plus the concurring votes of at least two of the non-permanent members.

10. For all these reasons, the four Sponsoring Governments agreed on the Yalta formula and have presented it to this Conference as essential if an international organization is to be created through which all peace-loving nations can effectively discharge their common responsibilities for the maintenance of international peace and security.

II

In the light of the considerations set forth in Part I of this statement, it is clear what the answers to the questions submitted by the Subcommittee should be, with the exception of Question 19. The answer to that question is as follows:

1. In the opinion of the Delegations of the Sponsoring Governments, the Draft Charter itself contains an indication of the application of the voting procedures to the various functions of the Council.

2. In this case, it will be unlikely that there will arise in the future any matters of great importance on which a decision will have to be made as to whether a procedural vote would apply. Should, however, such a matter arise, the decision regarding the preliminary question as to whether or not such a matter is procedural must be taken by a vote of seven members of the Security Council, including the concurring votes of the permanent members.

Committee Consideration of Interpretation of Sponsoring Governments and France. The report of the subcommittee to Committee III/1[1], along with the above Statement of Interpretation of the Sponsoring Governments, was submitted on June 9. There followed a full discussion of the questions raised by the original proposal of the Sponsoring Governments and their agreed interpretation which extended through four meetings of the Committee on June 9, 11 and 12.[2] The Statement of the Delegations of the Sponsoring Governments was severely criticized by many delegates on the ground that it did not answer all the questions submitted and that it took an unduly narrow view with regard to the field of application of the unqualified "majority of seven" rule. The position of those delegations adopting a critical attitude was best expressed in a printed memorandum presented by the Australian Delegate (Dr. Evatt). It read as follows: [3]

[1] *Ibid.*, Doc. 883, III/1/B/4.
[2] See *ibid.*, Doc. 897, III/1/42; Doc. 922, III/1/44; Doc. 936, III/1/45; and Doc. 956, III/1/47.
[3] *Ibid.*, *Summary Report of Sixteenth Meeting of Committee III/1, June 9, 1945,* Doc. 897, III/1/42, p. 9. References are to Dumbarton Oaks text, see p. 308.

VOTING PROCEDURE IN THE SECURITY COUNCIL

1. The issue now confronting the Committee is not purely one of interpretation nor purely one of policy, but is complex, comprising both elements. The question of interpretation is whether the Committee agrees with the views now expressed by the Sponsoring Governments regarding the application of the veto in the Security Council under Chapter VI, Section C. The question of policy is whether the voting formula should be clarified or amended in order to ensure an effective procedure for conciliation, i.e. the peaceful settlement of disputes between nations.

2. The question of interpretation turns on the meaning to be given to the phrase "procedural matters" in Chapter VI, Section C. On this point it is submitted that the joint statement is not satisfactory, for a number of reasons.

3. The interpretation given by the joint statement is not based on any consistent principle. In some respects it is unduly narrow, in others perhaps surprisingly wide. In its application to Chapter VIII, Section A, it is far more restrictive than the interpretation given by the representative of one of the Sponsoring Governments when the matter was last before the Committee.

4. The joint statement answers directly only one of the 22 questions, though these were asked at the suggestion of the Sponsoring Governments themselves. The answer they would have given to some of the questions is reasonably clear, but in others the matter is left altogether at large. In a few instances the correctness of the answer implied is open to grave question. Under paragraphs 3 and 4 of Chapter VIII, Section A, for example, the Security Council is not merely empowered, but is imperatively required, to take a particular course of action or make a certain choice. Where the Security Council's power is thus associated with a duty to exercise it, the decision is limited to questions of time and method, and could fairly be treated as procedural. Yet the joint statement plainly treats these decisions as subject to the veto.

5. The joint statement gives no weight to the fact that Section A is devoted almost wholly to the choice of one or other of a number of steps which were described in the Dumbarton Oaks text as "procedures" for the peaceful settlement of disputes. (Dumbarton Oaks Text, Chapter VIII, A, 5, and VIII, B, 1.) The context gives little justification for the narrow interpretation placed especially on Chapter VIII, Section A by the joint statement as contrasted with the broad interpretation placed on Chapter VI, Section D.

6. The net effect of the joint statement is that "consideration and discussion by the Council" of a dispute or situation is the only matter under Chapter VIII, Section A, that cannot be blocked by a permanent member. It is important to understand that the words "consideration and discussion" are used in the joint statement in a much narrower sense than they ordinarily bear. In ordinary speech "consideration" of a dispute would include calling for reports, hearing witnesses, or even the appointment of a commission of investigation. The joint statement, however, treats the veto as applicable to a decision to use any of those procedures. It is only "consideration and discussion" of a very preliminary and restricted character that is to be free of the veto. It may be said that, without veto, the Council can only discuss whether a dispute can be discussed, and can only investigate whether it should be investigated.

7. The importance of the fact that such consideration and discussion is free of the veto must not be underestimated, and the joint statement represents a substantial advance over a blanket veto. On the other hand, a system for the peaceful settlement of disputes in which everything except preliminary consideration and discussion of this limited character *is* to be subject to the veto is

not an effective method of conciliation. The only argument put forward in support of it by the joint statement is that all subsequent decisions "may well have major political consequences, and may even initiate a chain of events which might, in the end, require the Council under its responsibilities to invoke measures of enforcement under Chapter VIII, Section B." This is true. But it is for this very reason that the exercise of a veto to block conciliation of disputants — even where both disputants seek conciliation — will prevent the dispute from being composed and will be more likely to cause serious consequences in the way of a breach of the peace.

8. The matter stands at present in so confused a condition that, if the present text of the voting procedure stands without amendment, steps should be taken to secure the opinion of the International Court of Justice on the question of interpretation involved.

9. But the simpler, and preferable, course is to make sure by amendment that the veto is clearly inapplicable to any decision of the Security Council under the section dealing with the peaceful adjustment of disputes.

10. The matter of the veto assumes greater importance because of the fact that, under the present draft, each of the five great powers could block any amendment of the Charter.

In the course of Committee discussion, it became clear that many delegations would be more favorably inclined to the acceptance of the formula as it stood if there were some assurance that a General Conference to review the Charter would be held, and that such revision would not be subject to the rule of unanimity of the permanent members of the Security Council. The question of voting procedure thus came to be tied up in the minds of many with that of amendment procedure. Furthermore, there was discussion of the effect of abstention from voting by members of the Council and particularly of abstention from voting by permanent members as required under the circumstances referred to in paragraph 3. On the latter point, the Delegate of the United States explained that the abstention required under the paragraph could not be used to prevent a decision since it was clearly an exception to the rule of unanimity of the permanent members. In that situation a decision would be taken by seven affirmative votes with the concurrence of all permanent members not parties to the dispute.[1]

The issue chiefly pressed in Committee discussion was that of the voting procedure of the Council when performing conciliatory functions under the Chapter dealing with the pacific settlement of disputes. The position of the Sponsoring Governments was that unanimity of the permanent members was necessary here, except on the admittedly procedural questions of putting matters on the Council's agenda, and giving states the opportunity to be heard, since a decision ordering an investigation or making a recommendation might have major political consequences and might even initiate a chain of events which would lead to

[1] Ibid., Summary Report of the Twentieth Meeting of Committee III/1, June 13, 1945, Doc. 967, III/1/48, p. 2.

enforcement action by the Council. On the other hand, it was argued that where the Council was acting in a purely conciliatory capacity, without any power to bind interested parties, no one state should be in a position to prevent conciliatory action from being taken simply by interposing its objection. Numerous amendments were submitted to achieve this end. It was decided that the Committee should settle the issue by voting on an Australian amendment which read as follows: [1]

Add the following at the end of Chapter VI, Section C, paragraph 2 (of the Dumbarton Oaks Proposals):
"Decisions made by the Security Council in the exercise of any of its duties, functions and powers under Chapter VIII, Section A (Chapter VI of the Charter), shall be deemed to be decisions on procedural matters."

This amendment was acted upon by the Committee on June 12 and defeated by the following vote: 10 affirmative, 20 negative, and 15 abstentions.

Interpretation of the Article. While the attempt to modify the Yalta formula failed, and while the proposals of the Sponsoring Governments were finally accepted by Committee III/1, Commission III and the Conference, it was made clear in the course of Committee discussion and by the votes taken that no action was taken on the Statement of Interpretation of the Sponsoring Governments. That cannot therefore be regarded as the accepted interpretation of the Article, though as a matter of fact, due to the ability of any one permanent member of the Council to veto an interpretation contrary to it, there is a probability that the interpretations given in the statement will be followed.

The text of the paragraph says that a decision shall be taken on other than procedural matters by an affirmative vote of seven members including the concurring votes of the permanent members. This makes it quite clear that abstentions from voting will not affect the size of the majority required. This would seem to mean that any permanent member has a veto right and can exercise it, even by absenting himself or abstaining from voting. However, in any situation where the concluding proviso is applicable, the requirement of unanimity of the permanent members does not presumably extend to parties to the dispute. In such cases, the requirement would be that there must be an affirmative vote of seven members of the Security Council including the concurring votes of all permanent members who are not parties to the dispute. The rule also means that any group of five non-permanent members has the same veto power as is possessed by a permanent member. The Great Powers must have at least two of the other members voting with them. Politically this may not mean very much. It is highly unlikely

[1] *Ibid.*, *Summary Report of the Nineteenth Meeting of Committee III/1, June 12 1945*, Doc. 956, III/1/47, p. 7.

that the Great Powers will be unable to convince at least two of the other members to vote with them in a case they consider important.

The second and third paragraphs of Article 27 use the word "decisions." It should be kept in mind that the word "decisions" has two different meanings. In one sense "decisions" may be opposed to "recommendations." On the other hand, "decisions" may refer to votes of any character. The Council must also decide when to make a recommendation. It must decide whether to put a matter on the agenda. It must decide when to meet. It is clear from the wording of this Article, from the discussion in the Committee and from the answer given by the Sponsoring Governments to the questionnaire of the Subcommittee that the word "decisions" as used in paragraph 3 must be taken in a wider sense than the same word when used in Article 25.[1]

Exceptions to the General Rule. The paragraph states two important exceptions to the general principle. The one is that a state party to a dispute shall not vote when its case is being treated under Chapter VI. No state shall be judge in its own cause, not even a Great Power. It is indubitable progress that this is stated so clearly. The other exception is a decision of the Security Council under Article 52, paragraph 3, referring to action with respect to settlement of disputes under regional arrangements, where likewise a party is to abstain from voting.

There are also in the Charter other exceptions to the unanimity principle as applied to non-procedural matters. A decision of the Security Council, concurring with a decision of the General Assembly in the calling of a General Conference to review the Charter under Article 107, may be taken by a vote of any seven members. Under Article 10 of the Statute of the Court, judges are elected concurrently by the General Assembly and the Security Council, with the Security Council acting by an ordinary majority.

Procedure

ARTICLE 28

1. The Security Council shall be so organized as to be able to function continuously. Each member of the Security Council shall for this purpose be represented at all times at the seat of the Organization.

This paragraph introduces an important departure from League practice. Under the Covenant, the Council met "from time to time as occasion may require, and at least once a year." [2] The Rules of Procedure of the Council provided for periodical ordinary sessions. Under the 1933 Rules, the Council had four ordinary sessions, but since the fourth

---

[1] For comment on Article 25, see this volume, p. 122.
[2] *Covenant*, Article 4, paragraph 3.

followed immediately upon the third, the Council met in fact three times a year at intervals of four months. Extraordinary sessions were held on decision of the Council or at the request of any Member of the League "in the circumstances referred to in Articles 11, 15 and 17 of the Covenant." [1] There was no provision for permanent representation of the members of the Council at the seat of the League where the meetings of the Council were normally held.

While these provisions were flexible and gave reasonable assurance that a meeting of the Council would be held when the occasion required, a certain amount of delay was inevitable due to the fact that representatives often had considerable distances to travel to reach the Council's meeting place, not to mention the time required for preparations. The Charter gives assurance of prompter action by the Security Council by providing that it shall be organized so as to function continuously. This presumably refers to the administrative organization of the Council, a matter which will presumably be taken care of in connection with the organization of the Secretariat, as well as to the matter of member representation covered in the second sentence of the paragraph.

Every member of the Council shall be permanently represented at the seat of the Organization. The institution of the "permanent delegate" is not new in international life. Many members of the League of Nations had their permanent delegates in Geneva. [2] They were usually members of the diplomatic staffs. It is possible that the work of the Security Council will be considered so important that the permanent representative will be a person with greater political authority than a foreign service officer. However, it is more reasonable to assume that the permanent delegate referred to in this paragraph will in fact be the equivalent of a permanent diplomatic representative with rank of ambassador. More cannot be said about this before a practice is established.

The paragraph clearly implies that there shall be one central headquarters for all the principal and subsidiary organs of the United Nations, with the exception of the International Court of Justice, the seat of which is designated in Article 22 of the Statute. [3] In the report accompanying the recommendation of the Executive Committee to the Preparatory Commission, the view was expressed that the principle of centralization should be adopted to the extent that the seats of the specialized agencies should be concentrated in one place. [4] It was admitted, however, that

[1] Rules of the Council, see League of Nations, *Official Journal*, vol. 14, no. 7, Part I (July 1933), p. 900.

[2] See Potter, Pitman B., *Permanent Delegations to the League of Nations*, Geneva Research Centre, Geneva Special Studies, I, no. 8 (1930).

[3] See this volume, p. 369.

[4] *Report by the Executive Committee to the Preparatory Commission of the United Nations*, cited above.

the adoption of this principle would not exclude the possibility of any subsidiary organ or specialized agency having its permanent seat in another place if there were very strong reasons for making an exception.

No decision was taken at San Francisco concerning the location of the permanent headquarters. This matter was not even officially discussed, but was referred to the Preparatory Commission for recommendation.

2. The Security Council shall hold periodic meetings at which each of its members may, if it so desires, be represented by a member of the government or by some other specially designated representative.

A distinction seems to be made between the functioning and the meeting of the Council. As we have seen, the Covenant provided for meetings of the Council when occasion required, at least once a year. The Rules of Procedure specified the number and dates of ordinary meetings, and made provision for the calling of extraordinary sessions. Presumably the Rules of the Security Council will make provision for regular periodic sessions, while making it possible for extraordinary sessions to be called whenever necessary.

It is stated that each member of the Council may be represented by a "member of the government" or by some other specially designated representative. This would seem to be an unnecessary provision, since it can be assumed that each member is free to choose its own representative in any way it deems fit. The provision was apparently inserted to make clear, and emphasize, the possibility of meetings at which members may be represented by their foreign ministers or persons of comparable importance in order to bring such meetings within the framework of the United Nations Organization. One of the great advantages of the League system was that through provision for periodic sessions of the Council and Assembly the opportunity was afforded for foreign ministers to get together to discuss matters of common concern. The Charter seeks to retain the gains of the League system.

In the light of the provision of Article 23, paragraph 3, it is to be assumed that at the "periodic meetings" at which members are represented by "a member of the government or by some other specially designated representative," the "permanent representative" will for the time being cease to represent his government, and will presumably act in the capacity of adviser or alternate.

3. The Security Council may hold meetings at such places other than the seat of the Organization as in its judgment will best facilitate its work.

This paragraph needs no special comment. It is quite in accordance with the practice of international organizations and with the practical necessities. This was the practice of the Council of the League of Nations.

ARTICLE 29

The Security Council may establish such subsidiary organs as it deems necessary for the performance of its functions.

See provisions of Article 7, paragraph 2, and Article 22, and comment thereon.

ARTICLE 30

The Security Council shall adopt its own rules of procedure, including the method of selecting its President.

This Article follows customary international practice. It is quite clear that the Council must be able to make its own rules of procedure. The Council of the League of Nations did so in the absence of any special provision in the Covenant.

It is not stated that the President shall be elected by the Council for a special period. The first paragraph of the fourth article of the Rules of Procedure of the League Council provided that the presidency should rotate among the members according to their alphabetical order in the French language. The period of service of a President extended from the beginning of one ordinary session to the beginning of the next ordinary session.

ARTICLE 31

Any Member of the United Nations which is not a member of the Security Council may participate, without vote, in the discussion of any question brought before the Security Council whenever the latter considers that the interests of that Member are specially affected.

A comparison with Article 32 indicates that a distinction is made between the situation where a state has interests which are "specially affected" and one where a state is party to a dispute. Only in the second situation may a non-member state be invited to participate in the discussions of the Security Council.

The second point to be noted is that it is the Security Council, and not the Member itself, which decides whether the interests are "specially affected."

Article 4 of the Covenant of the League not only placed upon the Council the obligation to invite a Member not represented on the Council to send a representative during the consideration of matters specially affecting that Member, but also gave that Member a vote. Under the Charter, it is expressly stated that such participation is to be without the privilege of voting.

An invitation to a Member State under this Article is clearly a procedural matter to be decided according to the second paragraph of Article 27.

ARTICLE 32

Any Member of the United Nations which is not a member of the Security Council or any state which is not a Member of the United Nations, if it is a party to a dispute under consideration by the Security Council, shall be invited to participate, without vote, in the discussion relating to the dispute. The Security Council shall lay down such conditions as it deems just for the participation of a state which is not a Member of the United Nations.

This Article deals with the situation where the Security Council is dealing with a dispute brought before it under the terms of the Charter where one or more of the parties are not members of the Security Council and not necessarily Members of the United Nations.

In that situation, the Covenant of the League provided that any Member of the League not represented on the Council should be invited to send a representative to sit on the Council while the dispute was under consideration with the privilege of voting. In the case of non-member states, the provisions of Article 17 applied under which the non-member state was to be invited to accept the obligations of membership in the League for the purposes of the dispute "under such conditions as the Council may deem just." If the invitation was accepted, the provisions of Articles 12 to 16 of the Covenant were to be applied with such modifications as might be deemed necessary by the Council.

Under the Charter, the same general principle is laid down to cover the two situations, namely, that the Security Council shall invite the state to participate "without vote" in the discussion relating to the dispute. In the case of a state not a Member of the Organization the Security Council is to lay down such additional conditions as it may deem just for the participation of the state. The Charter provisions would thus appear to permit greater flexibility of treatment. The provision, common to Articles 31 and 32, by which participation is to be "without vote" would appear to be based on the view that the state invited to participate does not become for the purpose in question a member of the Security Council, but rather is invited to participate in order that its position may be fully expressed and defended.

Distinction between "Dispute" and "Question." It is to be noted that under the provisions of Articles 31 and 32 a distinction is made between a "dispute" and a "question." It is only in the case of a dispute to which it is a party that a state which is not a Member has a right to be invited to participate in the discussion relating thereto. This is consistent with the provision of Article 35, paragraph 2, which permits a non-member state to bring only disputes to which it is a party before the Security Council or the General Assembly.

The definition of the word "dispute" therefore becomes a matter of considerable importance. A dispute can properly be considered as a disagreement between two or more states which has reached a stage where the parties have formulated claims and counter-claims sufficiently definite to be passed upon by a court or other body set up for the purposes of pacific settlement. A "question," by contrast, is a matter which is before the Council for consideration which has not as yet assumed such a contentious character, or perhaps is not capable of developing to that extent. It might be a situation of the kind referred to in Articles 34, 35 and 36.[1] Or it might be any other matter before the Security Council for consideration under the terms of the Charter, such as the taking of enforcement action under Article 39 or the exercise of the Organization's functions in a strategic area, under the terms of Article 83. The term is intended to be general in scope.

Obviously, the decision will not in certain imaginable circumstances be an easy one to make. It is the function, however, of the Security Council to make the decision. Once, however, the Security Council has decided that a state not a member of the Council is a party to a dispute before it, it is obligated to invite the state to participate in the discussion relating to the dispute.

[1] On distinction between "dispute" and "situation," see comment on Article 34, this volume, p. 145.

CHAPTER VI

PACIFIC SETTLEMENT OF DISPUTES

ARTICLE 33

1. The parties to any dispute, the continuance of which is likely to endanger the maintenance of international peace and security, shall, first of all, seek a solution by negotiation, enquiry, mediation, conciliation, arbitration, judicial settlement, resort to regional agencies or arrangements, or other peaceful means of their own choice.

Scope of Obligation. This paragraph is an application of the principle laid down in Article 1, paragraph 1, and Article 2, paragraph 3. It imposes a duty upon the Members to seek in the first instance the pacific settlement of their disputes by means of their own choice. The Organization does not intervene, as a general principle, until it is clear that the Members cannot manage by themselves, cannot settle their dispute or disputes in such a way as to avoid endangering international peace and security. It should be emphasized, however, that, unlike Article I of the Paris Treaty for the Renunciation of War as an Instrument of National Policy (the Kellogg-Briand Peace Pact [1]) by which the parties agreed that the settlement of their disputes should "never be sought except by pacific means," this paragraph of Article 33 and Article 2, paragraph 3, positively obligate Members of the United Nations to "seek a solution" of their serious disputes by pacific means.

This paragraph does not, as it is phrased, apply to all disputes between Member States. It applies only to disputes "the continuance of which is likely to endanger the maintenance of international peace and security." This is the phraseology of the Dumbarton Oaks Proposals and was accepted at San Francisco by the technical committee and Conference without change. In the opinion of some, the obligation of the paragraph would have been brought more fully into line with the principle stated in Article 2, paragraph 3, if the paragraph had been rephrased to read somewhat as follows:

"The parties to any dispute shall, first of all, seek a solution by negotiation, enquiry, mediation, conciliation, arbitration, judicial settlement, resort to regional agencies or arrangements, or other peaceful means of their own choice, in such a manner that the maintenance of international peace and security will not be endangered."

[1] United States, *Treaties, Conventions,* etc., IV, 1923–1937, p. 5130.

This would have established, in the opinion of some, a clear and definite obligation so far as Member States were concerned, and would have made clearer the exact stage in the development of a given situation when the Security Council was to intervene. The paragraph as it stands places upon each Member an initial obligation to do something in a contingency the existence of which only an international agency can properly determine.

In defense of the present phraseology it can be stated that it is consistent with the basic purpose of the Organization to maintain peace and security. The intention is not to require Members to settle all their disputes by peaceful means. The possibility is admitted that certain disputes may continue unsettled until they are forgotten. It is only serious disputes "the continuance of which is likely to endanger the maintenance of international peace and security" with which the Organization is concerned. By Article 12 of the Covenant, Members of the League agreed "that, if there should arise between them any dispute likely to lead to a rupture, they will submit the matter either to arbitration or judicial settlement or to inquiry by the Council."

It may of course be difficult to decide whether a dispute is of such a nature that its continuance is likely to endanger the maintenance of international peace and security. The parties presumably have obligated themselves not to resort to force or the threat of force; if they show a readiness to respect this obligation, logically it is difficult to see how any dispute between them could endanger peace and security. However, it must be admitted that disputes can become so persistent and so bitter that they poison international relations and create a political climate that may tempt a peace-loving state to use means of force because the situation becomes unbearable, or that may permit states acting in good faith to become involved in a series of events which lead to the use of force without either party's initially desiring it. It is quite clear that a dispute of this kind ought to be dealt with by an international agency.

It should also be clear that a dispute between a very small and a very powerful state cannot be brushed aside as unimportant or lacking in danger from the point of view of its consequences to the peace. It is not sufficient to say that the small state would never endanger peace and security by attacking its powerful adversary. If the very strong power, to take a purely theoretical example, should seek to help itself and intimidate the small state, there would still be present a danger to the peace of the world. The expression "likely to endanger international peace and security" must be understood in relation to the principles of "justice" and "international law," recognized in the first paragraph of Article 1.

Action by the Security Council. The next question which arises is who will decide whether the continuance of a dispute is likely to endanger peace and security. It would seem that the opinion of one of the parties ought to suffice. If, however, the other party does not agree with this and does not want to have the dispute settled by one of the specified means, the Security Council can itself decide that a conflict has this character and take appropriate action. During the discussion of this paragraph in the technical committee of the Conference, the question was raised as to whether the use of the words "first of all" would be an obstacle to intervention by the Security Council at any time before recourse to the means enumerated in this paragraph were exhausted. The United States Delegate answered categorically that the sole purpose of the words in question was to assure that the parties would first make an endeavor to settle their disputes by peaceful means and that the Security Council should and must intervene in any dispute which threatened world peace.[1]

Means of Peaceful Settlement. The paragraph lists certain generally accepted means of peaceful settlement open to the parties. It is clear that the list is not meant to be exhaustive. With one exception, they fall into two groups:

(1) *Those means which do not make use of the element of compulsion, being based upon the principle of voluntary acceptance.* The enumerated means falling into this category are negotiation, enquiry, mediation and conciliation.

a. Negotiation is the first and most commonly used means for the pacific settlement of international disputes. This term covers all kinds of diplomatic discussions, exchanges of notes, etc. By this means the parties seek a solution by direct exchanges between themselves. Diplomatic annals are full of instances where such settlements have been successfully reached.

b. Enquiry is, strictly speaking, not a means of settlement at all. It is an effort to find a basis for a settlement. It sometimes happens that a disagreement between the parties can be eliminated if it is only possible to establish the facts. The use of this means was provided for by the Hague Conventions for the Pacific Settlement of International Disputes of 1899 and 1907. The value of an international commission of enquiry was shown in the conflict between Great Britain and Russia over the Dogger Bank incident during the Russo-Japanese war. Such commissions are provided for in a number of treaties.

c. Mediation is the action of an outside agency, state or person with a view to getting the parties together and helping them in a more or less informal way to find the basis for the settlement of their dispute. This means of peaceful settlement was also provided for in the Hague Conventions of 1899 and 1907. It has been utilized on important occa-

[1] UNCIO, *Summary Report of the Fifth Meeting of Committee III/2, May 15, 1945,* Doc. 356, III/2/11, p. 1–2.

sions, notably by President Theodore Roosevelt in bringing the Russo-Japanese War of 1904–5 to an end.

d. Conciliation is a means of pacific settlement effected through commissions or other international bodies, usually consisting of persons designated by agreement between the parties to the conflict. The efforts of the commission are directed towards finding a reasonable solution of the conflict that the parties can agree to. Among the treaties providing for the use of the means of conciliation were the Locarno Treaties of 1925 [1] and the General Convention of Inter-American Conciliation signed at Washington, January 5, 1929.[2]

(2) *Those means which make use of the element of compulsion so far as the proposed settlement is concerned.* Arbitration and judicial settlement fall into this category.

a. Arbitration is a method of pacific settlement by which the parties obligate themselves in advance to carry out the decision given by the arbitrator or arbitral tribunal. The rules to be applied are determined by the *compromis* or agreement by which the dispute is submitted to arbitration. The parties may stipulate that the decision be based on international law or they may agree that considerations of equity and justice be taken into account. The tribunal to which the dispute is submitted may be specially created under the terms of the agreement or it may be a tribunal already in existence. In any case the procedure of arbitration is essentially of an *ad hoc* character.

b. Judicial settlement means settlement by a permanent international tribunal such as the International Court of Justice, in accordance with judicial methods. It was a settled usage in the period between the World Wars to reserve this expression for settlement by reference to the Permanent Court of International Justice. It seems, therefore, only logical to interpret the expression as used in the Charter as referring to settlement by reference to the International Court of Justice. Such was also the intention of the Committee which drafted this Chapter. However, the Charter usage is not quite clear since Article 92 envisages the possibility of other "judicial" organs.

The Article also makes reference to "resort to regional agencies or arrangements" as a means of peaceful settlement. This expression must be understood in connection with the provisions of Article 52. It was inserted in this paragraph at the request of Committee III/4,[3] dealing with regional arrangements, and was part of a compromise worked out at the Conference with a view to integrating regional and global arrange-

---

[1] See *The Locarno Conference, October 5–16, 1925*, Boston, World Peace Foundation Publications IX, No. 1, 1926.

[2] United States, *Treaties, Conventions*, etc., IV, 1923–1937, p. 4763.

[3] UNCIO, *Report of Dr. V. K. Wellington Koo, Rapporteur of Committee III/4, to Commission III*, Doc. 904, III/4/13(1), p. 1–2.

ments. It does not add anything to the material content of the paragraph. All the other peaceful means enumerated in the paragraph can at the same time be provided for under regional arrangements or included in regional agencies.

Any attempt at the exhaustive enumeration of peaceful means of settlement in a paragraph of this kind may have serious consequences. It might lead to a restrictive interpretation. This is excluded in the present paragraph by the addition of the words "or other peaceful means of their own choice." It is, thereby, made quite clear that the parties are to have recourse to any conceivable peaceful means which may lead to the settlement of a dispute.

The words "of their own choice" refer not only to the choice of the parties at the moment of the settlement of the conflict, but also to a choice possibly made by the parties before the dispute has arisen. The words are really intended to express the thought that the dispute shall be settled by any peaceful means which the parties choose or may have agreed to use.

2. The Security Council shall, when it deems necessary, call upon the parties to settle their dispute by such means.

This paragraph possibly should have come after Article 34 and not before it. It cannot properly be understood without a reference to Article 34. The justification of the present arrangement is that the contingency in which the Council is to act is the failure of parties to a dispute to fulfill their obligations under paragraph 1.

It is to be noted by way of explanation of the apparent illogicality of the present arrangement that what is now Article 33 was paragraph 3 of Chapter VIII, Section A, of the Dumbarton Oaks Proposals, and then followed what have become Articles 34 and 35. This change of order was made on the ground that the general obligation laid down in the first sentence of paragraph 3 of Chapter VIII, Section A, of the Dumbarton Oaks text would most appropriately come at the beginning of the Chapter. The second sentence of the paragraph, which might better have been left in its original position, according to one principle of arrangement, was brought up with the first, and becomes paragraph 2 of Article 33.

The paragraph states that the Council shall "when it deems necessary" call upon the parties to settle their disputes by peaceful means of their own choice. It is clear that this duty of the Council only applies when the dispute is "likely to endanger" peace and security. If the dispute has no such character, the Council shall remain passive. It is also clear that ordinarily the Council will make such a decision after having investigated the dispute under Article 34. However, it may happen that the dispute is so obviously dangerous that the Security

Council can decide at once that its continuance endangers the peace of the world without entering into any formal investigation.

The expression "shall, when it deems necessary, call upon the parties," was carefully discussed. Some delegates favored the use of the word "may" so as to make it quite clear that this action was left entirely to the discretion of the Council and that the obligation of the parties under paragraph 1 was in no way dependent upon any action that the Security Council might take. Others wanted the word "shall" used without qualification so as to make it quite clear that a duty was incumbent on the Council. The present wording was a compromise between these two extremes. The right interpretation is that it is left to the discretion of the Council to decide when the situation is of such a character that it is necessary to call upon the parties. When the Council has decided that such a necessity exists, it is, however, the absolute duty of the Council to call upon the parties.

The Security Council is to "call upon" the parties to settle their disputes by "such means." The exact meaning to be attached to the words "call upon" is a matter of some doubt since the words are not commonly used in the Charter.[1] Obviously they have a stronger connotation than the word "recommend," and it would also appear that they are not as strong as the words "decide what measures shall be taken" used in Article 39. Apparently the intention is that the Security Council shall remind the parties of their obligations under the first paragraph in no uncertain terms. Does the use of the words "by such means" signify that the reminder is to be couched in the phraseology of the first paragraph, or may it be more specific, calling attention to specific means which the parties have agreed to use by agreement between them? The power of the Security Council would certainly appear to be broad enough to permit the second course.

ARTICLE 34

The Security Council may investigate any dispute, or any situation which might lead to international friction or give rise to a dispute, in order to determine whether the continuance of the dispute or situation is likely to endanger the maintenance of international peace and security.

It is to be particularly noted that the power of the Security Council to investigate under this Article applies to "any dispute," and to "any situation which might lead to international friction or give rise to a dispute." The broad phraseology used is reminiscent of Article 11 of the Covenant which, in paragraph 2, declared it to be "the friendly

---

[1] The expression is used in Articles 40, 41 and 44 in connection with enforcement action. See comment on its use in Article 41, this volume, p. 160.

right of each Member of the League to bring to the attention of the Assembly or of the Council any circumstance whatever affecting international relations which threaten to disturb international peace or the good understanding between nations upon which peace depends." Certainly this Article of the Charter gives the Security Council ample authority to concern itself with any dispute or situation well in advance of the time that it threatens the peace of the world with a view to determining whether its continuance "is likely to endanger the maintenance of international peace and security." This may be considered as one of the key provisions of the Charter since it permits the Council to make the inquiries and factual determinations necessary to the exercise of its preventive functions.

The power of the Security Council to investigate is limited by the final clause of the Article. It is not a general power of investigation that is conferred, but only the power to investigate in order to determine the answer to a particular question. Consequently, it would not appear that the Security Council would be justified at this stage in undertaking a thorough investigation such as would be necessary preliminary to the making of recommendations for the settlement of the dispute or the adjustment of the situation. It is nevertheless clear that, according to the interpretation of the Sponsoring Governments and France, the provisions of Chapter 27, paragraph 3, as to voting procedure are applicable.

The Security Council may undertake the investigation of a dispute or situation on its own initiative, following a formal request made in accordance with Article 35, or following action by the Secretary-General under the terms of Article 99.

The distinction between a "dispute" and a "situation" is made in several Articles of the Chapter. The latter appears to refer to a condition of affairs that arises in the relations between states at an earlier stage than the actual formulation of demands. If we accept the definition of "dispute" given in the comment on Article 32, then a "situation" of the kind here referred to might be said to exist when there is obviously a lack of complete harmony in the relations between states concerned and when the conduct of the parties reflects conflicting objectives and interests, but when as yet there has been no definite formulation of demands and definition of positions such as would be necessary to the existence of a dispute. Such a "situation" might very well lead to a "dispute," but not necessarily. It might develop directly into a serious threat to the peace without any such formulation of the respective claims of the parties as is necessary to the existence of a dispute in the technical sense. It is therefore desirable for the Security Council to deal with such situations, both to prevent serious disputes from arising and also to head off serious threats to or actual violations of the peace.

ARTICLE 35

1. Any Member of the United Nations may bring any dispute or any situation of the nature referred to in Article 34 to the attention of the Security Council or of the General Assembly.

The first paragraph of Article 35 applies only to Members of the United Nations. They may bring any dispute or any situation of the nature referred to in Article 34 to the attention of the Council or the Assembly. The distinction between "dispute" and " situation " has been explained. A Member has the right to bring any such dispute or situation to the attention of the Assembly or the Council, whether or not it is a party to the dispute or directly interested in the situation.

Under this paragraph Members of the United Nations have the same right as was enjoyed by Members of the League under the second paragraph of Article 11 of the Covenant.

It is to be noted that this paragraph uses the words "bring . . . to the attention of," as did Article 11 of the Covenant. In the discussion of this paragraph in Committee III/2 of the Conference, the question was raised as to whether this action would have the effect of formally bringing the matter before the body in question. It was proposed that the word "before" be substituted for the words "to the attention of." It was the sense of the subcommittee to which the proposal was referred, however, that this was a change of a purely formal nature, and that this would not modify the meaning of the paragraph. It was decided to retain the original phraseology.

2. A state which is not a Member of the United Nations may bring to the attention of the Security Council or of the General Assembly any dispute to which it is a party if it accepts in advance, for the purposes of the dispute, the obligations of pacific settlement provided in the present Charter.

The Dumbarton Oaks Proposals in Chapter VIII, Section A, paragraph 2, provided that "any state, whether member of the Organization or not, may bring any such dispute or situation (referring to the Dumbarton Oaks counterpart of Article 34) to the attention of the General Assembly or of the Security Council." In so far as the rights of Members were concerned, this proposal was adopted without question by UNCIO (see paragraph 1 of Article 35). Strong objection was raised, however, to placing Members and non-members on an equal basis in this respect. It was pointed out that this would permit any state which had been an enemy of any of the United Nations in World War II to have recourse to the Security Council or the General Assembly for the purpose of securing redress for an alleged wrong having its origin in the war or the peace settlement. It was also pointed out that it would permit a non-member interested in discrediting the Organization to bring disputes and situations before the Security Council and the General Assembly with that sole object in view.

The whole matter was considered very carefully by the drafting subcommittee of Committee III/2 and the present text incorporates in substance the recommendation of the subcommittee.[1] Three separate cases were envisaged: (1) where a non-member is party to the dispute; (2) where a non-member has interests which are directly affected by a situation which might lead to international friction or give rise to a dispute; and (3) where a non-member neither is a party to the dispute nor has interests directly affected by the situation. It was decided that only in the first case should a non-member be accorded the right, given generally under paragraph 1 to Members, and then only on condition that the state accept "in advance, for the purposes of the dispute, the obligations of pacific settlement provided in the present Charter." These include, notably, the obligation set forth in Article 2, paragraph 3.

The provisions of this paragraph would appear clearly to apply to all states not Members of the United Nations, including so-called "enemy states." While the whole matter was in process of discussion in Committee III/2 and before a final decision on the recommendation to be made to the Commission had been taken, the Greek Delegate proposed an amendment to Chapter VIII, Section A, paragraph 2, reading as follows:

It is understood that the enemy states in this war shall not have the right of recourse to the Security Council or the General Assembly before the treaties which end this war have been made effective.

This proposal was referred to Committee III/3 with the statement that Committee III/2 approved the proposal in principle.[2] The proposal was considered by Committee III/3 and the Committee decided against adopting the proposal as an amendment to Chapter XII of the Dumbarton Oaks Proposals,[3] but it was agreed to incorporate in the report of the Rapporteur the following statement:[4]

It is understood that the enemy states in this war shall not have the right of recourse to the Security Council or the General Assembly until the Security Council gives them this right.

To bring a dispute to the attention of the Security Council or the General Assembly would appear to be one form of having recourse to these

[1] Ibid., Report of the Rapporteur of Committee III/2, Doc. 1027, III/2/31(1), p. 3.
[2] Ibid., Summary Report of Fourth Meeting of Committee III/2, May 14, 1945, Doc. 321, III/2/9, p. 3.
[3] Ibid., Summary Report of Twenty-first Meeting of Committee III/3, June 19, 1945, Doc. 1111, III/3/51, p. 2.
[4] Ibid., Report of Committee III to Commission III on Chapter XII, Doc. 1095, III/3/50, p. 3–4.

bodies. It is highly doubtful, to put it mildly, if the provision of a statement incorporated in the report of a Committee Rapporteur, after refusal of the Committee to adopt the substance of the statement as a formal provision of the Charter, can be regarded as limiting in any way the explicit provisions of the Charter contained in this paragraph.

3. The proceedings of the General Assembly in respect of matters brought to its attention under this Article will be subject to the provisions of Articles 11 and 12.

See Articles 11 and 12 and comment. The principal point of course is that the division of function between Security Council and General Assembly there established is to be respected.

ARTICLE 36

1. The Security Council may, at any stage of a dispute of the nature referred to in Article 33 or of a situation of like nature, recommend appropriate procedures or methods of adjustment.

This paragraph deals with both situations and disputes, but only with those "the continuance of which is likely to endanger the maintenance of international peace and security." That is, it does not authorize the Security Council to take action with respect to all disputes and situations, but only those which present a certain degree of danger or seriousness.

If a dispute or a situation presents this serious character, the Security Council can intervene whether or not the parties to the dispute or the states involved in the situation are Members. The Council can in such cases recommend appropriate methods or procedures of adjustment. It cannot recommend any particular terms of settlement. It can only recommend to the interested parties the means by which in its judgment they can best adjust their conflict.

The Council may make recommendations "at any stage" of such a dispute or situation. This seems to give very wide power to the Council and conceivably will result in Council intervention while the parties are proceeding with their own efforts at settlement. However, the second paragraph of this Article makes it quite clear that the Council should ordinarily be guided in its action by what the parties have already agreed to or are in process of carrying out. It is clear that the Council will consider itself in a freer position in cases where the parties have not agreed to any procedure in advance.

Under this paragraph, the Council does not make a decision binding on the interested parties. It only recommends terms of settlement. The recommendations are not legally binding on the parties, although they may have the greatest political and moral weight.

2. The Security Council should take into consideration any procedures for the settlement of the dispute which have already been adopted by the parties.

This paragraph covers two different cases. If the parties have already started to settle their dispute in a certain way, the Council should give great weight to this circumstance in making its recommendation. If the parties can settle the matter among themselves, so much the better. If the International Court of Justice, an arbitral tribunal, a commission of conciliation, or any other body is already working on the case, this body should be allowed to complete its duties if consistent with the maintenance of peace and security.

The other case covered by this paragraph is that where treaties for pacific settlement have been concluded between the parties prior to the actual dispute. They may for instance have accepted the "optional clause" of the International Court of Justice [1] or they may be parties to agreements for obligatory arbitration. Such commitments the Council should take into consideration in making its recommendations.

It should be noted that the wording of the Article is such as to make its provisions hortatory instead of mandatory. It states that the Council "should take into consideration" the procedures adopted by the parties, but it does not say that the Council must be guided in its action by this consideration. It may well be that the Council, after having considered these procedures very carefully, will decide that other methods are more appropriate under the circumstances. The possibility of doing so is left open. The Council is allowed a certain discretion. Here, as elsewhere, a definite effort has been made to keep the provisions of the Charter flexible rather than rigid.

3. In making recommendations under this Article the Security Council should also take into consideration that legal disputes should as a general rule be referred by the parties to the International Court of Justice in accordance with the provisions of the Statute of the Court.

This paragraph refers to so-called "legal disputes." According to generally adopted terminology there are two chief classes of international disputes. In one group of conflicts the parties are in dispute over conflicting claims of legal right. The answer to such questions is sought in the established rules of international law, as described in Article 38 of the Statute of the International Court of Justice. This kind of conflict is called a legal dispute. For a more detailed definition of a legal dispute, see Article 36 of the Statute of the International Court of Justice. [2]

In the other class of disputes, sometimes referred to as "political," the disagreement relates not to the application of the rules of inter-

[1] See Article 36 of the *Statute*, this volume, p. 372.
[2] *Ibid.*

national law, but rather to the adequacy of the existing legal order. In other words, the disagreement arises from dissatisfaction with the applicability of the rules of law. The answer to the questions posed by the parties will not be looked for in international law, but in "justice" and "expediency."

The third paragraph of Article 36 says that in the case of legal disputes, the Security Council, in making recommendations of procedures to be followed, should, as a general rule, recommend to the parties that they submit their disputes to the International Court of Justice. The paragraph is not mandatory since it is implicitly recognized that circumstances may exist which will make this course inadvisable.

This paragraph is to be understood in relation to the discussion at San Francisco on obligatory jurisdiction of the International Court of Justice.[1] Chapter VIII, Section A, paragraph 6 of the Dumbarton Oaks Proposals provided that "justiciable disputes should normally be referred to the international court of justice." Numerous proposals were made at San Francisco to the effect that this reference should be made obligatory, thus achieving the result of obligatory jurisdiction for the Court over justiciable disputes. On the other hand, it was pointed out that the sentence was open to the interpretation that it envisaged the reference of disputes to the Court by the Security Council, a procedure without precedent since disputes in the past have been brought before international tribunals by the parties themselves. In the course of consideration by Committee II/3 it was decided to revise the provision so as to make it clear that the Security Council action envisaged was a recommendation to the parties, and to harmonize this revised text with the recommendation of Committee IV/1 on the question of the Court's obligatory jurisdiction. Furthermore, it was decided that the word "legal" described more accurately the category of disputes which was in question than the word "justiciable."

The present paragraph states that legal disputes should be referred to the Court "in accordance with the provisions of the Statute of the Court." It should be remembered that the Statute of the Court does not institute obligatory jurisdiction. Any Member of the United Nations may accept obligatory jurisdiction under defined conditions by a declaration made under the terms of Article 36 of the Statute. Obligatory jurisdiction may also be accepted under the terms of treaties and conventions referred to in Article 36, paragraph 1, and Article 37 of the Statute of the Court. This paragraph does not seek to introduce obligatory jurisdiction by the back door. The meaning of this provision must, therefore, be that the Council shall impress upon the parties their duty to submit their legal disputes to the Court if they have accepted the obligatory jurisdiction of the Court. In other cases the Council can only recommend

[1] See p. 259.

to the parties to go to the Court. It is always the parties and none other than the parties who can refer a case to the Court. This paragraph is really a special application of the principle laid down in the previous paragraph.

ARTICLE 37

1. Should the parties to a dispute of the nature referred to in Article 33 fail to settle it by the means indicated in that Article, they shall refer it to the Security Council.

This paragraph lays a definite duty on the parties to a dispute. The obligation refers only to disputes, not to situations. The obligation is further restricted to disputes "the continuance of which is likely to endanger the maintenance of international peace and security." When this provision was under consideration in the technical committee at San Francisco, the question was raised as to whether this provision was to be interpreted to mean that in case of failure of one party to agree to the reference of the dispute to the Council, the other party could so refer it and thus fully seise the Council of the dispute. The interpretation given which appeared to be accepted by the Committee was that this was the meaning intended.[1]

2. If the Security Council deems that the continuance of the dispute is in fact likely to endanger the maintenance of international peace and security, it shall decide whether to take action under Article 36 or to recommend such terms of settlement as it may consider appropriate.

This paragraph corresponds to the second sentence of paragraph 4 of Chapter VIII, Section A, of the Dumbarton Oaks Proposals. In its original form, no distinction was made between the action which the Security Council might take in the situation where it intervened on its own initiative and found that a continuance of the dispute was likely to threaten the maintenance of international peace and security, and that which it might take when the dispute came before it on reference by one or more parties following failure to settle it by means of their own choice. One of the amendments proposed by the Sponsoring Governments had as its purpose to enable the Security Council to recommend terms of settlement in the latter case.[2] This amendment was accepted by the technical committee and without modification of substance came finally to be expressed in the present form.

The difference between the two situations described above which would seem to justify giving the Security Council different authority in the two cases is that in the first situation, arising under Article 36,

[1] *UNCIO, Summary Report of Seventh Meeting of Committee III/2, May 17, 1945,* Doc. 433, III/2/15, p. 1.
[2] *Ibid., Amendments Proposed by the Governments of the United States, the United Kingdom, the Soviet Union and China.* Doc. 2, G/29, May 5, 1945, p. 4.

there has been no admission by one or more of the parties of failure to settle the dispute in accordance with the terms of Article 33. In this situation, the Council is restricted to assisting the parties in finding procedures or methods which will be successful. In the second situation, however, described in the first paragraph of Article 37, there has been failure of the parties to settle their dispute by means of their own choice, attested by the fact that one party has in effect asked the Council to take a hand. There would therefore be less point in the Council's seeking to aid the parties to find a means or procedure acceptable to them, though that course is open. In such a situation the Council should be able, it was felt, to actually recommend the terms of settlement.

It is clear that the Security Council has only the power to recommend the terms of settlement. There was considerable discussion at San Francisco of the exact implications of this grant of power. The fear was expressed that, particularly in view of the rather broadly phrased provisions of paragraphs 1 and 2 of Chapter VIII, Section B, of the Dumbarton Oaks Proposals, the Security Council might consider itself empowered to impose its recommendations upon the parties as means necessary to the maintenance of international peace and security. The interpretation given and accepted at UNCIO was that the recommendations made under this paragraph have no binding effect and can be given no binding effect by the Council under other provisions of the Charter.[1] This interpretation is given additional support by the phraseology of Articles 39 and 40 of the Charter.

ARTICLE 38

Without prejudice to the provisions of Articles 33 to 37, the Security Council may, if all the parties to any dispute so request, make recommendations to the parties with a view to a pacific settlement of the dispute.

This Article did not exist in the Dumbarton Oaks Proposals but was introduced at UNCIO at the suggestion of the Sponsoring Governments. The idea is to give the power to the Council to deal with disputes even before they have assumed such a serious character as to endanger the maintenance of peace and security, if the parties to the dispute so agree. The Article applies to all disputes irrespective of their character and the parties to them. It is assumed of course that they are international disputes. The only condition is that the parties shall have agreed to ask the Council to consider the dispute or disputes in question and to make recommendations with a view to their peaceful settlement.

[1] *Ibid., Summary Report of Ninth Meeting of Committee III/2, May 21, 1945,* Doc. 498, III/2/19, p. 2; *Report of the Rapporteur of Committee III/2,* Doc. 1027, III/2/31(1), p. 4.

The Article uses the word "recommendation" which means of course that the terms of settlement proposed will not be binding on the parties. This raises the question whether the Council is thereby barred from assuming the powers of an arbitral tribunal if the parties should so agree. It would not seem that any provision in the Charter could be intended to prohibit such action with a view to peaceful settlement.[1]

[1] The Council of the League of Nations exercised such a power when conferred on it by the terms of the Treaty of Lausanne. See Myers, D. P., *Handbook of the League of Nations*, Boston, World Peace Foundation, 1935, p. 317.

CHAPTER VII

ACTION WITH RESPECT TO THREATS TO THE PEACE, BREACHES OF THE PEACE, AND ACTS OF AGGRESSION

ARTICLE 39

The Security Council shall determine the existence of any threat to the peace, breach of the peace, or act of aggression and shall make recommendations, or decide what measures shall be taken in accordance with Articles 41 and 42, to maintain or restore international peace and security.

Comparison with Covenant Provisions. This Article represents a quite different approach to the problem of peace enforcement from that adopted in the Covenant of the League of Nations. Under the Covenant an attempt was made to define the contingency in which enforcement action was to take place and to specify the specific measures to be taken by Members of the League in case the contingency arose. It was provided in Article 10 that the Members should "respect . . . the territorial integrity and existing political independence of all Members of the League" and in Article 12 that they should in no case "resort to war" under certain specified conditions. In Article 16 provision was made for the immediate application by Members of certain specified economic and financial sanctions, should any Member "resort to war in disregard of its covenants under Articles 12, 13 or 15." The Council was empowered to make recommendations with regard to military, naval or air forces to be used to protect the covenants of the League. It must, however, be added that the provisions of Article 16 were not applied in practice in the specified manner. The League Assembly on October 4, 1921 adopted a series of rules recommended to it by its International Blockade Committee,[1] by which the principle of the progressive application of sanctions was substituted for that of the immediate application of the economic and financial measures specified in Article 16. This general principle was followed in the application of sanctions against Italy in 1935–1936.[2]

[1] League of Nations, *Resolutions and Recommendations Adopted by the Assembly During Its Second Session, Sept. 5–Oct. 5, 1921, Official Journal, Special Supplement,* no. 6, p. 24.

[2] On operation of League sanctions, see Highley, A. E., *The First Sanctions Experiment,* Geneva Research Centre, Geneva Studies, IX, No. 4 (July 1938); and Royal Institute of International Affairs, *International Sanctions,* N. Y., Oxford Univ. Press, 1938.

The Charter system proceeds in a different manner. In the first place the Security Council determines "the existence of any threat to the peace, breach of the peace, or act of aggression." It is left to the unrestricted judgment of the Security Council, subject to the principles set forth in Article 2, to decide what specific action constitutes any one of these specified acts. Furthermore the Security Council decides what measures shall be taken once a threat to the peace, breach of the peace or act of aggression has been found to exist. Its power in this respect is subject to the provisions of Articles 41 and 42. There is no attempt made in the Charter to provide for "automatic sanctions." Members of the United Nations are under no obligation to apply diplomatic, economic, financial or military sanctions against the state which has violated the peace or threatened to do so until the Security Council has determined the measures that are to be taken.

Responsibility of Security Council. Under the provisions of this Article the responsibility is placed exclusively upon the Security Council. At San Francisco proposals were advanced that the General Assembly should be associated with the Security Council in the performance of the functions specified in this Article. These proposals were supported by the argument that since the decisions taken would affect the interests of and involve commitments by all Members of the Organization, there should be opportunity for these Members through their representatives in the General Assembly to exercise some control over the decisions taken. The arguments advanced against associating the General Assembly with the Security Council were principally that the effective performance of the functions in question required vesting them in a small body and that in any case the Members of the Organization would be represented, since the Security Council would consist not only of permanent members but also of members elected by the General Assembly. Furthermore it was pointed out that to associate the General Assembly with the Security Council would result in a breakdown of the differentiation of functions of the two bodies, which had been made in the Dumbarton Oaks Proposals, and which had met with general approval. The arguments against associating the General Assembly with the Security Council proved to be conclusive and the Conference decided to accept in substance the recommendations of the Sponsoring Governments on this point.[1]

Proposal to Limit Council's Authority. There was also considerable opposition at San Francisco to giving the Security Council such broad discretionary authority, uncontrolled by precisely defined principles or standards. It was pointed out that the Security Council in the performance of its functions must be guided by the basic purposes and

---

[1] UNCIO, *Report of Mr. Paul-Boncour, Rapporteur, on Chapter VIII, Section B,* Doc. 881, III/3/46, p. 2.

principles of the Organization as set forth in Articles 1 and 2. This, however, was not regarded as satisfactory by some of the delegations and the proposal was made, which received considerable support, that a definition of aggression should be incorporated in the Charter.

The problem of defining aggression is an old one. The attempt made in the Covenant of the League of Nations has generally been regarded as inadequate. Other attempts were made in the Geneva Protocol of 1924 and in the Locarno Treaty of Guarantee of 1925. Treaties entered into by the Soviet Union with its neighbors before the war contained a more detailed definition of aggression.[1] At the time the Kellogg-Briand Pact of 1928 was under discussion the Government of the United States took the position that the definition of aggression was impracticable since it would be impossible to cover every possible case of aggression, and furthermore, the effect would be to make it possible for a would-be aggressor nation to use the definition for its own purposes. That in substance was the position taken at San Francisco. The proposals of the Bolivian and Philippine Delegations were defeated in the technical committee. The majority of the committee was apparently convinced by the arguments that the progress and technique of modern warfare made such a definition difficult. It was also felt that, such a list of cases being necessarily incomplete, the Council would have a tendency to consider the cases listed as being more important than the others, and that omissions would encourage the aggressor to use the definition to further its own purposes.[2]

"Recommendations" of the Security Council. The Article provides that the Security Council "shall make recommendations, or decide what measures shall be taken . . . to maintain or restore international peace and security." Considerable confusion had arisen in the minds of many over the use of the word "recommendations" in the corresponding part of the Dumbarton Oaks Proposals and this, taken together with the fact that paragraphs 1 and 2 of Chapter VIII, Section B of the Dumbarton Oaks Proposals were regarded by many as overlapping, led to a very thorough reconsideration of these paragraphs at UNCIO. The result was that paragraph 2 became Article 39, paragraph 1 was omitted, and a new provision was introduced and adopted by the Committee and the Conference which became Article 40. In the course of the discussion of the new proposals the following observations were made by the Belgian Delegate which, at his request, the Committee voted unanimously to include in its final report. Though the observations relate both to Articles 39 and 40, they are included at this point:[3]

[1] For specific proposals for the definition of aggression, see Eagleton, Clyde, "The Attempt to Define War," *International Conciliation*, no. 291, June 1933; Royal Institute of International Affairs, *International Sanctions*, cited above, p. 177.

[2] UNCIO, *Report of Mr. Paul-Boncour, Rapporteur, on Chapter VIII, Section B,* Doc. 881, III/3/46, p. 4.   [3] *Ibid.*, p. 6.

(1) In using the word "recommendations" in Section B, as already found in paragraph 5, Section A,[1] the Committee has intended to show that the action of the Council so far as it relates to the peaceful settlement of a dispute or to situations giving rise to a threat of war, a breach of the peace, or aggression, should be considered as governed by the provisions contained in Section A.[2] Under such an hypothesis, the Council would in reality pursue simultaneously two distinct actions, one having for its object the settlement of the dispute or the difficulty, and the other, the enforcement or provisional measures, each of which is governed by an appropriate section in Chapter VIII.

(2) It is the Committee's view that the power given to the Council under paragraphs 1 and 2[3] not to resort to the measures contemplated in paragraphs 3 and 4,[4] or to resort to them only after having sought to maintain or restore peace by inviting the parties to consent to certain conservatory measures, refers above all to the presumption of a threat of war. The Committee is unanimous in the belief that, on the contrary, in the case of flagrant aggression imperiling the existence of a Member of the Organization, enforcement measures should be taken without delay, and to the full extent required by circumstances, except that the Council should at the same time endeavor to persuade the aggressor to abandon its venture, by the means contemplated in Section A and by prescribing conservatory measures.

From these observations approved by the Committee it becomes clear that the intention of the Article is that the recommendations of the Security Council are to be made in connection with its efforts to achieve a pacific settlement under Chapter VI. Efforts at peaceful settlement will presumably continue even during the period when enforcement action is being taken. The decisions of the Security Council are to be taken only with regard to measures under Articles 41 and 42 necessary to restore peace once an act of aggression has occurred. Furthermore it becomes clear that the Security Council, faced with a case of flagrant violation of peace, should take these enforcement measures promptly although, as has already been pointed out, it can continue its endeavor to persuade the aggressor to abandon its venture.

Probable Frequency of Application. While the provisions of Article 39 are basic to the whole Charter system for the enforcement of peace, it must, nevertheless, be borne in mind that in actual practice there presumably will be few occasions when enforcement action will be taken. In the first place, the primary effort of the Security Council will be to deal with a dispute or situation in such a way as to prevent any overt violation of the peace. The functions of the Security Council under Chapter VI will first be put into play and in the great majority of cases, it is to be hoped, will be successfully exercised. In case of an immediate threat to the peace, the conservatory functions of the Council, more specifically provided for in Article 40, will be exercised. Only presum-

---

[1] Corresponding to Article 36, paragraph 1 of the Charter.
[2] Corresponding to Chapter VI of the Charter.
[3] Corresponding to Articles 39 and 40 of the Charter.
[4] Corresponding to Articles 41 and 42 of the Charter.

ably in case of actual violation of the peace or an act of aggression will enforcement measures be taken.

The possibility of taking such measures, however, will be limited by other provisions of the Charter. In the first place, during the transition period, according to the provisions of Article 106,[1] such action against enemy states will be taken by the signatories of the Moscow Four-Power Declaration of October 1943 and France. In the second place, no such action will presumably be taken against a permanent member of the Security Council since a permanent member by the exercise of the veto will be able to prevent such a decision from being taken. That leaves then, for the transitional period at least, a highly restricted field for the operation of the enforcement provisions of Chapter VII, and even after the transitional period above referred to, enforcement against any of the Great Powers will be practically excluded.

ARTICLE 40

In order to prevent an aggravation of the situation, the Security Council may, before making the recommendations or deciding upon the measures provided for in Article 39, call upon the parties concerned to comply with such provisional measures as it deems necessary or desirable. Such provisional measures shall be without prejudice to the rights, claims, or position of the parties concerned. The Security Council shall duly take account of failure to comply with such provisional measures.

There were no corresponding provisions in the Dumbarton Oaks Proposals. As stated in the comment on Article 39, the adoption of Article 40 was the result of a thorough reconsideration and revision of the first two paragraphs of Chapters VIII, Section B, of the Dumbarton Oaks Proposals. Under Article 40 as it stands the Security Council is specifically authorized to call upon the parties concerned to comply with such provisional measures as it deems necessary to the maintenance or restoration of peace.

The use of the words "call upon" under the circumstances envisaged in the Article suggests that the parties are expected to comply with the measures in question. It would seem that the words as used are more mandatory in character than the words as used in the second paragraph of Article 33, since in Article 40 the parties are called upon to comply with measures laid down by the Council, while in Article 33 they are called upon to agree among themselves which, with good faith on both sides, may not be found possible.

The provisional measures envisaged in this Article are not enumerated but may presumably include such measures as the withdrawal of armed

[1] See comment on Article 106, this volume, p. 286.

forces from specified areas, the acceptance of some form of international policing arrangement within a specified area, and the termination of retaliatory measures which have been taken in connection with a particular dispute or situation.

It is stated that the recommendation of such provisional measures will not prejudice "the rights, claims, or position of the parties concerned," but that the Security Council "shall duly take account of failure to comply with such provisional measures." Some would regard these two statements as contradictory. Failure to comply will not apparently, in any strictly legal sense, prejudice the rights, claims or positions of the parties. However, the last sentence would seem to mean, if it means anything, that the Security Council may allow its estimate of the situation and its decision with regard to enforcement measures to be taken to be influenced by such a failure. In that sense the position of a party may undoubtedly be prejudiced. Practically, this may lead in the end to the prejudice of legal rights as well if, as the result of enforcement action taken, a party feels constrained to accept terms of settlement which originally it refused to accept.

ARTICLE 41

The Security Council may decide what measures not involving the use of armed force are to be employed to give effect to its decisions, and it may call upon the Members of the United Nations to apply such measures. These may include complete or partial interruption of economic relations and of rail, sea, air, postal, telegraphic, radio, and other means of communication, and the severance of diplomatic relations.

This Article provides in part for the specific exercise of the authority conferred upon the Security Council under Article 39. It is to be noted that the Council is given the discretionary power to decide what measures "not involving the use of armed force" are to be used under the provisions of Article 39. This means that the Council is free to decide, first, whether such measures shall be used, and secondly, if so, what specifically these measures are to be. In this respect the provisions of the Article differ radically from Article 16 of the Covenant which placed upon all Members of the League the definite obligation to apply immediately the enumerated sanctions, all falling in the category of measures "not involving the use of armed force." No preliminary decision by the Council was necessary although it was found expedient in the application of sanctions against Italy in 1935 to establish a coordinating agency in order to increase the effectiveness of the measures taken by Members under this Article.[1]

[1] For account of application of sanctions against Italy, see Highley, and Royal Institute of International Affairs, *International Sanctions*, cited above.

The paragraph specifies certain measures which are included in the term "measures not involving the use of armed force." This enumeration, however, is not to be regarded as exhaustive and in no way as a limitation upon the powers of the Security Council.

The words "called upon" appear to be used in this Article in the same mandatory sense as in Article 40. The basic principle of the security provisions of the Charter, as distinguished from that of the Covenant of the League of Nations would be nullified if, after the Security Council had reached a decision regarding the application of measures not involving the use of armed force, discretion were left to Members of the Organization as to whether they should carry out those measures or not. This interpretation is also supported by the fact that this Article is a special application of the general principle of Article 39, which empowers the Security Council to "decide what measures shall be taken in accordance with Articles 41 and 42, to maintain or restore international peace and security."

ARTICLE 42

Should the Security Council consider that measures provided for in Article 41 would be inadequate or have proved to be inadequate, it may take such action by air, sea, or land forces as may be necessary to maintain or restore international peace and security. Such action may include demonstrations, blockade, and other operations by air, sea, or land forces of Members of the United Nations.

This Article like its predecessor provides specifically for the exercise of the authority conferred upon the Security Council under Article 39. It goes beyond any provision of the Covenant in requiring the use under certain conditions of military force in support of international peace and security. The Covenant, not only did not impose upon Member States a specific obligation to apply military sanctions as it did in the case of certain non-military sanctions, but it did not make it obligatory for Members of the League to carry out any measures which the Council might think desirable. Both under the provisions of Article 10 and Article 16, paragraph 2, the Council could only recommend measures to be taken, which Members of the League might or might not carry out. Furthermore, any recommendation of the Council had to be made by a unanimous vote of its members.

The Charter system goes beyond the League system in two respects. In the first place, it empowers the Security Council to take a decision with regard to the use of air, sea or land forces to maintain or restore international peace and security by less than a unanimous vote. Under the provisions of Article 27, paragraph 2, this decision may be taken by a vote of seven members of the Security Council with the concurrence of all the permanent members. In the second place, such a decision taken by the Security Council creates obligations for Members of the Organization which these Members are required faithfully to carry out according to the express provision of Article 25.

It is to be noted that in this Article it is stated that "it [the Security Council] may take such action," whereas in Articles 40 and 41 the Security Council is empowered to "call upon" the Members or parties. It is not believed that this difference of phraseology is intended to suggest any important difference in the procedures that are followed, the extent of the obligations which Members assume, or the powers of the Security Council under the two Articles. It is of course true, and the difference of phraseology may be intended to give recognition to this fact, that by the terms of Article 43 Members do by special agreement undertake to make available specified armed forces, facilities and assistance for the use of the Council under Article 42. Nevertheless, as Article 43 recognizes, in order for action to ensue it is necessary for the Security Council to call upon Members to make available the forces, facilities and assistance they have promised since these are normally under the control and direction of the governments of Member States. The difference of phraseology in the two Articles would, then, appear to have its explanation, if any logical explanation is to be found, not in the power of the Security Council or the nature of the obligation of Members, or the basic procedure that is followed, but rather in the extent to which the implementation of the obligation has been provided for in advance. In both cases, the Security Council in order to implement its decision, must call upon Member States, and in both cases the Members are obligated under the Charter, notably by the provisions of Article 25, to carry out the decisions taken.

This Article, together with the preceding Article, leaves to the Security Council a wide measure of discretion in the exercise of the power that is given to it. The Security Council may decide in a particular case that measures not involving the use of armed force will be adequate. In that case it will be only after such measures have been tried and have been proven by experience to be inadequate that the Security Council will decide to use military measures under this Article. In another situation the Security Council may decide that measures not involving the use of armed force will be inadequate. In that case it may decide that the use of armed force, immediately and from the beginning, is necessary. It can be assumed that ordinarily the use of armed force will be accompanied by the use of measures provided for in Article 41, although that will not of necessity be the case.

The question arises as to whether the Security Council may, under the provisions of Articles 39 and 42, require Members to provide "armed forces, assistance, and facilities" in excess of those specified in the "special agreement or agreements" referred to in Article 43. This question was raised in the course of the discussion in Committee III/3 at UNCIO and, speaking on behalf of the Sponsoring Governments, the Delegate of the United Kingdom gave assurance that the Security Council would not have that authority.[1] Since this interpretation by vote of the Committee was included in the Report of the Committee to Commission III and was approved by that body, and since it is expressly stated that it was after consideration of this and other observations that the Committee finally approved the texts of the articles of the Committee draft which became Articles 39 and 40 of the Charter, it can be fairly assumed that no Member of the Organization is obligated under Article 42 to employ "armed forces, assistance, and facilities" in excess of those specifically provided for in the "special agreement or agreements" mentioned in Article 43.

Article 42, by itself, does not specify from where the air, sea or land forces in question are to come. By the terms of Article 43, provision is made for their provision by Members, in accordance with the terms of "a special agreement or agreements." However, there is nothing in Article 42, as it stands, which would prevent the establishment and use of an independent international armed force under Security Council direction. It would of course be necessary for the Charter to be amended in other respects or for a supplementary agreement to be entered into (conceivably the special agreement or agreements referred to in Article 43 could accomplish the purpose) for such a force to become a reality, since under the Charter as it stands the Security Council does not have the power to recruit and organize such a force.

ARTICLE 43

1. All Members of the United Nations, in order to contribute to the maintenance of international peace and security, undertake to make available to the Security Council, on its call and in accordance with a special agreement or agreements, armed forces, assistance, and facilities, including rights of passage, necessary for the purpose of maintaining international peace and security.

Charter System for Assuring Availability of Necessary Force. This paragraph provides for the specific implementation of the obligation assumed by Members of the Organization to make contributions to the "air, sea or land forces" which the Security Council may decide are necessary to maintain or restore international peace and security. While efforts were made, following the establishment of the League, particularly under the leadership of France, to provide for such advance commitments to use specific forces in support of the Covenant of the

---

[1] UNCIO, *Report of Mr. Paul-Boncour, Rapporteur, on Chapter VIII, Section B*, Doc. 881, III/3/46, p. 7.

League, no general agreement among the Members was found possible. It was only to the extent that pairs of states agreed by treaties of mutual assistance and implementing military agreements to come to each other's assistance in case of attack by a third state and to subordinate the operation of these agreements to the basic principles of the League system that any provision of this kind was made for the implementation of the League security system.

The architects of the Charter were faced with the possibility of using three broad alternatives in providing for the use of military forces in the maintenance of international peace and security. One was to establish a permanent army of an international character, over and above national armies or even replacing them. The second was the establishment of a system of national contingents to be placed under international direction for specified purposes. A third was to provide for cooperative action by national forces under some form of over-all international direction but with national strategic direction and tactical command left intact. The third was substantially the system envisaged in the Covenant although never put into actual operation. The first was found unacceptable both at the time of the drafting of the Covenant and at the time of the drafting of the Charter because it involved too great an infringement upon national sovereignty. The second is substantially the system that has been adopted under the Charter.

Form and Content of Agreement. Under the system of the Charter the Members of the United Nations are to agree in advance to make available to the Security Council specific contingents of armed forces, specific facilities and other forms of assistance, "including rights of passage," for use in the maintenance of international peace and security. The paragraph which we are considering does not specify the exact scope of the agreement so far as the number of parties is concerned. It can, therefore, be assumed from the use of the words "a special agreement or agreements" that there may be one general agreement to which all Members of the United Nations are parties, or a general agreement supplemented by a number of more limited agreements, or finally a series of limited agreements which together would serve the purpose of a general agreement while permitting greater flexibility of treatment.

This paragraph, taken together with the preceding paragraphs of the Article, does not define in any exhaustive manner the content of the special agreement or agreements, or more particularly, the scope of the obligations to be assumed by Member States. The provisions of the paragraph are stated in general terms and would seem to suggest that the agreements should make available the specified forces, assistance and facilities for such use as the Security Council may desire.

It has been suggested that there can appropriately be included in such an agreement a provision to the effect that the forces of a particular

Member are to be used only within certain areas.[1] While this technically may be a correct interpretation of the paragraph, it is suggested that it would greatly hamper the work of the Security Council in carrying out its functions under Articles 39, 41 and 42 if states generally should insist upon such restrictions and particularly if this should be done by those states to which the Organization will naturally look for the forces necessary to effective military action. Furthermore the fact that it is expressly provided in Article 48, paragraph 1, that the action taken in a particular case or situation by the Security Council is to be taken by all the Members or some of them "as the Security Council may decide," seems to suggest that the Security Council is to have a wide latitude of judgment when the situation actually requiring action arises, which would not be the case if Members had specified in advance that their forces were to be used only in certain regions.

Position of States Not Members of Council. The special agreement or agreements in question are specifically to provide that the armed forces, assistance and facilities specified therein are to be made available to the Security Council "on its call." This provision, taken together with the provisions of Articles 39 and 42, would suggest that Members of the United Nations who are not members of the Security Council are in a somewhat less favorable position than those who are members of the Security Council. Furthermore, by virtue of the provision regarding voting procedure (Article 27, paragraph 3), non-permanent members are in a less favorable position than permanent members, since those states not permanently represented, while they will have the opportunity to take part in the discussion leading up to the decision, will not necessarily be included in the majority necessary to a decision.

At the United Nations Conference it was decided to equalize somewhat the positions of non-permanent members and non-members of the Security Council by providing that before a Member of the United Nations, not a member of the Security Council, is called upon to provide armed forces, it shall be given the opportunity to participate in the decisions of the Council concerning the use of that Member's contingents.[2] This, however, does not give the non-member of the Security Council any assurance that its armed forces will be used only with its consent since, while it is allowed to take part in the voting, its affirmative vote will not be necessary to a decision binding upon it according to the terms of Article 25. Consequently it may find itself in the position where it must assume heavy obligations in a given situation without having given its specific approval to the proposals before the Security Council. Its position, however, will be no worse than that of a non-permanent member of the Council.

[1] See testimony of John Foster Dulles in *Hearings . . . on The Charter of the United Nations*, etc., cited above, p. 653.　　[2] See Article 44 and comment, this volume, p. 168.

2. Such agreement or agreements shall govern the numbers and types of forces, their degree of readiness and general location, and the nature of the facilities and assistance to be provided.

This paragraph gives further detail with regard to the content of the special agreement or agreements referred to in paragraph 1. As a result of the discussions at the United Nations Conference the provisions of the original Dumbarton Oaks Proposals were made considerably more specific. Chapter VIII, Section B, paragraph 5 of the Proposals stated that such agreement or agreements should govern "the numbers and types of forces and the nature of the facilities and assistance to be provided." At San Francisco the words "their degree of readiness and general location" were inserted at the suggestion of the French Delegation. This means that under the agreement or agreements in question the Members of the United Nations are expected to commit themselves in some detail with regard to their specific contributions in definitely envisaged situations because it would seem to be only with respect to such situations that the location of armed forces can be determined with any degree of satisfaction.

When we consider the great, in fact, insuperable, difficulties that were experienced under the League system in establishing the criteria that were to be used in determining the maximum level of a nation's armaments,[1] and when we think of the equal difficulty that will no doubt be met in establishing criteria governing a Member's contributions of armed forces, facilities and assistance, it becomes clear that the making of the agreement or agreements provided for in paragraph 1, with the content indicated in paragraph 2, will be a difficult task, possibly requiring long and extended negotiations and discussions, not to mention delays that may occur at the ratification stage. The result of this may well be that the transitional security arrangements provided for in Articles 106 and 107 will be in operation for a fairly long period of time, since Article 106 specifies that they shall be operative "pending the coming into force of such special agreements referred to in Article 43 as in the opinion of the Security Council enable it to begin the exercise of its responsibilities under Article 42." [2]

3. The agreement or agreements shall be negotiated as soon as possible on the initiative of the Security Council. They shall be concluded between the Security Council and Members or between the Security Council and groups of Members and shall be subject to ratification by the signatory states in accordance with their respective constitutional processes.

This paragraph is the result of careful discussion by the technical committee at UNCIO and contains one or two rather important modifica-

[1] See Madariaga, Salvador de, *Disarmament*, N. Y., Coward, McCann, 1929 and Rappard, William E., *The Quest for Peace*, chap. V, cited above.
[2] See comment on Article 106, p. 286.

tions of the original Dumbarton Oaks Proposals. It eliminates certain ambiguities which undoubtedly existed in the Dumbarton Oaks text. It places upon the Security Council a responsibility which it did not clearly have under that text.

This paragraph makes it clear that the "agreement or agreements" referred to in paragraph 1 are to be negotiated on the initiative of the Security Council as soon as possible and not upon the independent initiatives of the Members of the United Nations. In the second place, it makes it clear that the "agreement or agreements" are to be concluded between the Security Council and Members or groups of Members. By presenting these alternatives it conforms to the provisions of Article 43, paragraph 1, which permits, as we have seen, one all-inclusive agreement or a series of limited agreements or a combination of the two.

The provision that the Security Council is to be party to the "agreement or agreements" is an interesting innovation in international practice. It was strongly doubted whether such a possibility existed under the Covenant of the League of Nations. It assumes that the Security Council has a capacity for entering into international commitments apart from that of its members. It represents an important advance in the development of an international authority. The paragraph also provides that the "agreement or agreements" in question shall be subject to ratification by the signatory states in accordance with their respective constitutional processes. This is a recognition, of which there are others in the Charter, of the principle that each state in taking action upon a proposed agreement can be expected to conform to its own domestic constitutional requirements and that every other signatory of the agreement in question should take cognizance of this fact.

All three paragraphs of this Article make use of the words "agreement or agreements." This terminology can be taken as having no special significance so far as the constitutional requirements of Members of the Organization are concerned. The term is to be regarded as a generic term covering all the more highly specialized forms of international contractual arrangements. So far as the Constitution of the United States is concerned, it would seem to be more a question of political expediency than of constitutional interpretation as to whether the agreement is to be treated as an executive agreement, requiring at most approval by or advance authorization by a joint resolution of the two Houses of Congress, or as a treaty requiring approval by a two-thirds vote of the United States Senate.[1]

[1] In his testimony before the Senate Foreign Relations Committee John Foster Dulles expressed the view that the term "special agreement or agreements" was synonymous with the word "treaty" thereby suggesting that approval by a two-thirds vote of the Senate was necessary. See *Hearings . . . on The Charter of the United Nations*, etc., cited above, p. 643.

See on this general subject Corwin, E. S., *The Constitution and World Organization*, N. J., Princeton Univ. Press, 1944, chap. III.

ARTICLE 44

When the Security Council has decided to use force it shall, before calling upon a Member not represented on it to provide armed forces in fulfillment of the obligations assumed under Article 43, invite that Member, if the Member so desires, to participate in the decisions of the Security Council concerning the employment of contingents of that Member's armed forces.

This provision was not in the original Dumbarton Oaks Proposals, nor was there anything of an equally specific nature in the Covenant of the League of Nations. In fact the exact situation here envisaged could not have arisen under the Covenant since, as we have seen, the Council had no authority to decide that the Members of the League were to use armed force for the maintenance of international peace and security.

This Article was inserted by UNCIO at the request of certain of the so-called "middle powers," acting under the leadership of Canada, who insisted that a Member of the Organization before being called upon to contribute armed forces under Articles 39 and 42 should have at least the same opportunity to take part in the discussions leading up to the decision of the Council and in the decision itself as a non-permanent member of the Council. In other words, to use the phrase coined by the Netherlands Delegate, the principle of "no military action without representation" was accepted.

It is to be noted, however, that this provision for special representation is limited to the case where it is proposed to call upon a Member to provide armed forces in fulfillment of obligations assumed under Article 43 and that Member specifically requests to be allowed to participate in the decision. The technical committee concerned with the matter at San Francisco expressly refused to accord the same privilege to a Member that is called upon to provide facilities or assistance on the ground that this would unduly hamper the work of the Security Council. It was, however, pointed out by way of reassurance to the Members particularly interested in this angle of the problem that the question of facilities and assistance was covered by the special agreements contemplated in Article 43 and that adequate provision for necessary consultations was to be found in Articles 31 and 47, paragraph 2.[1]

ARTICLE 45

In order to enable the United Nations to take urgent military measures, Members shall hold immediately available national air-force contingents for combined international enforcement action. The strength

---

[1] UNCIO, *Report of Mr. Paul-Boncour, Rapporteur, on Chapter VIII, Section B,* Doc. 881, III/3/46, p. 2–3.

and degree of readiness of these contingents and plans for their combined action shall be determined, within the limits laid down in the special agreement or agreements referred to in Article 43, by the Security Council with the assistance of the Military Staff Committee.

This Article, taken over practically intact from the Dumbarton Oaks Proposals, is intended to be a special application of the provisions of Article 43. In a sense it is what is left of a proposal originally sponsored in the course of the Dumbarton Oaks Conversations to establish a truly international air force under the direction of the Security Council. This Article is not to be interpreted as in any way restricting the provisions of Article 43. The purpose of Article 45 is to give "supplementary precision" to the provisions of Article 43 without in any way limiting its general scope.[1] It was because this interpretation was given to the Article that proposals made at San Francisco to include "mixed contingents" or "forces of all arms" were withdrawn.

It is to be noted that this Article envisages giving the Security Council some discretionary power in determining "the strength and degree of readiness" of national air force contingents. To this extent the Article would seem to go beyond the provisions of Article 43 and not merely give "supplementary precision" to it. However, it is stated that this power is to be exercised "within the limits laid down in the special agreement or agreements referred to in Article 43." Thus, the "special agreement or agreements" become the source of any additional authority with respect to national air force contingents which the Security Council may have. The Article does not place upon Members any direct obligation to include in the special agreement or agreements a grant of this special authority to the Council, though it strongly suggests that they should do so.

It is to be noted that the provisions of this Article were considered and adopted before the announcement was made of the use of the atomic bomb and before knowledge was available of the possible results of such use.

ARTICLE 46

Plans for the application of armed force shall be made by the Security Council with the assistance of the Military Staff Committee.

This provides for a Military Staff Committee constituted in accordance with the terms of Article 47, paragraph 2, to serve as a general staff responsible to the Security Council for over-all strategic planning. It follows closely the precedent of the Combined Chiefs-of-Staff evolved during World War II.[2]

[1] *Ibid.*, p. 10.
[2] See Announcement of War Department, February 6, 1942; *Documents on American Foreign Relations, IV, 1941–1942*, p. 245.

ARTICLE 47

1. There shall be established a Military Staff Committee to advise and assist the Security Council on all questions relating to the Security Council's military requirements for the maintenance of international peace and security, the employment and command of forces placed at its disposal, the regulation of armaments, and possible disarmament.

The functions of the Military Staff Committee are defined in this paragraph. These functions are threefold: (1) to advise and assist the Security Council on all questions relating to the Security Council's military requirements for the maintenance of international peace and security, which in effect means in connection with the negotiation of "special agreement or agreements" referred to in Article 43 and the taking of decisions under Article 42; (2) to advise and assist the Security Council in the strategic direction of the forces placed at its command under the provisions of Article 43; and (3) to advise and assist the Security Council in connection with the preparation of plans for "the establishment of a system for the regulation of armaments" under the terms of Article 26, and the exercise of any powers which may be conferred upon the Security Council in connection with the enforcement of any such system.

It will be seen that, generally speaking, the functions of the Military Staff Committee are of the same kind as those conferred upon the Permanent Military, Air and Naval Commission of the League of Nations under Article 9 of the Covenant. Since, however, the functions of the Security Council in respect to the maintenance of international peace and security are of a more advanced character than those of the League Council, the functions of the Military Staff Committee assume a considerably greater prominence and can be assumed in practice to be considerably more vital than those of the corresponding League organ.

There are many historical examples which show the importance of such staff discussions in preparing for joint military operations. Such discussions between the British and the French before World War I were an important factor in the successful stemming of the German attack. Under the League system, the French persistently stressed the need of such advanced planning to assure the effectiveness of whatever joint military action might be taken under the Covenant. Consultations between the military leaders of the United States and the United Kingdom in World War II took the advanced form of a Combined Chiefs-of-Staff organization, upon which, as has already been pointed out, the Charter provision is largely modelled, and the effectiveness of this staff cooperation was a very important factor in the successful conduct of the war. In fact, without it victory might not have been possible.

2. The Military Staff Committee shall consist of the Chiefs of Staff of the permanent members of the Security Council or their representatives. Any Member of the United Nations not permanently represented on the Committee shall be invited by the Committee to be associated with it when the efficient discharge of the Committee's responsibilities requires the participation of that Member in its work.

The question of membership was discussed at some length at the United Nations Conference. Considerable pressure was brought to bear by the smaller powers to secure wider representation upon the Committee. This pressure was successfully resisted. The arguments which appear to have been conclusive, apart from the firm stand taken by the Delegates of the Sponsoring Governments and France, were that the Committee must, by the very nature of its functions, be a small compact committee, and that the second sentence of this paragraph adequately safeguards the interests of any state which might have a special reason for representation. In the course of Committee discussion, while an amendment that the Military Staff Committee should be composed of the Chiefs of Staff of all the members of the Security Council was under consideration, numerous explanations were given of the plan proposed by the Sponsoring Governments which apparently had the effect of giving assurance to those who had earlier been critical, as the amendment was easily defeated. These explanations were as follows: [1]

1. Paragraph 9 (the paragraph under consideration) provided that members not permanently represented should be asked to join when appropriate.
2. The initiative for expanding the membership to meet a particular situation should be left to the Military Staff Committee; otherwise it might become as large as the Council itself.
3. If the forces of a country were used there was no question but that the military staff of that country would be consulted.
4. Because of the complex duties of the Committee, it was essential that its composition should be limited to the permanent Council members in order to avoid a committee with constantly changing membership.
5. Allied military machinery in this war was of the same type as that proposed in paragraph 9.
6. As a Chief of Staff, the Military Staff Committee's function would be to make decisions, and therefore, it should be a small group. The function of command was a different matter. No committee, large or small, could exercise command; and the selection of individuals for this purpose would be decided upon later.
7. The limitation of membership on the Military Staff Committee to the permanent members of the Council did not conflict with the pending Canadian amendment regarding representation of non-members in Council decisions.

3. The Military Staff Committee shall be responsible under the Security Council for the strategic direction of any armed forces placed at the disposal of the Security Council. Questions relating to the command of such forces shall be worked out subsequently.

[1] UNCIO, *Summary Report of Fourteenth Meeting of Committee III/3, May 26, 1945*, Doc. 628, III/3/33, p. 3–4.

This reaffirms, somewhat more specifically, one of the functions conferred under paragraph 1. It makes it clear, as stated in the comment above, that the function of the Military Staff Committee in connection with the employment and command of forces being used under the terms of Articles 39 and 42 is that of strategic direction instead of tactical command. It is specifically stated that questions relating to command are to be worked out subsequently but the assumption is perhaps justified that tactical command will more commonly be national.

4. The Military Staff Committee, with the authorization of the Security Council and after consultation with appropriate regional agencies, may establish regional subcommittees.

This paragraph was inserted at San Francisco with a view to giving opportunities for representation to the small states and, more particularly, with a view to tying up regional arrangements recognized in Chapter VIII with global security arrangements. Before setting up such regional subcommittees, the Military Staff Committee, acting under the authorization of the Security Council, must consult with appropriate regional agencies. However, the Staff Committee will have the final decision in each case. These regional subcommittees will conceivably have varied functions. They will assist the Military Staff Committee in the performance of its functions within regional areas. In addition, they may perform in relation to regional agencies for the maintenance of peace and security much the same functions that the Military Staff Committee performs under Article 47 for the Security Council. The subcommittees can thus make a useful contribution to the proper integration of the plans and activities of the regional agencies and the Security Council.

ARTICLE 48

1. The action required to carry out the decisions of the Security Council for the maintenance of international peace and security shall be taken by all the Members of the United Nations or by some of them, as the Security Council may determine.

This Article specifically adds to the flexibility of the enforcement arrangements set up under this chapter and to the discretionary authority vested in the Security Council in carrying out its functions. Recognizing the fact that certain Members of the United Nations may be more advantageously situated to take specific action in a particular contingency than others, the paragraph empowers the Security Council to determine whether in a particular case action shall be taken by all the Members of the United Nations or by some of them. Thus in a case where maintenance of peace and security have been violated by a western European state the Security Council might direct that the necessary action be taken by the western European neighbors of that state. Furthermore, it seems to be implied in this paragraph that the Security Council may not only designate certain Members to take action to the exclusion of other Members, but that it may also direct certain Members to take certain kinds of action while other Members are directed to take other appropriate kinds of action. Thus Members in close proximity to the violation of the peace may be required to take military action while those further removed may be required to apply political and economic measures only.

2. Such decisions shall be carried out by the Members of the United Nations directly and through their action in the appropriate international agencies of which they are members.

One of the problems arising from the fact that international organization is being attempted on a functional basis is that of adequate coordination of the activities of the numerous specialized agencies. The Organization provided for under the Charter is general in its functions and is therefore the agency which is to undertake this task of coordination.[1] However, as we shall see from an examination of the provisions of the Charter, there is no certain assurance that such coordination will be effective since it is to be achieved largely by agreement. One of the best assurances of coordination is no doubt to be found in the fact that generally speaking membership of the specialized agencies will be the same as that of the general Organization.

One situation in which coordination will be particularly necessary is that where enforcement action is being taken against a Member for violation of the peace or an act of overt aggression. In such a situation it will be necessary that the acts of all the specialized agencies shall be in harmony with the measures being taken by the Security Council. Thus if a decision is taken to apply economic and financial measures against a state which has violated the peace the International Bank for Reconstruction and Development should refrain from advancing any loans to the state in question or continuing payments on any loans made. The Charter does not provide that the specialized agencies shall be subject to the decisions of the Security Council in this respect. By the terms of this Article, however, it is provided that the Members of the Organization shall "through their action in the appropriate international agencies of which they are members," as well as directly, take necessary steps to carry out the decisions of the Security Council. Since the various specialized agencies will operate through organs upon which Members of the United Nations Organization are represented, this would appear to be an important assurance of the necessary coordination.

[1] See Articles 57 and 58, and comments thereon, this volume, p. 194–206.

ARTICLE 49

The Members of the United Nations shall join in affording mutual assistance in carrying out the measures decided upon by the Security Council.

This Article which simply reaffirms the principle of Article 2, paragraph 5, corresponds in a general way to Article 16, paragraph 3, of the Covenant of the League of Nations. It is general in scope and clearly applies to economic and financial assistance, which is further particularized in Article 50, and to military assistance.

In the course of the discussion of this principle in the technical committee concern was expressed by the Delegation of the Union of South Africa with regard to the sharing of expenses of enforcement action taken against a particular state. Although accepting the view that no specific provision should be put into the Charter covering this point, the Committee expressed the desire that the Organization should in the future seek to promote a system aiming at the "fairest possible distribution" of expenses incurred as a result of enforcement action.[1]

ARTICLE 50

If preventive or enforcement measures against any state are taken by the Security Council, any other state, whether a Member of the United Nations or not, which finds itself confronted with special economic problems arising from the carrying out of those measures shall have the right to consult the Security Council with regard to a solution of those problems.

This Article is to be understood as a special implementation of a part of the general principle stated in Article 49. In case any state "whether a Member of the United Nations or not" finds itself confronted with special economic difficulties as the result of taking action prescribed by the Security Council under the Articles of this Chapter that state has the right to consult with the Security Council concerning a possible solution or alleviation of the situation. In one respect this goes beyond the provisions of Article 49 since it admits the right of a non-member as well as of a Member to consult with the Security Council. The obligation of Article 49 to afford mutual assistance is limited to Members, which is proper in view of the fact that obligations under the Charter can only arise from membership. Article 50, however, defines a right which is made available not only to Members but also to non-members.

ARTICLE 51

Nothing in the present Charter shall impair the inherent right of individual or collective self-defense if an armed attack occurs against a

[1] UNCIO, *Report of Mr. Paul-Boncour, Rapporteur, on Chapter VIII, Section B,* Doc. 881, III/3/46, p. 12.

Member of the United Nations, until the Security Council has taken the measures necessary to maintain international peace and security. Measures taken by Members in the exercise of this right of self-defense shall be immediately reported to the Security Council and shall not in any way affect the authority and responsibility of the Security Council under the present Charter to take at any time such action as it deems necessary in order to maintain or restore international peace and security.

Background of Article. This Article, although included in the Chapter dealing with action with respect to threats to the peace, breaches of the peace and acts of aggression, was adopted at the United Nations Conference as a part of the arrangement for harmonizing the operation of regional arrangements and agencies with that of the general provisions of the Charter. More specifically it was the outcome of careful study and consideration of the best means of fitting the system of the American Republics into the United Nations, with special reference to obligations which had been assumed at the Mexico City Conference under the Act of Chapultepec.[1]

In the Dumbarton Oaks Proposals it was provided that the Security Council should, where appropriate, utilize regional arrangements or agencies for enforcement action under its authority, but no enforcement action was to be taken under such regional arrangements or by regional agencies without the authorization of the Security Council. As has already been explained, no agreement was reached at Dumbarton Oaks with regard to the vote necessary to a decision by the Security Council giving such authorization, and consequently the exact manner in which this provision of the original Proposals would operate could not be clearly envisaged although there was a general expectation that unanimity, at least of the Great Powers, would be required. By the Yalta formula which filled this particular gap in the original Dumbarton Oaks Proposals it was provided that a decision of the Security Council giving authorization for the taking of enforcement action under regional arrangements should be taken by the affirmative vote of seven members, including all of the permanent members of the Council. Thus it would be possible for any permanent member of the Security Council to veto any proposal for the taking of enforcement action under a regional arrangement to which that member was not a party.

Due to the progress that had been made in the development of an Inter-American system for the maintenance of peace and security a great deal of sentiment existed in the Western Hemisphere in favor of allowing a large measure of autonomy to the operation of such regional arrangements. This Inter-American system was based on a series of agreements which have been reached at Inter-American conferences,

[1] Department of State, *Bulletin, XII*, p. 339.

notably the Conventions of the Inter-American Conference for the Maintenance of Peace of 1936,[1] the Declaration of Lima of 1938,[2] and Declaration XV of the Second Meeting of Ministers of Foreign Affairs of 1940.[3] The basic principles of this system received their fullest development and expression in the Act of Chapultepec, adopted at the Mexico City Conference of February–March, 1945.

By the provisions of this Declaration the American Republics agreed that every attack by a state, whether a state of the Western Hemisphere or not, against the integrity or the inviolability of the territory, or against the sovereignty or the political independence of an American state, should be considered as an act of aggression; that consultation should take place in any case where an act of aggression of this nature had occurred or where there was reason to believe that it was being prepared; and that for the duration of the war and until a permanent treaty had been concluded, the parties to this Declaration should utilize such procedures as might be found necessary, including the use of armed force, to deal with such acts of aggression. It was also stated in the Act of Chapultepec, as a recommendation, that for the purpose of meeting threats or acts of aggression against any American republic following the establishment of peace, the Governments of the American Republics should consider the conclusion of a treaty "establishing procedures whereby such threats or acts may be met by: The use, by all or some of the signatories of said treaty of any one or more of the following measures; recall of chiefs of diplomatic missions; breaking of diplomatic relations; breaking of consular relations; breaking of postal, telegraphic, telephonic, radio-telephonic relations; interruption of economic, commercial and financial relations; use of armed force to prevent or repel aggression."[4] The announcement of the adoption of this Act by the American Republics brought to the fore the issue of how such a regional system was to be fitted into a general global system with sufficient assurance that the operation of the regional system would not be thwarted at every turn by states outside the Hemisphere.

Consideration of Problem of Regionalism at San Francisco. At the United Nations Conference various amendments were proposed with a view to making it possible for such a regional system for the maintenance of peace and security to enjoy autonomy within the global system. These proposals, advanced principally though by no means entirely by the Delegations of the Latin American Republics, took two lines. One

[1] *Report of the Delegation of the United States of America to the Inter-American Conference for the Maintenance of Peace, Buenos Aires, Argentina, December 1–23, 1936.* Washington, D.C., 1937, Department of State Publication (Conference Series 33) p. 116.

[2] *Documents on American Foreign Relations, I, 1938–1939*, p. 44.

[3] *Ibid., III, 1940–1941*, p. 76.

[4] Department of State, *Bulletin*, XII, p. 340.

was to secure a modification of the Dumbarton Oaks Proposals which would permit regional arrangements to function freely within certain limits without control by the global organization. The other was to seek changes in the Dumbarton Oaks Proposals, particularly as regards the voting procedure of the Council, which would make it possible for Council authorization for regional action to be forthcoming by something more closely approximating a straight majority vote of that body. These various proposals were referred by Committee III/4 to a subcommittee and in the course of the deliberations of this subcommittee draft texts were evolved which gave satisfaction to the Latin American Republics and to others desiring a greater autonomy for regional arrangements. These, of which one subsequently became the Article under consideration, were approved by the Committee [1] and were later included in the Charter.

The place of the Article in question in the Charter was discussed at some length at San Francisco. Committee III/4, which had undertaken to draft the Article, was, under its terms of reference, only empowered to make recommendations with regard to the content of Chapter VIII, Section C of the Dumbarton Oaks Proposals (Chapter VIII, under the new arrangement of the Charter). It, therefore, became technically necessary for the Committee to recommend this Article as a part of this Chapter or as a new Chapter dealing with a related matter. On the other hand, the Article in effect deals with the subject matter of Chapter VII (Chapter VIII, Section B of the Dumbarton Oaks Proposals) and was originally drafted with a view to inclusion as a final paragraph of that Chapter. The recommendation of the Committee was that "the question of the place where the new paragraph should be inserted in the Dumbarton Oaks Proposals should be referred to the Coordination Committee for final decision, with a recommendation, however, that it might constitute a new Section D of Chapter VIII." In the discussion of this matter in Committee the Delegate from the Soviet Union reiterated the view, previously expressed by him in a meeting of the subcommittee, that the adopted paragraph should appropriately be placed as the final paragraph of Section B, Chapter VIII of the Dumbarton Oaks Proposals, and the Chairman of the Committee ruled that this statement be referred to the Coordination Committee for its consideration.[2] The Coordination Committee decided that the Article should take its present position.

The Right of Self-Defense. The Article safeguards the right of self-defense which is referred to as being "inherent." By so doing it follows

[1] UNCIO, *Report of Dr. V. K. Wellington Koo, Rapporteur of Committee III/4, to Commission III*, Doc. 904, III/4/13(1), p. 3.
[2] *Ibid.*, p. 4; also *Summary Report of Fourth Meeting of Committee III/4, May 23, 1945*, Doc. 576, III/4/9, p. 4–5.

a long line of precedents where in connection with international agreements of this kind the right of self-defense has been tacitly or explicitly reserved. In connection with the Kellogg-Briand Pact of 1928 which contained no explicit reservation of the right of self-defense, the American Secretary of State, Mr. Kellogg, observed that the right was inherent and that there was no necessity of stating it expressly.[1]

The problem presented is a difficult one since any attempt to maintain international peace and security against disturbance by the unilateral action of one state of necessity involves restricting the right of any state to resort to the use of force. Since states commonly justify the resort to the use of armed force on the ground of self-defense, it becomes clear that as a practical matter the limitation of the right of any state to use force involves a definition of the permissive limits of self-defense. One approach to the problem is to seek to define specifically those acts which are regarded as constituting the unjustifiable use of force, or as it is more commonly termed, "aggression." As we have seen the architects of the Charter deliberately decided not to undertake a definition of aggression, leaving it to the Security Council to decide in each case whether a particular act constitutes a threat to the peace or a violation of the peace. We do find, however, in this Article some limits placed upon the unlimited exercise of this right of self-defense. It is, for example, stated that the right of self-defense which is here safeguarded is that which exists "if an armed attack occurs against a Member of the United Nations." Furthermore this right of independent action exists only "until the Security Council has taken the measures necessary to maintain international peace and security." However, it is not made clear who is to determine when this requirement has been satisfied.

Right of "Collective Self-Defense." The Article goes beyond safeguarding the inherent right of self-defense. It introduces the words "individual or collective," thereby making it clear that the right referred to is not only the right of an individual state to take action if an armed attack occurs against it, but also that of a group of states to take action when any member of that particular group is the victim of an armed attack. The reason for the word "collective" is obvious. It covers a situation which might arise under a regional arrangement such as the Act of Chapultepec or the peacetime agreement between the American Republics envisaged under Part II of that instrument. It is to be noted, however, that whereas the Act of Chapultepec refers both to acts of aggression and to threats of aggression, the provisions of Article 51 are more restricted, applying only to "an armed attack."

[1] Identic note of the Government of the United States to the Governments of Australia, Belgium, etc., and accompanying Draft Multilateral Treaty for the Renunciation of War, June 23, 1928, in *General Pact for Renunciation of War, Text of the Pact as Signed, Notes and Other Papers*, Washington, D. C., 1928.

Does the use of the word "collective" envisage exclusively action under a limited agreement such as the Act of Chapultepec or does it also permit action by two or more states without any definite commitment in advance, simply on the basis of common interest in meeting successfully a common danger? There does not appear to be anything in the commonly accepted meaning of the word or in the record of discussions at San Francisco to exclude the second possibility. In fact, in thus safeguarding the right of collective self-defense the Article provides the opportunity for Members of the United Nations to act together in self-defense if any armed attack occurs and if the Security Council fails to take the measures necessary to maintain or restore peace. Such failure can conceivably occur since, by the terms of Article 27, a decision of the Security Council must be concurred in by all the permanent members of the Council.

The Article as a Safeguard of the Monroe Doctrine. From the point of view of the United States, this Article has an added importance in that it provides at lease a partial basis for the continued application of a traditional policy of that country, namely, the Monroe Doctrine. It is probably open to some question whether under this Article the United States enjoys the full freedom of action to implement this policy which it would enjoy were it not a Member of the United Nations. The Monroe Doctrine originally laid down two principles: one was to the effect that the United States would look with disfavor upon any attempt on the part of European, later interpreted to include all non-American, countries to extend their political systems to the Western Hemisphere; the second brought any attempt on the part of a non-American state to colonize further the Western Hemisphere under a similar ban of disfavor.[1] In recent years the United States has indicated a willingness to place the enforcement of these principles, in the first instance, on a collective basis. By the Declaration of Lima of 1938 [2] all the American Republics announced their common concern and their determination to make effective their solidarity in opposing any threat to the peace, security or territorial integrity of any American Republic. At Havana in 1940 the American Republics stated that any attempt on the part of a non-American state against the integrity or the inviolability or against the territorial, the social or the political independence of any American state would be considered an act of aggression against all American states.[3] The provisions of the Act of Chapultepec have already been referred to.

These agreements, however, have not in effect touched the original right of the United States to take action in case the cooperative measures

[1] See Perkins, Dexter, *Hands Off*, Boston, Little, Brown, 1941.
[2] *Documents on American Foreign Relations, I, 1938–1939*, p. 44.
[3] *Ibid., III, 1940–1941*, p. 76.

provided for fail of their desired effect. The question which arises under Article 51 is whether by the terms of this Article the United States reserves the right to take necessary measures to resist acts falling into the two categories above referred to in the exercise of the inherent right of self-defense which the Article clearly recognizes within defined limits. The view has been expressed that there is nothing in the Charter which limits our right of self-defense or "that impairs the Monroe Doctrine as a doctrine which has been proclaimed, sustained, and recognized by the world as a doctrine of self-defense." [1] It is possible to accept this interpretation if it means that in case the United Nations fails in its efforts to maintain peace and security, the United States would have the right to take necessary action in self-defense. It would, however, seem clear that by becoming a Member of the United Nations and accepting the commitments of the Charter, even with the reservation contained in Article 51, the United States will not be free to take certain measures in the exercise of self-defense which we have felt free to take in the past. It will be necessary, first of all, to give the Security Council a chance to deal with the situation and it will be only in case of an armed attack that action can be taken in advance of or apart from any action which the Security Council may see fit to adopt. Of course any permanent member of the Security Council can, if it wishes to take a non-cooperative attitude, assure the failure of that body in the performance of its functions.

Effect on Authority of Security Council. The final question to be considered in connection with this Article is the amount of effective control by the Security Council which remains. It is to be borne in mind that under the regional provisions of the Dumbarton Oaks Proposals no enforcement action under regional arrangements was to be taken without the Security Council's authorization. Article 51 clearly opens the way to the taking of such measures by individual states or groups of states acting in agreement where the individual state or the members of a group are engaged in resisting an armed attack. This power of independent action exists until the Security Council has taken the measures necessary to maintain international peace and security. In view of the fact that a decision of the Security Council requires the concurrence of all the permanent members of the Council, it thus becomes clearly possible for any permanent member of the Security Council to postpone the taking of such measures if it seems in its interest to do so. The theory of the Article would appear to be that the Security Council will take measures which after a time will supersede those taken in individual or collective self-defense, or under regional arrangements. To maintain the principle of Security Council control and supervision, provi-

[1] See testimony of John Foster Dulles in *Hearings . . . on The Charter of the United Nations,* etc., cited above, p. 650–1.

sion is made that measures taken by individual Members in the exercise of self-defense shall be immediately reported to the Security Council and shall not in any way affect the authority and responsibility of the Security Council under the present Charter. It becomes clear, then, that whether or not this Article opens the way for wholly independent and autonomous action by Members or groups of Members, without effective control by the organ of the United Nations made responsible for the maintenance of international peace and security, will depend in practice upon the good faith shown by Members of the Organization and their ability to cooperate effectively.

CHAPTER VIII

REGIONAL ARRANGEMENTS

ARTICLE 52

1. Nothing in the present Charter precludes the existence of regional arrangements or agencies for dealing with such matters relating to the maintenance of international peace and security as are appropriate for regional action, provided that such arrangements or agencies and their activities are consistent with the Purposes and Principles of the United Nations.

Reasons for Inclusion. This paragraph lays down the general principle that "regional arrangements or agencies for dealing with such matters relating to the maintenance of international peace and security as are appropriate for regional action" are permissible under the Charter so long as they are consistent with the Purposes and Principles of the United Nations.

The express acceptance of this principle in the Charter was apparently dictated by a number of considerations. In the first place, it recognizes the undoubted fact that national interest and national capacity to exercise power effectively are governed, even in the era of air communications and travel, by geographical location, distances, natural barriers and economic and political development. The policies of states must take these fundamental factors into account and it would likewise seem to be prudent to base any international system on the admitted fact that states are less interested in and less capable of influencing the course of events in some parts of the world than in others. In the second place, that fact of gradation of national interests has found expression in national policies. The Monroe Doctrine is a policy of the United States based on a recognition of our special concern with the affairs of the Western Hemisphere. The failure of the United States to join the League of Nations was in large part due to the belief that we were being called upon to assume commitments that far exceeded our interests in certain areas.

Finally, in the historical evolution of international organization for purposes of peace and security the first emphasis has been on cooperation between those similarly situated with respect to interests which are to be served by such arrangements. The treaties of alliance entered into before 1914 were limited to those who faced a common danger of attack. Under the Covenant of the League of Nations, regional arrangements were entered into such as the Little Entente, the Balkan Entente and the Locarno Agreements. Briand's proposal for European Union[1] was a more ambitious attempt along this line. In fact the League itself tended to be primarily concerned with the affairs of Europe. Reference has already been made to the development of an Inter-American peace system. The League of Arab States is the latest example of such a regional arrangement.[2]

While these and other considerations can be advanced in support of recognition of regional arrangements in any global system for peace and security, there are undoubtedly other considerations, likewise based on historical experience, which point to the need for great caution in admitting such arrangements into a universal system. For one thing they have too often in the past been directed against particular states and have been the occasion for fear and suspicion instead of inspiring confidence and cooperation. Treaties of alliance were condemned by President Wilson as a weak reed upon which to base international peace and security. Furthermore, they tend to emphasize limited commitments, whereas modern war and the increasing interdependence of the modern world reduce the possibility of thinking in such terms. Recent experience has shown how war spreads to engulf all nations. It therefore becomes increasingly true that peace is indivisible. These considerations, therefore, point to the need of keeping commitments general, while limiting the application of the regional principle to the practical operation of peace machinery or the strategic use of enforcement measures in dealing with a threat to the peace or a violation of the peace.

Certainly this problem of regionalism was one of the most important faced at San Francisco. The exact nature of the balance that was struck and the way that balance is applied in practice may determine the future success of the Organization.

Meaning of "Regional Arrangements." The exact meaning of "regional arrangements or agencies" is not made clear although it is suggested by the qualifying words which follow and by the place that these provisions had in the Dumbarton Oaks Proposals that such arrangements or agencies will have to do with the matters covered by Chapters VI and VII of the Charter. In the course of the discussions at San Francisco a proposal was made by the Egyptian Delegation to introduce a defini-

---

[1] League of Nations, *Documents Relating to the Organization of a System of European Federal Union*, Geneva, League of Nations Document 1930. VII. 4; *Memorandum on the Organization of a Regime of European Federal Union addressed to Twenty-six Governments of Europe*, by M. Briand, Foreign Minister of France, *May 17, 1930*, N. Y., Carnegie Endowment, *International Conciliation*, Special Bulletin, June 1930.

[2] UNCIO, *The Pact of the League of Arab States, Signed in Cairo, March 22, 1945*, Doc. 72, III/4/1.

tion of regional arrangements into this Chapter.[1] The amendment proposed read as follows:

There shall be considered as regional arrangements organizations of a permanent nature grouping in a given geographical area several countries which, by reason of their proximity, community of interests or cultural, linguistic, historical or spiritual affinities, make themselves jointly responsible for the peaceful settlement of any disputes which may arise between them and for the maintenance of peace and security in their region, as well as for the safeguarding of their interests and the development of their economic and cultural relations.

This amendment was considered by the subcommittee of Committee III/4 and by the Committee and was rejected on the ground that while it "clearly defined obvious legitimate and eligible factors for a regional arrangement" it probably failed to cover all the situations which might be covered by regional arrangements.[2] The phrase "regional arrangements" as used in this and other articles of the Charter obviously does have a wider scope than the Egyptian amendment would admit. In Article 53, as we shall see, it is made to apply to mutual assistance treaties entered into between states which are wholly lacking in geographical propinquity or in the other common interests enumerated in the Egyptian proposal.

The question of extending the provisions regarding regional arrangements to include regional arrangements with regard to economic and social matters was discussed at San Francisco. The matter was not considered as coming within the competence of the Committee concerned with the drafting of the provisions of this Chapter.[3] The Committee on Economic and Social Cooperation decided against the regional approach to the matters with which it was concerned.[4]

Much of the comment on Article 51 bears on the general question of the place of regional arrangements in the Charter system.

2. The Members of the United Nations entering into such arrangements or constituting such agencies shall make every effort to achieve pacific settlement of local disputes through such regional arrangements or by such regional agencies before referring them to the Security Council.

This paragraph was introduced at the United Nations Conference as a part of the compromise there worked out for fitting a system of regional

---

[1] Ibid., Interim Report to Committee III/4 by Subcommittee III/4/A on the Amalgamation of Amendments, Doc. 533, III/4/A/9, May 23, 1945, p. 3.

[2] Ibid., Summary Report of Fifth Meeting of Committee III/4, June 8, 1945, Doc. 889, III/4/12, p. 1.

[3] Ibid., Interim Report to Committee III/4 on the Work of Subcommittee III/4/A, Doc. 335, III/4/A/5, p. 1; also Summary Report of Third Meeting of Committee III/4, May 15, 1945, Doc. 363, III/4/7, p. 1.

[4] Ibid., Summary Report of the Nineteenth Meeting of Committee II/3, June 4, 1945, Doc. 780, II/3/53, p. 3.

agencies and arrangements into the general system. It is to be interpreted in relation to the provisions of Article 33. Under Article 33 the
Members of the United Nations undertake in the first instance to seek
a solution of any dispute whose continuance is likely to endanger the
maintenance of international peace and security by peaceful means of
their own choice. A number of such peaceful means are listed including
"resort to regional agencies or arrangements." Under the provisions
of Article 33, however, no particular order of preference is indicated.

The provisions of the paragraph under consideration, however, specify
that Members of the United Nations, entering into such arrangements
or constituting such agencies, "shall make every effort to achieve pacific
settlement of local disputes through such regional arrangements or by
such regional agencies before referring them to the Security Council." It
thus gives priority to "resort to regional agencies or arrangements"
so far as "local disputes" are concerned.

The term "local disputes" is apparently to be interpreted as referring
to disputes which exclusively involve states which are parties to such
regional arrangements. The paragraph requires that before these are
brought before the Security Council by the parties to them, the parties
are to make every effort to settle them under such regional arrangements.
It places no obligations, however, upon the Security Council to refrain
from action.

**3. The Security Council shall encourage the development of pacific
settlement of local disputes through such regional arrangements or by
such regional agencies either on the initiative of the states concerned or
by reference from the Security Council.**

This paragraph, on the other hand, obligates the Security Council to
encourage the development of pacific settlement of local disputes, by
such regional agencies as have been agreed to or set up by the parties.
It specifies further that the Security Council is to do this either by
encouraging the parties concerned to use such procedures or by direct
reference of the disputes by the Security Council to regional agencies.
This idea of reference of disputes by the Security Council to regional
agencies seems to be a new one, not wholly in harmony with the procedures laid down in Chapter VI of the Charter. Under the Articles of
Chapter VI the Security Council only has the power to recommend
directly to the parties procedures to be followed in the settlement of their
disputes, or the actual terms of settlement. It is, therefore, difficult to
see how the Security Council can actually refer a dispute to a regional
agency except upon the agreement of the parties concerned. What is
apparently meant is that when the Security Council has before it a
local dispute, which has been called to its attention under the provisions
of Article 35, it is to refer the matter to the appropriate regional agency,

if such exists, on the basis of the undertaking into which the parties have entered under paragraph 2, for such action as the agency in question is empowered to take under the agreement establishing it. See also the provisions of Article 36, paragraphs 2 and 3, and comment.

4. This Article in no way impairs the application of Articles 34 and 35.

Under this Article the power of the Security Council to investigate a dispute either upon its own initiative or upon the initiative of a state, whether a Member of the United Nations or not, for the purpose of determining whether the continuance of the dispute or situation is likely to endanger the maintenance of international peace and security, is safeguarded. The absence of any reference to Articles 36 and 37 raises the question whether the provisions of this Article are intended to exclude any intervention by the Security Council for the purpose of recommending a procedure for settlement or for the purpose of recommending terms of settlement. The over-all responsibility placed upon the Security Council under Article 24 for the maintenance of international peace and security, taken together with the specific provisions of Articles 36 and 37, would seem to warrant the interpretation that under Article 52 there is no intention to deny to the Security Council the power to exercise its normal functions, if it becomes clear that the dispute is not being settled by regional arrangements or by regional agencies and that there is a situation in which the maintenance of international peace and security is actually endangered.

ARTICLE 53

1. The Security Council shall, where appropriate, utilize such regional arrangements or agencies for enforcement action under its authority. But no enforcement action shall be taken under regional arrangements or by regional agencies without the authorization of the Security Council, with the exception of measures against any enemy state, as defined in paragraph 2 of this Article, provided for pursuant to Article 107 or in regional arrangements directed against renewal of aggressive policy on the part of any such state, until such time as the Organization may, on request of the Governments concerned, be charged with the responsibility for preventing further aggression by such a state.

The General Principle. The first sentence of this paragraph, taken together with the second sentence down to the excepting clause, lays down the general principle that the Security Council shall, where it considers such action appropriate, utilize regional arrangements and agencies for enforcement action under Chapter VII but no enforcement action shall be taken under such regional arrangements or by such regional agencies without the authorization of the Security Council. Such authorization, by virtue of the provisions of Article 27, paragraph 3, can only be given by a vote of the Security Council concurred in by at least seven members, including all of the permanent members. As we have seen, this would enable a permanent member of the Security Council, outside the area where the regional arrangement applies and not a party to the regional arrangement, to prevent action from being taken under the arrangement even though all other members of the Security Council might be in favor. The provisions of Article 51 provide one avenue of escape from this possible situation as well as from any delays that might occur in connection with normal Council action. The provisions of this paragraph, beginning with the words "with the exception of," indicate two other conditions under which the general principle is not to apply.

Exception of Measures Taken Against Enemy State. The first exception relates to measures taken against any enemy state under the provisions of Article 107 of the Charter. Article 107 is one of the Articles dealing with transitional security arrangements and, by its terms, action in relation to any state which during the second World War has been an enemy of any signatory to the present Charter, taken or authorized as a result of the war by the governments having responsibility for such action under Article 106, is declared to be unaffected by and permissible under the present Charter.

The second exception is more vaguely defined and refers to "regional arrangements" directed against renewal of aggressive policy on the part of any such state. The use of the term "regional arrangements" does not seem too appropriate here since the arrangements to which reference is clearly made may be regarded as regional only in the sense that they are limited as to parties and are directed against a particular state. The parties to the arrangement may be far removed in any geographical sense. The arrangements here referred to include the Treaty of Alliance between the Soviet Union and the United Kingdom, signed at London on May 26, 1942,[1] the Agreement of Friendship and Mutual Assistance between the Soviet Union and the Czechoslovak Republic, signed at Moscow on December 12, 1943,[2] the Treaty of Alliance and Mutual Assistance between the Soviet Union and France, signed at Moscow, December 10, 1944,[3] and the Treaty of Friendship and Alliance between the Soviet Union and the Republic of China, signed at Moscow, August 14, 1945.[4] In each of these treaties the parties undertake to come to each other's assistance in case of attack by the enemy state or states against which it is directed. Only in the case of the United Kingdom-Soviet and the Chinese-Soviet treaties is there any attempt to fit

[1] *Documents on American Foreign Relations, IV, 1941–1942,* p. 254.
[2] *Ibid., VI, 1943–1944,* p. 642.
[3] *The United Nations Review,* V, no. 1, January 15, 1945, p. 9.
[4] *Ibid.,* V, no. 5, September 15, 1945, p. 229.

their provisions into a general security system such as is provided for under the Charter of the United Nations.

This exception in favor of "regional arrangements directed against renewal of aggressive policy" is to operate only until such time as the Organization may "on the request of the Governments concerned" be charged with the responsibility for preventing further aggression. It is interesting to note that the amendment proposed by the Sponsoring Governments covering this point used the words "by consent of" in place of the words "on the request of." [1] The significance of this change would appear to be that under the text as it stands the responsibility for initiative is placed upon the governments concerned and not upon the Organization itself. This would seem to place upon the governments themselves rather than upon the Organization the responsibility for deciding in the first instance whether these special arrangements, partaking very definitely of the character of treaties of alliance, should be allowed to operate without effective control by the Security Council.

2. The term enemy state as used in paragraph 1 of this Article applies to any state which during the Second World War has been an enemy of any signatory of the present Charter.

This paragraph repeats and makes applicable to paragraph 1 the definition which is to be found in Article 106.

ARTICLE 54

The Security Council shall at all times be kept fully informed of activities undertaken or in contemplation under regional arrangements or by regional agencies for the maintenance of international peace and security.

This Article was taken over intact from the Dumbarton Oaks Proposals. It provides that the Security Council shall be kept informed with regard to the activities undertaken or in contemplation under the regional arrangements or by regional agencies referred to in Article 52. It places a definite obligation upon Members and upon regional agencies. Such a provision would seem to be necessary to an effective control by the Security Council of the regional arrangements and agencies here referred to.

[1] UNCIO, *Terms of Reference of Committee III/4*, Doc. 269, III/4/5, p. 1 a.

CHAPTER IX

INTERNATIONAL ECONOMIC AND SOCIAL COOPERATION

ARTICLE 55

With a view to the creation of conditions of stability and well-being which are necessary for peaceful and friendly relations among nations based on respect for the principle of equal rights and self-determination of peoples, the United Nations shall promote:

a. higher standards of living, full employment, and conditions of economic and social progress and development;

b. solutions of international economic, social, health, and related problems; and international cultural and educational cooperation; and

c. universal respect for, and observance of, human rights and fundamental freedoms for all without distinction as to race, sex, language, or religion.

Relations of Economic and Social to Political Provisions of Charter. A question of basic importance is whether or not an organization established primarily for the maintenance of international peace and security should be limited to this function to the exclusion of other functions having to do with the promotion of economic and social well-being and respect for human rights. The decision embodied in the Dumbarton Oaks Proposals was to make the proposed international organization general, not only from the point of view of its membership but also from the point of view of its functions. It was agreed that any organization, established *primarily* for the purpose of maintaining international peace and security, must concern itself with the establishment of those conditions — economic, social and intellectual — which are necessary to the existence of a viable peace. In the absence of such conditions peace and security become precarious things, maintained only by the force which those possessing a selfish interest in the preservation of the *status quo* may be prepared to use.

It is significant that in the setting up of the League system at the conclusion of World War I a similar question arose and was answered in like manner. Part XIII of the Treaty of Versailles, the Constitution of the International Labor Organization, expressly asserted the dependence of international peace on social justice and provided for organized international cooperation with a view to the improvement of the conditions of labor.[1] The Preamble and Article 23 of the Covenant, while not containing nearly as detailed or carefully thought out provisions regarding economic and social cooperation as the pertinent Articles of the Charter, nevertheless recognized the need of cooperative action along these lines as part of any effective program for maintaining peace and provided the basis for the extensive work done by the League in the field of social and humanitarian activities, work which was to prove in the long run the most valuable part of the League's achievement.[2]

Certain provisions of the Preamble of the Charter and of Chapters I and IV, and more particularly the provisions of Chapters IX and X, give expression to this basic idea of the interdependence of international peace and security and conditions of economic and social well-being and human freedom. The provisions of Chapters IX and X provide the implementation of the objectives stated in Article 1, paragraph 3. In the Article now under consideration the interrelation among the objectives of the Organization is emphasized. It is stated that with a view to the creation of conditions of stability and well-being which are necessary for peaceful and "friendly relations among nations based on respect for the principle of equal rights and self-determination of peoples," the United Nations shall promote certain enumerated objectives. The words in quotes are taken verbatim from paragraph 2 of Article I; "peaceful . . . relations" expresses the general idea of paragraph 1; and the detailed objectives constitute a particularization of the broad purposes stated in paragraph 3.

Scope of Organization's Authority. The Article uses the word "promote" whereas the Dumbarton Oaks Proposals [3] employed a somewhat more cautious phraseology using the word "promote" in connection with "respect for fundamental rights and freedoms" but otherwise using the words "facilitate solutions of international . . . problems." The discussions at the United Nations Conference made it clear that there were two dominant interests which were sometimes in conflict. On the one hand, there was a general desire to make the organization an effective agency for achieving international cooperative action in dealing with certain specified matters in the attainment of declared purposes. On the other hand, there were some delegations which were obviously concerned lest the words used would provide the basis for intervention by the Organization in affairs regarded by them as being essentially within the domestic jurisdiction of a state.

[1] See Wilson, Francis G., *Labor in the League System*, Stanford Univ., Calif., Stanford Univ. Press, 1934.

[2] See McClure, Wallace, *World Prosperity as Sought through the Economic Work of the League of Nations*, N. Y., Macmillan, 1933; League of Nations Secretariat, *Ten Years of World Cooperation*, Geneva, 1930; Myers, Denys P., *Handbook of the League of Nations*, Boston, World Peace Foundation, 1935, p. 135–220.

[3] Chapter IX, Section A, paragraph 1, see this volume, p. 316.

The statement of purpose contained in Chapter IX, Section A, paragraph 1, of the Dumbarton Oaks Proposal was substantially revised at San Francisco, not only in the manner indicated above, but also by a revision, which was more than a rephrasing, of the specific purposes to be promoted. To remove any misgivings that might exist that this revised statement would permit interference in the domestic affairs of any Member, the technical committee dealing with economic and social cooperation (Committee II/3) agreed to include in its report the following statement:

The members of Committee 3 of Commission II are in full agreement that nothing contained in Chapter IX (Chapters IX and X of the Charter) can be construed as giving authority to the Organization to intervene in the domestic affairs of member states.[1]

Objectives. The objectives enumerated in Article 55 under *a* are in general self-explanatory. There was considerable discussion of the term "full employment" at the Conference. The drafting subcommittee of Committee II/3 originally recommended the use of the words "high and stable levels of employment." These words were defended as being more realistic and as establishing a goal capable of realization in fact. It was decided, however, by vote of the Committee that the words "full employment" should be used [2] since they had come to be widely accepted as defining the desired goal and since they did not imply a willingness to accept in advance the idea that a substantial amount of unemployment is inevitable.

The objectives listed under *b* represent a refinement of the provisions of the Dumbarton Oaks Proposals. While it probably would be agreed that "economic, social and other humanitarian" problems included "cultural," "health," and "education," it was thought better to have a more detailed enumeration. It was made clear in the course of Committee discussion that the word "economic" was to be interpreted to include, for instance, international trade, finance, communications and transport, and post-war economic reconstruction. It was also agreed that under the head of economic problems should be included the international problems of access to raw materials and capital goods. The Committee also made it clear that it interpreted the words under *b* to include international cooperation in the control of traffic in, and the suppression of the abuse of, opium and dangerous drugs.[3]

The objectives under *c* were taken over from the Dumbarton Oaks Proposals with two changes. One was the addition of the words "for

[1] UNCIO, *Report of the Rapporteur of Committee II/3*, Doc. 861, II/3/55 (1), p. 3–4.
[2] *Ibid.*, *Summary Report of Seventh Meeting of Committee II/3, May 16, 1945*, Doc. 381, II/3/16, p. 1–2.
[3] *Ibid.*, *Report of Rapporteur of Committee II/3*, Doc. 861, II/3/55(1), p. 3; *Revised Report of the Rapporteur of Commission II to the Plenary Session*, Doc. 1180, II/18(1), p. 4.

all without distinction as to race, sex, language or religion." This was one of the proposals of the Sponsoring Governments, and its adoption had the effect of defining more explicitly the application of the principle. The other change consisted of the insertion of the words "and observance of." This was thought by some to strengthen the statement by making it clear that something more than formal respect for the rights and freedoms in question is demanded; the actual observance of these rights and freedoms is also sought.

ARTICLE 56

All Members pledge themselves to take joint and separate action in cooperation with the Organization for the achievement of the purposes set forth in Article 55.

The Dumbarton Oaks Proposals contained no such pledge. Apparently it was to be assumed that the commitment of the Organization contained in the statement of purposes was enough. Some of the governments represented at San Francisco felt, however, that a more specific commitment was necessary to reenforce the statement of purposes and to make it clear that the Members obligated themselves to take individually the action necessary to make the cooperation effective. The original text proposed by the drafting subcommittee of Committee II/3 read as follows:

All Members pledge themselves to take separate and joint action and to cooperate with the Organization and with each other to achieve these purposes.[1]

The United States Delegate reserved her position on the question of phraseology and the matter was referred back to the subcommittee for reconsideration. The subcommittee then recommended the following phraseology:

All Members undertake to cooperate jointly and severally with the Organization for the achievement of these purposes.[2]

Several delegates objected to this phraseology on the ground that it did not contain the threefold pledge which the Committee had in principle approved, i.e. the pledge to take separate action, to take joint action, and to cooperate with the Organization.[3] It was voted to refer the matter back a second time to the drafting subcommittee. The phrase-

[1] *Ibid., Summary Report of Twelfth Meeting of Committee II/3, May 26, 1945,* Doc. 599, II/3/31, p. 1.
[2] *Ibid., Summary Report of the Fourteenth Meeting of Committee II/3, May 29, 1945,* Doc. 684, II/3/38, p. 4.
[3] *Ibid., Summary Report of Fifteenth Meeting of Committee II/3, May 30, 1945,* Doc. 699, II/3/40, p. 1–3.

ology which the subcommittee recommended the third time was found acceptable.[1]

From this abbreviated account of the history of the Article, it is clear that two opposing points of view were pressed at San Francisco. One was that each Member should pledge itself to take independent, separate national action to achieve the purposes set forth in Article 55. This was the view of the Australian Delegation, for example, and found expression in a proposed amendment which perhaps was the original inspiration of this Article. On the other hand, there was the view that such a pledge of separate national action went beyond the proper scope of the Charter which was concerned with encouraging international cooperation, and perhaps even infringed upon the domestic jurisdiction of Member States. This apparently was the view of the American Delegation.

The phraseology finally agreed to was a compromise and like most compromises is capable of more than one interpretation. The question arises with respect to the significance of the qualifying words. "In cooperation with the Organization" presumably refers to the Organization as a separate entity functioning through the appropriate organs, and not to its individual Members; otherwise "joint and separate action in cooperation with the Organization" becomes meaningless. If this is the proper interpretation, it would then appear that Members pledge themselves to cooperate with each other, and also to take joint and separate action along the lines of the recommendations of the organs of the United Nations Organization with a view to achieving the purposes in question. It does not make these recommendations binding but it does require that Member States should take a cooperative attitude toward them in their national action and in their relations with each other. Furthermore, if as the result of the initiative of the Organization, multipartite agreements are drafted and signed, Members, if signatories, are pledged to take action, in accordance with their constitutional procedures, to complete ratification, and, once ratification has occurred, to enact legislation and take other measures necessary to give effect to the terms of the agreement. The International Labor Organization, for example, has experienced considerable difficulty in getting action under conventions once they have been adopted by the Conference,[2] and this pledge is no doubt intended to apply to a like situation. See Article 64 and comment, p. 217.

[1] *Ibid., Summary Report of Seventeenth Meeting of Committee II/3, June 1, 1945,* Doc. 747, II/3/46, p. 1.

[2] See Tayler, William L., *Federal States and Labor Treaties,* N. Y., 1935; *Report of the Committee of Experts on the Application of Conventions,* London, July 27, 1945. *International Labor Conference,* 27th Session, Paris, 1945, Report VI. Appendix, Montreal, Canada, 1945; see also annual *Reports on the Application of Conventions* (Article 22 of the Constitution), International Labor Office, Geneva and Montreal, 1920–1945.

ARTICLE 57

1. The various specialized agencies, established by intergovernmental agreement and having wide international responsibilities, as defined in their basic instruments, in economic, social, cultural, educational, health, and related fields, shall be brought into relationship with the United Nations in accordance with the provisions of Article 63.

Basic Principles. In this paragraph we have recognition of two basic principles governing the United Nations approach to economic and social cooperation. These are (1) the principle that organization is to develop in response to functional need, without any attempt being made at one time to set up an organization which will be equipped to satisfy the many detailed needs that may arise; and (2) the principle that in the economic and social field the general international organization is to limit itself, so far as special-function organizations are concerned, to rendering assistance and coordinating their activities on the basis of agreements freely entered into on both sides. This permits the specialized agencies a large measure of autonomy and results in a more decentralized system than was envisaged under the League Covenant.[1]

Agencies with Wide International Responsibilities. What are the "various specialized agencies, established by intergovernmental agreement and having wide international responsibilities" to which the provisions of this article apply? There would appear to be agencies established by intergovernmental agreement which, because of the fact that their international responsibilities are not wide, are not covered by the provisions of this Article. In *Observations on Relationships with Specialized Agencies*, prepared by the Executive Committee of the Preparatory Commission and recommended for transmission to the General Assembly, the distinction is made between an "intergovernmental agency," the term used to describe any agency established by intergovernmental agreement whether it is to be brought into relationship with the United Nations Organization or not, and a "specialized agency," the term used to describe the particular type of intergovernmental agency coming within the definition of Article 57, that is, having wide international responsibilities as defined in its basic instrument.[2] Clearly, such recently established organizations as the United Nations Food and Agriculture Organization and the United Nations Educational, Scientific, and Cultural Organization are to be regarded as having "wide responsibilities" under the terms of this Article. The same can certainly be said of the International Labor Organization, established at the

---

[1] On advantages of such functional decentralization, see Mitrany, David, *A Working Peace System*, N. Y., Oxford Univ. Press, Post-War Problems, 1943, 56 p.

[2] *Report by the Executive Committee to the Preparatory Commission of the United Nations*, cited above, p. 102, note.

end of World War I, even though some opposition to bringing it into relationship with the United Nations Organization has arisen because of the basis of its organizational structure. On the other hand, there can be some question as to whether agencies such as the Universal Postal Union and the International Telegraphic Union are to be regarded as having "wide responsibilities" in the sense in which the words are here used. It would seem that in order for an agency to qualify as one having wide responsibilities it must have broader purposes and functions than the promotion of administrative cooperation within special technical fields such as postal communications, protection of industrial property, etc. Such an interpretation does not exclude, however, the possibility that the Organization will make recommendations under its broad powers in the non-political field with a view to bringing these organizations into a closer relationship with the Organization.

In its *Observations on Relationships with Specialized Agencies* above referred to, the Executive Committee of the Preparatory Commission commented as follows:

There were a large number of independent bureaux and agencies functioning before the war, and it is thought that more suitable organizational arrangements could be made for the exercise of the functions hitherto entrusted to many of them. It may be desirable for some to continue to function and to be brought into relationship with the United Nations. In a few cases, the process of merging pre-war agencies with newly established agencies is already taking place. The total number of older agencies should, however, be reduced and brought into a more rational and unified organizational structure. The following alternatives. might be followed in achieving this end:

(*a*) liquidation of the bureau or agency with a transfer of some or all of its functions to a specialized agency;

(*b*) liquidation of the agency and arrangements made for the exercise of its functions under appropriate commissions or committees within the United Nations;

(*c*) merger with another intergovernmental agency.[1]

The term "wide international responsibilities" apparently has a geographical connotation as well. An agency which is purely regional in membership and in the scope of its responsibilities is not to be regarded as subject to the provisions of this Article, though not outside the possible scope of recommendations by the General Assembly and the Economic and Social Council. This was the view taken in the Report of the Executive Committee to the Preparatory Commission.[2]

Nature and Scope of Obligation. This Article makes it mandatory upon the Organization and upon its Members to undertake to bring into relationship with it the various specialized agencies with wide international responsibilities, to which reference is made. This obligation applies not only to existing agencies but also to those which may be established in the future. It was stated in the Report of the Rapporteur

[1] *Ibid.*, p. 102.   [2] *Ibid.*

of Committee II/3 at the United Nations Conference that the wording of this Article was not intended "to preclude the Economic and Social Council from negotiating at its discretion, subject to the approval of the General Assembly, agreements bringing other types of intergovernmental agencies into relationship with the Organization." [1] This, however, is not an obligation but a discretionary power. As stated in the *Observations*, above quoted, "in addition to negotiating agreements with the specialized agencies which have wide international responsibilities, the Economic and Social Council may, at its discretion, negotiate agreements with such other intergovernmental agencies, including those of a regional character, as are not considered as being within the definition of Article 57, but which it is desirable to bring into relationship." [2]

Specialized Agencies Established or in Process of Establishment. A number of specialized agencies, established by intergovernmental agreement and having wide international responsibilities as defined in their basic instruments have already been, or are in the process of being established. These include:

(1) *The International Labor Organization.* This was established at the end of World War I under the terms of the treaties of peace as a part of the League system of international cooperation. The Constitution [3] provided for the establishment of a permanent organization for the improvement of labor conditions throughout the world. The Organization consists of a General Conference, a Governing Body, and an International Labor Office. In the Governing Body and the General Conference, employers and employees are represented along with governments. In many respects the International Labor Organization was tied into the League of Nations, notably by the provision that its expenses should be paid out of the general funds of the League.

The United States, although never joining the League of Nations, became a Member of the International Labor Organization in 1934 by executive agreement. The Organization continued to function on a limited basis during the war. At the 26th meeting of the General Conference held at Philadelphia in 1944, a Declaration of Aims and Purposes, known as the "Philadelphia Charter," [4] was adopted which sets forth the broad purposes of the Organization for the future. Fifty-two states were members of the Organization as of November 1, 1945, including 40 of the signatories of the United Nations Charter. [5]

[1] UNCIO, Doc. 861, II/3/55(1), p. 4.
[2] *Report by the Executive Committee to the Preparatory Commission of the United Nations*, cited above, p. 102.
[3] Part XIII of the Treaty of Versailles. On organization and activities of the I.L.O., see Wilson, cited above.   [4] Department of State, *Bulletin*, X, p. 482.
[5] The United Nations which are not members of the I.L.O. are the Soviet Union, the Ukranian S.S.R., the Byelorussian S.S.R., Paraguay, Nicaragua, Guatemala, El Salvador, Honduras, Saudi Arabia, Syria, Lebanon and the Philippine Commonwealth.

At the United Nations Conference, it was proposed that specific reference should be made in the Charter to the International Labor Organization as the agency which would be primarily concerned with promoting "improved labor standards, economic advancement and social security."[1] Committee II/3 voted, however, when it became obvious that there was strong opposition in certain quarters to such reference, to omit any such provision and even to omit a paragraph in the Draft Report of the Rapporteur containing such a reference.[2] It was apparent, however, that, for the most part, the delegations at San Francisco were prepared to recognize the International Labor Organization as the agency primarily responsible for promoting improved labor standards.

At the sixth meeting of Committee II/3 on May 15, 1945, the chairman of the Governing Body of the International Labor Organization informed the Committee that the Governing Body had adopted unanimously a statement affirming the desire of the International Labor Organization for association with the United Nations. He stated that the International Labor Organization needed enough freedom of action within the new framework to discharge its responsibilities and particularly to assure that the voice which the workers and employers exercised in world affairs through the Organization remained a real one. The Governing Body recognized, he said, that it would be necessary to alter the Constitution of the Organization in order to provide the necessary links with the United Nations, and was in course of examining the constitutional changes necessary to enable it to do its own work better.[3]

At the 27th Session of the International Labor Conference, held at Paris, October 15–November 5, 1945, the pledge of cooperation with the United Nations Organization in pursuit of the objectives set forth in the Charter, the Constitution of the International Labor Organization and the Declaration of Philadelphia was reaffirmed. It was stated to be the desire of the I.L.O. to enter into relations with the United Nations Organization on terms, to be determined by agreement, which would permit the I.L.O. "in which the representatives of workers and employers enjoy equal status with those of governments" to cooperate fully for the attainment of these ends, while retaining the authority necessary for the discharge of its responsibilities under its Constitution and the Declaration of Philadelphia. The Governing Body was authorized to enter into such agreements with the appropriate authorities of the United Nations, subject to the approval of the Conference, as might be necessary or desirable for this purpose. An Instrument for the Amend-

---

[1] UNCIO, *Proposed Amendments to the Dumbarton Oaks Proposals*, Doc. 157, II/3/5, p. 10, 14.

[2] *Ibid.*, *Draft Report of the Rapporteur of Committee II/3*, Doc. 823, II/3/55, June 6, 1945, p. 5; *Summary Report of Twenty-first Meeting of Committee II/3, June 8, 1945*, Doc. 876, II/3/58, p. 1–2.

[3] *Ibid.*, Doc. 346, II/3/13, p. 2 and Addendum, Doc. 804, II/3/12 (a).

ment of the Constitution of the International Labor Organization was adopted on November 5,[1] which, when it enters into force, will have the effect of severing all relations with the League of Nations,[2] and placing the I.L.O. on an autonomous basis, with the authority to enter into such relations with the United Nations Organization as are envisaged in this and other articles of the Charter. A resolution was also adopted supporting close collaboration and exchange of information with other specialized agencies.[3]

(2) *The United Nations Relief and Rehabilitation Administration.* This organization was established under an agreement signed at Washington, November 9, 1943,[4] and has the following purposes: (a) "to plan, coordinate, administer or arrange for the administration of measures for the relief of victims of war in any area under the control of any of the United Nations," and "to facilitate in such areas, so far as necessary to the adequate provision of relief," the production and transportation of necessary articles and the furnishing of necessary services; (b) "to formulate and recommend" measures for the coordination of purchasing, the use of ships, and other procurement activities for the above purposes; and (c) to study, formulate and recommend measures with respect to certain related matters.

The organization functions through a Council, on which each member has a representative; a Central Committee; certain special committees; and a Director-General with staff. The organization has its own budget. By the very nature of its functions, it is not to be regarded as permanent in nature, but for the period of its existence its relations to other specialized organizations and to the United Nations Organization will undoubtedly be of the greatest importance, particularly when it comes to dealing with problems of reconstruction. Forty-four states are members of UNRRA, all Members of the United Nations Organization.

(3) *The International Monetary Fund.* This organization is provided for under the terms of the Articles of Agreement of the International Monetary Fund, which is Annex A of the Final Act of the United Nations Monetary and Financial Conference, held at Bretton Woods, July 1–22, 1944.[5] Forty-four states were signatories of the Final Act. By the terms

[1] International Labor Conference, 27th Session, Paris, 1945, Instrument for the Amendment of the Constitution of the I.L.O. adopted November 5, 1945, Paris.

[2] *Ibid., Resolution Concerning the Relationship between the I.L.O. and the United Nations,* Paris, 1945.

[3] *Ibid., Resolution Concerning Reciprocal Relationship between the International Labor Organization and Other International Bodies,* Paris, 1945.

[4] United States, *Executive Agreement Series* 352, Washington, D. C., 1944, Department of State Publication 2075; *Documents on American Foreign Relations, VI, 1943–1944,* p. 251.

[5] *United Nations Monetary and Financial Conference, Bretton Woods, New Hampshire, July 1 to July 22, 1944, Final Act and Related Documents,* Washington, D. C., 1944, Department of State Publication 2187 (Conference Series 55), p. 28.

of Article XX, the Agreement was to enter into force when signed on behalf of governments having sixty-five percent of the total of the quotas set forth in Schedule A and when instruments of acceptance had been deposited on their behalf. The Agreement entered into force on December 27, 1945, following the signature of the Agreement and the deposit of instruments of acceptance by 29 governments, signatories of the Bretton Woods Final Act, whose subscriptions to the Fund amounted to 65 percent of the total. The Soviet Union has not as yet signed the Agreement and deposited its instrument of acceptance.

The principal purposes of the International Monetary Fund are: (1) "to promote international monetary cooperation through a permanent institution which provides the machinery for consultation and collaboration on international monetary problems"; (2) "to facilitate the expansion and balanced growth of international trade"; (3) "to promote exchange stability, to maintain orderly exchange arrangements among members, and to avoid competitive exchange depreciation"; and (4) "to assist in the establishment of a multilateral system of payments in respect of current transactions between members and in the elimination of foreign exchange restrictions which hamper the growth of foreign trade."

Except where otherwise provided, operations on account of the Fund are to be limited to transactions for the purpose of supplying a member with currency of another member in exchange for gold or for the currency of the member desiring to make the purchase. The extensive powers are to be exercised by a Board of Governors, upon which Members are to be equally represented; by the Executive Directors (not less than 12), to be appointed in such a way as to give the five Members with the largest quotas permanent representation; and by a Managing Director and staff. Voting power is to be related to the size of the national quota.

It is expressly provided that the Fund shall cooperate "within the terms of this Agreement with any general international organization and with public international organizations having specialized responsibilities in related fields." [1] Any arrangement for cooperation involving a modification of the Agreement can be effected only after amendment of the Agreement according to the terms of Article XVII.

(4) *The International Bank for Reconstruction and Development.* This is provided for under the terms of the Articles of Agreement constituting Annex B of the Bretton Woods Final Act, referred to above.[2] Forty-four states were signatories of the Final Act. By the terms of Article XI, the Agreement was to enter into force when it had been signed on behalf of governments whose minimum subscriptions comprised not less than sixty-five percent of the total subscriptions set forth in Schedule A and when instruments of acceptance had been deposited on their behalf. The Agreement entered into force on December 27, 1945, following the sig-

[1] Articles of Agreement, Article X, *ibid.*, p. 44.   [2] *Ibid.*, p. 68.

nature of the Agreement and the deposit of instruments of acceptance by 29 governments, signatories of the Bretton Woods Final Act, whose subscriptions to the Fund amounted to 65 percent of the total. The Soviet Union has not as yet signed the Agreement and deposited its instrument of acceptance.

The Bank will have the following primary purposes: (1) "to assist in the reconstruction and development of territories of members by facilitating the investment of capital for productive purposes"; (2) to promote private foreign investment, and, when private capital is not available for productive purposes on reasonable terms, to supplement private investments; and (3) "to promote the long-range balanced growth of international trade and the maintenance of equilibrium in balances of payments by encouraging international investment for the development of the productive resources of members." The operations of the Bank are to consist of making or facilitating loans for the specified purposes under conditions set forth in the Articles of Agreement. The Bank is to perform its functions through a Board of Governors, on which each member state will be represented, with voting power largely determined by the number of shares of stock held; the Executive Directors, of whom five shall be appointed by the member states having the largest number of shares; and a President, to be selected by the Executive Directors. Provision is made for an Advisory Council of not less than seven members, including representatives of industrial, commercial, agricultural and banking interests with as wide national representation as possible.

The relationship of the Bank to other international organizations is governed by provisions identical with those already described in the case of the Fund.[1] In addition, however, it is provided that "in making decisions on applications for loans or guarantees relating to matters directly within the competence of any international organization of the types specified in the preceding paragraph and participated in primarily by members of the Bank, the Bank shall give consideration to the views and recommendations of such organization." [2]

(5) *The United Nations Food and Agriculture Organization.* This Organization is provided for in the Constitution presented in the First Report of the Interim Commission on Food and Agriculture, published August 1, 1944.[3] The Interim Commission was established under agreement reached at the United Nations Conference on Food and Agriculture, held at Hot Springs, Virginia, May 3, 1943,[4] and was convened in Washington on July 15, 1943. Following acceptance by twenty of the

[1] Articles of Agreement, Article V, Section 8 Paragraph (*a*), *ibid.*, p. 82.

[2] Paragraph (*b*), *ibid.*

[3] *First Report to the Governments of the United Nations by the Interim Commission on Food and Agriculture*, Washington, D. C., August 1, 1944, p. 41.

[4] Department of State, *Bulletin*, VIII, p. 546.

states declared eligible for original membership, Members of the United Nations, the Constitution entered into force, and the Organization was formally established at a Conference convened in Quebec, October 16, 1945, when delegates of 30 nations, including the United States, signed the Constitution.[1]

The Organization has as its purposes the raising of levels of nutrition and standards of living, the securing of improvements "in the efficiency of the production and distribution of all food and agricultural products," and the bettering of the conditions of rural populations, "thus contributing toward an expanding world economy." The functions of the Organization are to "collect, analyze, interpret and disseminate information relating to nutrition, food and agriculture"; to promote and, where appropriate, recommend national and international action with respect to research, the improvement of education and administration, the conservation of natural resources, the improvement of methods of processing, marketing and distribution, the provision of adequate agricultural credit, and the adoption of international policies with respect to agricultural commodity arrangements; and to furnish such technical assistance as governments may request. The Organization performs these functions through a Conference in which each member state has one representative; an Executive Committee, of nine to fifteen members, to be appointed by the Conference; and a Director-General and staff.

Article XII of the Constitution provides that the Conference may enter into agreements with the competent authorities of "other public international organizations with related responsibilities" defining "the distribution of responsibilities and the methods of cooperation." More particularly, the Director-General may, subject to any decision of the Conference, "enter into agreements with other public organizations for the maintenance of common services, for common arrangements in regard to recruitment, training, conditions of service and other related matters, and for interchanges of staff." Article XIII provides that the Organization shall "in accordance with the procedure provided for in the following paragraph, constitute a part of the general international organization to which may be entrusted the coordination of the activities of international organizations with specialized responsibilities." The procedure prescribed is as follows:

Arrangements for defining the relations between the Organization and any such general organization shall be subject to the approval of the Conference. Notwithstanding the provisions of Article XX, such arrangements may, if approved by the Conference by a two-thirds majority of the votes cast, involve modification of the provisions of this Constitution: Provided that no such arrangements shall modify the purposes and limitations of the Organization as set forth in this Constitution.

[1] *Ibid.*, XIII, p. 619. The Soviet Union was not among the signatories and its representatives attended the conference as observers, *ibid.*, p. 726.

(6) *International Civil Aviation Organization.* This Organization is provided for under the terms of the Convention on International Civil Aviation, constituting Appendix II of the Final Act of the International Civil Aviation Conference, held at Chicago, November 1 to December 7, 1944.[1] The Convention was originally signed by representatives of 39 states. Of these 7 are not Members of the United Nations Organization. Six Members of the United Nations Organization, including the Soviet Union, were not signatories. An Interim Agreement signed by the representatives of 41 states provided for a provisional international organization pending the entrance into force of the Convention. By the terms of Article 91 of the Convention it is to enter into force on the thirtieth day after the deposit of the twenty-sixth instrument of ratification. As of January 10, 1946, one state, Poland, had deposited its instrument of ratification of the Convention.

The objectives of this Organization are set forth in some detail in the Convention and include, among others, the following: (1) to insure the "safe and orderly growth of international civil aviation throughout the world"; (2) to "encourage the development of airways, airports and air navigation facilities for international civil aviation"; (3) to meet world needs for safe, regular, efficient, and economical air transport; (4) and to promote generally the development of all aspects of international air transport. The functions vested in the Organization with a view to the furtherance of these purposes include investigation and research, the collection and publication of information, reporting on infractions of the Convention, adoption of international standards and recommended practices, and the making of recommendations to Member States. Provision is made for an Assembly with equal representation and equal voting power for all members; a Council composed of 21 members elected by the Assembly, with adequate representation of states important for purposes of air transport and of the different geographic areas; an Air Navigation Commission; and a Secretariat. The functions of these organs are defined in some detail. The Assembly is to vote the budget and decide the apportionment of expenses.

The Convention provides (Article 64) that the Organization may, "with respect to air matters within its competence directly affecting world security, by vote of the Assembly enter into appropriate arrangements with any general organization set up by the nations of the world to preserve peace." The Council, under the terms of Article 65, "may enter into agreements with other international bodies for the maintenance of common services and for common arrangements concerning personnel and, with the approval of the Assembly, may enter into such other arrangements as may facilitate the work of the Organization."

[1] *International Civil Aviation Conference, Chicago, Illinois, November 1 to December 7, 1944, Final Act and Related Documents*, Washington, D. C., 1945, Department of State Publication 2282 (Conference Series 64), p. 59.

(7) The *United Nations Educational, Scientific, and Cultural Organization* was provided for under the terms of an instrument signed at London on November 16, 1945, by representatives of 44 of the United Nations.[1] Article XV of the Constitution provides that it shall come into force when accepted by twenty of its signatories. A decision was taken at the Conference to establish the seat of the Organization in Paris, subject to the right of the General Conference to take a new decision by a two-thirds vote.

In the Preamble the Governments of the states parties to the Constitution "on behalf of their peoples" declare "that since wars begin in the minds of men it is in the minds of men that the defenses of peace must be constructed" and "that a peace based exclusively upon the political and economic arrangements of Governments would not be a peace which could secure the unanimous, lasting and sincere support of the peoples of the world and that the peace must, therefore, be founded, if it is not to fail, upon the intellectual and moral solidarity of mankind." For these and other stated reasons, the states parties to the Constitution, "believing in full and equal opportunities for education for all in the unrestricted pursuit of objective truth and in the free exchange of ideas and knowledge," declare themselves "agreed and determined to develop and to increase the means of communication between their peoples and to employ these means for the purposes of mutual understanding and a truer and more perfect knowledge of each other's lives."

In Article I of the Constitution the purpose of the Organization is stated to be "to contribute to peace and security by promoting collaboration among the nations through education, science and culture in order to further universal respect for justice, for the rule of law and for the human rights and fundamental freedoms which are affirmed for the peoples of the world without distinction of race, sex, language or religion by the Charter of the United Nations."

To realize this purpose, the Organization is to have the following functions:

(1) To "collaborate in the work of advancing the mutual knowledge and understanding of peoples through all means of mass communication and to that end recommend such international agreements as may be necessary to promote the free flow of ideas by word and image";

(2) To encourage popular education and the spread of culture by collaborating with members "at their request" in the development of educational activities, by collaboration to advance the ideal of equality of educational opportunity, and by suggesting educational methods best suited to prepare children for the responsibilities of freedom;

(3) To "maintain, increase and diffuse knowledge" by assuring the conservation and protection of the world's cultural inheritance, and by

---

[1] For text of Final Act, see Department of State, *Bulletin*, XIII, p. 801.

"encouraging cooperation among the nations in all branches of intellectual activity," including the international exchange of persons active in the fields of education, science and culture, and the exchange of publications, objects of artistic and scientific interest, and other materials of information, and by initiating methods of international cooperation calculated to give the people of all countries access to the printed and published materials produced by any of them.

Membership in the United Nations Organization carries with it the right to membership in the United Nations Educational, Scientific, and Cultural Organization. States which are not Members of the first may be admitted to the latter upon the recommendation of the Executive Board by a two-thirds vote of the General Conference. The functions of the Organization are to be performed by the General Conference, in which each Member is to be equally represented, the Executive Board, and the Director-General and his staff.

The Organization is to be brought into relationship with the United Nations Organization by an agreement made in accordance with the terms of Article 63 of the Charter. This agreement is to be subject to the approval of the General Conference of UNESCO. It is stated that the agreement shall provide for effective cooperation between the two Organizations in the pursuit of common purposes and "at the same time shall recognize the autonomy of this Organization within the fields of its competence as defined in this Constitution." It is specifically stated that the agreement may provide, among other things, for the approval of the budget of the Organization by the General Assembly of the United Nations.

Article XI of the Constitution authorizes the Organization to cooperate with other specialized intergovernmental organizations and agencies whose interests and activities are related to its purposes. To this end, the Director-General, acting under the general authority of the Executive Board, may establish effective working relationships with such organizations and agencies. Any formal arrangements are to be subject to the approval of the Executive Board.

Other Organizations. This list includes only those specialized organizations for the establishment of which agreements have been made, with one exception, during or since World War II. It does not include organizations (except for the I.L.O.) which were set up in the interwar period either as parts of the League system or to achieve certain of its purposes, and which in some cases will undoubtedly continue. Nor does it include organizations which in all likelihood will be provided for in agreements to come. In the course of the committee discussions at San Francisco, the United States expressed the hope, in which it was supported by the Canadian, Chinese, and Indian Delegates, that existing agencies intrusted with the supervision over existing or future agreements with regard to the control of the legitimate traffic in opium and other dangerous drugs and the suppression of the illicit traffic in and abuse of such drugs would be regarded as autonomous agencies to be brought into relationship with the United Nations.[1] No decision was taken at the United Nations Conference with respect to the continuation of the technical organizations of the League, such as the Economic and Financial Organization, the Health Organization,[2] and the Communications and Transit Organization.[3] This whole question was referred to the Preparatory Commission for recommendations. Furthermore, additional specialized agencies will undoubtedly be established, either to replace organizations which are allowed to pass from the picture, or to meet new needs. There appears, for example, to be good ground for believing that an international trade organization will be established to deal with matters of commercial policy and the regulation of international trade practices.

2. Such agencies thus brought into relationship with the United Nations are hereinafter referred to as specialized agencies.

This paragraph seems to assume that all the "specialized agencies" referred to in paragraph 1 of Article 57 will be brought into relationship with the United Nations in the manner described in Article 63. That clearly is the intention of Article 57 since, as we have seen, it is a definite obligation of Members to see that the agreements referred to in Article 63 are entered into.

ARTICLE 58

The Organization shall make recommendations for the coordination of the policies and activities of the specialized agencies.

The substance of this Article appeared in the Dumbarton Oaks Proposals as paragraph 7 of Chapter V, Section B, dealing with the functions and powers of the General Assembly. Its present form and position in the Charter resulted from a considerable rearrangement by the Coordination Committee of the draft recommended by Committee II/3. As

[1] UNCIO, *Summary Report of the Nineteenth Meeting of Committee II/3, June 4, 1945*, Doc. 780, 11/3/53, p. 4.

[2] There was general support at the United Nations Conference for an international health organization but it was not thought to be the proper function of the Conference to provide for such an organization, either by taking over the League of Nations Health Organization or by creating an entirely new organization. *Ibid., Summary Report of the Thirteenth Meeting of Committee II/3, May 28, 1945*, Doc. 658, 11/3/36, p. 1.

[3] By an agreement between the United States and other powers, signed at London on May 8, 1945, there was established the European Central Inland Transport Organisation, which will serve as a coordinating and consultative organ. "The Organization shall cooperate as may be required with the appropriate authorities and agencies of any one or more of the United Nations and with international organisations" (Article VII, par. 19). United States, *Executive Agreement Series* 458, Washington, D. C., 1945, Department of State Publication 2387.

the result of the changes made, the original proposal has not been altered except in form. Since, by the terms of Article 60, it is the General Assembly in which is vested original responsibility for the discharge of the functions of the Organization, it is the General Assembly which will have the responsibility for making the recommendations here referred to. However, the Economic and Social Council, acting under Article 63, paragraph 2, may also make such recommendations, but will do so "under the authority of the General Assembly." [1]

The "specialized agencies" referred to in this Article are those which have been brought into relationship with the United Nations according to the terms of Article 63.

It is to be noted that the authority of the Organization to coordinate the policies and activities of the specialized agencies is limited to the making of recommendations. These will undoubtedly have great weight, since the governments represented in the specialized agencies will for the most part be the same governments that are represented in the General Assembly of the United Nations. However, differences in the voting rules of the various organs of the Organizations and of the specialized agencies may create difficulties in this connection.

The provisions of this Article are sufficiently general to cover the matter of budgetary control. This is specifically dealt with, however, in another part of the Charter, Article 17, paragraph 3. See comment on Article 17, paragraph 3, and Article 63, paragraph 1.

ARTICLE 59

The Organization shall, where appropriate, initiate negotiations among the states concerned for the creation of any new specialized agencies required for the accomplishment of the purposes set forth in Article 55.

A basic assumption of the Charter system, as we have already seen, is that the needs of international cooperation for special purposes should be met as those needs arise by agreement of the interested parties. Certain of these needs have already been met. Others are in the process of being met. Considerable areas remain where the establishment of specialized agencies will probably be needed. Under the terms of the Charter, the Members of the United Nations recognize the need of cooperative action in these fields, and pledge themselves to take joint action to achieve specified purposes. It is to be assumed, then, that on the initiative of the Members themselves, and even of non-members, new specialized agencies required for the accomplishment of the purposes set forth in Article 55 will be created. In addition, however, the Organization itself, acting through the General Assembly and the Economic

---

[1] *Charter of the United Nations*, Article 60.

and Social Council, is given the function of initiating negotiations among the states concerned with a view to the creation of such agencies. The specific powers necessary to the performance of this function are conferred upon the General Assembly by Articles 10 and 13 and upon the Economic and Social Council by Article 62.

At San Francisco, there were numerous proposals for the establishment of specialized agencies, such as an international health agency (proposed by the Brazilian Delegation), an International Organization for Cultural Cooperation (proposed by the French Delegation), an International Institute for Educational, Social, Cultural, and Intellectual Cooperation (proposed by the Venezuelan Delegation), and an International Office of Migration (proposed by the Panamanian Delegation). The French Delegation pressed with particular earnestness for the setting up of an international organization to deal with problems of equal access to raw materials and capital goods. The technical committee decided, however, that there should be no mention in the Charter of the creation of any particular specialized organization. It was thought that it would be misleading to mention one or two fields without mentioning others, and that it would be better to leave the whole matter to the informed judgment of the General Assembly and the Economic and Social Council.[1]

In its *Observations on Relationships with Specialized Agencies*, the Executive Committee of the Preparatory Commission suggested the following alternatives as being available under the Charter for developing international cooperation and agencies in fields where these are not as yet adequate for the attainment of the purposes of the Organization:

(a) the initiation of negotiations among the states concerned for the creation of a new specialized agency, in accordance with Article 59 of the Charter;

(b) the establishment of a commission or committee by the Economic and Social Council (under Article 68);

(c) the creation of a subsidiary organ by the General Assembly, in accordance with Article 22 of the Charter;

(d) a recommendation by the Economic and Social Council to an existing specialized or other intergovernmental agency to undertake additional functions (under Article 62).[2]

ARTICLE 60

Responsibility for the discharge of the functions of the Organization set forth in this Chapter shall be vested in the General Assembly and, under the authority of the General Assembly, in the Economic and Social Council, which shall have for this purpose the powers set forth in Chapter X.

[1] UNCIO, *Report of the Rapporteur of Committee II/3*, Doc. 861, II/3/55 (1), p. 5.
[2] *Report by the Executive Committee to the Preparatory Commission of the United Nations*, cited above, p. 102.

In the previous Articles of this Chapter, functions of the United Nations in respect to international economic and social cooperation are defined. Article 60 lays down the principle that responsibility for the discharge of these functions is vested in the General Assembly and, under its authority, in the Economic and Social Council. Thus while the Security Council is made primarily, not exclusively, responsible for the maintenance of international peace and security, it is the General Assembly which is made responsible for the promotion of human welfare and freedom. This Article, together with Articles 10, 13 and 14, provides the basis for the expectations of many that the General Assembly will become in time the dominant agency of the United Nations, since in the years to come, as political conditions become more stable, people are bound to be primarily concerned with matters of human freedom and welfare.

Under the Covenant of the League, the Council was not excluded from directly concerning itself with matters in this field. Under the Charter, however, the function of the Security Council is restricted to peace and security matters. The Economic and Social Council in which is vested the exercise of executive powers and functions in this field is to act "under the authority of the General Assembly."

The provision for a separate Economic and Social Council represents an important departure by the Charter from the League system.[1] The Covenant provided for one Council with broad powers which became differentiated in practice from those of the Assembly in such a manner that the Council became in a sense the "executive" organ of the League while the Assembly was the "legislative" body. One result of this arrangement was that since the Great Powers insisted on permanent representation on the Council, largely because of its political functions, they also acquired a privileged position when that organ was dealing with social and economic affairs. This dominance of the Council by the Great Powers was thought by many to constitute a drag on the economic and social work of the League. Furthermore, since the Council was primarily a political organ, its exercise of economic and social functions was open to the objection that its members allowed political considerations to influence them unduly when the Council was called upon to deal with economic and social problems.

Following the collapse of the League security system and the progressive deterioration of the international political situation in the years 1936 to 1939, an attempt was made to salvage the League as an agency for economic and social cooperation by establishing a separate economic and social organization within the League framework. The so-called

[1] For discussion of the Economic and Social Council, particularly its place in international economic cooperation, see Finer, Herman, *The United Nations Economic and Social Council*, Boston, World Peace Foundation, 1945.

Bruce Committee, appointed by the Council on May 27, 1939, issued a report on August 22 of that year [1] in which after reviewing the nature and extent of the economic and social work of the League, it recommended that the Assembly should set up a new organ to be known as the Central Committee for Economic and Social Questions, to which would be entrusted the direction and supervision of the work of the League Committees dealing with economic and social questions. It was proposed that this Committee should consist of the representatives of twenty-four states chosen by the Assembly and that eight unofficial members should be co-opted on the ground of their special competence and authority. This report was adopted by the Assembly but never put into effect.[2]

On the basis of League experience up to that time, the Bruce Committee concluded that the establishment of such a Central Committee on Economic and Social Questions, distinct from the Council, would increase the efficiency of the League's work in the social and economic field, and, in particular, would bring this part of the League's work under the supervision of an agency "which should be both effective and representative," would provide more effective coordination of the activities of the different specialized organizations in the field, would "add fresh vigor and efficiency" to the work through increasing public knowledge of it and making it the primary interest of the directing organ, and would give non-member states the opportunity of the fullest cooperation in the work "as well as in its direction and supervision." It is obvious of course that not all of these considerations are equally valid today but certain of them were undoubtedly influential in leading to the establishment of a separate Economic and Social Council.

[1] Special Supplement to the *Monthly Summary of the League of Nations*, August 1939; also published as League of Nations Document 1939. General. 3, N. Y., Columbia Univ. Press, agents.

[2] The decision in 1940 to send part of the Economic, Financial and Transit Departments on mission to Princeton, N. J. for the duration of the war greatly facilitated the research and publication program on post-war problems and policies in these fields. The activities are carried on by a Director and twelve officials, assisted by a staff of economists and statisticians, and secretarial assistants. Besides the work at Princeton, twelve officials of the Economic Intelligence Service are pursuing, in Geneva, publication of statistical bulletins and yearbooks.

CHAPTER X

THE ECONOMIC AND SOCIAL COUNCIL

Composition

ARTICLE 61

1. The Economic and Social Council shall consist of eighteen Members of the United Nations elected by the General Assembly.

The provisions of this Article should be compared with Article 23 defining the composition of the Security Council. From this comparison it will be seen that whereas in the Security Council, by the explicit provisions of the Charter, the Great Powers are given a privileged position. in the case of the Economic and Social Council there is no special provision assuring Great Powers membership. This represents an advance over the League system from the point of view of the application of the principle of equality since under the Covenant of the League the Council, which performed functions of a character comparable to those conferred upon the Economic and Social Council, was constituted in such a way as to give the great powers permanent membership. As has been explained in the comment on Article 60, one reason why the proposal to establish a separate Economic and Social Council met with such wide support was that it made possible the application of the principle of equality of representation to the composition of the council dealing with economic and social matters.

This paragraph provides that the members of the Economic and Social Council shall be elected by the General Assembly. Not only are there no provisions assuring membership to particular states but also there are no criteria incorporated in the Charter for the guidance of the General Assembly which might be expected to have the effect of assuring certain states membership in the Council. In the Constitution of the International Labor Organization there is the provision that eight of the government representatives on the Governing Body shall be appointed by the Member States of chief industrial importance. At San Francisco a proposal was made by the Canadian and French Delegations which was intended to assure Members of chief industrial importance membership in the Council. These proposals were withdrawn, however, when it became clear that the prevailing view of the delegations was that no such formal discrimination should be established.[1]

[1] UNCIO, *Summary of Report of Ninth Meeting of Committee II/3, May 21, 1945,* Doc. 493, II/3/21, p. 2.

It was the view of the technical committee, accepted by the Conference, that the General Assembly should be left absolutely free in the election of members of the Council. It was, however, assumed in the course of discussion that industrially important states would naturally be elected to membership, and, since members of the Council are declared eligible for immediate re-election, the same result in fact can be achieved as if certain members were given permanent membership. In principle, however, the freedom of action of the General Assembly is safeguarded.

2. Subject to the provisions of paragraph 3, six members of the Economic and Social Council shall be elected each year for a term of three years. A retiring member shall be eligible for immediate re-election.

The Dumbarton Oaks Proposals provided for three-year terms without any provision, however, for overlapping of membership. It was felt at San Francisco that it was desirable to have some assurance of continuity of membership, other than that contained in the provision permitting re-election. See comment above on additional significance of provision permitting re-election of a member whose term is expiring.

3. At the first election, eighteen members of the Economic and Social Council shall be chosen. The term of office of six members so chosen shall expire at the end of one year, and of six other members at the end of two years, in accordance with arrangements made by the General Assembly.

In order to carry out the principle of rotation it was necessary, of course, to decide upon some mechanism by which the members of the Council after the initial elections might be placed in the three categories. Consideration was given to a plan whereby originally there would be three classes of members, to be elected for terms of one, two and three years respectively. It was considered desirable, however, that initially all members should be elected without designation as to whether their terms were to run for one, two or three years, and that subsequently arrangement would be made to divide the members elected into the three categories. The drafting subcommittee of Committee II/3 proposed that this determination should be made by drawing lots. It was finally decided, however, that the specific plan to be followed should be determined by the General Assembly.

4. Each member of the Economic and Social Council shall have one representative.

This accords with the rule of Article 23, paragraph 3, applying to the Security Council and that of Article 86, paragraph 2, applying to the Trusteeship Council.

Functions and Powers

ARTICLE 62

1. The Economic and Social Council may make or initiate studies and reports with respect to international economic, social, cultural, educational, health, and related matters and may make recommendations with respect to any such matters to the General Assembly, to the Members of the United Nations, and to the specialized agencies concerned.

The provisions of this Article and of the following Articles relating to the functions and powers of the Economic and Social Council constitute considerable elaboration of the comparable provisions of the Dumbarton Oaks Proposals. Members of Committee II/3 of the United Nations Conference at San Francisco were in agreement in seeking to strengthen the provisions of the Charter for economic and social cooperation, and particularly to strengthen the position of the Economic and Social Council, by introducing a much more detailed and, in some respects, more comprehensive definition of the functions and powers of that body.

This particular paragraph is a case in point. Under the terms of paragraph 1*b* of Chapter IX, Section C, of the Dumbarton Oaks Proposals the Economic and Social Council was to be empowered "to make recommendations, on its own initiative, with respect to international economic, social and other humanitarian matters." At San Francisco this provision was expanded in three respects. In the first place the Council is specifically empowered to "make or initiate studies and reports" with respect to such matters. It was felt that this specific grant of authority was needed to provide an adequate basis for the power to make recommendations although it might clearly be argued that it was implied in the power to make recommendations. This power to make and initiate studies and reports was used extensively by the organs of the League of Nations to provide important factual material which was available to League organs and to Members.

In the second place, the Article specifies in greater detail the matters with regard to which the Economic and Social Council may make or initiate studies and reports and make recommendations. The words "cultural," "educational" and "health" were inserted to cover specifically matters which were perhaps covered by implication by the more general phraseology of the Dumbarton Oaks Proposals, but the delegates at San Francisco were insistent that they should be included to avoid any possibility of doubt. This elaboration was in line with changes made in other Articles of the Charter, notably Article 1, paragraph 3, and Article 13, paragraph 1.

In the third place, this paragraph makes it clear that the recommendations to be made by the Economic and Social Council may be directed to the General Assembly, to the Members of the United Nations, or to the specialized agencies concerned. Since the Economic and Social Council functions under the authority of the General Assembly, it might, perhaps, have been assumed in the absence of such particularization that recommendations were to be made only to the General Assembly.

Since the General Assembly has the responsibility under the terms of Articles 13 and 60 of making recommendations to Members and the specialized agencies, the question arises as to whether conflicting recommendations are not possible. The answer would seem to be that the Economic and Social Council, in performing the functions and powers vested in it under Articles 62 and 66, acts "under the authority of the General Assembly" (Article 60) and therefore must conform to general directives of that organ. In case of conflict, the General Assembly has the power to resolve the conflict in its favor.

2. It may make recommendations for the purpose of promoting respect for, and observance of, human rights and fundamental freedoms for all.

It is to be noted that under the terms of this paragraph the Economic and Social Council is not specifically empowered "to make or initiate studies and reports." There is nothing in the record of the discussions at San Francisco to indicate that there was any intention to differentiate between the powers of the Economic and Social Council under paragraph 1 and its powers under paragraph 2. This particular paragraph was introduced as a result of a proposal made by the Sponsoring Governments themselves. It would seem that the grant of power to make recommendations for the enumerated purposes would necessarily imply the power to make or initiate studies leading up to the making of recommendations. It would also seem to be implied, particularly in the light of provisions of the previous paragraph, that these recommendations may be directed to the General Assembly, to the Members of the United Nations or to any specialized agency which may be concerned with these matters.

3. It may prepare draft conventions for submission to the General Assembly, with respect to matters falling within its competence.

No provision for the granting of such power was contained in the original Dumbarton Oaks Proposals. Under the Constitution of the I.L.O. the General Conference is empowered to draw up draft conventions for submission to the Member States. The Assembly of the League of Nations at its second session declared itself competent to draft conventions by direct action and did so in four instances, although there was no specific grant of such authority in the Covenant.[1] At the United

[1] See Burton, Margaret E., *The Assembly of the League of Nations*, Chicago, Univ. of Chicago Press, 1941, p. 243–66.

Nations Conference one of the amendments proposed by the Australian Delegation was to the effect that the Economic and Social Council should be empowered to initiate conventions dealing with the matters enumerated in the statement of purposes.

The question of explicitly empowering the General Assembly to initiate draft conventions was considered by another Committee, namely Committee II/2, and was decided in the negative, although, as it has been pointed out in connection with the comment on Article 13, it would appear that such power is implicit in the other powers given to that body. When the matter of empowering the Economic and Social Council to prepare draft conventions for submission to the General Assembly was before Committee II/3 for discussion, attention was called to the action taken by Committee II/2 on a more general question, but the Committee nevertheless felt that it was able to deal with the more limited proposition before it and voted unanimously in favor of the text as found in substance in this paragraph. It can be assumed, it would seem, that this specific grant of authority is quite in line with the provisions of the Charter relating to the general powers of the General Assembly for reasons given earlier.[1]

4. It may call, in accordance with the rules prescribed by the United Nations, international conferences on matters falling within its competence.

This is also a new provision inserted at San Francisco in response to a proposal of the Australian Delegation. The Australian proposal was to the effect that the Economic and Social Council should be empowered to call a conference in case of an economic emergency to consider and recommend action for safeguarding and promoting the economic and social purposes of the Charter.[2] In the course of consideration by the technical committee and its drafting subcommittee the view prevailed that there was no good reason for limiting this grant of power to an emergency situation. It was decided that this grant of power to call international conferences should extend to all matters falling within the competence of the Council but that the power should be exercised according to rules to be prescribed by the United Nations, that is, by the General Assembly. The authority conferred upon the Economic and Social Council by this paragraph is comparable to that vested in the League Council under the more general provisions of the Covenant which made it possible for that body to call international conferences, such as the International Economic Conference held at Geneva in May 1927, when circumstances seemed to warrant it.

[1] See comment on Article 13, this volume, p. 101.
[2] UNCIO, *Proposed Amendments to the Dumbarton Oaks Proposals*, Doc. 157, II/3/5, p. 21.

ARTICLE 63

1. The Economic and Social Council may enter into agreements with any of the agencies referred to in Article 57, defining the terms on which the agency concerned shall be brought into relationship with the United Nations. Such agreements shall be subject to approval by the General Assembly.

Under the provisions of this paragraph the Economic and Social Council is specifically empowered to enter into agreements with various specialized agencies referred to in Article 57, defining the relationships of these agencies to the United Nations. This paragraph thus provides for the implementation of the first paragraph of that Article. In the course of Committee discussions at San Francisco it was made clear that the initiative in the making of such agreements might be taken by the specialized agencies themselves.[1] The effect of the paragraph then is not to limit the initiative in the making of such agreements to the Economic and Social Council but rather to empower the Economic and Social Council to represent the United Nations in the making of these agreements. The agreements are to be subject to approval by the General Assembly.

The content of the agreement defining the terms on which a given agency is to be brought into relationship with the United Nations Organization is of course a matter for negotiation. Some of the items which will be included are suggested by the provisions of different articles of the Charter. Other items may be included because it is found that the agreement provides the best method of dealing with the matters concerned. After all, the Charter places no limitation on the range of matters to be covered, other than the limitations placed upon the special agency by its constitution and upon the United Nations Organization by the Charter. The purpose of the agreement presumably will be to establish the kind of relationship which will be most conducive to the attainment of common purposes, while allowing to the specialized agency that measure of autonomy which is necessary to the most effective performance of its special functions and responsibilities.

In its *Observations on Relationships with Specialized Agencies*, the Executive Committee of the Preparatory Commission listed a number of subjects which were deemed appropriate for inclusion in the agreements or for suitable action by the General Assembly or the Economic and Social Council. The list included subjects to which specific reference is made in the Charter as well as others to which no specific reference is made. It was explained that all or most of the items enumerated in both categories "should figure in the agreements with those specialized

[1] *Ibid., Summary Report of Sixteenth Meeting of Committee II/3, May 31, 1945,* Doc. 725, II/3/42, p. 1–2.

agencies whose range of functions with regard to economic, social or related matters is extensive, but all should not necessarily figure in the agreements with specialized agencies whose range of functions is less extensive." [1]

The subjects suggested for inclusion are the following: reciprocal representation (Article 70); exchange of information and documents; liaison, in case headquarters are in different places; participation of specialized agencies in activities of a Coordination Commission, proposed to be established by the Economic and Social Council; proposal of agenda items; rules of procedure; consideration of recommendations of General Assembly and Economic and Social Council (Articles 58, 62 and 63); reports by specialized agencies (Article 64); assistance in carrying out decisions of Security Council (Articles 41 and 48); assistance to Trusteeship Council (Article 91); requests for advisory opinions (Article 96); requests for information by the International Court of Justice (Article 34 of the Statute); budgetary and financial relations (Article 17, paragraph 3); common fiscal services; personnel arrangements; privileges and immunities (Article 105); establishment of administrative tribunal; provision for common technical services; central statistical service; and location of headquarters.

The importance of these agreements is clear in view of the fact that they are to provide the legal basis for the exercise by the General Assembly and the Economic and Social Council of the coordinating functions which are vested in these organs of the United Nations. The intergovernmental agreements which have thus far been negotiated or entered into with a view to establishing such specialized agencies have made provision in a number of instances for participation in such agreements by the agencies concerned. The specific provisions contained in intergovernmental agreements thus far made are given in the comment on Article 57 above.

2. It may coordinate the activities of the specialized agencies through consultation with and recommendations to such agencies and through recommendations to the General Assembly and to the Members of the United Nations.

This paragraph corresponds to paragraph 1 *c* of Chapter IX, Section C of the Dumbarton Oaks Proposals. It provides, however, that the recommendations to be made by the Economic and Social Council may be directed not only to the agencies concerned but also to the General Assembly and to the Members of the United Nations. It thus broadens the scope of the Council's activities and increases considerably the potential effectiveness of the Council as a coordinating body. Notwith-

[1] *Report by the Executive Committee to the Preparatory Commission of the United Nations,* cited above, p. 103.

standing the fact, however, that the Council is empowered to make recommendations directly to Members of the United Nations, the likelihood is very great that its recommendations will be directed in the first instance to the General Assembly, and that the General Assembly will make such recommendations as are to be directed to the Members of the Organization. This would seem to be the logical development in view of the fact that the primary responsibility for the discharge of the functions which the Organization assumes under Article 58 is vested in the General Assembly itself.

ARTICLE 64

1. The Economic and Social Council may take appropriate steps to obtain regular reports from the specialized agencies. It may make arrangements with the Members of the United Nations and with the specialized agencies to obtain reports on the steps taken to give effect to its own recommendations and to recommendations on matters falling within its competence made by the General Assembly.

It is to be noted that this empowers the Council to "take appropriate steps" and to "make arrangements" without, however, placing upon the specialized agencies or upon the Members of the United Nations any obligation to cooperate on their side in achieving the desired result. As has been pointed out above, the obligations of the specialized agencies and the procedures to be followed will presumably be defined by the agreements referred to in paragraph 1 of Article 63.

The nature of the arrangements to be made with the Members of the United Nations to obtain reports on steps taken to give effect to recommendations of the Council and the General Assembly is somewhat less clear. Presumably one means, and the most effective means, would be to get Members of the United Nations to agree under an agreement initiated by the Council to make the reports in question either at regular intervals or upon request. The Article as it stands does not, however, place upon Members of the United Nations the obligation to make such reports.

The experience of international organizations in the past, particularly the I.L.O., shows how important it is that information should be available upon the steps actually taken by Member States to give effect to recommendations of the kind here referred to. The I.L.O. has found that the drafting and adoption of labor conventions to be submitted to Member States for their consideration as recommendations of the Conference often present fewer difficulties than obtaining favorable action by Member States subsequently. The Economic and Social Council is given no authority to take coercive action against any Member of the United Nations or against any agency which refuses to carry out its recommendations or those of the General Assembly. It is, however, important to the exercise of any moral suasion that full facts should be available with regard to the steps which have been taken.

2. It may communicate its observations on these reports to the General Assembly.

This empowers the Economic and Social Council to communicate its observations on these reports to the General Assembly for such action as that body may see fit to take. This provision would seem to be unnecessary in view of the fact that the General Assembly as the organ under whose authority the Economic and Social Council acts should be able, in the absence of any specific provision, to require such reports from the Council. Such observations may have great value in providing the basis for Assembly discussions.

ARTICLE 65

The Economic and Social Council may furnish information to the Security Council and shall assist the Security Council upon its request.

The substance of this Article was contained in the Dumbarton Oaks Proposals. The phraseology has been somewhat modified. The first part of the Article empowers the Economic and Social Council to give information to the Security Council. The second part places upon the Council the obligation to assist the Security Council upon its request. This second part of the Article presumably covers the furnishing of information but might conceivably extend to other forms of assistance although any assistance given would presumably have to be in line with the Council's general functions and powers under the Charter.

One of the objections commonly made to having two separate councils, as the Charter provides, is that it opens the way to conflicts and lack of cooperation between the two organs in dealing with matters of common concern. This danger is thought to be particularly likely to arise when one of the two organs, as is the case under the Charter, is relatively independent and not responsible to the representative body to which the other must answer. This Article attempts to deal with that situation in part by assuring the Security Council the cooperation of the Economic and Social Council in matters that come within its competence. Presumably it is left to the Security Council to decide the form of assistance which the Economic and Social Council is to give and the Economic and Social Council is obligated to give the form of assistance required unless it finds itself in the position where it cannot so act for lack of authority.

Since the powers of the Economic and Social Council are limited for the most part to fact-finding and making recommendations, it becomes clear that the assistance which the Economic and Social Council will be called upon to give will be largely of the nature referred to in the first part of this Article. The Security Council may, however, in addition to asking for information in the usual sense of the term, also ask advice upon technical matters concerning which the Economic and Social Council will be thought to have special competence, as for example, in connection with the application of economic and financial measures under Article 41. Conceivably, too, it may ask the Economic and Social Council to take such action as it is empowered to take under agreements made with the specialized agencies.

ARTICLE 66

1. The Economic and Social Council shall perform such functions as fall within its competence in connection with the carrying out of the recommendations of the General Assembly.

The reason for this paragraph is not clear. In view of the relationship of the Economic and Social Council to the General Assembly established by Article 60, it would seem obvious that the Council is to perform functions in connection with the carrying out of the recommendations of the General Assembly. The use of the words "as fall within its competence" would not seem to constitute any special limitation in view of the fact that paragraph 3 recognizes the power of the General Assembly to assign to the Council functions not otherwise specified in the Charter.

The ambiguity of the paragraph is largely the result of last-minute changes by the Coordination Committee of the text recommended by Committee II/3. The technical committee recommendation, following more closely the original Dumbarton Oaks text as to arrangement, placed this general grant of authority at the beginning of the enumeration of the Council's functions and powers. Besides, both in the original Dumbarton Oaks text and in the Committee draft, the power conferred was "to carry out, within the scope of its functions, recommendations of the General Assembly." There is a serious question as to whether the text of the Charter actually conveys the meaning intended by the original Committee text, since the phraseology of this paragraph and its place in the Chapter suggests that the power that is granted is more limited and less important than the Committee's text would have indicated.

2. It may, with the approval of the General Assembly, perform services at the request of Members of the United Nations and at the request of specialized agencies.

This paragraph is new in the sense that there was no provision of a comparable nature in the Dumbarton Oaks Proposals. It makes it possible for the Economic and Social Council to perform special services at the request of the Members of the United Nations and at the request of the specialized agencies such as were performed by the technical services of the League of Nations for Members of the League. China, for example, in the thirties received special assistance from the League in connection with the development of its health and communications services. This kind of assistance can be rendered to Members of the United Nations by the Economic and Social Council in the future, provided, of course, the General Assembly gives its consent.

3. It shall perform such other functions as are specified elsewhere in the present Charter or as may be assigned to it by the General Assembly.

This paragraph is to be considered in connection with provisions of Article 60. That Article states that the Economic and Social Council in carrying out the functions placed upon it shall "have for this purpose the powers set forth in Chapter X." That might be interpreted as restricting the power of the Economic and Social Council and, more particularly, the import of the words "under the authority of the General Assembly." This paragraph of Article 66 makes it clear, however, that the effect of this reference is not restrictive since the Council is specifically authorized to perform such other functions as may be assigned to it by the General Assembly in the exercise of powers and functions vested in it by the Charter.

Voting

ARTICLE 67

1. Each member of the Economic and Social Council shall have one vote.

Compare with the provisions of Article 18, paragraph 1, and Article 27, paragraph 1, applying to the General Assembly and the Security Council respectively.

2. Decisions of the Economic and Social Council shall be made by a majority of the members present and voting.

While the General Assembly can only decide important matters such as those enumerated in Article 18, paragraph 2, by a two-thirds vote of the members present and voting, decisions that need to be taken in connection with the exercise of its functions under Chapters IX and X can presumably be taken by a majority of those present and voting. The rule of this paragraph is therefore fully in harmony with the rule governing the voting procedure of the General Assembly.

The Constitution of the I.L.O. provides that, except where there is provision to the contrary, decisions shall be taken by a majority vote. The adoption of proposed labor conventions for submission to Members of the Organization requires a two-thirds vote of the General Conference. It is to be noted that the decisions of the Economic and Social Council will generally be of such a nature as not to create any specific obligations for Members. The decisions will be on proposals to organize studies, make recommendations, and call conferences.

Procedure

ARTICLE 68

The Economic and Social Council shall set up commissions in economic and social fields and for the promotion of human rights, and such other commissions as may be required for the performance of its functions.

The interpretation of this Article presents some difficulty due in part to the circumstances under which it was drafted. The Dumbarton Oaks Proposals provided in Chapter IX, Section D, paragraph 1, that the Economic and Social Council should set up an economic commission, a social commission and such other commissions as might be required. At the United Nations Conference in San Francisco considerable pressure was brought to bear to extend the number of commissions specifically referred to. In particular the proposal was made that a commission for the promotion of fundamental human rights should be included in the list. It was recognized, however, that it was necessary to leave some discretion to the Council since all specific needs could not be foreseen. As a compromise it was agreed to add the commission for the promotion of human rights to the list of commissions whose establishment is obligatory and to empower the Economic and Social Council to set up such additional commissions as may be required for the performance of its functions. This leaves a certain amount of latitude to the Economic and Social Council with regard to the specific commissions to be established, not to mention the inevitable latitude which is left to the Council in determining the specific functions which these commissions are to perform in their relation to the other organs of the United Nations and to the specialized agencies.

The Executive Committee of the Preparatory Commission in its report on the organization of the Economic and Social Council gave careful consideration to the problem of establishing commissions under this Article. In reaching its conclusions regarding the number and character of the commissions which should be set up immediately, it was guided by five major considerations: [1]

1. The specific fields in which international economic and social cooperation is required are diverse and call for treatment by more or

[1] *Ibid.*, p. 50.

less specialized bodies. In some of these fields international governmental agencies exist or are contemplated.[1] In others, specialized functions might be entrusted to commissions or committees of the Economic and Social Council. Undesirable duplication should be avoided.

2. Complex economic and social problems of the gravest urgency, arising out of the war, will demand immediate attention by the Economic and Social Council.

3. Provision will have to be made for the continuance of certain functions and activities of the League of Nations.

4. There is need for flexibility in the number of commissions, the scope of their activities, and the powers delegated to them.

5. Due consideration should be given to the importance of coordinating activities in fields which are closely related.

Taking these considerations into account the Executive Committee recommended the establishment of the following Commissions:

(a) Commission on Human Rights,
(b) Economic and Employment Commission,
(c) Temporary Social Commission,
(d) Statistical Commission,
and possibly
(e) Demographic Commission,
(f) Temporary Transport and Communications Commission.

It was decided at San Francisco to omit one provision contained in the Dumbarton Oaks Proposals. This was the requirement that the commissions should consist of experts. It was felt that it might be desirable to appoint to these commissions persons other than experts and that the Economic and Social Council should be given freedom to decide what was wise.

ARTICLE 69

The Economic and Social Council shall invite any Member of the United Nations to participate, without vote, in its deliberations on any matter of particular concern to that Member.

This Article should be compared with Article 31. By the latter, a Member of the United Nations which is not a member of the Security Council may participate without vote in the discussion of any question when the Council considers that the interests of that Member are specially affected. By the Article under consideration, the Economic and

[1] The Executive Committee assumed that the following subjects would fall within the responsibility of specialized agencies: (a) relief and rehabilitation; (b) monetary cooperation and international investment; (c) trade policies; (d) food and agricultural policies; (e) labor standards, welfare and related social questions; (f) educational and cultural cooperation; (g) health; (h) some aspects of transport; (i) some aspects of communications. See comment on Article 57, this volume, p. 194.

Social Council is obligated to invite any Member which is not a member of that body to participate, without vote, in its deliberations on any matter of particular concern to that Member. Thus under Article 31 the Member which is not a member of the Security Council has the right to participate in the discussion, if it so desires, if the Council finds that its interests are specially affected, while under Article 69, in a similar situation, the Economic and Social Council is required to invite a Member to participate. The result would appear to be substantially the same in the two cases.

The Dumbarton Oaks Proposals contained no provision on the subject. The drafting subcommittee of Committee II/3 at the Conference proposed a paragraph reading as follows:

The Economic and Social Council may invite any Member of the Organization to participate without vote in its deliberations if it considers that the interest of that Member may be specially affected by such deliberations.[1]

It was proposed during Committee discussion that the word "shall" be substituted for the word "may." Some delegates took the view that this would in practice greatly increase the size of the Council since every Member of the Organization would be affected to some extent by the deliberations of the Council. They thought this would in fact destroy the effectiveness of the Council. It was pointed out that any Member could submit written statements. Others, however, argued that it was possible to distinguish between those situations where all were more or less concerned with the matters under discussion, and those situations where there would be matters under discussion of particular concern to certain states. After reconsideration, the drafting subcommittee recommended a new text with substantially the present phraseology.

It thus would appear that the use of the words "of particular concern" is intended to indicate an interest of special magnitude or different in kind from that which the ordinary Member would have. The question naturally arises, which is not expressly answered by the terms of the Article, as to who is to decide whether a Member has an interest entitling it to an invitation. Presumably this question will be decided by the Council.

ARTICLE 70

The Economic and Social Council may make arrangements for representatives of the specialized agencies to participate, without vote, in its deliberations and in those of the commissions established by it, and for its representatives to participate in the deliberations of the specialized agencies.

[1] UNCIO, *Summary Report of the Sixteenth Meeting of Committee II/3*, Doc. 725, II/3/42, p. 4.

This Article has to do with the relations between the Economic and Social Council and the specialized agencies. The Council is empowered to make arrangements, presumably under the agreements referred to in Article 63, for representatives of the specialized agencies to participate, without vote, in its deliberations and those of the commissions established by it, and for its representatives to participate in the deliberations of the specialized agencies. Precedents for this were to be found in the practice of certain organs of the League of Nations, and more recently in the rules of the San Francisco Conference which permitted representatives of the League of Nations, the International Labor Organization, the Permanent Court of International Justice, the Food and Agriculture Organization and the United Nations Relief and Rehabilitation Administration to participate under certain conditions in the discussions of technical committees of the Conference, without vote. It is a natural and convenient method of establishing effective liaison, and should prove to be an important means of coordinating the activities of the specialized agencies among themselves and with the United Nations.

ARTICLE 71

The Economic and Social Council may make suitable arrangements for consultation with non-governmental organizations which are concerned with matters within its competence. Such arrangements may be made with international organizations and, where appropriate, with national organizations after consultation with the Member of the United Nations concerned.

This Article goes one step further, and beyond what has been customary in the past, in making formal provision for consultation with non-governmental organizations which are concerned with the matters under discussion. Such arrangements are to be made with national organizations, however, only after consultation with the Member of the United Nations concerned.

The question of the relation of private organizations to intergovernmental organizations has arisen in the past. The International Association for Labor Legislation, organized at Paris in 1900, included private national organizations as well as governments. Under the Constitution of the International Labor Organization, national employer and employee organizations are entitled to be represented in the General Conference. The United Nations Conference on International Organization decided not to admit representatives of private international organizations in a consultative capacity. The Government of the United States invited some fifty private national organizations to send representatives to the Conference to serve unofficially in the capacity of consultants to the United States Delegation.

ARTICLE 72

1. The Economic and Social Council shall adopt its own rules of procedure, including the method of selecting its President.

This requires no comment. It is a customary rule. See Articles 21 and 30 applying to the General Assembly and Security Council respectively.

2. The Economic and Social Council shall meet as required in accordance with its rules, which shall include provision for the convening of meetings on the request of a majority of its members.

This paragraph leaves the time and frequency of meetings entirely to the discretion of the Council. The sole requirement is that the rules of the Council shall provide for the convening of meetings on the request of a majority of the members.

CHAPTER XI

DECLARATION REGARDING NON–SELF–GOVERNING TERRITORIES

ARTICLE 73

Members of the United Nations which have or assume responsibilities for the administration of territories whose peoples have not yet attained a full measure of self-government recognize the principle that the interests of the inhabitants of these territories are paramount, and accept as a sacred trust the obligation to promote to the utmost, within the system of international peace and security established by the present Charter, the well-being of the inhabitants of these territories, and to this end:

a. to ensure, with due respect for the culture of the peoples concerned, their political, economic, social, and educational advancement, their just treatment, and their protection against abuses;

b. to develop self-government, to take due account of the political aspirations of the peoples, and to assist them in the progressive development of their free political institutions, according to the particular circumstances of each territory and its peoples and their varying stages of advancement;

c. to further international peace and security;

d. to promote constructive measures of development, to encourage research, and to cooperate with one another and, when and where appropriate, with specialized international bodies with a view to the practical achievement of the social, economic, and scientific purposes set forth in this Article; and

e. to transmit regularly to the Secretary-General for information purposes, subject to such limitation as security and constitutional considerations may require, statistical and other information of a technical nature relating to economic, social, and educational conditions in the territories for which they are respectively responsible other than those territories to which Chapters XII and XIII apply.

Scope of Application. This Article, taken together with Article 74, lays down a set of principles to be respected by all Members of the United Nations in their administration of territories whose peoples have not attained a full measure of self-government. The purpose of these Articles and the scope of their application are to be distinguished sharply from those of the Articles of Chapter XII and XIII which have in view the creation of a special international regime for certain territories and which apply only to those territories that are placed under this regime by agreement of the interested states. This *Declaration Regarding*

Non-Self-Governing Territories goes beyond any international agreement that has hitherto been in force in the definiteness and scope of its provisions. By Article 23 of the Covenant, Members of the League undertook "to secure just treatment of the native inhabitants of territories under their control."

In the *Proposed Working Paper* [1] which was submitted to the technical committee of the Conference (Committee II/4) as a basis for discussion, and which incorporated the ideas found in proposals made by various governments, more especially those of Australia, China, France, the United Kingdom and the United States, the phrase "inhabited by peoples not yet able to stand by themselves under the strenuous condition of the modern world" was used in describing the territories to which the Declaration would be applicable. This phrase was taken without change from Article 22 of the Covenant of the League of Nations.

Objection was raised to its use in the Charter on the following grounds: that the words were outmoded, having been drafted in the light of conditions prevailing twenty-five years ago; that, from the military point of view, very few countries, if any, were able to stand alone in protecting themselves; that few countries were economically self-sufficient; and that the words would be highly objectionable to certain peoples. It was furthermore pointed out that among dependent peoples there are those who are undeveloped and those with a long heritage of civilization. These two categories should be differentiated. The question was raised as to whether the phrase included peoples within metropolitan areas. The consensus of opinion in the Committee was to the effect that inclusion was not intended but it was admitted that the wording was ambiguous on this point. The Committee left to the drafting subcommittee the matter of finding an improved phraseology which would reflect the mind of the Committee as expressed in the discussion.[2] The phraseology finally adopted by the Committee was the one which now appears in the Article, "whose peoples have not yet attained a full measure of self-government."

Chapter XI contains no provision excluding from the application of its terms territories which are or may become Members of the United Nations. It would seem, then, that the phrase used in describing territories to which the provisions of this Chapter are applicable is sufficiently broad to include such countries as India and the Philippines, which at the time of the adoption of the Charter did not enjoy full self-government.

It is clear from the Article that the provisions apply not only to territories at present under the administration of Members but also to such

---

[1] See this volume, p. 328.

[2] UNCIO, *Summary Report of the Eleventh Meeting of Committee II/4, May 31, 1945,* Doc. 712, II/4/30, p. 2–3.

territories as may be acquired in the future. It would also appear that, except where there is express provision to the contrary, provisions of this Chapter apply to trust territories as well.

Obligations Assumed by Administering State. With respect to non-self-governing territories, Members recognize the principle that "the interests of the inhabitants are paramount." They "accept as a sacred trust the obligation to promote . . . the well-being of the inhabitants of these territories," and, to this end, they obligate themselves to do the specific things listed under *a, b, c, d* and *e.*

The obligations assumed under *a* are very broad in nature. The first is "to ensure, with due respect for the cultures of the peoples concerned, their political, economic, social, and educational advancement." The qualifying clause is intended to safeguard native cultures which often, particularly under systems of direct rule, have been pushed to one side in favor of the cultures of the colonizing powers. This practice, while it has often led to more rapid advances in certain respects than could be achieved under practices more respectful of native cultures, has often resulted in weakening the basis for autonomous development and ultimate self-government.

The second obligation under *a* is to ensure "the just treatment" of the inhabitants of these territories. Obviously, this is a very general term which will lend itself to a variety of interpretations. It follows very closely the phraseology of Article 23(b) of the Covenant. Presumably it is intended to protect the inhabitants of the territories in question against arbitrary and discriminatory treatment. The term "just treatment" is presumably used in a broad social sense and not in a legal sense, and consequently does not provide the basis for any legal claim by the inhabitants of the territories in question against the states having responsibilities for administration.

The third obligation is "to ensure . . . their protection against abuses." This wording is very vague as there is no specification of particular abuses. The Covenant of the League of Nations provided that in territories to be placed under B and C mandates, "abuses such as the slave trade, the arms traffic and the liquor traffic" were to be prohibited. In the course of the discussion of this provision in Committee II/4, the Netherlands Delegate drew attention to three grievances which were acutely felt by dependent peoples: (1) failure to protect their land, particularly arable land; (2) forced labor; and (3) the humiliation caused by the assertion of racial superiority. He asked the Delegate of the United States to give an assurance that the provisions of this Article implied an obligation to deal with these abuses. The United States Delegate stated in reply that he would regard it as clear "that the abuses you refer to are included in the abuses against which the people concerned are to be protected and the obligation referred to in paragraph 1 (corresponding to Article 73) covers the situation." These questions and the answer given were recorded in the Report of the Rapporteur.[1]

The obligation under *b* was the subject of long discussion at the Conference and the phraseology finally agreed to was arrived at only after considerable difficulty. To understand its true import it is necessary to examine the positions taken and the actual evolution of the text. In the *Proposed Working Paper*, the following phraseology was used: "to develop self-government in forms appropriate to the varying circumstances of each territory." The Delegate of China proposed in Committee that the following phraseology be substituted:

To promote development towards independence or self-government as may be appropriate to the particular circumstances of each territory.[2]

In support of this change it was argued that independence was an aim of many dependent peoples and that its attainment should not be excluded from the terms of the Charter. Attention was called to the fact that the goal was recognized in Article 22 of the Covenant and that certain territories placed under League mandates had actually become independent states. The hopes of dependent peoples would receive a heavy blow, it was argued, if a step backward were taken now. Furthermore, it was pointed out, the right of self-determination is recognized in Article I of the Charter.

Against the proposed change it was argued that the word "independence" means different things to different peoples, that its use would lead to confusion and uncertainty, that the ultimate result would be the creation of a large number of small states when the emphasis should be on the interdependence of peoples, and that the use of "self-government" alone did not exclude the possibility of independence. Following informal consultations, the Chinese Delegate agreed to withdraw his amendment on condition that independence be included among the objectives of the trusteeship system.[3] Further consideration of the matter in the light of proposals made by the Australian and Philippine Delegations led to the submission by the drafting subcommittee of the present text. In the discussion 'of this text the Philippine Delegate stated that he interpreted the words "to assist them in the progressive development of their free political institutions" to refer to independence. The Delegate of the United Kingdom said that his government had never ruled out independence as a possible goal for dependent territories

---

[1] *Ibid., Summary Report of Fifteenth Meeting of Committee II/4, June 18, 1945*, Doc. 1090, II/4/43, p. 3–4; *Report of the Rapporteur of Committee II/4*, Doc. 1115, II/4/44 (1) (a), p. 13.

[2] *Ibid., Summary Report of Sixth Meeting of Committee II/4, May 17, 1945*, Doc. 404, II/4/17, p. 2.

[3] *Ibid., Summary Report of Eleventh Meeting of Committee II/4, May 31, 1945*, Doc. 712, II/4/30, p. 1–2

in appropriate cases but objected to putting it forward as a universal co-equal alternative goal for all territories. The new paragraph as drafted was unanimously adopted.[1]

The obligation contained in subparagraph c needs no special comment.

The obligations set forth in subparagraph d are related to those contained in a but refer more particularly to the use of methods of scientific inquiry and cooperation between national administrations and international bodies in the development of programs for the achievement of broad social and economic purposes. It would seem fairly clear that the Anglo-American Caribbean Commission offers a model of the kind of constructive cooperative action which this subparagraph has in view.[2] The British Government was reported to have proposed at San Francisco the establishment of a system of regional commissions modelled on the Anglo-American Caribbean Commission.[3] Such commissions would conduct studies and discussions with a view to giving advice and making recommendations to the colonial administrative authorities. They would not directly exercise governmental or administrative authority. It is to be noted that in this subparagraph "specialized international bodies" is used instead of "specialized agencies," suggesting that the term is broader than the term "specialized agencies" as used in Article 57, and includes bodies such as regional commissions modelled on the Anglo-American Caribbean Commission or other bodies of a similar character, as well as bodies such as the Food and Agriculture Organization which comes under the Charter designation of "specialized agencies."

The obligation set forth in subparagraph e is intended to provide the factual basis for determining whether Members live up to their other obligations under this Article. The territories to which Chapters XII and XIII apply are expressly excluded from the application of this particular obligation. The obligation to transmit information of a technical nature, i.e. to make reports, to the Secretary-General is subject "to such limitation as security and constitutional considerations may require." Since it is presumably left to each Member to interpret this limitation for itself, it is obviously open to very broad interpretation. Nevertheless, the principle laid down by this paragraph represents an important step forward, even though in fact it can be largely nullified by a non-cooperative attitude on the part of the Members. The Charter provides no means for dealing with such an attitude, except of course the power which the General Assembly has to focus public attention on the situation and express to the recalcitrant Member the disapproval of that body and of world opinion.

[1] Ibid., Report of Fifteenth Meeting of Committee II/4, June 19, 1945, Doc. 1090, II/4/43, p. 2.
[2] See Report of the Anglo-American Caribbean Commission to the Governments of the United States and Great Britain for the year 1944, Washington, D. C. (810 Eighteenth St., N. W.); also for the year 1942–43.   [3] New York Times, June 3, 1945, p. 25.

ARTICLE 74

Members of the United Nations also agree that their policy in respect of the territories to which this Chapter applies, no less than in respect of their metropolitan areas, must be based on the general principle of good-neighborliness, due account being taken of the interests and well-being of the rest of the world, in social, economic, and commercial matters.

While Article 73 obligates Members to recognize the interests of the inhabitants of non-self-governing territories as paramount and to promote their well-being, this Article commits them in respect to these territories to the "general principle of good neighborliness." Obviously this is at most a guiding principle of policy without any specific legal content. It recognizes in a general sort of way that other countries have interests in these territories which if adversely affected by policies followed by the administering state give them legitimate ground for complaint. It requires Members to take these interests into account in formulating policies for the territories in question. But it does not give to other countries any legal protection against policies and practices which might be generally regarded as unneighborly.

The Article would appear to be directed particularly against discriminatory policies such as the closed-door in commercial policy, imperial preference, discriminatory immigration restrictions and exclusion of or discrimination against the nationals of countries other than the administering state in the granting of concessions.

CHAPTER XII

INTERNATIONAL TRUSTEESHIP SYSTEM

ARTICLE 75

The United Nations shall establish under its authority an international trusteeship system for the administration and supervision of such territories as may be placed thereunder by subsequent individual agreements. These territories are hereinafter referred to as trust territories.

This Article provides for the establishment of an international trusteeship system comparable to the mandatory system which was established under Article 22 of the Covenant.[1] It lays down the general principle that such a system shall be established and indicates broadly the area of its application, leaving to subsequent Articles the detailed implementation of the principle.

The Dumbarton Oaks Proposals contained no provisions on this matter. It was understood that this was one of the questions left over for further study and subsequent negotiation, and that it was to be placed on the agenda of the United Nations Conference. The matter was considered at the Yalta Conference by the Heads of the Governments of the Soviet Union, the United Kingdom and the United States, and agreement was reached on the following policy:

(1) That the five governments with permanent seats in the Security Council should consult each other prior to the United Nations Conference on providing machinery in the World Charter for dealing with territorial trusteeships which would apply only to (a) existing mandates of the League of Nations; (b) territory to be detached from the enemy as a result of this war; and (c) any other territory that may voluntarily be placed under trusteeship. (2) That no discussions of specific territories were to take place during the preliminary consultations on trusteeships or at the United Nations Conference itself. Only machinery and principles of trusteeship should be formulated at the Conference for inclusion in the Charter, and it was to be a matter for subsequent agreement as to which territories within the categories specified above would actually be placed under trusteeship.[2]

[1] On the League mandate system, see Wright, Quincy, *Mandates under the League of Nations*, Chicago, Univ. of Chicago Press, 1930; and League of Nations, *The Mandates System, Origin — Principles — Application*, Geneva, 1945, League of Nations Document 1945. VI. A. 1, N. Y., Columbia Univ. Press, agents.

[2] *Charter of the United Nations, Report to the President on the Results of the San Francisco Conference*, etc., cited above, p. 128.

When the San Francisco Conference convened, the Sponsoring Governments had as yet reached no agreement on a set of proposals covering the establishment of a trusteeship system to be submitted to the Conference. Proposals were submitted by the Governments of Australia,[1] China,[2] France,[3] the Union of Soviet Socialist Republics,[4] the United Kingdom,[5] and the United States.[6] Subsequently, on the request of the Chairman of the technical committee dealing with the matter (Committee II/4), and in order to expedite its work, the Delegate of the United States presented a *Proposed Working Paper for Chapter on Dependent Territories and Arrangements for International Trusteeship*, with the understanding that the acceptance of this document by the Committee as the basis for discussion did not constitute an approval by the Committee of the substance of the Paper or affect in any way positions taken by delegates. The Working Paper was accepted by the Committee with these understandings.[7]

On the basis of this Working Paper, the Committee, with the assistance of a drafting subcommittee, drafted its recommendations for the Charter provisions relating to the establishment of an international trusteeship system, and the related *Declaration Regarding Non-Self-Governing Territories*.[8] The text recommended by the Committee was extensively revised by the Coordination Committee as to the arrangement of material but not as to substance.

ARTICLE 76

The basic objectives of the trusteeship system, in accordance with the Purposes of the United Nations laid down in Article 1 of the present Charter, shall be:

   a. to further international peace and security;

   b. to promote the political, economic, social and educational advancement of the inhabitants of the trust territories, and their progressive development towards self-government or independence as may be appropriate to the particular circumstances of each territory

[1] UNCIO, *Amendments to the Dumbarton Oaks Proposals Submitted on Behalf of Australia*, Doc. 2, G/14 (1), p. 6.

[2] *Ibid.*, *Draft Proposal of the Chinese Delegation on International Territorial Trusteeship*, Doc. 2, G/26 (e).

[3] *Ibid.*, *Chapter —, International Trusteeship, French Preliminary Draft*, Doc. 2, G/26 (a).

[4] *Ibid.*, *Amendments of the Soviet Delegation to the United States Draft on Trusteeship System*, Doc. 237, G/26 (f).

[5] *Ibid.*, *Territorial Trusteeship. United Kingdom Draft of Chapter for Inclusion in United Nations Charter*, Doc. 2, G/26 (d).

[6] *Ibid.*, *Arrangements for International Trusteeship. Additional Chapter Proposed by the United States*, Doc. 2, G/26 (c).

[7] *Ibid.*, Doc. 323, II/4/12; *ibid.*, *Summary Report of the Fifth Meeting of Committee II/4, May 15, 1945*, Doc. 364, II/4/13, p. 2.

[8] *Ibid.*, *Report of the Rapporteur of Committee II/4*, Doc. 1115, 11/4/44 (1) (a), p. 8.

and its peoples and the freely expressed wishes of the peoples concerned, and as may be provided by the terms of each trusteeship
agreement;

   c. to encourage respect for human rights and for fundamental
freedoms for all without distinction as to race, sex, language, or religion, and to encourage recognition of the interdependence of the
peoples of the world; and

   d. to ensure equal treatment in social, economic, and commercial
matters for all Members of the United Nations and their nationals,
and also equal treatment for the latter in the administration of justice,
without prejudice to the attainment of the foregoing objectives and
subject to the provisions of Article 80.

Comparison with Objectives of League Mandates System. It is interesting to compare this statement of objectives with the objectives of the
League mandates system as described in Article 22 of the Covenant.
The purposes of the League system were not brought together in any one
place and generalized as is done in the Charter. The promotion of the
"well-being and development of such peoples" was recognized as a
general over-all purpose. In the case of communities referred to in paragraph 4 (Class A mandates), the attainment of independence was obviously a principal objective. In the case of peoples referred to in paragraph 5 (Class B mandates) other objectives were set forth: "freedom of
conscience and religion," "the prohibition of abuses such as the slave
trade, the arms traffic and the liquor traffic," "the prevention of the
establishment of fortifications of military and naval bases and of
military training of the natives for other than police purposes and the
defense of territory" and securing "equal opportunities for the trade
and commerce of other Members of the League." In the case of those
territories referred to in paragraph 6 (Class C mandate) only those purposes relating to the interests of the indigenous population were recognized. Furthermore, by the terms of Article 23, paragraph *b*, the
Members of the League "undertake to secure just treatment of the
native inhabitants of territories under their control."

   The Charter obviously goes considerably beyond the League in its
provisions with regard to the basic purposes of the trusteeship system.
This statement of purposes follows rather closely the statement of fundamental obligations set forth in the *Declaration Regarding Non-Self-
Governing Territories.* There are, however, important differences to be
noted, which result primarily from the fact that the Declaration is to
be regarded as applying primarily to non-self-governing territories
which are not placed under international trusteeship arrangements,
and which are and for a long time may remain parts of the territorial
domain of the governing state and subject to its jurisdiction, while the
statement of objectives in Article 76 applies to territories which are
placed under an international regime with the administering authority

exercising only the powers of trustee as defined in the trusteeship agreement.

Objectives Analyzed. The objective stated in subparagraph *a* requires no comment.

The first part of subparagraph *b* corresponds closely to the first objective stated in Article 73, subparagraph *a*. The second objective corresponds to subparagraph *b* of that Article, but has a different phraseology which is to be particularly noted as these two texts were the result of a compromise referred to above,[1] and were intended to express somewhat different ideas. Under Article 73 *b* Members are obligated to develop "self-government" and "to assist them [the peoples of non-self-governing territories] in the progressive development of their free political institutions." This is not an obligation to give independence to these peoples at some future time, but only an obligation to develop "self-government" and "free political institutions" which may, but will not necessarily, take the form of "independence," using that term in the sense of the severance of all political ties with another state, or at least the right to do so. Under subparagraph *b* of Article 76, however, the basic objective of the trusteeship system is declared to be the "progressive development towards self-government or independence" of the peoples of the trust territories. Thus, "self-government," which may include independence but not necessarily, and "independence" become equal alternative objectives. The factors determining which of these objectives should be pursued are "the particular circumstances of each territory and its people," "the freely expressed wishes of the peoples concerned," and "the terms of each trusteeship agreement."

The first objective stated in subparagraph *c* does not have a specific counterpart in the Declaration, though presumably "just treatment" and "protection against abuses" cover much of what is more specifically stated here. The phraseology used is taken from paragraph 3 of Chapter I. There is apparently no special significance to be attached to the somewhat abbreviated form used, i.e. "to encourage" in place of "to promote and encourage." As we have already seen, Article 22 of the Covenant provided only for the guarantee of freedom of conscience and religion, and that only in territories to be placed under Class B and C Mandates, though the provisions of Class A Mandates did incorporate like guarantees. See comment on Article 1, paragraph 3, for discussion of meaning of the terms "human rights" and "fundamental freedoms."

The second objective stated in subparagraph *c* is of an extremely general character. It emphasizes the necessity of recognition by all peoples of their essential interdependence as a condition to any effective international cooperation for the attainment of the specific purposes of this and other Articles of the Charter.

[1] See comment on Article 73, this volume, p. 226.

Subparagraph *d* states two objectives which relate to the interests of the Members of the United Nations, as distinguished from the interests of the indigenous populations. In territories under trusteeship agreements "equal treatment in social, economic, and commercial matters" and in "the administration of justice" is to be ensured to all Members of the United Nations and their nationals. The principle of equality of economic opportunity was applied to the Congo Basin by the Berlin Convention of 1885.[1] It was recognized in Article 22 of the Covenant in so far as territories placed under Class B Mandates were concerned and was also included in Class A Mandates though this was not specifically required by the provisions of the Covenant.[2] As for Class C mandated territories there was no provision for this guarantee and the mandate agreements omitted all reference to it with the result that the territories were in this respect assimilated to colonial areas. In principle, then, this provision represents a considerable advance over previous practice.

The provision for equality of treatment in social matters is new and its exact meaning is not clear. Equal treatment in the administration of justice is a principle commonly recognized in international agreements and relates primarily to procedural matters.

The qualification at the end of subparagraph *d* needs a word of comment. The words "without prejudice to the attainment of the foregoing objectives" are apparently intended to make it possible for discriminatory policies to be pursued, as, for example, bilateral trade arrangements making it possible for the goods of one Member to enter the territory on more favorable terms than those of another in return for special favors granted, if such arrangements seem to be necessary to the economic development of the country. It is a safeguard which may be necessary but which nevertheless opens the way for seriously weakening, if not destroying, the principle which it is sought to establish, particularly as there is no effective international control over the administering authority provided for in the Charter.

The second qualification contained in *d* declares the objectives here set forth "subject to the provisions of Article 80" which conserves existing rights pending the making of trusteeship agreements. Since the objectives of this Article apply only to territories which have been made trust territories as the result of such agreements, this reservation has the effect of saying that only to the extent agreed upon in individual trust agreements shall existing rights be affected by the provisions of this Article. The rights referred to in Article 80 include, among others, the rights enjoyed under League mandate arrangements now in force.

[1] *British and Foreign State Papers*, 76, p. 4–20.
[2] See Wright, cited above, Chaps. XV and XVI and Appendix II, p. 593–616.

ARTICLE 77

1. The trusteeship system shall apply to such territories in the following categories as may be placed thereunder by means of trusteeship agreements:

    a. territories now held under mandate;

    b. territories which may be detached from enemy states as a result of the Second World War; and

    c. territories voluntarily placed under the system by states responsible for their administration.

This paragraph indicates the categories of territories to which the trusteeship system is to apply. However, the system does not become automatically applicable to these territories once the Charter enters into force. It becomes applicable only following agreement between "the states directly concerned," as the second paragraph of this Article and Article 79 make clear.

Territories under Mandate. Falling in the category of territories now held under mandate are all territories which were placed under mandate in accordance with the terms of Article 22 of the Covenant and for which the mandates have not subsequently been terminated. These originally included the following:

Class A Mandates

Territory	Mandatory
The Lebanon	France
Syria	France
Palestine	United Kingdom
Trans-Jordan	United Kingdom
Iraq	United Kingdom

Class B Mandates

Togoland	United Kingdom
The Cameroons	United Kingdom
Tanganyika Territory	United Kingdom
Togoland	France
The Cameroons	France
Ruanda-Urundi	Belgium

Class C Mandates

South West Africa	Union of South Africa
The Marianas, Caroline, and Marshall Islands	Japan
New Guinea (Northeastern part), New Ireland, New Britain and the Solomon Islands	Australia
Nauru	British Empire; through Australia
Western Samoa	New Zealand

The independence of Iraq was established on October 3, 1932, following approval by the Council of the League of Nations of an agreement between the United Kingdom and Iraq. In 1936, treaties of friendship and alliance were negotiated between France and Syria and Lebanon for application when the independence of these two countries was established. While the French Government had not recognized at the time that its responsibilities under the League mandates system were ended, both Syria and Lebanon [1] were admitted to participation in the San Francisco Conference, are among the signatories of the Charter, and, under the provisions of Article 78, are placed outside the categories of territories to which the trusteeship system may apply.

The mandate held by Japan for the Marianas, the Carolines and the Marshall Islands was never treated by the League as terminated or affected in any way by Japan's withdrawal from the League in March 1935 or by the outbreak of World War II. The mandate was originally conferred by the Supreme Council, consisting of the Principal Allied and Associated Powers in World War I (France, Italy, Japan, the United Kingdom and the United States) by decision of May 7, 1919. The termination of the mandate can presumably be achieved by agreement of these states, and since two of them are among the enemy states in World War II, their consent can be obtained under the terms of peace.

Territories Detached from Enemy States. The second category includes territories detached from enemy states as the result of World War II. It is not expressly restricted to territories which would fall in the category of "non-self-governing territories," but the reasonable assumption is that such a restriction will be applied in practice. The Italian colonies of Eritrea, Somaliland and Libya will fall into this category if the decision is taken to detach them from Italy, together with such other territories as it may be decided to take from that country. The same would be true of the insular possessions of Japan (excluding the mandated territories) and of Korea which was detached from the Japanese Empire pursuant to the terms of the Cairo Communiqué of December 1, 1943,[2] and the Potsdam Declaration of August 2, 1945.[3]

Territories Voluntarily Placed under System. The third category includes all territories without further qualification which are "voluntarily" placed under the system by the states responsible for their administration. In a sense, the use of the word "voluntarily" here is misleading since it will be by agreement voluntarily entered into by the interested parties that all territories, including those falling into the first

---

[1] By the terms of the Anglo-French agreement of December 13, 1945 the complete independence of Syria and the Lebanon was confirmed by France, and both British and French troops will be evacuated from those countries. *New York Times*, December 14, 1945, p. 1.

[2] Department of State. *Bulletin*, IX, p. 393.

[3] *Ibid.*, XIII, p. 153.

two categories, will be brought under the trusteeship system. There is, however, the implication that in the case of territories falling into the first two categories, the states directly concerned should enter into the agreements necessary to bring them under the system while in the case of territories falling into the third category there is no suggestion whatever of obligation. While the door is open to any Member which possesses a colony to place it by agreement under the trusteeship system, there can be no allegation of breach of faith or violation of the spirit of the Charter if it refuses to do so.

2. It will be a matter for subsequent agreement as to which territories in the foregoing categories will be brought under the trusteeship system and upon what terms.

The provisions of Article 22 of the Covenant, while not committing the Members of the League of Nations in any legal sense to placing specific territories under mandate, did by the specific references contained in paragraphs 4, 5 and 6 commit Members, at least in a moral sense, to place these territories under the mandates system. The provisions of Article 77, however, emphasize the fact that the trusteeship system shall apply only to the extent determined by subsequent agreement. While the difference from a strictly legal point of view between the Covenant and Charter provisions is not apparent, it would seem that the Charter places greater emphasis on the agreement stage and makes the conclusion of these agreements appear to be a voluntary matter subject to less moral compulsion than was implied in the Covenant.

For content of and parties to agreements, see Article 79 and comment.

ARTICLE 78

The trusteeship system shall not apply to territories which have become Members of the United Nations, relationship among which shall be based on respect for the principle of sovereign equality.

This Article specifically excludes from the application of the trusteeship system territories which have become Members of the United Nations. It would appear to be obvious that a Member entitled to the benefit of the principle of sovereign equality, under Article B, paragraph 1, cannot at the same time be a trust territory. Nevertheless, it was thought desirable to make this explicit for the reassurance of certain participants in the San Francisco Conference whose international status had not been completely clarified. Thus, Lebanon and Syria, though participants in the Conference and signatories of the Charter, were still regarded by France as technically subject to League Class A Mandates. Ethiopia, following its conquest by Italy in 1936, was proclaimed a part of the Italian Empire. British troops invaded Ethiopia in June 1940, when Italy declared war, and the Emperor, Haile Selassie, returned to his capital on May 5, 1941. An agreement and military convention signed between Great Britain and Ethiopia on January 31, 1942 placed under British military administration certain areas bordering on French Somaliland and all the railways in Ethiopia. On October 9, 1942 Ethiopia joined the United Nations.

ARTICLE 79

The terms of trusteeship for each territory to be placed under the trusteeship system, including any alteration or amendment, shall be agreed upon by the states directly concerned, including the mandatory power in the case of territories held under mandate by a Member of the United Nations, and shall be approved as provided for in Articles 83 and 85.

This Article establishes the rule that the terms of trusteeship for each trust territory, as well as the fact of a particular territory's being designated a trust territory, are to be agreed upon by the states directly concerned. This extends to any alteration or amendment of the terms.

Provisions of Trust Agreement. The detailed provisions of each trusteeship agreement will presumably be such as to give effective application to the terms of the Charter, especially Chapters XII and XIII.

Under the League system, mandates fell into three categories, "A," "B" and "C," the provisions of each being determined to a large extent by the terms of Article 22 of the Covenant relating to each class. Certain clauses, however, were common to all mandates. The mandatory power was given full power of administration and legislation subject to the terms of the mandate. It was placed under an obligation to make an annual report to the Council giving full information as to the measures taken to carry out the provisions of the mandate. It agreed that if any dispute should arise with any other Member of the League as to the interpretation or application of the mandate, such dispute, if not settled by negotiation, should be submitted to the Permanent Court of International Justice. Any modification of the mandate required the consent of the Council.[1]

Presumably the trusteeship agreements referred to in this Article will contain provisions covering the following matters, among others: the territory to which the agreement is to apply (Article 77); the nature of the administering authority (Article 81); the designation of any area, the whole or part of the territory in question, as strategic (Article 82); the obligations assumed by the administering authority; the responsibility of the administering authority in the maintenance of peace and security (Article 84); the organ by which the functions of the United

---

[1] League of Nations, *The Mandates System*, etc., cited above, p. 24.

Nations are performed (Articles 83 and 86); annual report by administering authority to the appropriate organ of the United Nations (Article 88); periodic visits and other procedures for keeping the appropriate organs of the United Nations informed (Article 87); settlement of disputes regarding interpretation and application of the agreement; revision of the agreement (Article 79); and termination of the agreement. There will no doubt be considerable variation in the detailed provisions of particular agreements because of the requirements of special circumstances which it will be necessary to take into account.

Parties to the Agreements. It is stated that the agreements here referred to shall be between "the states directly concerned" (Article 79). This raises important and difficult questions of interpretation. Who are "the states directly concerned" in the case of territories held under League mandates? Article 79 and the report of the Conference technical committee [1] make it clear that the mandatory state is to be regarded as a party to the agreement in each case. That being so, it will be possible for the mandatory state to refuse to enter into such an agreement, and, with the League of Nations presumably no longer in existence, the mandatory will in fact assume the role of colonial administrator with none of the safeguards originally intended. Are the states who constituted the Principal Allied and Associated Powers at the time the original assignment of Mandates was made to be regarded as "states directly concerned"? Are the members of the League of Nations Council, which under the Covenant was made responsible for securing observance of the terms of the mandates, to be so regarded? And what about the Members of the League? It is clear that there are serious difficulties involved here, and since an agreement between the states directly concerned is required before any mandated territory can be placed under the trusteeship system, long delays may well ensue, and no assurance is provided that any such territories will be so disposed of.[2]

A similar problem arises in connection with territories detached from enemy states as the result of World War II, though here the technical difficulties would appear to be considerably less. Presumably the "states directly concerned" include at least those of the "Big Five" who have been at war with the enemy state in question. Are other Members of the United Nations to be included as well? Agreement among the United Nations may be difficult to obtain, and, in particular, the Member whose forces are in actual occupation of the territory may be reluctant to yield it up, though under the terms of the Atlantic Charter, the principles of which were accepted by the signatories of the Declaration by

[1] UNCIO, *Draft Report of the Rapporteur of Committee II/4*, Doc. 1091, II/4/44.
[2] For discussion of title to mandated territories, see Wright, cited above, p. 319; for discussion at San Francisco, see UNCIO, *Summary Report of Eighth Meeting of Committee II/4, May 22, 1945*, Doc. 512, II/4/21, p. 1.

United Nations of January 1, 1942, the United Nations seek "no aggrandizement, territorial or other."

Approval of Agreements. As stated in Articles 83 and 85 to which reference is made, the trusteeship agreement, once it has been negotiated, must be approved by the Security Council, in so far as it relates to strategic areas, and by the General Assembly for all areas not designated as strategic.

If the agreement is entered into by the states directly concerned without any consultation with the Trusteeship Council in advance, or without any advance consideration of the matter by the General Assembly or the Security Council, these organs may find themselves in the position where in fact their freedom of decision is considerably restricted. It may well be that the practical alternative presented will be that of approval of the agreement as it stands or no agreement at all. This would greatly weaken the effectiveness of United Nations control of the administration of trust territories. It would seem desirable that some procedure be worked out by which the appropriate organ or organs of the United Nations might have the opportunity to consider the matter and express their views on desirable terms of the agreement before the "states directly concerned" actually commit themselves.

ARTICLE 80

1. Except as may be agreed upon in individual trusteeship agreements, made under Articles 77, 79 and 81, placing each territory under the trusteeship system, and until such agreements have been concluded, nothing in this Chapter shall be construed in or of itself to alter in any manner the rights whatsoever of any states or any peoples or the terms of existing international instruments to which Members of the United Nations may respectively be parties.

The purpose of this Article is conservatory, that is, to safeguard existing rights pending the entrance into force of the trusteeship agreements provided for in Articles 77, 79 and 81. It is intended to apply particularly to rights in mandated territories.

The question of the protection of existing rights was the subject of extensive discussion at the Conference. The original proposal contained in paragraph 5 of Section B of the Working Paper was that "except as may be agreed upon in individual trusteeship arrangements, placing each territory under the trusteeship system, nothing in this chapter should be construed in and of itself to alter in any manner the rights of any state or any peoples in any territory." [1] This was criticized by some delegates on the ground that it protected the rights of mandatory

---

[1] *Ibid., Proposed Working Paper for Chapter on Dependent Territories and Arrangements for International Trusteeship*, Doc. 323, II/4/12, p. 2; this volume, p. 328.

powers and was a deviation from the basic purpose of the trusteeship system which was to further the welfare of dependent peoples. It was argued that the protection given should be extended only to the rights of inhabitants, that the mandatory had only duties, not rights. As regards the inhabitants of certain mandated territories, the view appeared to be held that the proposal did not go far enough in protecting rights enjoyed under the mandate system, particularly the right of communities referred to in paragraph 4 of Article 22 of the Covenant to have their independence provisionally recognized and to have their wishes treated "as a principal consideration in the selection of the mandatory." Other delegates took the view that the mandatory power equally had rights which should be protected.

The Delegate of the United States stated that the proposal under consideration was intended to mean "that all rights, whatever they may be, remain exactly the same as they exist — that they are neither increased or diminished by the adoption of this Charter. Any change is left as a matter for subsequent agreements." [1] To meet some of the objections that had been raised, though not all, a new draft was presented toward the end of the Conference, substantially the text of the Charter. The United States Delegate, who presented the draft, stated that among the "rights" protected were included any rights set forth in paragraph 4 of Article 22 of the Covenant.[2]

The Delegate for Iraq moved an alternative text which read as follows:

(a) In the event of any territory being placed under the trusteeship system, nothing in this Chapter should be construed in and of itself to alter in any manner the rights of any state in any territory or to diminish the rights of the people of that territory.

(b) Notwithstanding anything contained in this Chapter, in the event of the transfer to the trusteeship system of any territory now administered on the basis of Paragraph 4 of Article 22 of the Covenant of the League of Nations, such trusteeship shall not apply to such a territory save within the limits and for the purposes laid down in the aforementioned paragraph of the Covenant.[3]

The Committee decided by a vote of 32 to 5 in favor of the present text, while accepting the interpretation given by the Delegate of the United States. It thus appears that among the rights to be protected in mandated territories are to be included the rights of mandatory powers, the rights of other states and the rights of peoples other than the inhabitants of the mandated territory. Such rights as the peoples of particular mandated territories have, as for example under paragraph 4 of Article 22 of the Covenant, are equally protected.

[1] *Ibid., Summary Report of Tenth Meeting of Committee II/4, May 24, 1945,* Doc. 580, II/4/24, p. 2.

[2] *Ibid., Summary Report of Thirteenth Meeting of Committee II/4, June 8, 1945,* Doc. 877, II/4/35, p. 3.

[3] *Ibid.*

2. Paragraph 1 of this Article shall not be interpreted as giving grounds for delay or postponement of the negotiation and conclusion of agreements for placing mandated and other territories under the trusteeship system as provided for in Article 77.

The meaning of this paragraph is apparent. It is obviously intended to prevent a mandatory from using the protection of its rights as an excuse for refusing to enter into a trusteeship agreement. There is no sanction provided, however, and no means of coercing a mandatory into concluding a trusteeship agreement.

ARTICLE 81

The trusteeship agreement shall in each case include the terms under which the trust territory will be administered and designate the authority which will exercise the administration of the trust territory. Such authority, hereinafter called the administering authority, may be one or more states or the Organization itself.

Nature of Administering Authority. It is to be noted that whereas under the League system, according to the provisions of Article 22, the practice was for single states to act as mandatories, this Article permits an alternative method. The administering authority for a given territory may be one or more states or the Organization itself. It is to be noted that it is not specifically stated that the administering authority, if a state, must be a Member. It therefore cannot be assumed that membership will be a prerequisite. There was some objection in committee to permitting the Organization to act as administering authority on the grounds that this was likely to prove ineffective in practice. The point was not pressed, however, and under the terms of the Article, direct administration by the Organization is permissible.

Termination of Trust Agreement. Neither in this Article nor in any other Article of the Charter is there any provision regarding the termination of the status of trusteeship or covering the cases of the withdrawal from the Organization of a state acting as administrative authority under a trusteeship agreement, or of the commission of an act of aggression by such a state. The League Covenant contained no express provision applicable to these situations.

As regards the termination of a mandate the practice of the League was to permit this on two conditions: (1) the existence in the territory concerned of *de facto* conditions justifying the presumption that the country had reached the stage of development where it was able "to stand by itself under the strenuous conditions of the modern world"; and (2) the provision of certain guarantees.[1] In the case of Iraq, which was the only mandated territory to have its status officially terminated

[1] League of Nations, *The Mandates System,* etc., cited above, p. 118.

and to be admitted to the League, the guarantees took the form of a treaty between the mandated territory and the mandatory and of a declaration signed by the Government of Iraq.

When the question arose of the consequences for the mandates system of the Japanese invasion of Manchuria in 1931 and subsequent Japanese withdrawal from the League, a course of inaction was followed. In this case, there was the aggravating circumstance that Japan, in addition to committing an act of aggression and withdrawing from the League, clearly failed to live up to her obligations under the terms of Article 22 and of the mandate.

In the course of Committee consideration at San Francisco, the Delegate of Egypt moved that provisions embodying the following principles be included in this Chapter:

That in all trust territories, within its competence, the General Assembly shall have the power to terminate the status of trusteeship, and declare the territory to be fit for full independence, either at the instance of the Administering Authority, or upon the recommendation of any member of the Assembly.

That whenever there is any violation of the terms of the trusteeship arrangements by the administering authority, or when the administering power has ceased to be a Member of the United Nations, or has been suspended from membership, the Organization shall take the necessary steps for the transfer of the territory under trusteeship to another administering authority, subject to the provisions of Articles 2 and 6 above.[1]

It was argued against this proposal that a provision for the termination or transfer of a trusteeship without the consent of the administering authority would be contrary to the voluntary basis upon which the system was to rest. It was contended that on the basis of League experience a provision for the termination of a trusteeship through recognition of independence was unnecessary and might be left to individual agreements. With regard to the matter of termination as a penalty for maladministration or as a consequence of the administering authority ceasing to be a Member, it was argued that the case was covered by other provisions of the Charter, notably by the provisions empowering the Security Council to deal with disputes and situations likely to endanger the peace. Moreover, it was pointed out that there were great practical difficulties in the way of enforcing penalties.

As a result of this discussion the Chairman of Committee II/4 (the Delegate of New Zealand) asked the Delegates of the United States and the United Kingdom to prepare a statement for inclusion in the Rapporteur's report on two questions which the discussion had suggested. In the light of this action, the Delegate of Egypt withdrew his motion,

---

[1] UNCIO, *Summary Report of Fourteenth Meeting of Committee II/4, June 15, 1945*, Doc. 1018, II/4/38, p. 5. Articles 2 and 6, here referred to, became Articles 76 and 81 of the Charter.

and no formal vote was taken on it. The statement [1] which was submitted by the Delegates of the United States and Great Britain was as follows:

1. *If a State administering a trust territory commits an act of aggression, what consequences will follow in relation to its trust?* — The powers of the Security Council as defined in Chapter VIII [2] of the Charter are not limited to dealing with acts of aggression. The Security Council may investigate any situation which may lead to international friction or give rise to a dispute, in order to determine whether its continuance is likely to endanger the maintenance of international peace and security. Any Member of the United Nations may bring any such situation to the attention of the General Assembly or of the Security Council. If the Security Council should in any particular case decide that the continuance of the situation is in fact likely to endanger the maintenance of international peace and security it may recommend appropriate procedures or methods of adjustment. In this way a Trustee State which showed signs of aggressive intentions or had committed an aggression could be dealt with, whether it were still a Member of the Organization or not. In general, however, the same considerations apply as are explained in reply to Question 2, namely that the action to be taken in such a case can only be decided upon at the time and in the light of all relevant circumstances.

2. *If a State withdraws from the United Nations Organization and continues to hold a trust territory under the Charter, how is the Organization to continue to exercise its responsibilities with respect to the administration of that trust territory?* — If a State withdraws for reasons which reflect no discredit upon it, and if it declares its willingness to continue to abide by the terms of the Trusteeship system, although itself ceasing to be a member of the General Assembly or Trusteeship Council, there should be no reason for transferring the trust territory. There is no inherent reason why the system of annual reports, petitions, periodic visits, etc. could not continue in such circumstances and the Administering Authority could be given the opportunity (though not compelled) to attend meetings of the Trusteeship Council when matters affecting its Trust Territories are under consideration. Moreover, if after ceasing to be a Member of the United Nations, the Administering Authority committed violations of the Trust, any measures which are provided elsewhere in the Charter against Member States could be invoked equally against the State in question. If, however, the State were allowed to withdraw for other reasons, or were expelled, and did not voluntarily consent to the transfer of the Trust to another authority, the resulting situation could only be judged by the General Assembly and the Security Council on its merits in the light of all the circumstances prevailing at the time. It is impossible to make provision in advance for such a situation.

It was decided that while this statement should not be regarded as an expression of the views of the Committee, it should be appended to the Rapporteur's report.[3]

---

[1] *Ibid., Report of the Rapporteur of Committee II/4*, Doc. 1115, II/4/44 (1) (a), p. 14–15.

[2] Chapter VIII of the Dumbarton Oaks Proposals. This was broken down into Chapters VI, VII and VIII of the Charter as finally adopted.

[3] *Ibid., Summary Report of Sixteenth Meeting of Committee II/4, June 20, 1945*, Doc. 1143, II/4/46, p. 1.

ARTICLE 82

There may be designated, in any trusteeship agreement, a strategic area or areas which may include part or all of the trust territory to which the agreement applies, without prejudice to any special agreement or agreements made under Article 43.

This Article, taken together with Article 83, provides for a special regime for those areas in which a Member or Members of the United Nations, or the United Nations as a group, may have special interests of a strategic character. Presumably the interest in question may result either from the defense requirements of a particular state or states or from the needs of the Organization as a whole for maintaining peace and security as determined by the Security Council.

The situation which apparently gave rise to this differentiation between territories placed under trusteeship agreements, subject to the authority of the General Assembly, and those placed under the authority of the Security Council because of the designation of a strategic area or areas, was the need of finding some device by which the principle of non-aggrandizement laid down in the Atlantic Charter might be respected while at the same time the special security requirements of certain Members of the United Nations would be satisfied. The United States, for example, after the experience of attack without warning at Pearl Harbor, was inclined to insist upon a measure of control over areas in the Pacific in the interest of national defense. However, by the terms of the Atlantic Charter the United States Government was committed to the principle of territorial non-aggrandizement.

The special significance of the designation of a particular area as strategic is made clear in Article 83. It means that functions of the Organization, including the approval of the terms of the agreement and their alteration or amendment, are to be performed by the Security Council. On the Security Council any one of the permanent members, including the United States, will be in a position to veto any action by that body. A permanent member will consequently be in a better position to protect its special national interests on the Security Council than in the General Assembly where decisions are taken by a majority vote or a special two-thirds majority vote. In addition to the protection that a permanent member of the Security Council interested in a particular strategic area will derive from the fact that its consent is necessary to any agreement bringing the area under the trusteeship system, there is the added guarantee that with respect to the supervision of the administration of such an area no action can be taken by the Security Council without its approval.

In addition to safeguarding the special security interests of permanent members of the Security Council, this arrangement can be said to harmonize with the general peace and security system of the Charter since it places on the Security Council, primarily responsible for the maintenance of international peace and security, the responsibility for the exercise of Organization trusteeship functions in those areas which are of strategic value in the organization of international peace and security. It thus gives assurance that the areas in question will be administered with due regard to the requirements of enforcement action under Chapters VII and VIII.

It is stated that this Article in no way affects the obligations of Members under Article 43 which provides for a special agreement or agreements defining the terms under which Members place at the disposition of the Security Council armed forces, assistance and facilities for use in the maintenance of international peace and security.

ARTICLE 83

1. All functions of the United Nations relating to strategic areas, including the approval of the terms of the trusteeship agreements and of their alteration or amendment, shall be exercised by the Security Council.

This paragraph simply provides for the substitution of the Security Council for the General Assembly in the performance of the functions of the United Nations in respect to strategic areas. The reasons and consequences of this were explained in the comment on Article 82.

While the Security Council is substituted for the General Assembly as the organ responsible for the performance of the functions of the United Nations relating to strategic areas in trust territories, there is nowhere in the Charter a specific grant of powers to be used in carrying out these functions comparable to that contained in Article 87 for the General Assembly. It would seem that the possession of such powers would be necessary to the effective exercise by the Security Council of its functions under this Article, and furthermore, by a reasonable interpretation might be implied from the wording of this Article.

2. The basic objectives set forth in Article 76 shall be applicable to the people of each strategic area.

The meaning of this is self-explanatory.

3. The Security Council shall, subject to the provisions of the trusteeship agreements and without prejudice to security considerations, avail itself of the assistance of the Trusteeship Council to perform those functions of the United Nations under the trusteeship system relating to political, economic, social, and educational matters in the strategic areas.

By the terms of this paragraph the Security Council is to avail itself of the assistance of the Trusteeship Council in performing those functions of the United Nations relating to political, economic, social and educational matters in the strategic areas designated under the terms of Article 82. There was some discussion in the technical committee at the Conference as to whether this should be made obligatory or facultative. It was argued that the Security Council must be given some discretion in the matter and in recognition of this need two safeguards were inserted. One states that this obligation is subject to the provisions of the trusteeship agreements and the other that it is "without prejudice" to security considerations. This would indicate then that security considerations within the special areas designated are to be paramount even though they may involve neglect of other purposes stated in Article 76.

ARTICLE 84

It shall be the duty of the administering authority to ensure that the trust territory shall play its part in the maintenance of international peace and security. To this end the administering authority may make use of volunteer forces, facilities, and assistance from the trust territory in carrying out the obligation towards the Security Council undertaken in this regard by the administering authority, as well as for local defense and the maintenance of law and order within the trust territory.

This Article places upon the administering authority the obligation to see to it that the trust territory plays its part in the maintenance of international peace and security and it empowers the administering authority to this end to make use of "volunteer forces, facilities and assistance from the trust territory" in carrying out any obligation undertaken toward the Security Council. These forces and facilities may also be used for the purposes of local defense and the maintenance of law and order within the trust territory.

Under the League mandates system, insofar as territories under Class B and Class C mandates were concerned, mandatories were obligated to prevent "the establishment of fortifications of military and naval bases" and "military training of the natives for other than police purposes and the defense of territory." The meaning of the words "defense of territory" was not clear and led to disagreement between the Members of the League as to whether natives given military training might be used for defense of the territory of the mandatory power.[1] Nothing was said about their use in connection with carrying out League obligations.

The Charter makes it clear that while compulsory military training cannot be instituted, volunteer forces may be recruited and trained and used not only for local defense and police purposes but also for carrying out commitments under the Charter entered into by the administering

[1] See Wright, cited above, p. 39, 115.

authority for the maintenance of peace. It would seem then that such forces cannot be used by the administering authority for defense of its own territory, except by decision of the Security Council.

ARTICLE 85

1. The functions of the United Nations with regard to trusteeship agreements for all areas not designated as strategic, including the approval of the terms of the trusteeship agreements and of their alteration or amendment, shall be exercised by the General Assembly.

This paragraph represents a change from the method of control provided in the Covenant of the League. The terms of Article 22 of the Covenant provided that the Council should define the terms of the mandates except where previously determined by agreement of the Members of the League. In practice the agreements were invariably submitted to the Council for its approval. Furthermore, it was to the Council that the mandatory reported on its administration, and the Council was the organ responsible under the Covenant for performing League functions in respect to mandated territories. However, the Assembly had the opportunity in connection with its consideration of the Secretary-General's report to review the administration of mandated territories, and did not hesitate to criticize it and make recommendations.

Under the Charter system it is the General Assembly which is made responsible for the performance of these functions except for those areas designated as strategic, where the functions are to be performed by the Security Council. This places the United Nations control of the operation of the trusteeship system on a broader basis than was the case with the League mandatory system and gives to the smaller nations which are perhaps more likely to be disinterested a relatively greater share in the international supervision that is established.

2. The Trusteeship Council, operating under the authority of the General Assembly, shall assist the General Assembly in carrying out these functions.

Under the Covenant system a Permanent Mandates Commission was established to advise the Council on all matters relating to the observance of the mandate. Under the Charter system the Trusteeship Council is primarily responsible to the General Assembly although, according to the terms of Article 83, paragraph 3, the Security Council is to make use of it.

CHAPTER XIII

THE TRUSTEESHIP COUNCIL

Composition

ARTICLE 86

1. The Trusteeship Council shall consist of the following Members of the United Nations:
   a. those Members administering trust territories;
   b. such of those Members mentioned by name in Article 23 as are not administering trust territories; and
   c. as many other Members elected for three-year terms by the General Assembly as may be necessary to ensure that the total number of members of the Trusteeship Council is equally divided between those Members of the United Nations which administer trust territories and those which do not.

Composition of the Council. Under the Covenant, the Permanent Mandates Commission consisted of experts appointed by the Council, the majority of members being nationals of non-mandatory states. The Trusteeship Council is organized on a different principle. It is composed in the same manner as the Economic and Social Council and consists of Members of the United Nations. It is referred to in Article 7 as one of the principal organs of the United Nations. It is from the point of view of the Organization a more independent and important body than was the Permanent Mandates Commission. It is intended, however, to function under the authority of the General Assembly and is, therefore, responsible in the exercise of its functions to that body.

The Trusteeship Council consists of three categories of members: (1) Members of the United Nations administering trust territories, (2) Members of the United Nations mentioned by name in Article 23, that is, the original permanent members of the Security Council, which are not administering trust territories, and (3) as many additional members elected for three-year terms by the General Assembly as may be necessary to make the number of members administering trust territories equal to the number which are not. This means that the total number of members of the Council will be variable, depending in the last analysis upon the number of Members which are made responsible for the administration of trust territories.

The way in which the Trusteeship Council is constituted under this paragraph was bound to create a difficulty when it came to the setting up of the organ in the first instance. The provisions of this paragraph cannot be fully applied until agreements have been entered into establishing trust territories and indicating what Members are to administer trust territories. Until these agreements are made there inevitably has to be a choice between postponing the setting up of the Trusteeship Council until the trusteeship agreements envisaged in Article 79 are made, and setting it up on a purely provisional basis. The Executive Committee of the Preparatory Commission, accepting the second alternative, recommended that there should be established "in accordance with Article 22 of the Charter, a temporary Trusteeship Committee to perform certain of the functions assigned by the Charter to the Trusteeship Council, pending its establishment." [1]

Balance between Administering and Non-Administering Members. It is to be noted that the balance between states administering trust territories and those not administering trust territories on the Trusteeship Council is different from that which existed between mandatories and non-mandatories on the Permanent Mandates Commission. On the Commission representatives of non-mandatory powers were in the majority which might be interpreted as giving a guarantee of greater independence of action than does the principle of equality which is used in determining the composition of the Trusteeship Council.

The Working Paper adopted by Committee II/4 as the basis for discussion provided that the Council should consist of specially qualified representatives "designated (*a*) one each by the states administering trust territories, and (*b*) one each by an equal number of other states named for three-year periods by the General Assembly." [2] In operation this arrangement could have resulted in one or more of the permanent members of the Security Council not having representation on the Trusteeship Council. Of course this possibility exists in the case of the Economic and Social Council under the plan for its constitution contained in the Charter. The nature of the matters with which the Trusteeship Council would be dealing, however, apparently led to a demand that a modification be introduced which would assure the permanent members of the Security Council membership at all times. A revised text was submitted by the Delegate of the United States. [3] This provided for constituting the Council in the manner provided in Article 86. A pro-

[1] *Report by the Executive Committee to the Preparatory Commission of the United Nations,* cited above, p. 55. Three delegations objected to this recommendation on the ground that it was not authorized by the Charter and would be unconstitutional.

[2] UNCIO, Doc. 323, II/4/12, p. 3.

[3] *Ibid., Summary Report of Thirteenth Meeting of Committee II/4, June 8, 1945,* Doc. 877, II/4/35, p. 4.

posal was then made in Committee to reintroduce the original idea of an equal balance between elected and non-elected members. It was argued that the permanent members of the Security Council resembled the administering states in that they were interested parties, and that the peoples of the trust territories would be better protected if half of the members of the Trusteeship Council were elected by the General Assembly. Against this proposal it was argued that there was "no distinction in humanitarian purpose" between the three categories but only "of practical experience," and that "what was required on the Trusteeship Council was the greatest possible sum of knowledge and wisdom." The proposal was defeated by a vote of 31 to 8.[1]

2. Each member of the Trusteeship Council shall designate one specially qualified person to represent it therein.

This suggests that from the point of view of the expert character of its members the Trusteeship Council is not to differ materially from the Permanent Mandates Commission. A "specially qualified person" would seem to be for all practical purposes an expert, that is, a person who by virtue of training and experience is entitled to have his opinions deferred to on all matters which come before the Council for action.

Functions and Powers

ARTICLE 87

1. The General Assembly and, under its authority, the Trusteeship Council, in carrying out their functions, may:
    a. **consider reports submitted by the administering authority;**
    b. **accept petitions and examine them in consultation with the administering authority;**
    c. **provide for periodic visits to the respective trust territories at times agreed upon with the administering authority; and**
    d. **take these and other actions in conformity with the terms of the trusteeship agreements.**

The powers that are given to the General Assembly and, under its authority, to the Trusteeship Council by the terms of this Article cover those powers which were vested in the League of Nations Council and the Permanent Mandates Commission under the Covenant of the League of Nations [2] and in addition make provision for periodic visits to the trust territories which were not permitted under the League mandates system. It was the contention of the mandatory powers that inquiries on the spot conducted under the direction of the Permanent Mandates Commission would have the effect of weakening the authority of the

[1] *Ibid.*, p. 5.
[2] On powers vested in the League Council and the manner in which these powers were exercised, see Wright, cited above, p. 126 ff.

mandatory. The withholding of this power deprived the Commission of an important means of establishing the facts which were necessary to the adequate performance of its duties. It made the Commission largely dependent upon the reports and oral explanations of the representatives of the mandatory powers.

While the General Assembly and the Trusteeship Council may make provision for periodic visits to the trust territories, there is one important provision attached to the grant of power, namely that the visits must be carried out "at times agreed upon with the administering authority." This makes it possible for the administering authority to prevent any such visits from taking place, but in view of the probable reaction to such a refusal it is unlikely that any administering authority which is a Member of the United Nations will resort to such extreme measures. This provision then represents a definite advance over the League system.

Certain other provisions of this Article deserve words of comment. The use of the words "under its authority," repeated from Article 85, paragraph 2, emphasizes that the Trusteeship Council in performing the functions here enumerated is to act under the direction and supervision of the General Assembly. The power to "consider reports" is to be understood as involving the power to discuss and to make recommendations.[1] Of course, it would be denying the General Assembly and the Trusteeship Council any effective means of carrying out the responsibilities placed on them by the terms of Article 85 if clause *a* were given a restricted interpretation which denied to these organs the power to do more than discuss and cogitate.

The power expressly accorded to accept petitions and examine them "in consultation with the administering authority" was not explicitly given by the Covenant to any organ of the League, but the Council adopted the procedure in 1923. Such petitions were frequently presented. Certain conditions were laid down to which petitions must conform in order to be considered.[2] The Provisional Rules of Procedure for the Trusteeship Council, recommended by the Executive Committee to the Preparatory Commission, contained rules with regard to petitions which were obviously inspired by League experience. Thus Rule 38 provided that the Council should reject petitions or parts thereof "(a) if they are trivial in nature, couched in abusive terms, or submitted anonymously; and (b) if they contain complaints which are incompatible with the provisions of Chapters XII and XIII of the Charter or the trusteeship agreements." The Provisional Rules admitted the possibility of oral as well as written petitions.[3]

---

[1] On meaning of word "consider" as used in Charter, see this volume p. 98.
[2] See Wright, cited above, p. 169.
[3] *Report by the Executive Committee to the Preparatory Commission of the United Nations*, cited above, p. 61.

Clause *d* authorizes the General Assembly and the Trusteeship Council to "take these and other actions in conformity with the terms of the trusteeship agreements." This might be interpreted in two ways. It can be regarded as adding to the powers of the two organs by providing that the powers enumerated in this Article may be extended by the terms of the trusteeship agreements. If this was the intention, it is not clear why "in conformity with" should be made to condition "these" as well as "other actions," as is clearly the case. On the other hand, this clause can be interpreted as having definitely restrictive possibilities, as saying in effect that actions of the two organs under this Article and other Articles of the Charter, in trusteeship matters, must conform to the terms of the individual trusteeship agreements in individual cases. The second interpretation would appear to be warranted by the history of the text. The original Working Paper closed the enumeration of the powers of the two organs with the words "and to take other action in conformity with the trusteeship arrangements." [1] This was subsequently revised in the United States draft by the insertion of a comma after "action," thereby making the qualifying phrase apply to all the powers enumerated.[2] It would thus appear that the purpose of the clause is to make it clear that the General Assembly and the Trusteeship Council in performing the trusteeship functions of the United Nations in respect to any given trust territory must act in conformity with the terms of the trusteeship agreement by which that trust territory is set up.

ARTICLE 88

The Trusteeship Council shall formulate a questionnaire on the political, economic, social and educational advancement of the inhabitants of each trust territory, and the administering authority for each trust territory within the competence of the General Assembly shall make an annual report to the General Assembly upon the basis of such questionnaire.

By the terms of this Article each administering authority is obligated to make an annual report to the General Assembly upon the administration of the territories for which it is responsible. This differs from the League system in that the report goes to the Assembly directly instead of to the Council. However, in the case of areas designated as strategic the practice will follow that of the League since it will be to the Security Council that the administering authority will presumably report in such cases.

In order to secure uniform reports and to be certain that all the points upon which information is desired are covered, the Trusteeship Council is given the power, in fact is required, to formulate a questionnaire upon

---

[1] UNCIO, Doc. 323, II/4/12, p. 3. [2] *Ibid.*, p. 7.

which the report of the administering authority is to be based. This, too, represents a considerable advance over the League system and if the terms of the Article are carried out, reports submitted by the administering authorities should be much more satisfactory than they were in many cases under the League mandates system.

It is to be noted that the Article specifies in some detail the content of the questionnaire. This detailed description was inserted largely upon the insistence of the smaller powers with a view to giving still another guarantee that full publicity will be given to the record of each administering authority in carrying out its trust under the trust agreement.

Voting

ARTICLE 89

1. Each member of the Trusteeship Council shall have one vote.
2. Decisions of the Trusteeship Council shall be made by a majority of the members present and voting.

This article is similar to Article 67, which governs voting in the Economic and Social Council. The same comment applies.

Procedure

ARTICLE 90

1. The Trusteeship Council shall adopt its own rules of procedure, including the method of selecting its President.
2. The Trusteeship Council shall meet as required in accordance with its rules, which shall include provision for the convening of meetings on the request of a majority of its members.

This is similar to Article 72, which applies to the Economic and Social Council. The same comment applies.

ARTICLE 91

The Trusteeship Council shall, when appropriate, avail itself of the assistance of the Economic and Social Council and of the specialized agencies in regard to matters with which they are respectively concerned.

While leaving a certain measure of discretion to the Trusteeship Council this Article makes it the duty of the Council to avail itself of the assistance of the Economic and Social Council and of the specialized agencies in regard to matters with which they are respectively concerned. The desirability of such a practice is obvious. The Article represents another attempt to secure proper coordination of the activities of the organs of the United Nations and of the specialized agencies in their relations with the United Nations Organization.

CHAPTER XIV

THE INTERNATIONAL COURT OF JUSTICE

ARTICLE 92

The International Court of Justice shall be the principal judicial organ of the United Nations. It shall function in accordance with the annexed Statute, which is based upon the Statute of the Permanent Court of International Justice, and forms an integral part of the present Charter.

History of the Chapter. No attempt was made in the Dumbarton Oaks Conversations to draft the statute of an international court. It was agreed that there 'should be an international court of justice which would constitute the principal judicial organ of the Organization, but it was not decided whether it should be a new court or the old Permanent Court of International Justice with its Statute revised. Shortly after the Crimea Conference in February 1945, when the date of the San Francisco Conference was set, the Sponsoring Governments invited the Members of the United Nations to send representatives to a preliminary meeting in Washington to prepare a draft of a statute for the proposed court to be submitted to the Conference as a basis for discussion. Thus was constituted the United Nations Committee of Jurists which met in Washington from April 9 to 20, 1945.

This Committee, taking into account the Statute of the Permanent Court of International Justice and the experience of that tribunal,[1] prepared a report for submission to the Conference.[2] This report included a Draft Statute following closely the arrangement and, in the main, the substance of the Statute of the Permanent Court. On points where there were differences of opinion which the Committee was unable to resolve, the Committee presented alternative texts. This draft was used as the basis of discussion by Committee IV/1 of the United Nations Conference. This Committee in addition had the benefit of the advice of two members of the Permanent Court (Judge Gustavo Guerrero, the President of the Court, and Judge Manley O. Hudson), who were invited by the Committee to attend its meetings.

The Court as a Principal Organ. Article 92 states that the International Court of Justice shall be "the principal judicial organ" of the United Nations. This means, first of all, that the Court is one of the

[1] For review of the Court's work, see Hudson, Manley O., *The Permanent Court of International Justice, 1920–1942: A Treatise*, N. Y., Macmillan, 1943, 807 p.

[2] *The United Nations Committee of Jurists*, Jurists 86, G/73, April 25, 1945.

organs of the Organization,[1] and secondly, that the connection between the Court and the Organization is organic. Thereby the problem of whether or not the Court is to be a separate and independent body is solved. It is not separate. Its fate is intimately linked with that of the other organs of the Organization. This is a realization of the oneness of international organization. Respect for law and order is a condition for the functioning of any political organization. Even an international court cannot operate in a political vacuum. If the political climate of the world is bad, the Court will suffer as well as other international institutions.

This first sentence of Article 92 also signifies that the International Court shall not, of necessity, be the only judicial organ of the Organization. The Charter thus leaves the door open for other — and subsidiary — judicial organs of a regional or functional character.[2]

A New Court. Opinions were sharply divided on the question whether the Permanent Court of International Justice should be continued or a new court set up.[3] The Dumbarton Oaks Proposals had left the question open.[4] Certain delegates felt that it was desirable to maintain the continuity of international judicial institutions as much as possible. They were of the opinion that the Permanent Court of International Justice had represented such a great advance in international relations that it must not be thrown overboard. They felt also that the Permanent Court was a living organism that should be kept. Hundreds of international conventions referred to this Court and recognized it as the tribunal to which parties were to refer their disputes. Furthermore its record justified its continuance.

Other delegates, while admitting the importance of these arguments, felt nevertheless that it was better to start with a clean slate. They argued that the Court would be so intimately linked with the United Nations that it should preferably be a new court created by this Organization. Their chief argument was that the old Court could not continue in any case. Elections had not been held for a long time. The old machinery for elections could not be employed again. Particular stress was laid on the membership of the Court. Certain states which were not Members of the United Nations were members of the Permanent Court and would not belong, in the beginning at least, to the new court. There were also Members of the United Nations who had not accepted the Permanent Court of International Justice. It was, therefore, better to have a completely new court. A subsidiary argument was that the traditions and experience of the Permanent Court of International

[1] See Article 7, paragraph 1.

[2] See Articles 52, 95.

[3] See UNCIO, *Report of the Rapporteur of Committee IV/1*, Doc. 913, IV/1/74 (1), p. 3.

[4] See Chapter VII, paragraph 3, this volume, p. 313.

Justice were already a part of the world inheritance and would live on in the new court and be utilized just as if it had been continued.[1]

Consequently, it was decided to create a new court. This of course means that the International Court of Justice will be established and will function on the basis of its Statute. This forms an integral part of the Charter and is annexed to it. It is based on the Statute of the Permanent Court of International Justice which will presumably be terminated by action of the parties to it.[2] This is not the place to give an extensive commentary on the Statute. That must form the subject of a separate study. It is so like the old Statute that studies of that document provide a useful introduction to the understanding of the new.[3] However, certain matters will be treated briefly here, namely, (1) the question of obligatory jurisdiction, (2) the method of electing judges, and (3) amendments to the Statute.

The Question of Obligatory Jurisdiction. The question of obligatory jurisdiction was extensively discussed at the Conference. It had earlier been considered by the United Nations Committee of Jurists in Washington. Furthermore, the question had been carefully considered at the time of the establishment of the Permanent Court of International Justice. The Draft Statute proposed by the Committee of Jurists,[4] appointed by the Council under Article 14 of the Covenant, had contained a provision for obligatory jurisdiction. In discussions in the League Council and Assembly, it was argued that this went too far in that some Members would be unwilling to accept compulsory jurisdiction. Consequently, the Statute, as submitted to the Members of the League, provided for voluntary jurisdiction in principle, but had appended to it a protocol the acceptance of which conferred obligatory jurisdiction upon the Court as between states accepting it and subject to certain other conditions.

The decision taken on this question at the Conference and the reasons therefor can best be described in the words of the Report of the Rapporteur of Committee IV/1 to Commission IV:

> The debate revealed a sharp division of opinion on the general question. On one side stress was placed on the progress made since 1920 under the Statute of the Permanent Court of International Justice; at one time or another 45 states exercised the option to confer compulsory jurisdiction on the Court, though in instances this was for limited periods of time and subject to reservations. The discussion in the First Committee showed, in the words of a subcommittee, "the existence of a great volume of support for extending the international legal order

[1] For report of Committee discussion, see UNCIO, *Report of the Rapporteur of Committee IV/1*, Doc. 913, IV/1/74 (1), p. 3.

[2] See recommendation of the Executive Committee to the Preparatory Commission, *Report of the Executive Committee to the Preparatory Commission of the United Nations*, cited above, p. 67.   [3] See Hudson, cited above.

[4] *Permanent Court of International Justice, Draft Scheme*, Boston, World Peace Foundation, League of Nations series, III (1920), Special Number.

by recognizing immediately throughout the membership of the new Organization the compulsory jurisdiction of the Court."

On the other side, the delegates of some states stated that their governments might find it difficult or impossible at this time to accept the compulsory jurisdiction of the Court, and they expressed their preference for the maintenance of the optional feature of Article 36. They felt that the adoption of this course would leave the way open for substantial advance toward the goal of universal jurisdiction, and that the Court would be placed on a firmer basis if the acceptance by states depended on their willing exercise of the option.

In an endeavor to reconcile the two points of view represented by the alternative texts proposed by the Committee of Jurists, much support was given to the third draft above mentioned, providing for immediate acceptance of compulsory jurisdiction subject to stated reservations. Some of the delegates supporting optional jurisdiction were, however, unable to accept this compromise. Other suggestions were made for amending the text of Article 36 in the optional form by incorporating permitted reservations, with or without liberty to add others. These suggestions were also rejected.

A subcommittee which made a report on the subject recommended the retention of the text in the Statute of the Permanent Court of International Justice with two changes designed to take into account the various views expressed by members of the Committee. The reference to "any of the classes" of legal disputes in paragraph 2 of Article 36 was omitted. A new paragraph 4 was inserted to preserve declarations made under Article 36 of the old Statute for periods of time which have not expired, and to make these declarations applicable to the jurisdiction of the new Court. In concluding its report, the subcommittee made the following statement:

"The desire to establish compulsory jurisdiction for the Court prevailed among the majority of the Subcommittee. However, some of these delegates feared that insistence upon the realization of that ideal would only impair the possibility of obtaining general accord to the Statute of the Court, as well as to the Charter itself. It is in that spirit that the majority of the Subcommittee recommends the adoption of the solution described above."

The following statement from the subcommittee's report should also be noted:

"The question of reservations calls for an explanation. As is well known, the article has consistently been interpreted in the past as allowing states accepting the jurisdiction of the Court to subject their declarations to reservations. The subcommittee has considered such interpretation as being henceforth established. It has therefore been considered unnecessary to modify paragraph 3 in order to make express reference to the right of the states to make such reservations." [1]

Furthermore, Committee IV/1 adopted unanimously a resolution asking the Conference to recommend to Members of the United Nations that they proceed as soon as possible to make declarations under Article 36, recognizing the obligatory jurisdiction of the Court.[2] The Conference agreed to this action at its plenary session of June 25, 1945.[3]

[1] UNCIO, *Report of the Rapporteur of Committee IV/1*, Doc. 913, IV/1/74(1), p. 10.
[2] *Ibid., Recommendation Adopted by Committee IV/1*, Doc. 870, IV/1/73.
[3] *Ibid., Verbatim Minutes of the Ninth Plenary Session, June 25, 1945*, Doc. 1210, P/20, p. 16.

The Election of Judges. The procedure for electing judges was considered very carefully at the Conference. Two alternative methods were discussed: (a) election by the Security Council and the General Assembly, voting concurrently; and (b) election by the General Assembly. The first was the method used under the Statute of the Permanent Court of International Justice and was finally adopted for the International Court of Justice for reasons which can best be given in the words of the Rapporteur of Committee IV/1:

Some delegates wished to retain the method that prevailed in the old Court so that Judges would be elected by the General Assembly and the Security Council, each acting independently of the other. It was believed that this method had worked well in the past, and that it would tend to secure the election of the best judges, irrespective of their nationality. Some delegates, on the other hand, held that this method gave double votes to states represented both in the General Assembly and in the Security Council. Therefore it was proposed that the elections should be by the General Assembly alone. The Committee finally reconciled these two views by deciding that both bodies should take part in the election, that an absolute majority should be required in each body, and that no distinction should be made between permanent and non-permanent members in the voting in the Security Council.[1]

For details of the method of election finally adopted, see Articles 2–15 of the Statute.[2]

Amendment of the Statute. The question of the process by which the Statute is to be amended was given careful consideration at San Francisco. The Statute of the Permanent Court of International Justice did not contain any rule for its own revision. For that reason, a new conference had to be held at any time when it was desired to amend the Statute and the changes had to be ratified by all the signatories.

The new Statute has avoided this pitfall by stating in Article 69 that the Statute shall be amended in the same way as the Charter of which it is a part,[3] subject however to any provisions which the General Assembly upon recommendation of the Security Council may adopt concerning the participation of states which are parties to the Statute but not Members of the United Nations. The Statute does not state specifically whether the provisions of Article 109 of the Charter, under which a General Conference may be called to review the Charter, also apply to the Statute, but since this Article is included in Chapter VIII (Amendments), it is to be assumed that all provisions of the Chapter are equally applicable. Article 70 of the Statute gives the Court itself the power to propose amendments. In the words of the Rapporteur of Committee IV/1, the provision "gives an opportunity for the Statute of the Court

---

[1] *Ibid., Verbatim Minutes of Second Meeting of Commission IV, June 15, 1945,* Doc. 1007, IV/12, p. 3–4.

[2] This volume, p. 365–8.

[3] See Articles 108 and 109 of the Charter.

to be watched and developed by those best able to understand the nature of the work of the Court and to adapt the Statute to the changing needs of the times." [1]

ARTICLE 93

1. All Members of the United Nations are *ipso facto* parties to the Statute of the International Court of Justice.

Under this provision, a state cannot be a Member of the Organization without at the same time being a party to the Statute of the Court. This was possible under the Covenant of the League of Nations and the Statute of the Permanent Court.

After the Committee of Jurists had prepared the Draft Statute for the Permanent Court, the question was raised in Council and Assembly discussions whether the Statute might be adopted and made binding on Members of the League without their individual consents. It was decided to submit the Statute as an international agreement to be adhered to by eligible states. The Soviet Union became a Member of the League in 1934 without ever adhering to the Statute of the Permanent Court.

The Statute of the Permanent Court permitted "states or Members of the League of Nations" to be parties in cases before it.[2] It declared the Court open to Members of the League and to states mentioned in the annex to the Covenant, and to other states under conditions laid down by the Council.[3] The Statute of the International Court of Justice contains similar provisions.[4]

2. A state which is not a Member of the United Nations may become a party to the Statute of the International Court of Justice on conditions to be determined in each case by the General Assembly upon the recommendation of the Security Council.

This makes it possible for a state which is not a Member of the United Nations to become a party to the Statute. The General Assembly, acting on the recommendation of the Security Council, is to determine "in each case" the conditions under which this can be done. This paragraph recognizes the desirability of extending as widely as possible the specific commitments of the Statute and the use of the procedures there laid down for the peaceful settlement of disputes. It recognizes, too, in its requirement that the General Assembly act upon the recommendation of the Security Council, the special responsibility of that body for the maintenance of international peace and security.

---

[1] UNCIO, *Verbatim Minutes of Second Meeting of Commission IV, June 15, 1945,* Doc. 1007, IV/12, p. 5.

[2] *Charter of the United Nations*, Article 34.

[3] *Ibid.*, Article 35.   [4] *Ibid.*, Articles 34 and 35.

Under the League system there was no specific provision either in the Covenant or in the Statute of the Permanent Court governing the adherence to the Statute of a state which was not a Member of the League. Such adherence however was admittedly possible without any control by the Council or Assembly. Experience, however, in connection with the attempted adherence of the United States to the Statute demonstrated that there were difficult questions involved.[1] Should the non-member be allowed to participate in the election of judges, and if so, in what way? What obligations, if any, under the Covenant would the non-member assume? To what extent would the non-member be bound by advisory opinions, and to what extent should it be permitted to veto requests for such opinions? Under what conditions might the non-member withdraw from the arrangement? These and other questions which had to be considered in connection with the proposed United States adherence to the Statute of the Permanent Court will have to be considered in the application of this paragraph and presumably will be covered by the conditions laid down by the General Assembly on recommendation of the Security Council.

ARTICLE 94

1. Each Member of the United Nations undertakes to comply with the decision of the International Court of Justice in any case to which it is a party.

It is an established principle of international law that the decision of an international court is binding upon the parties. This paragraph is a special application of this principle and of the general principle laid down in the second paragraph of Article 2 of the Charter. This principle is again laid down in Article 60 of the Statute. Neither the Charter nor the Statute contains any provision regarding the conditions, if any, under which a judgment may be regarded as not binding. The validity of certain arbitral decisions has been contested in the past on such grounds as excess of power. Article 60 of the Statute says that the judgment is "final and without appeal." Article 61 provides, however, for revision of the judgment by the Court itself under certain conditions.

2. If any party to a case fails to perform the obligations incumbent upon it under a judgment rendered by the Court, the other party may have recourse to the Security Council, which may, if it deems necessary, make recommendations or decide upon measures to be taken to give effect to the judgment.

Judging from past experience, this paragraph is not likely to have great importance in practice. It has happened very rarely that states

[1] See Hudson, cited above, chap. 11.

have refused to carry out the decisions of international tribunals. The difficulty has always been in getting states to submit their disputes to a tribunal. Once they have done so, they have usually been willing to accept even an adverse judgment.[1] In no case did the parties refuse to carry out a judgment of the Permanent Court of International Justice. Of course if the compulsory jurisdiction of the Court is generally accepted the situation may be changed since the willingness of parties to accept court judgments and arbitral awards in the past has been without doubt related to the fact of voluntary submission.

It was argued at the United Nations Conference that the principle of respect for judgments was of the highest importance to the new international order and ought to be implemented by the Charter. Article 13, paragraph 4, of the Covenant provided that in the event of any failure to carry out an arbitral award or judicial decision, "the Council shall propose what steps should be taken to give effect thereto." Even though there was objection in the technical committee to the inclusion of a similar proposal in the Charter on the ground that the matter was outside the competence of the Committee, it received strong support [2] and was adopted.

The phraseology of the paragraph raises an important question of interpretation. Does it confer upon the Security Council power additional to that conferred under the terms of Chapter VII? Does it, in other words, empower the Security Council to take appropriate action, upon the request of one of the parties to a dispute, to obtain respect for the judgment of the Court by the other party, even though there may be no threat to the peace or violation of the peace?

Dr. Leo Pasvolsky, in his testimony before the Senate Committee on Foreign Relations, expressed the view that the grant of power to the Security Council in this paragraph is subject to other provisions of the Charter defining the Council's power. In other words, according to this interpretation, the Security Council can act under this paragraph only within the scope of its powers as defined in Chapters V, VI and VII of the Charter. Quoting Dr. Pasvolsky:

The Council may proceed, I suppose, to call upon the country concerned to carry out the judgment, but only if the peace of the world is threatened, and if the Council has made a determination to that effect. It is the party, not the Court, that goes to the Council. It is the aggrieved party, the party which is willing to abide by the determination of the Court when the other party is not willing to so abide. The Council is not a sheriff in the sense that the Council enforces the Court's decision when the Court asks it to enforce it. The Council simply handles a political situation which arises out of the fact that the judgment of the Court is not being carried out by one of the parties.[3]

[1] See Hambro, Edvard, *L'exécution des sentences internationales*, Liége, 1936.
[2] UNCIO, *Summary Report of Twentieth Meeting of Committee IV/1/71, June 7, 1945*, p. 2–3.
[3] *Hearings . . . on The Charter of the United Nations*, etc., cited above, p. 287.

From the record of the discussion in Committee IV/1 at the Conference it is not clear what was the interpretation placed upon the words of this paragraph by the members of the Committee. Their principal concern seems to have been to make sure that the aggrieved party had recourse to the Security Council.[1] The words used, however, would seem to suggest action beyond that which might be required to keep the peace or restore peace, since in the situation where the provisions of this paragraph would likely be invoked, the state refusing to carry out the terms of a judgment would not necessarily be threatening the peace in any way, except in so far as the refusal to carry out a legal obligation might be so interpreted.

ARTICLE 95

Nothing in the present Charter shall prevent Members of the United Nations from entrusting the solution of their differences to other tribunals by virtue of agreements already in existence or which may be concluded in the future.

This paragraph contains an affirmation of the general principle laid down in the first paragraph of Article 33. The Members of the United Nations are at complete liberty to solve their disputes as they deem fit so long as they do so in a way that does not endanger the maintenance of international peace and security.

ARTICLE 96

1. The General Assembly or the Security Council may request the International Court of Justice to give an advisory opinion on any legal question.

This paragraph gives to the Security Council and to the General Assembly a very broad authority to ask the Court for legal advice. Such is the character of an "advisory opinion." Such an opinion will have the greatest prestige and moral force, but the Council or the Assembly will be under no obligation to follow the advice given. In spite of the great weight to be attached to such an opinion, it may happen that political realities make it unwise to accept it or that it has been possible to settle the matter by a compromise in such a way that the parties are satisfied. The experience of the League shows that such opinions may be of the greatest usefulness, and that such opinions are not likely to be lightly disregarded.

The question upon which the advisory opinion is requested may relate to a dispute which is before the Security Council under the provisions

[1] UNCIO, *Summary Report of Twentieth Meeting of Committee IV/1, June 7, 1945,* Doc. 864, IV/1/71, p. 2–3.

of Chapter VI, especially Articles 37 and 38. In the case of a legal dispute, the Council might well make the advisory opinion of the Court its recommendation to the parties, and such a recommendation would undoubtedly have greater weight than one not supported by the authority of the Court. In fact, judging by the experience of the League the parties will be prepared to show essentially the same deference to recommendations of that nature as to judgments of the Court, largely because of the safeguards contained in Chapter IV of the Statute in respect to the Court's procedure in advisory cases.[1]

2. Other organs of the United Nations and specialized agencies, which may at any time be so authorized by the General Assembly, may also request advisory opinions of the Court on legal questions arising within the scope of their activities.

This paragraph is a complete innovation. Under the League system it was only the Council and the Assembly which could ask for advisory opinions. By this paragraph the specialized agencies and the organs of the United Nations, other than the General Assembly and the Security Council, are given a limited right to ask for opinions on legal questions arising within the scope of their activities, if they are so authorized by the General Assembly. It is not quite clear from the text whether the authorization has to be given for each individual case or whether a general authorization can be given to any given organ or agency. The logic of experience would seem to indicate that the authorization should be general. The report of the technical committee's discussion supports this interpretation.[2] The Committee refused to adopt a proposal to substitute the words "in each case" for the words "at any time." Furthermore, if that is not the proper interpretation, it might as well be provided, as in the League Covenant, that only the Council or the Assembly has the right to ask for an opinion, since each case would have to be considered separately anyway.

Under the League system, the Council in many cases acted as a go-between in transmitting to the Court requests for advisory opinions relating to matters within the competence of specialized agencies. This was particularly true of requests for advisory opinions on questions relating to the International Labor Organization. Of the twenty-seven requests for advisory opinions addressed to the Court, six originated with the Governing Body of the I.L.O. A system of general authorizations under

---

[1] On experience with advisory opinions under the League system, see Hudson, cited above, chap. 22. See also Goodrich, Leland M., "The Nature of the Advisory Opinion of the Permanent Court of International Justice," *American Journal of International Law*, XXXII (October 1938), p. 738.

[2] UNCIO, *Summary Report of Twentieth Meeting of Committee IV/1*, Doc. 864, IV/1/71, p. 3–4.

which specially designated organs of the United Nations, other than
the General Assembly and the Security Council, or specialized agencies
may apply to the Court directly for advisory opinions would appear to
be the purpose of this paragraph.[1]

[1] In its *Observations on Relationships with Specialized Agencies*, the Executive
Committee of the Preparatory Commission expressed the following opinion:
"In the light of these provisions (paragraph 2 of Article 96), it will be for the
General Assembly to decide whether a general authorization, if requested, should be
given to any of the specialized agencies to enable them to make requests for advisory
opinions directly to the Court, without recourse to the General Assembly in each
instance. The General Assembly should also consider whether a provision relating to
a general authorization should be included in the initial or subsidiary agreements
with the agencies concerned. It is assumed that the General Assembly could at any
time revoke a general authorization." *Report by the Executive Committee to the
Preparatory Commission of the United Nations*, cited above, p. 105.

CHAPTER XV

THE SECRETARIAT

ARTICLE 97

The Secretariat shall comprise a Secretary-General and such staff as the Organization may require. The Secretary-General shall be appointed by the General Assembly upon the recommendation of the Security Council. He shall be the chief administrative officer of the Organization.

Deputy Secretaries-General. This Article was discussed at great length at the United Nations Conference on account of a proposal introduced by the Sponsoring Governments to make specific provision for a number of Deputy Secretaries-General to be appointed by the General Assembly upon the recommendation of the Security Council. This proposal was strongly opposed by many delegates for several reasons. It was openly admitted by some of the delegates of the Great Powers that the Secretary-General would in reality hold a position of very great political authority. These delegates maintained that the higher posts in the Secretariat would also be of the highest political importance and that they ought, for that very reason, to be treated as political positions. They imagined one deputy acting for the Council, one for the Assembly, one for the Economic and Social Council, and so on. They wanted to have political control of these high functionaries.

Other delegates, particularly those representing Belgium, Canada, the Netherlands, New Zealand and Norway, were perfectly well aware of the need for deputies. However, they were against fixing either their number or their terms of office in the Charter. They felt that it was impossible at this date to know how many such functionaries would be needed. They felt that their number should not be fixed in such a way that it could only be changed through the cumbersome procedure of amendment. They felt also that the deputies should be appointed by the Secretary-General like the other members of the staff. It would, they claimed, undermine the authority of the Secretary-General if he should have as his immediate subordinates people elected or appointed as he is himself. This would, in their eyes, destroy the homogeneous character of the Secretariat. Finally they did not want to have political nomination of staff members. They wanted to have all the members of the staff from the top down behave and feel like international civil

opinions and send it back to me at your earliest convenience
(better by air mail).

I repeat I am sorry that I have taken some of your very
valuable moments.

With best regards.

Yours sincerely,

University Park,
Nottingham,
NG7 2RD.

Dear Sir,

I may please be excused for taxing upon your valuable time.

I beg to inform you that I am a research student here, and I am working on "Trends in Pakistan's External Relations", I would like to have the seasoned views of our national leaders for my research work. A country's foreign policy and internal policy are interwoven. You are one of those few national leaders who have been trying hard for long to give a definite shape to the destiny of the nation, and I would highly value your views on different aspects of Pakistan's foreign policy.

I am, therefore, sending you herewith a questionnaire. I should be highly obliged if you would kindly spare a few moments to fill in the questionnaire with your enlightened

servants. For these reasons they fought against the proposed amendment and defeated it.

This, however, does not mean that there will be no Deputy Secretaries-General, Under Secretaries or other high officials. They will certainly be needed and they will be appointed in due time under the rules laid down in Article 101.

Powers of General Assembly and Security Council. The Secretary-General is to be appointed by the General Assembly on the recommendation of the Security Council. The use of the word "appoint" instead of the word "elect" is intended to emphasize the administrative character of his duties. It is clear that the Assembly can reject a candidate recommended by the Security Council. If it does so, it cannot appoint a Secretary General of its own choice, but must wait for the Council to make a new recommendation.

The General Assembly, according to the third paragraph of Article 18, makes its appointment by a simple majority. The Security Council, in making its recommendation, is governed by the provisions of the third paragraph of Article 27. This follows both from the wording of the paragraph on voting and from the Committee discussions at the United Nations Conference.[1] A recommendation thus requires the agreement of the permanent members of the Security Council.

Term of Secretary-General. This Article does not contain any indication as to the term of the Secretary-General. The Sponsoring Governments had proposed a three-year term with re-election permitted. This proposal was accepted by the technical committee after considerable opposition had been expressed. It then appeared that the Security Council in recommending a candidate for the position would be governed by the rule of a majority of any seven members. When, following the appeal of the Soviet Delegation to the Steering Committee, the decision regarding the voting procedure of the Security Council was reversed so as to make it possible for any permanent member to veto a particular proposed candidate, Committee I/2 reversed its earlier approval of the proposal to limit the term of service of the Secretary-General and voted in favor of the omission of any provision on this point. The argument advanced in support of this action was that the necessity of unanimous agreement of the permanent members of the Security Council for re-election every three years would either deprive the Secretary-General of his independence or force him to leave his office at a time when his experience would be most useful to the Organization.[2]

There is consequently no provision in the Charter governing the term of office of the Secretary-General or the eligibility of a particular incum-

[1] UNCIO, *Report of the Rapporteur of Committee I/2, on Chapter X (The Secretariat),* Doc. 1155, I/2/74 (2), p. 2–4.
[2] *Ibid.*

bent for re-election.[1] The whole matter is thus left to future agreement between the General Assembly and the Security Council, it being understood that the unanimity of the permanent members is necessary to any decision of the Security Council on this matter.

ARTICLE 98

The Secretary-General shall act in that capacity in all meetings of the General Assembly, of the Security Council, of the Economic and Social Council, and of the Trusteeship Council, and shall perform such other functions as are entrusted to him by these organs. The Secretary-General shall make an annual report to the General Assembly on the work of the Organization.

This Article does not require much explanation. The language of the Article is kept sufficiently broad to cover all functions of the Secretary-General under other Articles. It should also be stated that it was the unanimous opinion of the subcommittee that drafted this Article and of the technical committee that the Secretary-General can delegate his powers to members of his staff as the occasion requires.

The last sentence of this Article places upon the Secretary-General the obligation to make an annual report to the General Assembly on the work of the Organization. This is to be considered in connection with the provisions of Article 15 which state that the General Assembly "shall receive and consider" reports from the Security Council and the other organs of the United Nations.

The practice of the League of Nations was for the Secretary-General to report annually to the Assembly on all aspects of the League's work. This annual report was of the greatest value in that it provided the General Assembly with the factual basis for an intelligent discussion and review of the League's work. A considerable part of each Assembly session was devoted to this general review of the work of the past year. It is to be expected that under this provision of the Charter, a similar practice will be developed.

There is a question as to whether the requirement of "annual reports" from the Security Council and "reports" from the other organs of the United Nations will be satisfied by the annual report of the Secretary-General. The annual report of the Secretary-General of the League covered the activities of all League organs, including technical organizations and commissions such as the Economic and Financial Organization and the Permanent Mandates Commission. It would seem that such

---

[1] The Executive Committee of the Preparatory Commission recommended that the first Secretary-General be appointed for a term of five years, "the appointment being open at the end of that period for a further five-year term." *Report by the Executive Committee to the Preparatory Commission of the United Nations*, cited above, p. 72.

a practice might develop under the provisions of the Charter in so far as annual reports are concerned, even though there is clear legal basis for separate reports by the different organs. Such separate reports, if that is the practice which is to be followed, will be prepared, however, by the Secretary-General and his staff in the exercise of functions described in this Article.

ARTICLE 99

The Secretary-General may bring to the attention of the Security Council any matter which in his opinion may threaten the maintenance of international peace and security.

This paragraph gives a certain political discretion to the Secretary-General. If no state wishes to bring a certain matter to the attention of the Organization, the Secretary-General may still do so, and if he is a man with personal authority and moral courage, this power may be of real significance. It will undoubtedly have the effect of adding to the political importance of the office.

It is left entirely to the Secretary-General's discretion whether he shall exercise this power or not. In the course of subcommittee consideration of the matter at the Conference, it was proposed that the word "may" be changed to "shall." This proposal was withdrawn. It was agreed that the authority to bring to the attention of the Security Council any matter which in his opinion might threaten international peace and security should be exercised at the discretion of the Secretary-General and should not be imposed upon him as a duty. Committee I/2 accepted this view.[1]

During the discussion one of the delegates proposed that it should be the right of the Secretary-General not only to bring the question to the attention of the Security Council but also to the attention of the General Assembly. This proposal was rejected since it was felt that it might destroy the balance between the Council and the Assembly. It had already been decided that the Council should have the primary responsibility for the maintenance of peace and security. For that reason it was thought desirable that the Secretary-General's power should extend only to bringing matters to the attention of the Security Council.[2]

It was also proposed during the discussion to enlarge the scope of the action of the Secretary-General under this paragraph so as to include a reference to infringements or violations of the Principles of the Charter. It was felt, however, that this would place too heavy a responsibility on the Secretary-General and the amendment was defeated.[3]

[1] UNCIO, *Report of Rapporteur of Committee I/2 on Chapter X (The Secretariat)*, Doc. 1155, I/2/74 (2), p. 7. See also, *Summary Report of Seventeenth Meeting of Committee I/2, June 1, 1945*, Doc. 732, I/2/50 and *Summary Report of Eighteenth Meeting of Committee I/2, June 2, 1945*, Doc. 762, I/2/53.
[2] *Ibid.*   [3] *Ibid.*

ARTICLE 100

1. In the performance of their duties the Secretary-General and the staff shall not seek or receive instructions from any government or from any other authority external to the Organization. They shall refrain from any action which might reflect on their position as international officials responsible only to the Organization.

This paragraph is divided into two parts. The first prohibits members of the staff from seeking or receiving instructions from any government or other authority outside the Organization. The intention of this paragraph is to ensure the complete independence of the staff. This matter — like other matters relating to the Secretariat — was discussed at great length in the technical committee. A group of delegates from the smaller countries attached the greatest importance to the creation of a real international civil service. Several of these delegates had had long experience as officials of the League of Nations and of the International Labor Organization, and brought to the discussions all the authority of their experience. They took the position that it was of the utmost importance that the staff be under strict obligations to act as international civil servants and not as the servants of their governments from the moment they took office. This was stressed in the League of Nations and the International Labor Organization where the higher officials had to take an oath of loyalty to the organization.[1] This will undoubtedly be demanded in the new Organization.[2] The aim is to create a real international civil service in the best sense of the word.

The second part of this paragraph states the rule that the Secretary-General and the members of his staff shall not commit any action which may reflect on their position as international officials responsible only to the Organization. This provision will need careful consideration in the future. It will no doubt receive detailed application in the staff regulations.[3] Certain consequences of the rule are quite clear. The officials should not engage in political activities as long as they remain members of the United Nations Secretariat. They should not, for instance, be candidates for political office in their own countries while they are still international officials. In general, they should not engage in any activities incompatible with their jobs. But, of course, they cannot be required to sever completely their ties with their own country.

[1] For detailed discussion of League practice, see Ranshofen-Wertheimer, Egon F., *The International Secretariat: A Great Experiment in International Administration*, Washington, D. C., Carnegie Endowment for International Peace, 1945.

[2] See Draft Provisional Staff Regulations, Regulation 2, *Report by the Executive Committee to the Preparatory Commission of the United Nations*, cited above, p. 89.

[3] See Regulations 5–8, *ibid*.

On the contrary, they are better international civil servants if they are at the same time in close touch with their own country and understand political currents and public opinion in their home countries. They can do very useful work as liaison officers between the Organization and their home governments.

Because they are international, and not national, functionaries, they presumably will be able to continue in their posts even if the country whose citizenship they claim should be expelled or if its rights and privileges of membership should be suspended.

2. Each Member of the United Nations undertakes to respect the exclusively international character of the responsibilities of the Secretary-General and the staff and not to seek to influence them in the discharge of their responsibilities.

This paragraph expresses the reverse side of the principle of the first paragraph. The Secretary-General and the staff must promise not to seek or accept instructions from the outside. The natural and necessary complement of this rule is that the Member States must agree to respect the "exclusively" international character of the responsibilities of the Secretary-General and his staff. The wording is strong and is meant to be. The responsibility of the Secretary-General and the staff — as well as their loyalty — is and must be international, and nothing but international. This might involve Members of the Organization and staff members in serious conflicts. One can think of many possibilities of such conflict, as for example in the matter of military service, which was under discussion in the subcommittee. However, the Charter could only state the general principle and not elaborate the detailed application.

A special problem is raised by the fact that in the performance of his duties a staff member might be required to engage in action which under the laws of his state would be deemed treasonable. Such, for example, might be the case if a staff member engaged in the preparation of plans for military action against the state of his nationality under the enforcement provisions of the Charter. The seriousness of the problem was recognized in Committee discussion. This paragraph is clearly intended to cover that situation, but in practice the individual might find himself in an unenviable position.

The paragraph also states that Members shall not seek to influence the Secretary-General and the staff in performance of their duties. This is also a consequence of the first paragraph. This rule does not, necessarily, preclude the government of a Member from conferring with its nationals on the staff. This becomes entirely a question of discretion. The cardinal principle is, however, — and this cannot be too strongly emphasized — that the members of the staff owe loyalty exclusively to the Organization.

ARTICLE 101

1. The staff shall be appointed by the Secretary-General under regulations established by the General Assembly.

The Covenant of the League provided [1] that the secretaries and staff of the Secretariat should be appointed by the Secretary-General "with the approval of the Council." In practice, however, the control of staff matters came to be shifted to the Assembly as the result of making the Supervisory Commission, originally appointed by the Council, a committee of the Assembly.[2] This paragraph then does not represent any radical break with League practice.

2. Appropriate staffs shall be permanently assigned to the Economic and Social Council, the Trusteeship Council, and, as required, to other organs of the United Nations. These staffs shall form a part of the Secretariat.

The Dumbarton Oaks Proposals made provision in Chapter IX (*Arrangements for International Economic and Social Cooperation*) that the Economic and Social Council should have a permanent staff which was to constitute a part of the Secretariat of the Organization. The Conference Committee dealing with this matter adopted the proposal and so recommended to the Conference. Similarly, the Committee dealing with trusteeship matters recommended that there should be a permanent staff of the Trusteeship Council which should constitute a part of the Secretariat of the Organization. When these two recommendations came before the Coordination Committee, it was decided to combine them into one paragraph to be included in this Article. The phraseology reflects the original concern with providing staffs for the separate organs of the United Nations. It suggests the possibility, as does the phraseology of Article 98, of a staff organization which will lack the measure of integration, unified control and flexibility which many would argue is necessary to effectiveness of operation.

The Secretariat of the League of Nations was for administrative purposes divided into a number of sections and services.[3] These were organized on the basis of subject matter and the nature of the services to be rendered. Both the Council and the Assembly made use of the services of these sections. The specialized organs and agencies of the League were serviced by special sections of the Secretariat. The Mandates

[1] Article 6, paragraph 3.
[2] See Ranshofen-Wertheimer, cited above, p. 21. For Draft Provisional Staff Regulations recommended by the Executive Committee to the Preparatory Commission, see *Report by the Executive Committee to the Preparatory Commission of the United Nations*, cited above, p. 88.
[3] See *Essential Facts about the League of Nations*, Geneva Information Service, 1939, p. 95; also Ranshofen-Wertheimer, cited above, p. 99.

Commission, for example, was serviced by the Mandates Section. This form of organization was a natural development; it was not prescribed by any provision in the Covenant. The exact significance of the words "permanently assigned" in the paragraph under discussion is not clear. If they mean that needed secretarial services are to be permanently available, no issue can be taken. If, on the other hand, it is intended to place the emphasis on the separateness of the staffs of the different organs, the results may be quite unsatisfactory, as the experience of the League would seem to point to the need of an opposite emphasis.

This matter was given careful consideration by the Executive Committee of the Preparatory Commission. Two views were expressed with regard to the basic organizational principle to be followed: (1) that there should be a unified Secretariat organized on a functional basis; and (2) that each of the principal organs of the United Nations should have its own secretariat. The Committee adopted the first view by a large majority. Its recommendation in part was:

8. that the Secretariat be organized on a functional basis, each administrative unit being at the disposal of any organ of the United Nations for the performance of work falling within its competence;

9. that the principal units of the Secretariat be known as Departments, and should, in the first instance, be eight in number, namely:

(i) Department for the Maintenance of International Peace and Security,
(ii) Economic Department,
(iii) Social Department,
(iv) Department for Trusteeship and Information from Non-Self-Governing Territories,
(v) Legal Department,
(vi) Personnel and Administration Department,
(vii) Treasury Department,
(viii) Information Department;

10. that the Assistant Secretaries-General be the heads of Departments;[1]

The Committee of the Executive Committee on the Organization of the Secretariat, in its Report, interpreted Article 101, paragraph 2, to mean that "the Secretary-General has full authority to move staff at his discretion within the Secretariat, but must always provide the Economic and Social Council, the Trusteeship Council and, as required, the other organs of the United Nations with adequate specialized staff, which will form part of the Secretariat." [2]

3. The paramount consideration in the employment of the staff and in the determination of the conditions of service shall be the necessity of securing the highest standards of efficiency, competence, and integrity. Due regard shall be paid to the importance of recruiting the staff on as wide a geographical basis as possible.

[1] *Report by the Executive Committee to the Preparatory Commission of the United Nations,* cited above, p. 72.　　　　[2] *Ibid.,* p. 76.

This establishes the general principle that the paramount consideration in recruiting personnel and in determining the conditions of service is to be the efficient performance of staff duties and not political expediency. In other words, those specific qualities of personnel which are usually demanded in the organization of an efficient national administrative service are to be given proper recognition. Positions are not to be regarded as "spoils" to be divided among the more influential Members with a view to advancing the national interests of those states. Of course, it is not enough to state that officials must be endowed with these qualities. It will also be necessary to create working conditions, both material and spiritual, which will attract the highest type of person. Staff members must be assured a certain independence in their work and the opportunity for advancement. They must be given adequate salaries, assured tenure, and opportunities for vacations.[1]

It is also stated that the staff should be recruited on as wide a geographical basis as possible. This principle might on occasion conflict with the principle enunciated in the first sentence of this paragraph. In a sense it is a concession to political considerations. However, it is stated here as a consideration of a secondary nature. The main thing is to get a good staff. If this staff can be made international, not only in outlook, in loyalty and in work, but also in composition, this should be done. It is easy to see that the Secretariat will command greater confidence if it is also international in this respect. The League of Nations took this principle of geography into consideration to a very great extent. There are those who feel that the effectiveness of the League Secretariat was restricted by this fact. A balance has to be struck.

It is clear from the provisions of Article 8 that women and men are equally eligible for positions on the staff and are guaranteed equality of treatment as to pay, opportunities for promotion, and other conditions of employment.

[1] The recommendations of the Executive Committee of the Preparatory Commission on the organization of the Secretariat contained detailed proposals to achieve these results. *Ibid.*, p. 71 ff.

CHAPTER XVI

MISCELLANEOUS PROVISIONS

ARTICLE 102

1. Every treaty and every international agreement entered into by any Member of the United Nations after the present Charter comes into force shall as soon as possible be registered with the Secretariat and published by it.

No provision of this nature was included in the Dumbarton Oaks Proposals. Article 18 of the League Covenant contained a provision of this general character. There was strong support both at the Conference and outside for the inclusion in the Charter of such a provision.

The text of the Charter is not identical with that of the Covenant. The Covenant provision read as follows:

Every treaty or international engagement entered into hereafter by any Member of the League shall be forthwith registered with the Secretariat and shall as soon as possible be published by it.

The Charter requirement that registration be "as soon as possible" would seem to be somewhat weaker than the Covenant requirement that it be done "forthwith." Nevertheless, the obligation to register is clear in both cases, and since it is an obligation placed upon the parties, it is perhaps somewhat more realistic to use the Charter language. The Charter, like the Covenant, uses the phrase "entered into" which implies of course the completion of the procedure prescribed in the agreement for its entrance into force, or in the absence of such prescription, the deposit or exchange of ratifications by the parties.

The term "every treaty and every international agreement" is of course very comprehensive, covering in general every type of international agreement, irrespective of the technical designation which may be given to it. The word "agreement" is to be understood as including unilateral engagements of an international character which have been accepted by the state in whose favor such an engagement has been entered into.[1]

However, according to the interpretation of the United States Delegation, this does not prevent the Organization from limiting somewhat

---

[1] UNCIO, *Report of the Rapporteur of Committee IV/2*, Doc. 933, IV/2/42 (2), p. 3.

the application of the general rule in practice. This view finds expression in the *Report to the President . . . by the Chairman of the United States Delegation, the Secretary of State:* [1]

The second issue involved was the scope of the obligation; should the obligation to register cover every international agreement or only certain ones? Experience had indicated that the registration of every international agreement is unnecessary because many of them are of minor importance and of temporary effect. Such, for example, are numerous agreements between governments for the purchase and sale of commodities and the regulation of financial transactions. A more serious problem was the question whether military agreements concluded with the Security Council for the purpose of carrying out its duties under Chapter VII of the Charter should be registered. There was a realization of the fact that detailed arrangements about the disposition of forces at a time when security measures were actually being taken could not be made public. Accordingly, although the obligation to register is stated in general terms, it was contemplated that regulations would be worked out in practice by the General Assembly concerning the registration or non-registration of particular types of agreements.

The propriety of thus limiting the application of the obligation would seem to be questionable in the light of the discussion at the Conference as officially reported. It is true that the word "agreements" was used in place of the word "engagements," since the latter word might be taken to include instruments, such as commercial contracts by a state to buy goods. There is, however, nothing in the official record to indicate that there is any exception to the obligation as it stands.

The obligation to register extends to every treaty or international agreement entered into by a Member, whether the other party is a Member or not. It is understood that non-members may register treaties and agreements to which they are parties if they so desire. The United States registered its treaties with the League of Nations after 1934.

The treaties and agreements thus registered are to be published by the Secretariat. This means that the excellent work begun by the League of Nations will be continued. The League *Treaty Series*, running to 204 volumes, containing 4822 separate agreements, provides an invaluable collection for the use of governments and scholars alike.

The obligation to register treaties and agreements is limited to those entered into after the Charter came into force on October 24, 1945. However, it is clear that this Article does not prevent the Members from registering earlier treaties. This no doubt will be done as was done under the Covenant of the League of Nations. Such a practice would of course help to bridge the gap between the League *Treaty Series* and the United Nations series. The Executive Committee of the Preparatory Commission took note of the desirability of avoiding a gap between the League of Nations series and the United Nations series, and recommended that

[1] Department of State Publication 2349 (Conference Series 71), p. 154.

all governments, whether or not Members of the United Nations, be invited "to send for publication by the Secretariat of the United Nations, treaties and international agreements, concluded in recent years but before the date of the entry into force of the Charter, which have not been included in the *Treaty Series* of the League of Nations." [1]

2. No party to any such treaty or international agreement which has not been registered in accordance with the provisions of paragraph 1 of this Article may invoke that treaty or agreement before any organ of the United Nations.

Article 18 of the League Covenant stated broadly that no treaty was binding until it had been registered. This Article was never applied, but it created certain theoretical difficulties. The second paragraph of Article 102 of the Charter is more modest. It states only that an unregistered treaty may not be invoked before an organ of the United Nations.

Interpreted strictly, this paragraph would not exclude the possibility that an unregistered treaty or agreement to which a Member is a party will have considerable effect in any situation where it is not invoked by one of the parties. It would, for example, appear to be possible for the Security Council in the performance of its functions to take account of such a treaty or agreement on its own initiative. Furthermore, the use of the term "before any organ of the United Nations" suggests the possibility that such a treaty or agreement can actually be invoked by one of the parties before a special arbitral tribunal set up under the terms of Articles 33 or 52 of the Charter. This of course depends on the interpretation that is given to the words in question. However, it is clear that the paragraph lays down a much more limited rule than did the corresponding text of the Covenant. It represents a more modest approach to the problem and states an attainable objective.

ARTICLE 103

In the event of a conflict between the obligations of the Members of the United Nations under the present Charter and their obligations under any other international agreement, their obligations under the present Charter shall prevail.

This Article deals with the situation where the obligations of a Member under the Charter are in conflict with the obligations of that Member under another international agreement. This situation may conceivably take three forms: (1) that where there is a conflict between the obligation of a Member under the Charter and the obligation of that same Member resulting from an agreement with another Member, contracted

[1] *Report by the Executive Committee to the Preparatory Commission of the United Nations,* cited above, p. 68.

before the entrance into force of the Charter; (2) that where the conflict is between the obligation of a Member under the Charter and the obligation of that same Member resulting from an agreement with another Member contracted after the entrance into force of the Charter; and (3) that where the conflict is between the obligation of a Member under the Charter and the obligation of that same Member resulting from an agreement contracted with a non-member state, before the entrance into force of the Charter.

Under the terms of the Covenant of the League of Nations [1] the Members severally agreed that the Covenant abrogated "all obligations or understandings *inter se*" which were inconsistent with the terms of the Covenant, and they undertook not to enter into any engagements in the future inconsistent with the terms thereof. This provision covered the first two situations referred to above where the parties concerned were Members of the League. It did not, however, fully cover the situation where one party to the special agreement was not a Member and was therefore not bound by the terms of the Covenant. To take care of this situation more particularly, the second paragraph of Article 20 provided that in case any Member of the League, before becoming a Member, contracted an obligation inconsistent with the terms of the Covenant, it was the duty of that Member "to take immediate steps to procure its release from such obligations."

The Dumbarton Oaks Proposals contained no provisions relative to this matter. The whole problem was carefully considered by the Committee on Legal Problems (Committee IV/2) at the United Nations Conference and agreement was reached on a text, which after some revision as to phraseology by the Coordinating Committee, was adopted by the Conference.

So far as the first situation referred to above is concerned, the Article applies the established principle of international law that a later agreement between the same parties supersedes an earlier agreement. Thus obligations under the Charter clearly supersede obligations which Members have contracted among themselves before the Charter's entrance into force.

The Article clearly covers the second situation by stating that obligations under the Charter shall prevail over obligations "under any other international agreement" without qualification as to time of contracting. This is recognition of the principle that the obligation of a multipartite agreement prevails as against an obligation under an agreement between certain of the parties, even though later in time, since parties to a multipartite agreement cannot modify their obligations thereunder except with the consent of the other parties or by the procedure prescribed in the agreement itself.

[1] *Covenant*, Article 20.

The Article also applies in the third situation. While the Committee recognized that according to international law it is not ordinarily possible to provide in any convention for rules binding on third parties, it felt that it was of the highest importance to the Organization that the performance of Member's obligations under the Charter in specific cases should not be hindered by obligations they had assumed to non-member states.[1] The Charter thus assumes the character of basic law of the international community. Non-members, while they have not formally accepted it, are nevertheless expected to recognize this law as one of the facts of international life and to adjust themselves to it.

It is to be noted that this Article does not provide for the automatic abrogation of obligations inconsistent with the terms of the Charter. The rule is put in such form as to be operative only when there is an actual conflict. The nature of the conflict has not been defined but "it would be enough that a conflict should arise from the carrying out of an obligation of the Charter. It is immaterial whether the conflict arises because of intrinsic inconsistency between the two categories of obligations or as the result of the application of the provisions of the Charter under given circumstances." [2]

ARTICLE 104

The Organization shall enjoy in the territory of each of its Members such legal capacity as may be necessary for the exercise of its functions and the fulfillment of its purposes.

The question of the legal capacity of international organizations is a very complicated one. It has been a matter of concern to the League of Nations and other international organizations.[3] It is quite clear that an international organization may be seriously hampered in the performance of its functions by not being able to enter into contracts, hold property, appear in court, and engage in other acts having legal validity in the territory of its members. It is not possible nor necessary to enter into a detailed discussion of this matter here. It is enough to state that this Article imposes upon Members the duty of attributing a certain measure of legal personality to the Organization, enough to permit it to exercise its functions and fulfill its purposes. The way in which this is to be done is left to the governments of the Members. Some of them

[1] UNCIO, *Report of the Rapporteur of Committee IV/2*, Doc. 933, IV/2/42 (2), p. 6.
[2] *Ibid.*, p. 5–6.
[3] Compare the *League of Nations Covenant*, Article 7, paragraph 5, and the *modus vivendi* between the League and Switzerland of September 18, 1926, League of Nations Document C. 555. 1926. V. See also, Article XV in the Constitution of the United Nations Food and Agriculture Organization; Article 47 of the International Civil Aviation Convention of December 7, 1944; Article IX of the Agreement establishing an International Monetary Fund; and Article VII of the Agreement establishing the International Bank for Reconstruction and Development.

may be able to make arrangements of an administrative nature. Others may have to adopt new legislation. That is a matter of no consequence as far as the Charter is concerned. The Members are required, however, to do what is necessary even though changes in their constitutions may be involved.

ARTICLE 105

1. The Organization shall enjoy in the territory of each of its Members such privileges and immunities as are necessary for the fulfillment of its purposes.

This paragraph refers to the Organization considered as a distinct entity, including all the organs established under the Charter and all bodies and organs which may subsequently be established by virtue of the powers conferred by the Charter.[1] Not included are the specialized agencies referred to in Article 57 established by separate intergovernmental agreements. The privileges and immunities to which these agencies are entitled are determined by the agreements constituting them and by the general principles of international law. Article 7, paragraph 5, of the League Covenant provided that "the buildings and other property occupied by the League or its officials or by representatives attending its meetings shall be inviolable."

The question of privileges and immunities for the United Nations is of the greatest importance for the country in which the United Nations has its seat. In the case of the League of Nations, detailed arrangements were worked out in agreements concluded between the Secretary-General and the Swiss Government.[2] The Committee of the Executive Committee of the Preparatory Commission concerned with the permanent headquarters of the Organization in its report on considerations affecting the selection of the same recommended an agreement between the United Nations and the host state which would provide for the enjoyment by the United Nations of the privileges and immunities necessary to the performance of its functions. These would include the inviolability of buildings and property owned or occupied by the United Nations or its organs.[3]

While the question of privileges and immunities arises in the greatest degree in the host Member, the same question arises as between the Organization and all its Members. The difference is one of degree rather than of kind. Committee IV/2 of the United Nations Conference, while refusing to undertake to establish a complete list of the privileges and

---

[1] UNCIO, *Report of the Rapporteur of Committee IV/2*, Doc. 933, IV/2/42 (2), p. 2.
[2] League of Nations Document C. 555. 1926. V, printed in League of Nations, *Official Journal, VII* (1926), p. 1422.
[3] *Report by the Executive Committee to the Preparatory Commission of the United Nations*, cited above, p. 115.

immunities to be enjoyed under paragraph 1 and 2 of Article 105, laid down the basic principle "that no Member state may hinder in any way the working of the Organization or take any measures the effect of which might be to increase its burdens, financial or other." [1]

2. Representatives of the Members of the United Nations and officials of the Organization shall similarly enjoy such privileges and immunities as are necessary for the independent exercise of their functions in connection with the Organization.

This paragraph states the same general principle with reference to the representatives of Members and officials of the Organization.

Article 7, paragraph 2, of the League Covenant provided that "representatives of the Members of the League and officials of the League when engaged in the business of the League shall enjoy diplomatic privileges and immunities." The Covenant thus expressly accepted an established international law standard. There is a large measure of agreement on the nature and extent of these privileges and immunities, the result of international agreements and developing international practice.[2] The Charter standard is a somewhat different one. Under the Charter the privileges and immunities to be enjoyed by representatives of Members and officials of the Organization are to be such as "are necessary for the independent exercise of their functions in connection with the Organization."

The matter received careful study by the Committee of the Executive Committee of the Preparatory Commission dealing with legal questions. The Executive Committee recommended to the Preparatory Commission that the results of this study be communicated to the General Assembly for its consideration. Two paragraphs from that report are here quoted in full: [3]

Privileges and Immunities

7. In this report the expression "diplomatic privileges and immunities" is used for convenience to describe the whole complex of privileges and immunities which are in fact accorded to diplomatic envoys. While it will clearly be necessary that all officials, whatever their rank, should be granted immunity from legal process in respect of acts done in the course of their official duties, whether in the country of which they are nationals or elsewhere, it is by no means necessary that all officials should have diplomatic immunity. On the contrary, there is every reason for confining full diplomatic immunity to the cases where it is really justified. Any excess or abuse of immunity and privilege is as detrimental to the interests of the international organisation itself as it is to the countries

[1] UNCIO, *Report of the Rapporteur of Committee IV/2*, Doc. 933, IV/2/42 (2), p. 3.
[2] See Harvard Research in International Law, "Diplomatic Privileges and Immunities," *American Journal of International Law*, XXIX (1932), Doc. Sup. p. 89, et seq.; Satow, Sir E., *A Guide to Diplomatic Practice*, 2nd and rev. ed., I, p. 249 ff.
[3] *Report by the Executive Committee to the Preparatory Commission of the United Nations*, cited above, p. 70–71.

who are asked to grant such immunities. In the case of existing specialised agencies, the practice has up to now been to confine diplomatic immunity to the senior official of the agency concerned and those of his assistants, whose rank is equivalent to that of Deputy Secretary-General. (In the case of the I.L.O. the range of officials to whom diplomatic immunity has been accorded is somewhat wider.) It is also a principle that no official can have, in the country of which he is a national, immunity from being sued in respect of his non-official acts and from criminal prosecution. It is further most desirable that both the United Nations and all specialised agencies should adopt the principle that privileges and immunities are only given to their officials in the interests of the Organisation in whose service they are, and in no way for the benefit of the individual concerned, and that, in consequence, the Secretary-General both can waive immunity and will in fact do so in every case where such a course is consistent with the interests of the United Nations. This rule has long been in force in the International Labour Organisation. It has been accepted by most of the new specialised agencies which have come into being. Similarly, it is desirable that where the United Nations or a specialised agency concludes contracts with private individuals or corporations, it should include in the contract an undertaking to submit to arbitration disputes arising out of the contract, if it is not prepared to go before the Courts. Most of the existing specialised agencies have already agreed to do this.

Taxation of Officials in the State of which they are nationals

8. The provisions in the agreements or constitutions of the new specialised agencies, while providing in general that no taxation should be levied on the salaries of officials, leave complete latitude to governments to tax the salaries of officials who are their own nationals or persons resident in their territory. As a result, the Act of Parliament of the United Kingdom which was passed to enable the United Kingdom to give effect to its obligations as regards privileges and immunities for international organisations (the Diplomatic Privileges Extension Act, 1944) excepts from the immunity from income tax the salaries of those international officials who are both British subjects and whose usual place of abode is in the United Kingdom. A similar practice has been followed in certain other countries. It is, however, a matter for consideration whether this latitude or this exception are (*sic*) really sound. One of its effects is that some of the members of the staff have salaries which are tax free, because being resident outside their own states they do not fall under the income tax provisions of their own state, while other officials doing the same work for the same nominal salary are subject to income tax. This has led to certain administrative difficulties and has indeed raised the question whether the United Nations should not pay some special allowance to those of its employees who are paying income tax, in order to produce equality.

3. The General Assembly may make recommendations with a view to determining the details of the application of paragraphs 1 and 2 of this Article or may propose conventions to the Members of the United Nations for this purpose.

The General Assembly may make recommendations, presumably to Members, with a view to determining the details of the application of paragraphs 1 and 2 of this Article, or may propose conventions to the Members of the United Nations for this purpose.

The Executive Committee of the Preparatory Commission recommended that Members of the United Nations should be reminded that, by the terms of Article 105, "the obligation to accord to the United Nations, its officials and the representatives of its Members all privileges and immunities necessary for the accomplishment of its purposes, operates from the coming into force of the Charter and is therefore applicable even before the General Assembly has made the recommendations referred to in paragraph (3) of the Article, or the conventions there mentioned have been concluded."[1] It was also recommended that a study of the question of privileges and immunities, made by a committee of the Executive Committee, should be referred to the General Assembly for its consideration.

If the provisions of paragraphs 1 and 2 are to be applied with due regard for the interests of the Organization and in a uniform manner, it would seem highly desirable that the General Assembly act under this paragraph. Furthermore, of the two alternative courses open, the second, i.e. the proposal of a convention or conventions to Members for their acceptance, would seem most likely to achieve the desired result.

[1] *Ibid.*, p. 69.

CHAPTER XVII

TRANSITIONAL SECURITY ARRANGEMENTS

ARTICLE 106

Pending the coming into force of such special agreements referred to in Article 43 as in the opinion of the Security Council enable it to begin the exercise of its responsibilities under Article 42, the parties to the Four-Nation Declaration, signed at Moscow, October 30, 1943, and France, shall, in accordance with the provisions of paragraph 5 of that Declaration, consult with one another and as occasion requires with other Members of the United Nations with a view to such joint action on behalf of the Organization as may be necessary for the purpose of maintaining international peace and security.

This Article must be considered along with Article 107 which is intimately linked up with it. It is intended to provide the basis for the necessary action to maintain international peace and security during the period when the normal Charter arrangements are in the process of being developed.

Length of Transitional Period. The powers and duties of the Security Council with respect to enforcement action to maintain peace and security are laid down in Chapter VII and specially in Articles 39, 41 and 42. The taking of action under Article 42 depends upon the existence of special agreements concluded under the terms of Article 43. A considerable period of time is bound to elapse, if we take the most optimistic view, between the entrance into force of the Charter and the entrance into force of the special agreement or agreements provided for in Article 43. The situation during that period will be that, while the United Nations is in existence, the Security Council, primarily responsible for the maintenance of peace and security, will not have the means at its disposal for performing its function to maintain international peace and security. Article 106 aims at providing for the maintenance of peace and security during this period. The special responsibilities placed upon the signatories of the Moscow Declaration and France will be operative until such time as the Security Council deems that the agreements referred to in Article 43 "enable it to begin the exercise of its responsibilities under Article 42." The decision of the Security Council as to whether it is able to begin the exercise of its responsibilities under Article 42 will be a decision of substance that must be taken under the provisions of the third paragraph of Article 27, and will consequently require unanimity of the permanent members.

However, the text as finally adopted by the Conference does at least specify who is to make the decision as to when the transitional period is to end. The original proposal of the Sponsoring Governments was that the transitional arrangement should remain in operation "pending the coming into force of the special agreement or agreements referred to in Chapter VIII, Section B, paragraph 5" of the Dumbarton Oaks Proposals. The question was raised in the course of the discussion of the technical committee as to whether this meant that all the special agreements would have to come into force.[1] Delegates of certain of the Sponsoring Governments explained that the intention of the framers was that the Council should be able to undertake its responsibilities and that all of the agreements need not be in force. It was finally decided, however, to clarify the meaning of the text by specifying that it is for the Security Council to decide when the situation is such that it can assume responsibility.

Responsibilities of "The Big Five." The Article states that during this transitional period the parties to the Moscow Declaration [2] and France shall, in accordance with the provisions of paragraph 5 of that Declaration, "consult with one another and as occasion requires with other Members of the United Nations with a view to such joint action on behalf of the Organization as may be necessary for the purposes of maintaining international peace and security." Article 5 of the Declaration reads as follows:

That for the purpose of maintaining international peace and security pending the re-establishment of law and order and the inauguration of a system of general security, they will consult with one another and as occasion requires with other Members of the United Nations with a view to joint action on behalf of the community of nations.

The phraseology of the Charter Article follows very closely that of the Article of the Declaration.

In the course of the Committee discussions there was special interest expressed by many delegates as to the meaning of the words "joint action on behalf of the Organization." Would the Security Council during this transitional period be responsible for the pacific settlement of disputes or would that also be a responsibility of the signatories of the Moscow Declaration and France? What would be the role of the Security Council during this period?

[1] UNCIO, *Summary Report of Sixteenth Meeting of Committee III/3, May 30, 1945,* Doc. 704, III/3/36, p. 3.
[2] For text, see this volume, p. 307. The parties were the United States, the United Kingdom, the Soviet Union and China.

Both the United Kingdom and the United States Delegates expressed the view that the Security Council would be responsible during the interim period for the peaceful settlement of disputes.[1] The United States Delegate expressed the view that during the interim period the Security Council would perform all its functions under the Charter in so far as it was able to do so.[2] He further explained that the meaning of the words "joint action" might, in his opinion, be deduced from the reference in the Dumbarton Oaks text to Chapter VIII, Section B, paragraph 5, of the Dumbarton Oaks Proposals. Consequently, the joint action referred only to the exercise of those functions of the Security Council the exercise of which would be suspended pending the conclusion of the special agreements. This explanation was included in the Report of Committee 3 to Commission III,[3] and would thus appear to be the interpretation accepted by the Committee.

While this Article gives special power to and places special responsibility on a few Members of the United Nations during the transitional period, the arrangement would appear to be fundamentally consistent with the general theory of the Charter, since it places upon the permanent members of the Security Council, the Members of the Organization who will presumably be the chief contributors of military power, the responsibility for taking military enforcement action during this interim period. Two guarantees are provided against the arbitrary use of this power: first, the requirement that the signatories of the Moscow Declaration and France shall consult with each other, and that they shall "as occasion requires" consult with the other Members of the United Nations; and second, the requirement that the action shall be joint, that is, action to which the five powers agree.

Obligations of Other Members. The question arises whether the other Members of the United Nations are obliged to assist the five powers in carrying out the measures taken under the terms of this Article. All Members are obligated, according to the terms of Article 2, paragraph 5, to give "every assistance" to the United Nations in any action it takes "in accordance with the terms of the present Charter," and not to assist any state against which the United Nations is taking preventive or enforcement action. It can be argued that this double obligation will apply to action taken under this Article since the five powers will act "on behalf of the Organization." However, the more specific obligations under Article 25 and Chapter VII cannot be considered as applying. These provisions refer definitely to formal Council decisions.

---

[1] UNCIO, *Summary Report of Sixteenth Meeting of Committee III/3*, May 30, 1945, Doc. 704, III/3/36, p. 3.

[2] *Ibid.*, p. 4.

[3] *Ibid., Report of Committee 3 to Commission III on Chapter XII*, Doc. 1095, III/3/50, p. 3.

ARTICLE 107

Nothing in the present Charter shall invalidate or preclude action, in relation to any state which during the Second World War has been an enemy of any signatory to the present Charter, taken or authorized as a result of that war by the Governments having responsibility for such action.

General Scope. The purpose and effect of this Article is to leave to those governments primarily responsible for the defeat of any enemy state the determination of the terms of peace and in general the taking of necessary control measures. This does not preclude the possibility of placing on the Organization responsibilities of this kind, if the states at war with and responsible for the military defeat of the enemy state so agree. The Conference, however, adopted the Article with full realization that the action here referred to would probably be taken, at least for an initial period of uncertain length, by the governments chiefly responsible for the military defeat of the enemy and without any limitation being placed upon them in respect to such action by the terms of the Charter. It is quite clear that other Members are not bound in any way to support measures taken under this Article as the measures here in question are not being taken "on behalf of the Organization" as is the case under Article 106.

Discussion at San Francisco. This Article, like the preceding one, was extensively discussed in Committee III/3 of the Conference. The phraseology of the text proposed by the Sponsoring Governments was criticized on the ground that its meaning was not clear. It read as follows: [1]

No provision of the Charter should preclude action taken or authorized in relation to enemy states as a result of the present war by the Governments having responsibility for such action.

While those who objected to this text were not able to get the Delegates of the Sponsoring Governments to agree to a new text giving complete satisfaction to them, they did obtain individual interpretations which were included in the Report of the Committee. These interpretations, given by the Delegate of the United Kingdom, were as follows:

1. *Enemy States* are those which, on the day of the signature of the Charter, are still at war with any one of the United Nations.
2. *The present war* is to be understood as a series of wars which began on or before September 3, 1939 and which are still in progress.
3. *"Action taken or authorized."* It would be impossible to limit this action, as proposed by the Australian Delegate, to that decided upon in an armistice, a peace treaty, or a joint declaration like the Declaration of Moscow, because

[1] Chapter XII, paragraph 2, of the *Dumbarton Oaks Proposals,* see this volume, p. 318.

responsibility, as envisaged in paragraph 2, could fall upon a State which is party to none of these acts.

As to the exact meaning of the expression "action taken or authorized," the Delegate of the United Kingdom declared that, in his opinion, the distinction is made between "positive" and "negative" action; that is to say, between action with respect to enemy States by the governments responsible for this action, and the action which the responsible governments had authorized other governments to take.[1]

The Committee report states that "after these explanations" the text of paragraph 2 was adopted.[2] Subsequently the text was revised by the Coordination Committee in the interest of greater clarity and in conformity with this interpretation.

The phraseology of the Article leaves many questions open. Who are "the governments having responsibility for such action"? Does the phrase include all Members of the United Nations at war with a particular enemy state? How long does this freedom in dealing with the enemy state last? Will it end at the latest with the admission of the enemy state as a Member of the United Nations? Certainly it would seem that the answer to this question must be in the affirmative.

[1] UNCIO, *Report of Committee 3 to Commission III on Chapter XII*, Doc. 1095, III/3/50, p. 4.
[2] *Ibid.*

CHAPTER XVIII

AMENDMENTS

ARTICLE 108

Amendments to the present Charter shall come into force for all Members of the United Nations when they have been adopted by a vote of two thirds of the members of the General Assembly and ratified in accordance with their respective constitutional processes by two thirds of the Members of the United Nations, including all the permanent members of the Security Council.

Adoption of Amendments by General Assembly. This Article first lays down a rule governing the adoption of proposed amendments preliminary to submission to the Members for ratification. It states that such proposals shall be adopted by the General Assembly by a two-thirds majority. The General Assembly may adopt such proposals without any recommendation being made by the Security Council. This rule did not create any great difficulty at the United Nations Conference although certain delegates spoke in favor of a three-fourths vote and others favored a simple majority for the adoption of amendments.

It is to be noted that the vote required in the General Assembly is "two thirds of the members" as compared with "two-thirds majority of the members present and voting" required on "important questions" by the terms of Article 18. The phraseology used in Article 108 would appear to be intentionally different, and to have as its purpose an assurance that the proposed amendment has sufficient support to make likely its ratification by two thirds of the Members. If the phraseology of Article 18 had been used, it would be possible for a proposed amendment to be adopted by a bare majority, or even less than a majority vote of the total membership, the number of votes necessary for a two-thirds majority under Article 18 being determined by the total number of members "present and voting."

Entrance into Force. Article 108 also states that amendments thus adopted shall enter into force when they are ratified by two thirds of the Members, including the Members with permanent seats on the Security Council. This is a change from the Dumbarton Oaks Proposals.[1] The Proposals stipulated that amendments, adopted by a two-

---

[1] Chapter XI, see this volume, p. 317.

thirds majority vote of the General Assembly, should enter into force when ratified by the states with permanent seats on the Security Council and by a majority of the other Members of the United Nations. However, the requirement of "two thirds of the Members," including the permanent members of the Council, was accepted at the United Nation's Conference as being more democratic and reducing somewhat the privileged position of the permanent members. The difference is not enormous. There were fifty states represented at the United Nations Conference. Including Poland, one can count on fifty-one Members to begin with. According to the Dumbarton Oaks Proposals an amendment could enter into force following ratification by the five permanent members of the Security Council plus a majority of the remaining forty-six. This would amount to ratification by twenty-nine states altogether. According to the adopted procedure, it will be necessary to have the ratifications of two-thirds of fifty-one or thirty-four Members, inclusive of Members with permanent seats on the Council.

Special Position of Permanent Members of Security Council. The proposal which created the greatest difficulty was that by which ratification by all the five permanent members of the Security Council would be necessary to the entrance into force of any amendment. Here the same arguments were repeated which had already been used in Committee III/1 of the Conference concerning the "veto right" or "priority of concord" of the "Great Powers." See comments on Article 27.

The arguments in Committee I/2 were even stronger at times, since certain states claimed that they had agreed to — or abstained from voting against — the stipulations of Article 27 because of the belief that the privileged position of the permanent members of the Security Council would be of short duration. They claimed that the present Article perpetuated this position of inequality and they stated that because of this they must contemplate the possibility of withdrawal.[1]

Position of Non-Ratifying Members. The provision which requires the ratification of a proposed amendment by all the permanent members of the Council as a condition of its entering into force makes the process of amendment difficult. The provision that amendments shall enter into force when adopted by a two-thirds vote of the Assembly and ratified by two-thirds of the Members inclusive of the states with permanent membership on the Security Council may from the point of view of non-ratifying Members make the process too easy. This imposes rather serious obligations on Members who have not voted in favor of, and have refused to ratify, the amendment in question. The provision actually means that all Members, except the five permanent members of the Security Council, endorse a blank check obligating themselves to accept in advance certain international commitments which their duly accred-

[1] For comment on question of withdrawal, see p. 86.

ited representatives have voted against and which the constitutional authorities of the state after mature consideration have refused to ratify. This rule is a complete innovation in international life which was adopted because of the desire to make the United Nations a living and developing organism.

Other solutions were possible. It would have been possible to choose the solution adopted by the League of Nations which stated in Article 26 that amendments should enter into effect when ratified by the permanent members of the Council and by a majority of the Members of the League whose representatives composed the Assembly, provided, however, that a Member which signified its dissent would not be bound, but would cease to be a Member of the League. It would also have been possible to divide the amendments into two categories, and to have adopted the rule laid down in Article XX of the Constitution of the Food and Agriculture Organization of the United Nations:

1. Amendments to this Constitution involving new obligations for member nations shall require the approval of the Conference by a vote concurred in by a two-thirds majority of all the members of the Conference and shall take effect on acceptance by two-thirds of the member nations for each member nation accepting the amendment and thereafter for each remaining member nation on acceptance by it.

2. Other amendments shall take effect on adoption by the Conference by a vote concurred in by a two-thirds majority of all the members of the Conference.

The United Nations Conference adopted Article 108 in full awareness of these and other alternatives and after having discussed the matter very fully. There can be no doubt whatsoever about the fact that states which vote against proposed amendments and refuse to ratify them are bound by them if they are ratified by two thirds of the Members, inclusive of the states with permanent membership on the Council. This explains why the matter of amendment was so intimately linked up with the possibility of withdrawal from the Organization.[1]

Article 109

1. A General Conference of the Members of the United Nations for the purpose of reviewing the present Charter may be held at a date and place to be fixed by a two-thirds vote of the members of the General Assembly and by a vote of any seven members of the Security Council. Each Member of the United Nations shall have one vote in the conference.

There are differences of opinion concerning the results of any international conference, as indeed concerning any human enterprise. The United Nations Conference was no exception. Most delegates were of the opinion that the Conference was a success and that the Charter

[1] *Ibid.*

did not fall short of what might have been expected. Some delegates, however, were frankly disappointed. The feature that was found particularly objectionable to them was the special position accorded to certain so-called "Great Powers." Certain delegates even went so far as to say that they could not bring the Charter back to their countries with any hope of obtaining its ratification if it were not made quite clear that the Charter in its present form was a first step and that revision with a view to eliminating its most objectionable features and in general strengthening it would be undertaken within a reasonable time. For this reason it was decided to set up machinery for a complete revision of the Charter at a future date. Such conferences are known in the constitutional life of certain states. Such a special conference would give the opportunity to review the whole Charter in the light of the experience gained in the intervening period.

There was no great opposition to the idea as such. A proposal of the Sponsoring Governments to implement this idea was given general support in principle, but certain questions of detail evoked the most lively discussion. These questions will be treated under the second and third paragraphs of this Article.

The date and place of the General Conference are to be fixed by agreement of the General Assembly and the Security Council. The Assembly must take its decision by vote of two thirds of its members. The Sponsoring Governments had proposed a three-fourths vote but acceded to the demand of the smaller states for a smaller majority. It is to be noted that the requirement is different from that of Article 18, paragraph 2, which speaks of "a two-thirds majority of the Members present and voting." [1] The Security Council takes its decision by a vote of any seven members, which means that the "Great Power" veto does not apply. This was also a concession to the smaller states. It is stated specifically that each Member of the United Nations shall have one vote in the General Conference.

2. Any alteration of the present Charter recommended by a two-thirds vote of the conference shall take effect when ratified in accordance with their respective constitutional processes by two thirds of the Members of the United Nations including all the permanent members of the Security Council.

It is specified that decisions of the General Conference shall be taken by a two-thirds majority. This was the rule adopted and followed by the United Nations Conference on International Organization. However, changes in the Charter adopted by the Conference do not become by that fact alone binding on Members. They are "recommendations" which Members can ratify or refuse to ratify as they deem fit. The

---

[1] See comment on Article 108, p. 291.

problem of ratification created the chief difficulty. The "Big Five" demanded that ratification by all the permanent members of the Security Council should be required. This was the logical consequence of the stand taken by them when the voting procedure of the Council was being considered. It is clear that the special power which they enjoy under the terms of that Article might be destroyed if it were possible for amendments to enter into force following ratification by a part of the total membership with no special requirement of ratification by each permanent member of the Council.

It was, consequently, decided that no amendment should enter into force without being ratified by all the permanent members of the Council. It was also decided that ratification by two thirds of the Members of the Organization should be required, the permanent members included. The requirement thus corresponds to that for amendments under Article 108. This means in fact that the process of amending the Charter is substantially the same whether amendments are voted in a session of the General Assembly, according to Article 108, or in a General Conference, according to Article 109. Therefore, the General Conference procedure would seem to have greater psychological than substantial importance.

3. If such a conference has not been held before the tenth annual session of the General Assembly following the coming into force of the present Charter, the proposal to call such a conference shall be placed on the agenda of that session of the General Assembly, and the conference shall be held if so decided by a majority vote of the members of the General Assembly and by a vote of any seven members of the Security Council.

It was quite clear to the Delegates at the United Nations Conference that the proposal for a General Conference submitted by the Sponsoring Governments did not give any real guarantee that the Charter would be amended if such a Conference were held. Moreover, it was not even certain that a Conference would be held. Several of the delegates thought that the Charter should contain additional guarantees. In particular they proposed that the Charter should contain a provision that a Conference would be held by a certain time if no decision to hold one earlier had been taken. Public opinion could then be convinced that there was a real and practical chance that the Charter would be revised in the near future. Some delegates proposed that the General Conference should be held within five years of the entry into force of the Charter; others proposed seven; and still others proposed ten years.

On the other hand, certain of the delegates were very much against fixing a date. They claimed that it was impossible to know in advance when it would be wise to hold such a Conference. Only in the light of future events could it be told when it was desirable to review the Charter with a view to general revision. An acceptable compromise was finally found in the text of this paragraph. In the first place, this introduces a time limit of a kind. It is not stated that a Conference will necessarily be called at the end of any period of time. The only thing that is definitely stated is that the question of calling a General Conference shall be put on the agenda of the tenth annual session of the General Assembly following the coming into force of the Charter. Strictly speaking this in itself gives no additional assurance since the agenda of the Assembly will presumably contain any item which any Member wants discussed if it comes within the Assembly's competence. Such, at any rate, was the practice of the League of Nations, it being stated in the *Rules of Procedure of the Assembly* [1] that "all items proposed by a Member of the League" should be included in the agenda.

However, there is in this paragraph one concession which may have some importance. If a General Conference is not held before the tenth annual session of the General Assembly, the question of holding one is not only automatically placed on the agenda of the Assembly, but the Assembly may decide in favor of holding one by a majority vote of its members, as contrasted with a two-thirds vote required under paragraph 1. It is to be noted, however, that the majority vote required in the Assembly is not the same as that provided for in Article 18. This paragraph specifies "a majority vote of the members of the General Assembly" while Article 18, paragraph 3, uses the words "a majority of the members present and voting."

The decision of the General Assembly to hold a General Conference, taken under this paragraph, must be concurred in by a decision of the Security Council, taken by the affirmative vote of any seven members. This of course means that no permanent member, by its sole opposition, can prevent a General Conference from being held. Nor can a permanent member block a Conference recommendation.

However, no revision of the Charter recommended by a General Conference can, under the terms of paragraph 2 of this Article, enter into force unless ratified by all the permanent members of the Security Council. As we have seen, there was strong opposition to this at the United Nations Conference on the part of the delegates of certain of the smaller states. These delegates proposed that it might be left to the General Conference to decide the method of ratification of the amendments it might adopt. The representatives of the Sponsoring Governments and France, however, took the position that their governments could not enter upon the great responsibilities and obligations of membership which they were prepared to accept if forced to take

---

[1] League of Nations Document C.144.M.92.1937, Rule 4, Section 2.

the risk that these responsibilities might be increased without their consent.[1]

The question of the right of withdrawal from the Organization came under consideration in connection with this whole matter, since certain delegates pointed to the need of reserving the right of withdrawal if the provisions regarding revision of the Charter did not prove to be effective in practice.[2]

[1] UNCIO, *Report of the Rapporteur of Committee I/2 on Chapter XI (Amendments)*, Doc. 1154, I/2/73 (2), p. 8.

[2] See comment, p. 86.

CHAPTER XIX

RATIFICATION AND SIGNATURE

ARTICLE 110

1. The present Charter shall be ratified by the signatory states in accordance with their respective constitutional processes.

Ratification is the act by which the proper authority of the state sanctions an international agreement. The procedure is determined by the constitution of each state. The Charter expressly recognizes this fact. In the United States the ratification of all treaties requires Senate approval by a two-thirds majority. Other international agreements may be entered into by executive action alone, or by executive action coupled with Congressional authorization or approval by a majority vote of both Houses.

2. The ratifications shall be deposited with the Government of the United States of America, which shall notify all the signatory states of each deposit as well as the Secretary-General of the Organization when he has been appointed.

This paragraph is of a purely technical nature and does not require any comment.

3. The present Charter shall come into force upon the deposit of ratifications by the Republic of China, France, the Union of Soviet Socialist Republics, the United Kingdom of Great Britain and Northern Ireland, and the United States of America, and by a majority of the other signatory states. A protocol of the ratifications deposited shall thereupon be drawn up by the Government of the United States of America which shall communicate copies thereof to all the signatory states.

This paragraph states that the Charter shall come into force when the five permanent members of the Security Council and a majority of the other Members have ratified it and deposited their ratifications in accordance with the provisions of paragraph 2. The intention of this provision is to assure that the Organization will come into being with sufficiently strong support. The experience of the League of Nations lies behind this provision.

The Charter, together with the Statute of the International Court of Justice, came into force on October 24, 1945.[1] A Protocol of Deposit of Ratifications was signed by the Secretary of State of the United States on that day.[2] Facsimile copies of the Protocol were furnished by the Government of the United States to the other signatories of the Charter.

4. The states signatory to the present Charter which ratify it after it has come into force will become original Members of the United Nations on the date of the deposit of their respective ratifications.

See comment on Article 3.

Deposit of ratifications by all the signatories was completed on December 27, 1945. The dates of ratification and the dates of deposit of ratification are given in the following table:

	RATIFIED	RATIFICATION DEPOSITED
Argentina	Sept. 8	Sept. 24
Australia	Oct. 4	Nov. 1
Belgium	Dec. 19	Dec. 27
Bolivia	Oct. 17	Nov. 14
Brazil	Sept. 8	Sept. 21
Byelorussian S.S.R.	Aug. 30	Oct. 24
Canada	Nov. 1	Nov. 9
Chile	Sept. 18	Oct. 11
China	Aug. 24	Sept. 28
Colombia	Oct. 24	Nov. 5
Costa Rica	Aug. 9	Nov. 2
Cuba	Oct. 13	Oct. 15
Czechoslovakia	Sept. 19	Oct. 19
Denmark	Sept. 11	Oct. 9
Dominican Republic	Aug. 24	Sept. 4
Ecuador	Dec. 14	Dec. 21
Egypt	Oct. 13	Oct. 22
Ethiopia	Oct. 11	Nov. 13
France	Aug. 14	Aug. 31
Greece	Sept. 28	Oct. 25
Guatemala	Oct. 15	Nov. 21
Haiti	Aug. 17	Sept. 27
Honduras	Dec. 13	Dec. 17
India	Oct. 18	Oct. 30
Iran	Sept. 23	Oct. 16
Iraq	Nov. 1	Dec. 21
Lebanon	Sept. 4	Oct. 15
Liberia	Oct. 17	Nov. 2
Luxembourg	Sept. 11	Oct. 17
Mexico	Oct. 17	Nov. 7
Netherlands	Nov. 16	Dec. 10
New Zealand	Aug. 7	Sept. 19
Nicaragua	July 6	Sept. 6

[1] Department of State, *Bulletin*, XIII, p. 679.   [2] See p. 385.

	RATIFIED	RATIFICATION DEPOSITED
Norway	Nov. 16	Nov. 27
Panama	Oct. 27	Nov. 13
Paraguay	Sept. 28	Oct. 12
Peru	Oct. 15	Oct. 31
Philippines	Sept. 21	Oct. 11
Poland	Oct. 16 [1]	Oct. 24
El Salvador	July 12	Sept. 26
Saudi Arabia	Sept. 30	Oct. 18
Syria	Aug. 30	Oct. 19
Turkey	Aug. 24	Sept. 28
Ukrainian S.S.R.	Aug. 22	Oct. 24
Union of South Africa	Oct. 19	Nov. 7
Union of Soviet Socialist Republics	Aug. 20	Oct. 24
United Kingdom	Sept. 20	Oct. 20
United States	Aug. 8	Aug. 8
Uruguay	Dec. 15	Dec. 18
Venezuela	Nov. 2	Nov. 15
Yugoslavia	Aug. 24	Oct. 19

ARTICLE 111

The present Charter, of which the Chinese, French, Russian, English and Spanish texts are equally authentic, shall remain deposited in the archives of the Government of the United States of America. Duly certified copies thereof shall be transmitted by that Government to the Governments of the other signatory states.

The League of Nations Covenant was drawn up in two languages. The two texts were equally authentic. In practice, certain discrepancies were found to exist between them. The United Nations Charter was signed in five languages. This Article states that the five language texts shall be equally authentic. This will create difficult problems of interpretation if there prove to be discrepancies between the different texts. It is reasonable to expect such discrepancies, especially when we bear in mind the great pressure under which the work of translation was done,[2] as well as the inevitable difficulty of expressing exact shades of meaning in different languages. If such difficulties should arise, it will be necessary to go back to the documentation and discussions of the Conference in order to see what light they throw on the intentions of the Members. It would appear that for purposes of establishing intent, the English text will be the more important since English was the most commonly used language of the Conference and the language in which the Charter was first drafted.

[1] Signed *Charter* October 15, 1945.
[2] Kirk, Grayson, and Chamberlain, Lawrence, "The Organization of the San Francisco Conference," *Political Science Quarterly*, LX (September 1945), p. 340.

Many international treaties and agreements contain special stipulations regarding their interpretation. This was true, for instance, of the Constitution of the International Labor Organization though not of the Covenant of the League of Nations. Article 423 of the I.L.O. Constitution provided that "any question or dispute relating to the interpretation" of the Constitution should be referred for decision to the Permanent Court of International Justice. This provision proved, however, in practice to be largely a dead letter though questions of interpretation did come before the Court under the advisory opinion procedure. The Agreements for the establishment of the International Monetary Fund (Article XVIII) and for the International Bank for Reconstruction and Development (Article IX) have elaborate rules for interpretation, giving the power to the Executive Directors. The Convention on Civil Aviation, signed at Chicago on December 7, 1944, has provisions (Articles 84 to 86) giving the power of interpretation to the Council, with right of appeal to an arbitral tribunal or the Permanent Court of International Justice. Article XVII of the Constitution of the United Nations Food and Agriculture Organization provides for the reference of any matter of interpretation to "an appropriate international court or arbitral tribunal in the manner prescribed by rules to be adopted by the Conference."

The Charter does not contain any such rules. There are several possibilities. The first is for the parties to the dispute to refer any question arising between them to the International Court of Justice for decision. This is not ruled out by any provision of the Statute. If done, it must be by agreement of the parties to the dispute. If they have accepted the Optional Clause, one party alone could bring the question before the Court. Other states may intervene according to the rules laid down in Articles 62 and 63 of the Statute of the Court. Since, however, any question relating to the interpretation of the Charter will concern all Members, it is unlikely that questions of interpretation will be handled in this manner.

Another solution is for the appropriate organ of the United Nations to request an advisory opinion of the Court, according to the terms of Article 96 of the Charter. This suggests that the question of interpretation will normally be raised before an organ of the United Nations and that that organ will in the first instance have the function and responsibility of making a decision. It would certainly be appropriate for the organ to ask the Court to give an advisory opinion on the question since it would undoubtedly be a question of a legal nature.

As against the purely judicial approach, it is argued that the interpretation of the Charter is as much a political as a juridical function, and that therefore it must be left to the various organs of the United Nations and to Members to determine the meaning of the document in the light of circumstances. Every organ naturally will have to decide questions of its own competence and procedure, and Members, in their individual capacities and as members of organs, will find it necessary to express judgments on questions of interpretation. Differences of opinion as to what particular parts of the Charter mean may require formal amendments for their settlement.

The question of interpretation was discussed at considerable length at the United Nations Conference, but no real solution was found. The following statement was included in the final report of Committee IV/2:

In the course of the operations from day to day of the various organs of the Organization, it is inevitable that each organ will interpret such parts of the Charter as are applicable to its particular functions. This process is inherent in the functioning of any body which operates under an instrument defining its functions and powers. It will be manifested in the functioning of such a body as the General Assembly, the Security Council, or the International Court of Justice. Accordingly, it is not necessary to include in the Charter a provision either authorizing or approving the normal operation of this principle.

Difficulties may conceivably arise in the event that there should be a difference of opinion among the organs of the Organization concerning the correct interpretation of a provision of the Charter. Thus, two organs may conceivably hold and may express or even act upon different views. Under unitary forms of national government the final determination of such a question may be vested in the highest court or in some other national authority. However, the nature of the Organization and of its operation would not seem to be such as to invite the inclusion in the Charter of any provision of this nature. If two Member States are at variance concerning the correct interpretation of the Charter, they are of course free to submit the dispute to the International Court of Justice as in the case of any other treaty. Similarly, it would always be open to the General Assembly or to the Security Council, in appropriate circumstances, to ask the International Court of Justice for an advisory opinion concerning the meaning of a provision of the Charter. Should the General Assembly or the Security Council prefer another course, an *ad hoc* committee of jurists might be set up to examine the question and report its views, or recourse might be had to a joint conference. In brief, the Members or the organs of the Organization might have recourse to various expedients in order to obtain an appropriate interpretation. It would appear neither necessary nor desirable to list or to describe in the Charter the various possible expedients.

It is to be understood, of course, that if an interpretation made by any organ of the Organization or by a committee of jurists is not generally acceptable it will be without binding force. In such circumstances, or in cases where it is desired to establish an authoritative interpretation as a precedent for the future, it may be necessary to embody the interpretation in an amendment to the Charter. This may always be accomplished by recourse to the procedure provided for amendment.[1]

IN FAITH WHEREOF the representatives of the Governments of the United Nations have signed the present Charter.

DONE at the city of San Francisco the twenty-sixth day of June, one thousand nine hundred and forty-five.

[1] UNCIO, *Report of the Rapporteur of Committee IV/2*, Doc. 933, IV/2/42 (2), p. 7–8.

PART III

DOCUMENTS

(1) *Declaration of Principles, Known as the Atlantic Charter, by the President of the United States and the Prime Minister of the United Kingdom, August 14, 1941* [1]

JOINT DECLARATION of the President of the United States of America and the Prime Minister, Mr. Churchill, representing His Majesty's Government in the United Kingdom, being met together, deem it right to make known certain common principles in the national policies of their respective countries on which they base their hopes for a better future for the world.

First, their countries seek no aggrandizement, territorial or other;

Second, they desire to see no territorial changes that do not accord with the freely expressed wishes of the peoples concerned;

Third, they respect the right of all peoples to choose the form of government under which they will live; and they wish to see sovereign rights and self-government restored to those who have been forcibly deprived of them;

Fourth, they will endeavor, with due respect for their existing obligations, to further the enjoyment by all States, great or small, victor or vanquished, of access, on equal terms, to the trade and to the raw materials of the world which are needed for their economic prosperity;

Fifth, they desire to bring about the fullest collaboration between all nations in the economic field with the object of securing, for all, improved labor standards, economic advancement and social security;

Sixth, after the final destruction of the Nazi tyranny, they hope to see established a peace which will afford to all nations the means of dwelling in safety within their own boundaries, and which will afford assurance that all the men in all the lands may live out their lives in freedom from fear and want;

Seventh, such a peace should enable all men to traverse the high seas and oceans without hindrance;

Eighth, they believe that all of the nations of the world, for realistic as well as spiritual reasons must come to the abandonment of the use of force. Since no future peace can be maintained if land, sea or air armaments continue to be employed by nations which threaten, or may threaten, aggression outside of their frontiers, they believe, pending the establishment of a wider and permanent system of general security,

[1] In Message of the President (Roosevelt) to the Congress, August 21, 1941, House Doc. No. 358, 77th Cong., 1st sess.; *Documents on American Foreign Relations, IV, 1941–1942*, p. 10.

that the disarmament of such nations is essential. They will likewise aid and encourage all other practicable measures which will lighten for peace-loving peoples the crushing burden of armaments.

(2) *Declaration by United Nations, January 1, 1942* [1]

A JOINT DECLARATION *by the United States of America, the United Kingdom of Great Britain and Northern Ireland, the Union of Soviet Socialist Republics, China, Australia, Belgium, Canada, Costa Rica, Cuba, Czechoslovakia, Dominican Republic, El Salvador, Greece, Guatemala, Haiti, Honduras, India, Luxembourg, Netherlands, New Zealand, Nicaragua, Norway, Panama, Poland, South Africa, Yugoslavia.*

The Governments signatory hereto,

Having subscribed to a common program of purposes and principles embodied in the Joint Declaration of the President of the United States of America and the Prime Minister of the United Kingdom of Great Britain and Northern Ireland dated August 14, 1941, known as the Atlantic Charter,

Being convinced that complete victory over their enemies is essential to defend life, liberty, independence and religious freedom, and to preserve human rights and justice in their own lands as well as in other lands, and that they are now engaged in a common struggle against savage and brutal forces seeking to subjugate the world,

DECLARE:

(1) Each Government pledges itself to employ its full resources, military or economic, against those members of the Tripartite Pact and its adherents with which such government is at war.

(2) Each Government pledges itself to cooperate with the Governments signatory hereto and not to make a separate armistice or peace with the enemies.

The foregoing declaration may be adhered to by other nations which are, or which may be, rendering material assistance and contributions in the struggle for victory over Hitlerism.

DONE at Washington   *January First, 1942*

[The signatories to the Declaration by United Nations are as listed above.

The adherents to the Declaration by United Nations, together with the date of communication of adherence, are as follows:

Mexico	June 5, 1942	Iraq	Jan. 16, 1943
Philippines	June 10, 1942	Brazil	Feb. 8, 1943
Ethiopia	July 28, 1942	Bolivia	Apr. 27, 1943

[1] *Executive Agreement Series* 236; *Documents on American Foreign Relations, IV, 1941–42*, p. 203.

Iran	Sept. 10, 1943	Venezuela	Feb. 16, 1945
Colombia	Dec. 22, 1943	Uruguay	Feb. 23, 1945
Liberia	Feb. 26, 1944	Turkey	Feb. 24, 1945
France	Dec. 26, 1944	Egypt	Feb. 27, 1945
Ecuador	Feb. 7, 1945	Saudi Arabia	Mar. 1, 1945
Peru	Feb. 11, 1945	Syria	Mar. 1, 1945
Chile	Feb. 12, 1945	Lebanon	Mar. 1, 1945.]
Paraguay	Feb. 12, 1945		

(3) *Declaration of Four Nations on General Security, Moscow, October 30, 1943* [1]

THE GOVERNMENTS of the United States of America, the United Kingdom, the Soviet Union and China:

united in their determination, in accordance with the Declaration by the United Nations of January 1, 1942, and subsequent declarations, to continue hostilities against those Axis powers with which they respectively are at war until such powers have laid down their arms on the basis of unconditional surrender;

conscious of their responsibility to secure the liberation of themselves and the peoples allied with them from the menace of aggression;

recognizing the necessity of ensuring a rapid and orderly transition from war to peace and of establishing and maintaining international peace and security with the least diversion of the world's human and economic resources for armaments;

jointly declare:

1. That their united action, pledged for the prosecution of the war against their respective enemies, will be continued for the organization and maintenance of peace and security.

2. That those of them at war with a common enemy will act together in all matters relating to the surrender and disarmament of that enemy.

3. That they will take all measures deemed by them to be necessary to provide against any violation of the terms imposed upon the enemy.

4. That they recognize the necessity of establishing at the earliest practicable date a general international organization, based on the principle of the sovereign equality of all peace-loving states, and open to membership by all such states, large and small, for the maintenance of international peace and security.

5. That for the purpose of maintaining international peace and security pending the re-establishment of law and order and the inauguration of a system of general security, they will consult with one another and as occasion requires with other members of the United Nations with a view to joint action on behalf of the community of nations.

6. That after the termination of hostilities they will not employ their

[1] Department of State, *Bulletin*, IX, p. 308; *Documents on American Foreign Relations, VI, 1943–1944*, p. 229.

military forces within the territories of other states except for the purposes envisaged in this declaration and after joint consultation.

7. That they will confer and cooperate with one another and with other members of the United Nations to bring about a practicable general agreement with respect to the regulation of armaments in the post-war period.

V. MOLOTOV
ANTHONY EDEN
CORDELL HULL
FOO PING-SHEUNG

(4) *Proposals for the Establishment of a General International Organization, Dumbarton Oaks, Washington, October 7, 1944* [1]

THERE SHOULD BE established an international organization under the title of The United Nations, the Charter of which should contain provisions necessary to give effect to the proposals which follow.

CHAPTER I. PURPOSES

The purposes of the Organization should be:

1. To maintain international peace and security; and to that end to take effective collective measures for the prevention and removal of threats to the peace and the suppression of acts of aggression or other breaches of the peace, and to bring about by peaceful means adjustment or settlement of international disputes which may lead to a breach of the peace;

2. To develop friendly relations among nations and to take other appropriate measures to strengthen universal peace;

3. To achieve international cooperation in the solution of international economic, social and other humanitarian problems; and

4. To afford a center for harmonizing the actions of nations in the achievement of these common ends.

CHAPTER II. PRINCIPLES

In pursuit of the purposes mentioned in Chapter I the Organization and its members should act in accordance with the following principles:

1. The Organization is based on the principle of the sovereign equality of all peace-loving states.

[1] Department of State, *Bulletin*, XI, p. 368; see also *Dumbarton Oaks Documents on International Organization*, Washington, D. C., Department of State Publication 2192 (Conference Series 56). The text of provisions relative to voting procedure in the Security Council (chap. VI, sec. C) as agreed upon at the Crimea Conference and announced by the Secretary of State on March 5, 1945 is included.

2. All members of the Organization undertake, in order to ensure to all of them the rights and benefits resulting from membership in the Organization, to fulfill the obligations assumed by them in accordance with the Charter.

3. All members of the Organization shall settle their disputes by peaceful means in such a manner that international peace and security are not endangered.

4. All members of the Organization shall refrain in their international relations from the threat or use of force in any manner inconsistent with the purposes of the Organization.

5. All members of the Organization shall give every assistance to the Organization in any action undertaken by it in accordance with the provisions of the Charter.

6. All members of the Organization shall refrain from giving assistance to any state against which preventive or enforcement action is being undertaken by the Organization.

The Organization should ensure that states not members of the Organization act in accordance with these principles so far as may be necessary for the maintenance of international peace and security.

CHAPTER III. MEMBERSHIP

1. Membership of the Organization should be open to all peace-loving states.

CHAPTER IV. PRINCIPAL ORGANS

1. The Organization should have as its principal organs:
  a. A General Assembly;
  b. A Security Council;
  c. An international court of justice; and
  d. A Secretariat.

2. The Organization should have such subsidiary agencies as may be found necessary.

CHAPTER V. THE GENERAL ASSEMBLY

Section A. Composition. All members of the Organization should be members of the General Assembly and should have a number of representatives to be specified in the Charter.

Section B. Functions and Powers. 1. The General Assembly should have the right to consider the general principles of cooperation in the maintenance of international peace and security, including the principles governing disarmament and the regulation of armaments; to discuss any questions relating to the maintenance of international peace and security brought before it by any member or members of the Organization or by the Security Council; and to make recommendations with regard to any such principles or questions. Any such questions on which action is necessary should be referred to the Security Council by the General Assembly either before or after discussion. The General Assembly should not on its own initiative make recommendations on any matter relating to the maintenance of international peace and security which is being dealt with by the Security Council.

2. The General Assembly should be empowered to admit new members to the Organization upon recommendation of the Security Council.

3. The General Assembly should, upon recommendation of the Security Council, be empowered to suspend from the exercise of any rights or privileges of membership any member of the Organization against which preventive or enforcement action shall have been taken by the Security Council. The exercise of the rights and privileges thus suspended may be restored by decision of the Security Council. The General Assembly should be empowered, upon recommendation of the Security Council, to expel from the Organization any member of the Organization which persistently violates the principles contained in the Charter.

4. The General Assembly should elect the non-permanent members of the Security Council and the members of the Economic and Social Council provided for in Chapter IX. It should be empowered to elect, upon recommendation of the Security Council, the Secretary-General of the Organization. It should perform such functions in relation to the election of the judges of the international court of justice as may be conferred upon it by the statute of the court.

5. The General Assembly should apportion the expenses among the members of the Organization and should be empowered to approve the budgets of the Organization.

6. The General Assembly should initiate studies and make recommendations for the purpose of promoting international cooperation in political, economic and social fields and of adjusting situations likely to impair the general welfare.

7. The General Assembly should make recommendations for the coordination of the policies of international economic, social, and other specialized agencies brought into relation with the Organization in accordance with agreements between such agencies and the Organization.

8. The General Assembly should receive and consider annual and special reports from the Security Council and reports from other bodies of the Organization.

Section C. Voting. 1. Each member of the Organization should have one vote in the General Assembly.

2. Important decisions of the General Assembly, including recommendations with respect to the maintenance of international peace and

security; election of members of the Security Council; election of members of the Economic and Social Council; admission of members, suspension of the exercise of the rights and privileges of members, and expulsion of members; and budgetary questions, should be made by a two-thirds majority of those present and voting. On other questions, including the determination of additional categories of questions to be decided by a two-thirds majority, the decisions of the General Assembly should be made by a simple majority vote.

Section D. Procedure. 1. The General Assembly should meet in regular annual sessions and in such special sessions as occasion may require.

2. The General Assembly should adopt its own rules of procedure and elect its President for each session.

3. The General Assembly should be empowered to set up such bodies and agencies as it may deem necessary for the performance of its functions.

CHAPTER VI. THE SECURITY COUNCIL

Section A. Composition. The Security Council should consist of one representative of each of eleven members of the Organization. Representatives of the United States of America, the United Kingdom of Great Britain and Northern Ireland, the Union of Soviet Socialist Republics, the Republic of China, and, in due course, France, should have permanent seats. The General Assembly should elect six states to fill the non-permanent seats. These six states should be elected for a term of two years, three retiring each year. They should not be immediately eligible for re-election. In the first election of the non-permanent members three should be chosen by the General Assembly for one-year terms and three for two-year terms.

Section B. Principal Functions and Powers. 1. In order to ensure prompt and effective action by the Organization, members of the Organization should by the Charter confer on the Security Council primary responsibility for the maintenance of international peace and security and should agree that in carrying out these duties under this responsibility it should act on their behalf.

2. In discharging these duties the Security Council should act in accordance with the purposes and principles of the Organization.

3. The specific powers conferred on the Security Council in order to carry out these duties are laid down in Chapter VIII.

4. All members of the Organization should obligate themselves to accept the decisions of the Security Council and to carry them out in accordance with the provisions of the Charter.

5. In order to promote the establishment and maintenance of international peace and security with the least diversion of the world's

human and economic resources for armaments, the Security Council, with the assistance of the Military Staff Committee referred to in Chapter VIII, Section B, paragraph 9, should have the responsibility for formulating plans for the establishment of a system of regulation of armaments for submission to the members of the Organization.

[*Section C. Voting.*[1] 1. Each member of the Security Council should have one vote.

2. Decisions of the Security Council on procedural matters should be made by an affirmative vote of seven members.

3. Decisions of the Security Council on all other matters should be made by an affirmative vote of seven members including the concurring votes of the permanent members; provided that, in decisions under Chapter VIII, Section A, and under the second sentence of Paragraph 1 of Chapter VIII, Section C, a party to a dispute should abstain from voting.]

Section D. Procedure. 1. The Security Council should be so organized as to be able to function continuously and each state member of the Security Council should be permanently represented at the headquarters of the Organization. It may hold meetings at such other places as in its judgment may best facilitate its work. There should be periodic meetings at which each state member of the Security Council could if it so desired be represented by a member of the government or some other special representative.

2. The Security Council should be empowered to set up such bodies or agencies as it may deem necessary for the performance of its functions including regional subcommittees of the Military Staff Committee.

3. The Security Council should adopt its own rules of procedure, including the method of selecting its President.

4. Any member of the Organization should participate in the discussion of any question brought before the Security Council whenever the Security Council considers that the interests of that member of the Organization are specially affected.

5. Any member of the Organization not having a seat on the Security Council and any state not a member of the Organization, if it is a party to a dispute under consideration by the Security Council, should be invited to participate in the discussion relating to the dispute.

CHAPTER VII. AN INTERNATIONAL COURT OF JUSTICE

1. There should be an international court of justice which should constitute the principal judicial organ of the Organization.

2. The court should be constituted and should function in accordance with a statute which should be annexed to and be a part of the Charter of the Organization.

[1] See footnote 1, p. 308.

3. The statute of the court of international justice should be either (a) the Statute of the Permanent Court of International Justice, continued in force with such modifications as may be desirable, or (b) a new statute in the preparation of which the Statute of the Permanent Court of International Justice should be used as a basis.

4. All members of the Organization should *ipso facto* be parties to the statute of the international court of justice.

5. Conditions under which states not members of the Organization may become parties to the statute of the international court of justice should be determined in each case by the General Assembly upon recommendation of the Security Council.

CHAPTER VIII. ARRANGEMENTS FOR THE MAINTENANCE OF INTERNATIONAL PEACE AND SECURITY INCLUDING PREVENTION AND SUPPRESSION OF AGGRESSION

Section A. Pacific Settlement of Disputes. 1. The Security Council should be empowered to investigate any dispute, or any situation which may lead to international friction or give rise to a dispute, in order to determine whether its continuance is likely to endanger the maintenance of international peace and security.

2. Any state, whether member of the Organization or not, may bring any such dispute or situation to the attention of the General Assembly or of the Security Council.

3. The parties to any dispute the continuance of which is likely to endanger the maintenance of international peace and security should obligate themselves, first of all, to seek a solution by negotiation, mediation, conciliation, arbitration or judicial settlement, or other peaceful means of their own choice. The Security Council should call upon the parties to settle their dispute by such means.

4. If, nevertheless, parties to a dispute of the nature referred to in paragraph 3 above fail to settle it by the means indicated in that paragraph, they should obligate themselves to refer it to the Security Council. The Security Council should in each case decide whether or not the continuance of the particular dispute is in fact likely to endanger the maintenance of international peace and security, and, accordingly, whether the Security Council should deal with the dispute, and, if so, whether it should take action under paragraph 5.

5. The Security Council should be empowered, at any stage of a dispute of the nature referred to in paragraph 3 above, to recommend appropriate procedures or methods of adjustment.

6. Justiciable disputes should normally be referred to the international court of justice. The Security Council should be empowered to refer to the court, for advice, legal questions connected with other disputes.

7. The provisions of paragraphs 1 to 6 of Section A should not apply to situations or disputes arising out of matters which by international law are solely within the domestic jurisdiction of the state concerned.

Section B. Determination of Threats to the Peace or Acts of Aggression and Action With Respect Thereto. 1. Should the Security Council deem that a failure to settle a dispute in accordance with procedures indicated in paragraph 3 of Section A, or in accordance with its recommendations made under paragraph 5 of Section A, constitutes a threat to the maintenance of international peace and security, it should take any measures necessary for the maintenance of international peace and security in accordance with the purposes and principles of the Organization.

2. In general the Security Council should determine the existence of any threat to the peace, breach of the peace or act of aggression and should make recommendations or decide upon the measures to be taken to maintain or restore peace and security.

3. The Security Council should be empowered to determine what diplomatic, economic, or other measures not involving the use of armed force should be employed to give effect to its decisions, and to call upon members of the Organization to apply such measures. Such measures may include complete or partial interruption of rail, sea, air, postal, telegraphic, radio and other means of communication and the severance of diplomatic and economic relations.

4. Should the Security Council consider such measures to be inadequate, it should be empowered to take such action by air, naval or land forces as may be necessary to maintain or restore international peace and security. Such action may include demonstrations, blockade and other operations by air, sea or land forces of members of the Organization.

5. In order that all members of the Organization should contribute to the maintenance of international peace and security, they should undertake to make available to the Security Council, on its call and in accordance with a special agreement or agreements concluded among themselves, armed forces, facilities and assistance necessary for the purpose of maintaining international peace and security. Such agreement or agreements should govern the numbers and types of forces and the nature of the facilities and assistance to be provided. The special agreement or agreements should be negotiated as soon as possible and should in each case be subject to approval by the Security Council and to ratification by the signatory states in accordance with their constitutional processes.

6. In order to enable urgent military measures to be taken by the Organization there should be held immediately available by the members of the Organization national air force contingents for combined international enforcement action. The strength and degree of readiness of

these contingents and plans for their combined action should be determined by the Security Council with the assistance of the Military Staff Committee within the limits laid down in the special agreement or agreements referred to in paragraph 5 above.

7. The action required to carry out the decisions of the Security Council for the maintenance of international peace and security should be taken by all the members of the Organization in cooperation or by some of them as the Security Council may determine. This undertaking should be carried out by the members of the Organization by their own action and through action of the appropriate specialized organizations and agencies of which they are members.

8. Plans for the application of armed force should be made by the Security Council with the assistance of the Military Staff Committee referred to in paragraph 9 below.

9. There should be established a Military Staff Committee the functions of which should be to advise and assist the Security Council on all questions relating to the Security Council's military requirements for the maintenance of international peace and security, to the employment and command of forces placed at its disposal, to the regulation of armaments, and to possible disarmament. It should be responsible under the Security Council for the strategic direction of any armed forces placed at the disposal of the Security Council. The Committee should be composed of the Chiefs of Staff of the permanent members of the Security Council or their representatives. Any member of the Organization not permanently represented on the Committee should be invited by the Committee to be associated with it when the efficient discharge of the Committee's responsibilities requires that such a state should participate in its work. Questions of command of forces should be worked out subsequently.

10. The members of the Organization should join in affording mutual assistance in carrying out the measures decided upon by the Security Council.

11. Any state, whether a member of the Organization or not, which finds itself confronted with special economic problems arising from the carrying out of measures which have been decided upon by the Security Council should have the right to consult the Security Council in regard to a solution of those problems.

Section C. Regional Arrangements. 1. Nothing in the Charter should preclude the existence of regional arrangements or agencies for dealing with such matters relating to the maintenance of international peace and security as are appropriate for regional action, provided such arrangements or agencies and their activities are consistent with the purposes and principles of the Organization. The Security Council should encourage settlement of local disputes through such regional arrangements or by such regional agencies, either on the initiative of the states concerned or by reference from the Security Council.

2. The Security Council should, where appropriate, utilize such arrangements or agencies for enforcement action under its authority, but no enforcement action should be taken under regional arrangements or by regional agencies without the authorization of the Security Council.

3. The Security Council should at all times be kept fully informed of activities undertaken or in contemplation under regional arrangements or by regional agencies for the maintenance of international peace and security.

CHAPTER IX. ARRANGEMENTS FOR INTERNATIONAL ECONOMIC AND SOCIAL COOPERATION

Section A. Purpose and Relationships. 1. With a view to the creation of conditions of stability and well-being which are necessary for peaceful and friendly relations among nations, the Organization should facilitate solutions of international economic, social and other humanitarian problems and promote respect for human rights and fundamental freedoms. Responsibility for the discharge of this function should be vested in the General Assembly and, under the authority of the General Assembly, in an Economic and Social Council.

2. The various specialized economic, social and other organizations and agencies would have responsibilities in their respective fields as defined in their statutes. Each such organization or agency should be brought into relationship with the Organization on terms to be determined by agreement between the Economic and Social Council and the appropriate authorities of the specialized organization or agency, subject to approval by the General Assembly.

Section B. Composition and Voting. The Economic and Social Council should consist of representatives of eighteen members of the Organization. The states to be represented for this purpose should be elected by the General Assembly for terms of three years. Each such state should have one representative, who should have one vote. Decisions of the Economic and Social Council should be taken by simple majority vote of those present and voting.

Section C. Functions and Powers of the Economic and Social Council. 1. The Economic and Social Council should be empowered:

a. to carry out, within the scope of its functions, recommendations of the General Assembly;

b. to make recommendations, on its own initiative, with respect to international economic, social and other humanitarian matters;

c. to receive and consider reports from the economic, social and other organizations or agencies brought into relationship with the Organization, and to coordinate their activities through consultations with, and recommendations to, such organizations or agencies;

d. to examine the administrative budgets of such specialized organizations or agencies with a view to making recommendations to the organizations or agencies concerned;

e. to enable the Secretary-General to provide information to the Security Council;

f. to assist the Security Council upon its request; and

g. to perform such other functions within the general scope of its competence as may be assigned to it by the General Assembly.

Section D. Organization and Procedure. 1. The Economic and Social Council should set up an economic commission, a social commission, and such other commissions as may be required. These commissions should consist of experts. There should be a permanent staff which should constitute a part of the Secretariat of the Organization.

2. The Economic and Social Council should make suitable arrangements for representatives of the specialized organizations or agencies to participate without vote in its deliberations and in those of the commissions established by it.

3. The Economic and Social Council should adopt its own rules of procedure and the method of selecting its President.

CHAPTER X. THE SECRETARIAT

1. There should be a Secretariat comprising a Secretary-General and such staff as may be required. The Secretary-General should be the chief administrative officer of the Organization. He should be elected by the General Assembly, on recommendation of the Security Council, for such term and under such conditions as are specified in the Charter.

2. The Secretary-General should act in that capacity in all meetings of the General Assembly, of the Security Council, and of the Economic and Social Council and should make an annual report to the General Assembly on the work of the Organization.

3. The Secretary-General should have the right to bring to the attention of the Security Council any matter which in his opinion may threaten international peace and security.

CHAPTER XI. AMENDMENTS

Amendments should come into force for all members of the Organization, when they have been adopted by a vote of two-thirds of the members of the General Assembly and ratified in accordance with their respective constitutional processes by the members of the Organization having permanent membership on the Security Council and by a majority of the other members of the Organization.

CHAPTER XII. TRANSITIONAL ARRANGEMENTS

1. Pending the coming into force of the special agreement or agreements referred to in Chapter VIII, Section B, paragraph 5, and in accordance with the provisions of paragraph 5 of the Four-Nation Declaration, signed at Moscow, October 30, 1943, the states parties to that Declaration should consult with one another and as occasion arises with other members of the Organization with a view to such joint action on behalf of the Organization as may be necessary for the purpose of maintaining international peace and security.

2. No provision of the Charter should preclude action taken or authorized in relation to enemy states as a result of the present war by the Governments having responsibility for such action.

NOTE

In addition to the question of voting procedure in the Security Council referred to in Chapter VI, several other questions are still under consideration.

WASHINGTON, D. C.
    October 7, 1944.

(5) *Report of Crimea Conference, February 11, 1945* [1]

(Excerpts)

FOR THE PAST eight days, Winston S. Churchill, Prime Minister of Great Britain, Franklin D. Roosevelt, President of the United States of America, and Marshal J. V. Stalin, Chairman of the Council of People's Commissars of the Union of Soviet Socialist Republics, have met with the Foreign Secretaries, Chiefs of Staff, and other advisors in the Crimea.

[A list of participants in addition to the three heads of governments follows here in the original.]

The following statement is made by the Prime Minister of Great Britain, the President of the United States of America, and the Chairman of the Council of People's Commissars of the Union of Soviet Socialist Republics on the results of the Crimean Conference:

. . . .

UNITED NATIONS CONFERENCE

We are resolved upon the earliest possible establishment with our allies of a general international organization to maintain peace and security. We believe that this is essential, both to prevent aggression

---

[1] Department of State, *Bulletin,* XII, p. 213.

and to remove the political, economic and social causes of war through the close and continuing collaboration of all peace-loving peoples.

The foundations were laid at Dumbarton Oaks. On the important question of voting procedure, however, agreement was not there reached. The present Conference has been able to resolve this difficulty.

We have agreed that a conference of United Nations should be called to meet at San Francisco in the United States on April 25, 1945, to prepare the charter of such an organization, along the lines proposed in the informal conversations at Dumbarton Oaks.

The Government of China and the Provisional Government of France will be immediately consulted and invited to sponsor invitations to the conference jointly with the Governments of the United States, Great Britain and the Union of Soviet Socialist Republics. As soon as the consultation with China and France has been completed, the text of the proposals on voting procedure will be made public.

MEETINGS OF FOREIGN SECRETARIES

Throughout the Conference, besides the daily meetings of the heads of governments and the Foreign Secretaries, separate meetings of the three Foreign Secretaries, and their advisors have also been held daily.

These meetings have proved of the utmost value and the Conference agreed that permanent machinery should be set up for regular consultation between the three Foreign Secretaries. They will, therefore, meet as often as may be necessary, probably about every three or four months. These meetings will be held in rotation in the three capitals, the first meeting being held in London, after the United Nations Conference on World Organization.

UNITY FOR PEACE AS FOR WAR

Our meeting here in the Crimea has reaffirmed our common determination to maintain and strengthen in the peace to come that unity of purpose and of action which has made victory possible and certain for the United Nations in this war. We believe that this is a sacred obligation which our Governments owe to our peoples and to all the peoples of the world.

Only with the continuing and growing cooperation and understanding among our three countries and among all the peace-loving nations can the highest aspiration of humanity be realized — a secure and lasting peace which will, in the words of the Atlantic Charter, "afford assurance that all the men in all the lands may live out their lives in freedom from fear and want."

Victory in this war and establishment of the proposed international organization will provide the greatest opportunity in all history to create in the years to come the essential conditions of such a peace.

Signed: WINSTON S. CHURCHILL
FRANKLIN D. ROOSEVELT
February 11, 1945.   J. STALIN

(6) *Invitation to United Nations Conference Called to Meet at San Francisco, April 25, 1945, issued March 5, 1945* [1]

THE GOVERNMENT of the United States of America, on behalf of itself and of the Governments of the United Kingdom of Great Britain and Northern Ireland, the Union of Soviet Socialist Republics and the Republic of China, invites the Government of (name of Government invited was inserted here) to send representatives to a conference of the United Nations to be held on April 25, 1945, at San Francisco in the United States of America to prepare a charter for a general international organization for the maintenance of international peace and security.

The above-named Governments suggest that the conference consider as affording a basis for such a charter the proposals for the establishment of a general international organization, which were made public last October as a result of the Dumbarton Oaks Conference, and which have now been supplemented by the following provisions for Section C of Chapter VI:

(Provisions omitted here, see p. 312.)

Further information as to arrangements will be transmitted subsequently. In the event that the Government of (name of Government invited was inserted here) desires in advance of the Conference to present views or comments concerning the proposals, the Government of the United States of America will be pleased to transmit such views and comments to the other participating Governments.

(7) *Chinese Proposals on Dumbarton Oaks Proposals, May 1, 1945* [2]

The four Governments sponsoring the United Nations Conference on International Organization at San Francisco have agreed to support the following proposals put forward by the Chinese Government:

[1] Department of State, *Bulletin*, XII, p. 394.
[2] The United Nations Conference on International Organization (hereafter referred to as UNCIO), *Comments and Proposed Amendments Concerning the Dumbarton Oaks Proposals Submitted by the Delegations to the United Nations Conference on International Organization, May 7, 1945*, Doc. 1 (English) G/1(a).

"1. The Charter should provide specifically that adjustment or settlement of international disputes should be achieved with due regard for principles of justice and international law.

"2. The Assembly should be responsible for initiating studies and making recommendations with respect to the development and revision of the rules and principles of international law.

"3. The Economic and Social Council should specifically provide for the promotion of educational and other forms of cultural cooperation."

These proposals were developed during the course of the Chinese phase of the Dumbarton Oaks Conversations last fall and were agreed to at that time by the United States, the United Kingdom and China. They have now been considered with the Soviet Government and that Government has agreed to join in sponsoring the proposals for presentation to the San Francisco Conference.

(8) *Amendments Proposed by the Governments of the United States, the United Kingdom, the Soviet Union, and China, May 5, 1945* [1]

THE DELEGATIONS of the four Governments which participated in the Dumbarton Oaks Conversations, the United States, the United Kingdom, the Soviet Union, and China, have consulted together concerning amendments to the Dumbarton Oaks Proposals which each of them desired to submit. The proposed amendments on which the four find themselves in agreement are submitted to the Conference as joint proposals. Such further amendments as each of these Governments may wish to propose will be presented separately.

(NOTE: Amendments are indicated by using light italic type for added passages and heavy italic type for deleted passages.)

CHAPTER I. PURPOSES

1. To maintain international peace and security; and to that end to take effective collective measures for the prevention and removal of threats to the peace and the suppression of acts of aggression or other breaches of the peace, and to bring about by peaceful means, *and with due regard for principles of justice and international law*, adjustment or settlement of international disputes which may lead to a breach of the peace.

2. To develop friendly relations among nations *based on respect for the principle of equal rights and self-determination of peoples* and to take other appropriate measures to strengthen universal peace;

3. To achieve international cooperation in the solution of international economic, social, *cultural* and other humanitarian problems *and*

[1] UNCIO, Doc. 2 (English) G/29; Department of State, *Bulletin*, XII, p. 851.

promotion and encouragement of respect for human rights and for fundamental freedoms for all without distinction as to race, language, religion or sex; and

CHAPTER II. PRINCIPLES

1. The Organization is based on the principle of the sovereign equality of all **peace-loving states** *its members.*

3. All members of the Organization shall settle their *international* disputes by peaceful means in such a manner that international peace and security are not endangered.

New paragraph to be added following paragraph 6, to take the place of paragraph 7 of Chapter VIII, Section A, which would be deleted:

Nothing contained in this Charter shall authorize the Organization to intervene in matters which are essentially within the domestic jurisdiction of the State concerned or shall require the members to submit such matters to settlement under this Charter; but this principle shall not prejudice the application of Chapter VIII, Section B.

CHAPTER V. THE GENERAL ASSEMBLY

Section B. Functions and Powers

6. The General Assembly should initiate studies and make recommendations for the purpose of promoting international cooperation in political, economic, **and** social *and cultural* fields *to assist in the realization of human rights and basic freedoms for all, without distinction as to race, language, religion or sex and also for the encouragement of the development, of international law* **and of adjusting situations likely to impair the general welfare.**

New paragraph to follow paragraph 7:

The General Assembly should examine the administrative budgets of such specialized agencies with a view to making recommendations to the agencies concerned.

CHAPTER VI. THE SECURITY COUNCIL

Section A. Composition

The Security Council should consist of one representative of each of eleven members of the Organization. Representatives of the United States of America, the United Kingdom of Great Britain and Northern Ireland, the Union of Soviet Socialist Republics, the Republic of China, and, in due course, France, should have permanent seats. The General Assembly should elect six states to fill the non-permanent seats, *due regard being specially paid in the first instance to the contribution of members of the Organization towards the maintenance of international peace and security and towards the other purposes of the Organization, and also to equitable geographical distribution.* These six states should be elected for a term of two years, three retiring each year. They should not be immediately eligible for re-election. In the first election of the non-permanent members three should be chosen by the General Assembly for one-year terms and three for two-year terms.

SECTION D. PROCEDURE

2. The Security Council should be empowered to set up such bodies or agencies as it may deem necessary for the performance of its functions. **including regional sub-committees of the Military Staff Committee.**

5. Any member of the Organization not having a seat on the Security Council and any state not a member of the Organization, if it is a party to a dispute under consideration by the Security Council, should be invited to participate in the discussion relating to the dispute. *In the case of a non-member, the Security Council should lay down such conditions as it may deem just for the participation of such a non-member.*

CHAPTER VII. AN INTERNATIONAL COURT OF JUSTICE

The provisions of Chapter VII of the Dumbarton Oaks Proposals should be adjusted to bring it into conformity with the recommendations of Commission IV in light of the report of the Jurists Committee.

CHAPTER VIII. ARRANGEMENTS FOR THE MAINTENANCE OF INTERNATIONAL PEACE AND SECURITY INCLUDING PREVENTION AND SUPPRESSION OF AGGRESSION

SECTION A. PACIFIC SETTLEMENT OF DISPUTES

The following new paragraph should be inserted before Paragraph 1 of Section A of Chapter VIII:

Without prejudice to the provisions of paragraphs 1–5 below, the Security Council should be empowered, if all the parties so request, to make recommendations to the parties to any dispute with a view to its settlement in accordance with the principles laid down in Chapter II, Paragraph 3.

2. Any state, whether member of the Organization or not, may bring any such dispute or situation to the attention of the General Assembly or of the Security Council. *In the case of a non-member, it should be required to accept, for the purposes of such dispute, the obligations of pacific settlement provided in the Charter.*

4. If, nevertheless, parties to a dispute of the nature referred to in paragraph 3 above fail to settle it by the means indicated in that para-

graph, they should obligate themselves to refer it to the Security Council. *The If the* Security Council *should in each case decide whether or not deems that* the continuance of the particular dispute is in fact likely to endanger the maintenance of international peace and security, *and, accordingly, whether the Security Council should deal with the dispute, and, if so, whether it should take action under paragraph 5 it shall decide whether to take action under paragraph 5 or whether itself to recommend such terms of settlement as it may consider appropriate.*

7. *The provisions of paragraph 1 to 6 of Section A should not apply to situations or disputes arising out of matters which by international law are solely within the domestic jurisdiction of the state concerned.*

(NOTE: This paragraph would be replaced by the new paragraph proposed for addition following paragraph 6, Chapter II, Principles.)

SECTION B.   DETERMINATION OF THREATS TO THE PEACE OR ACTS OF AGGRESSION AND ACTION WITH RESPECT THERETO

1. Should the Security Council deem that a failure to settle a dispute in accordance with procedures indicated in paragraph 3 of Section A, or in accordance with its recommendations made under paragraphs *4 or 5* of Section A, constitutes a threat to the maintenance of international peace and security, it should take any measures necessary for the maintenance of international peace and security in accordance with the purposes and principles of the Organization.

2. In general the Security Council should determine the existence of any threat to the peace, breach of the peace or act of aggression and should make recommendations or decide upon the measures *set forth in paragraphs 3 and 4 of this Section* to be taken to maintain or restore peace and security.

Insert the following paragraph between paragraphs 2 and 3:

Before making the recommendations or deciding upon the measures for the maintenance or restoration of peace and security in accordance with the provisions of paragraph 2, the Security Council may call upon the parties concerned to comply with such provisional measures as it may deem necessary or desirable in order to prevent an aggravation of the situation. Such provisional measures should be without prejudice to the rights, claims or position of the parties concerned. Failure to comply with such provisional measures should be duly taken account of by the Security Council.

9. There should be established a Military Staff Committee the functions of which should be to advise and assist the Security Council on all questions relating to the Security Council's military requirements for the maintenance of international peace and security, to the employment and command of forces placed at its disposal, to the regulation of

armaments, and to possible disarmament. It should be responsible under the Security Council for the strategic direction of any armed forces placed at the disposal of the Security Council. The Committee should be composed of the Chiefs of Staff of the permanent members of the Security Council or their representatives. Any member of the Organization not permanently represented on the Committee should be invited by the Committee to be associated with it when the efficient discharge of the Committee's responsibilities requires that such a state should participate in its work. Questions of command of forces should be worked out subsequently. *The Military Staff Committee, with the authorization of the Security Council, may establish regional subcommittees of the Military Staff Committee.*

CHAPTER IX. ARRANGEMENTS FOR INTERNATIONAL ECONOMIC AND SOCIAL COOPERATION

Section A. Purpose and Relationships

1. With a view to the creation of conditions of stability and well-being which are necessary for peaceful and friendly relations among nations *based on respect for the principle of equal rights and self-determination of peoples,* the Organization should facilitate solutions of international economic, social, *cultural,* and other humanitarian problems and promote respect for human rights and *for* fundamental freedoms *for all without distinction as to race, language, religion or sex.* Responsibility for the discharge of this function should be vested in the General Assembly, and under the authority of the General Assembly, in an Economic and Social Council.

Section C. Functions and Powers of the Economic and Social Council

1. The Economic and Social Council should be empowered:
Insert after paragraph *a,* new paragraph as follows:
To make recommendations for promoting respect for human rights and fundamental freedoms;
  b. To make recommendations, on its own initiative with respect to international economic, social, *cultural* and other humanitarian matters;
  c. To receive and consider reports from the economic, social, *cultural* and other organizations or agencies brought into relationship with the Organization, and to coordinate their activities through consultations with, and recommendations to, such organizations or agencies;

SECTION D. ORGANIZATION AND PROCEDURE

1. The Economic and Social Council should set up *an economic commission, a social commission and such other commissions as may be required* commissions in the fields of economic activity, social activity, cultural activity, promotion of human rights and any other field within the competence of the Council. These commissions should consist of experts. There should be a permanent staff which should constitute a part of the Secretariat of the Organization.

CHAPTER X. THE SECRETARIAT

1. There should be a Secretariat comprising a Secretary-General, *four deputies* and such staff as may be required. *The Secretary-General should be the chief administrative officer of the Organization. He should be elected by the General Assembly, on recommendation of the Security Council, for such term and under such conditions as are specified in the Charter.* The Secretary-General and his deputies should be elected by the General Assembly on recommendation of the Security Council for a period of three years, and the Secretary-General should be eligible for re-election. The Secretary-General should be the chief administrative officer of the Organization.

4. In the performance of their duties, the Secretary-General and the staff should be responsible only to the Organization. Their responsibilities should be exclusively international in character, and they should not seek or receive instructions in regard to the discharge thereof from any authority external to the Organization. The members should undertake fully to respect the international character of the responsibilities of the Secretariat and not to seek to influence any of their nationals in the discharge of such responsibility.

CHAPTER XI. AMENDMENTS

1. The present Charter comes into force after its ratification in accordance with their respective constitutional processes by the members of the Organization having permanent seats on the Security Council and by a majority of the other members of the Organization.

NOTE: The existing text of Chapter XI would become paragraph 2.

2. A general conference of the members of the United Nations may be held at a date and place to be fixed by a three-fourths vote of the General Assembly with the concurrence of the Security Council voting in accordance with the provisions of Chapter VI, Section C, paragraph 2, for the purpose of reviewing the Charter. Each member shall have one vote in the Conference. Any alterations of the Charter recommended by a two-thirds vote of the

Conference shall take effect when ratified in accordance with their respective constitutional processes by the members of the Organization having permanent membership on the Security Council and by a majority of the other members of the Organization.

(a) Additional Amendments to the Dumbarton Oaks Proposals Agreed to by the Governments of the United States, United Kingdom, the Soviet Union and China, May 11, 1945 [1]

The Delegations of the four Governments which participated in the Dumbarton Oaks Conversations, the United States, the United Kingdom, the Soviet Union, and China, have now agreed to two further amendments to the Dumbarton Oaks Proposals in addition to those included in Document 2, G/29, May 5, 1945. These additional amendments are as follows:

CHAPTER V. THE GENERAL ASSEMBLY

SECTION B. FUNCTIONS AND POWERS

New paragraph to follow paragraph 6.

Subject to the provisions of paragraph 1 of this Section, the General Assembly should be empowered to recommend measures for the peaceful adjustment of any situations, regardless of origin, which it deems likely to impair the general welfare or friendly relations among nations, including situations resulting from a violation of the Purposes and Principles set forth in this Charter.

CHAPTER VIII. ARRANGEMENTS FOR THE MAINTENANCE OF INTERNATIONAL PEACE AND SECURITY INCLUDING PREVENTION AND SUPPRESSION OF AGGRESSION

SECTION C. REGIONAL ARRANGEMENTS

2. The Security Council should, where appropriate, utilize such arrangements or agencies for enforcement action under its authority. But no enforcement action should be taken under regional arrangements or by regional agencies without the authorization of the Security Council *with the exception of measures against enemy states in this war provided for pursuant to Chapter XII, paragraph 2, or, in regional arrangements directed against renewal of aggressive policy on the part of such states, until such time as the Organization may, by consent of the Governments concerned, be charged with the responsibility for preventing further aggression by a state now at war with the United Nations.*

(NOTE: Amendments are indicated by using light italic type for added passages.)

[1] UNCIO, Doc. 2 (English) G/29(a).

(9) *Working Paper for Chapter on Dependent Territories and Arrangements for International Trusteeship, May 15, 1945* [1]

(This paper is not proposed by any government at this time and does not constitute a withdrawal of the proposals put forward by any government.)

(NOTE: This draft deals with principles and mechanism only and makes no assumption about the inclusion of any specific territory.)

(NOTE: Section A might be considered for inclusion in the Chapter on Principles.)

A. GENERAL POLICY

1. States members of the United Nations which have responsibilities for the administration of territories inhabited by peoples not yet able to stand by themselves under the strenuous conditions of the modern world accept the general principle that it is a sacred trust of civilization to promote to the utmost the well-being of the inhabitants of these territories within the world community, and to this end:

   (*i*) to insure the economic and social advancement of the peoples concerned;

   (*ii*) to develop self-government in forms appropriate to the varying circumstances of each territory; and

   (*iii*) to further international peace and security.

2. States members also agree that their policy in respect to such territories, no less than in respect to their metropolitan areas, must be based on the general principle of good-neighborliness, due account being taken of the interests and well-being of other members of the world community, in social, economic, and commercial matters.

B.   TERRITORIAL TRUSTEESHIP SYSTEM

1. The Organization should establish under its authority an international system of trusteeship for the administration and supervision of such territories as may be placed thereunder by subsequent individual agreements and set up suitable machinery for these purposes.

2. The basic objectives of the trusteeship system should be: (*a*) to further international peace and security; (*b*) to promote the political, economic, and social advancement of the trust territories and their inhabitants and their progressive development toward self-government in forms appropriate to the varying circumstances of each territory; and (*c*) to insure equal treatment in social, economic, and commercial matters for all members of the United Nations, without prejudice to the attainment of (*a*) and (*b*) above, and subject to the provisions of paragraph 5 below.

[1] UNCIO, Commission II. General Assembly, Committee 4, Trusteeship System, Doc. 323 (English), II/4/12.

3. The trusteeship system should apply only to such territories in the following categories as may be placed thereunder by means of trusteeship arrangements: (*a*) territories now held under mandate; (*b*) territories which may be detached from enemy states as a result of this war; and (*c*) territories voluntarily placed under the system by states responsible for their administration. It would be a matter for subsequent agreement as to which territories would be brought under a trusteeship system and upon what terms. The trusteeship system should not apply to territories which have become members of the United Nations.

4. The trusteeship arrangement for each territory to be placed under trusteeship should be agreed upon by the states directly concerned and should be approved as provided for in paragraphs 8 and 10 below.

5. Except as may be agreed upon in individual trusteeship arrangements placing each territory under the trusteeship system, nothing in this chapter should be construed in and of itself to alter in any manner the rights of any state or any peoples in any territory.

6. The trusteeship arrangements in each case should include the terms under which the territory will be administered and designate the state which should exercise the administration of the territory or designate the United Nations Organization itself to exercise the administration of the territory.

7. In addition, there may also be designated, in the trusteeship arrangement, a strategic area or areas which may include part or all of the territory to which the arrangement applies.

8. All functions of the Organization relating to such strategic areas, including the approval of the trusteeship arrangements and their alteration or amendment, should be exercised by the Security Council. The basic objectives as provided for in paragraph B. 2 above should be applicable to the people of each strategic area. The Security Council may avail itself of the assistance of the Trusteeship Council provided for in paragraph 11 below to perform those functions of the Organization under the trusteeship system relating to political, economic, and social matters in the strategic areas, subject to the provisions of the trusteeship arrangements.

9. It shall be the duty of the state administering any trust territory to insure that the territory shall play its part in the maintenance of international peace and security. To this end the state shall be empowered to make use of volunteer forces, facilities, and assistance from the territory in carrying out the obligations undertaken by the state for the Security Council in this regard and for local defense and the maintenance of law and order within the territory.

10. The functions of the Organization with regard to trusteeship arrangements for all areas not designated as strategic should be exercised by the General Assembly.

11. In order to assist the General Assembly to carry out those func·tions under the trusteeship system not reserved to the Security Council, there should be established a Trusteeship Council which would operate under its authority. The Trusteeship Council should consist of specially qualified representatives, designated (*a*) one each by the states administering trust territories, and (*b*) one each by an equal number of other states named for three-year periods by the General Assembly.

12. The General Assembly, and under its authority, the Trusteeship Council, in carrying out their functions, should be empowered to consider reports submitted by the administering state to accept petitions and examine them in consultation with the administering state, to make periodic visits to the respective territories at times agreed upon with the administering state, and to take other action in conformity with the Trusteeship arrangements.

13. The administering authority in each trust territory within the competence of the General Assembly should make an annual report to the General Assembly upon the basis of a questionnaire formulated by the Trusteeship Council.

(10) *Statement by the Delegations of the Four Sponsoring Governments on Voting Procedure in the Security Council, June 7, 1945* [1]

Specific questions [2] covering the voting procedure in the Security Council have been submitted by a Sub-Committee of the Conference Committee on Structure and Procedures of the Security Council to the Delegations of the four Governments sponsoring the Conference — the United States of America, the United Kingdom of Great Britain and Northern Ireland, the Union of Soviet Socialist Republics, and the Republic of China. In dealing with these questions, the four Delegations desire to make the following statement of their general attitude towards the whole question of unanimity of permanent members in the decisions of the Security Council.

I

1. The Yalta voting formula recognizes that the Security Council, in discharging its responsibilities for the maintenance of international peace and security, will have two broad groups of functions. Under Chapter VIII, the Council will have to make decisions which involve its taking direct measures in connection with settlement of disputes, adjustment of situations likely to lead to disputes, determination of threats to the peace, removal of threats to the peace, and suppression of breaches of the peace. It will also have to make decisions which do

[1] UNCIO, Doc. 852 (English) III/1/37 (1); Department of State, *Bulletin*, XII, p. 1047.
[2] See Questionnaire, p. 333.

not involve the taking of such measures. The Yalta formula provides that the second of these two groups of decisions will be governed by a procedural vote — that is, the vote of any seven members. The first group of decisions will be governed by a qualified vote — that is, the vote of seven members, including the concurring votes of the five permanent members, subject to the proviso that in decisions under Section A and a part of Section C of Chapter VIII parties to a dispute shall abstain from voting.

2. For example, under the Yalta formula a procedural vote will govern the decisions made under the entire Section D of Chapter VI. This means that the Council will, by a vote of any seven of its members, adopt or alter its rules of procedure; determine the method of selecting its President; organize itself in such a way as to be able to function continuously; select the times and places of its regular and special meetings; establish such bodies or agencies as it may deem necessary for the performance of its functions; invite a member of the Organization not represented on the Council to participate in its discussions when that Member's interests are specially affected; and invite any state when it is a party to a dispute being considered by the Council to participate in the discussion relating to that dispute.

3. Further, no individual member of the Council can alone prevent consideration and discussion by the Council of a dispute or situation brought to its attention under paragraph 2, Section A, Chapter VIII. Nor can parties to such dispute be prevented by these means from being heard by the Council. Likewise, the requirement for unanimity of the permanent members cannot prevent any member of the Council from reminding the members of the Organization of their general obligations assumed under the Charter as regards peaceful settlement of international disputes.

4. Beyond this point, decisions and actions by the Security Council may well have major political consequences and may even initiate a chain of events which might, in the end, require the Council under its responsibilities to invoke measures of enforcement under Section B, Chapter VIII. This chain of events begins when the Council decides to make an investigation, or determines that the time has come to call upon states to settle their differences, or makes recommendations to the parties. It is to such decisions and actions that unanimity of the permanent members applies, with the important proviso, referred to above, for abstention from voting by parties to a dispute.

5. To illustrate: in ordering an investigation, the Council has to consider whether the investigation — which may involve calling for reports, hearing witnesses, dispatching a commission of inquiry, or other means — might not further aggravate the situation. After investigation, the Council must determine whether the continuance of the

situation or dispute would be likely to endanger international peace and security. If it so determines, the Council would be under obligation to take further steps. Similarly, the decision to make recommendations, even when all parties request it to do so, or to call upon parties to a dispute to fulfill their obligations under the Charter, might be the first step on a course of action from which the Security Council could withdraw only at the risk of failing to discharge its responsibilities.

6. In appraising the significance of the vote required to take such decisions or actions, it is useful to make comparison with the requirements of the League Covenant with reference to decisions of the League Council. Substantive decisions of the League of Nations Council could be taken only by the unanimous vote of all its members, whether permanent or not, with the exception of parties to a dispute under Article XV of the League Covenant. Under Article XI, under which most of the disputes brought before the League were dealt with and decisions to make investigations taken, the unanimity rule was invariably interpreted to include even the votes of the parties to a dispute.

7. The Yalta voting formula substitutes for the rule of complete unanimity of the League Council a system of qualified majority voting in the Security Council. Under this system non-permanent members of the Security Council individually would have no "veto." As regards the permanent members, there is no question under the Yalta formula of investing them with a new right, namely, the right to veto, a right which the permanent members of the League Council always had. The formula proposed for the taking of action in the Security Council by a majority of seven would make the operation of the Council less subject to obstruction than was the case under the League of Nations rule of complete unanimity.

8. It should also be remembered that under the Yalta formula the five major powers could not act by themselves, since even under the unanimity requirement any decisions of the Council would have to include the concurring votes of at least two of the non-permanent members. In other words, it would be possible for five non-permanent members as a group to exercise a "veto." It is not to be assumed, however, that the permanent members, any more than the non-permanent members, would use their "veto" power wilfully to obstruct the operation of the Council.

9. In view of the primary responsibilities of the permanent members, they could not be expected, in the present condition of the world, to assume the obligation to act in so serious a matter as the maintenance of international peace and security in consequence of a decision in which they had not concurred. Therefore, if a majority voting in the Security Council is to be made possible, the only practicable method is to provide, in respect of nonprocedural decisions, for unanimity of the permanent

members plus the concurring votes of at least two of the non-permanent members.

10. For all these reasons, the four sponsoring Governments agreed on the Yalta formula and have presented it to this Conference as essential if an international organization is to be created through which all peace-loving nations can effectively discharge their common responsibilities for the maintenance of international peace and security.

II

In the light of the considerations set forth in Part 1 of this statement, it is clear what the answers to the questions submitted by the Subcommittee should be, with the exception of Question 19. The answer to that question is as follows:

1. In the opinion of the Delegations of the Sponsoring Governments, the Draft Charter itself contains an indication of the application of the voting procedures to the various functions of the Council.

2. In this case, it will be unlikely that there will arise in the future any matters of great importance on which a decision will have to be made as to whether a procedural vote would apply. Should, however, such a matter arise, the decision regarding the preliminary question as to whether or not such a matter is procedural must be taken by a vote of seven members of the Security Council, including the concurring votes of the permanent members.

(a) Questionnaire on Exercise of Veto in Security Council, May 22, 1945 [1]

(Note: It is provided under Chapter VI (C), paragraph 3, that in all questions under VIII (A) a party to a dispute shall abstain from voting. Therefore unless otherwise indicated the veto referred to in each question below is the veto of a permanent member who is *not* a party to a dispute.)

Under new Paragraph 1 of Chapter VIII (A), prepared by the sponsoring Governments:

"Without prejudice to the provisions of paragraphs 1–5 below, the Security Council should be empowered, if all the parties so request, to make recommendations to the parties to any dispute with a view to its settlement in accordance with the principles laid down in Chapter II, Paragraph 3."

---

[1] From UNCIO, *Memorandum from the Secretary of Subcommittee III/1/B to the Members on the Subcommittee of the Delegations of China, United Kingdom, Union of Soviet Socialist Republics and the United States of America on a List of Questions Submitted by the Representatives of Delegations Other Than Those of the Sponsoring Governments, June 8, 1945,* Doc. 855 (English) III/1/B/2(a); Department of State, *Bulletin,* XII, p. 1044.

(1) If the parties to a dispute request the Security Council to make recommendations with a view to its settlement, would the veto be applicable to a decision of the Security Council to exercise its power to investigate the dispute for that purpose?

(2) If the Security Council has investigated a dispute under this paragraph, would the veto be applicable to a decision of the Security Council to recommend to the Parties certain terms, with a view to the settlement of the dispute?

Under present Paragraph 1 of Chapter VIII (A):

"1. The Security Council should be empowered to investigate any dispute, or any situation which may lead to international friction or give rise to a dispute, in order to determine whether its continuance is likely to endanger the maintenance of international peace and security."

(3) If the attention of the Security Council is called to the existence of a dispute, or a situation which may give rise to a dispute, would the veto be applicable to a decision of the Security Council to exercise its power to investigate the dispute or situation?

(4) If the Security Council has investigated the dispute, would the veto be applicable to a decision by the Security Council that the continuance of the dispute is likely to endanger the maintenance of international peace and security?

Under present Paragraph 3 of Chapter VIII (A):

"3. The parties to any dispute the continuance of which is likely to endanger the maintenance of international peace and security should obligate themselves, first of all, to seek a solution by negotiation, mediation, conciliation, arbitration or judicial settlement, or other peaceful means of their own choice. The Security Council should call upon the parties to settle their dispute by such means."

(5) If the Security Council has decided that the continuance of a dispute is likely to endanger the maintenance of international peace and security, would the veto be applicable to a decision of the Security Council to call upon the parties to settle their dispute by the means indicated in Paragraph 3?

Under Paragraph 4 of Chapter VIII (A) as proposed to be amended by the sponsoring Governments:

"4. If, nevertheless, parties to a dispute of the nature referred to in Paragraph 3 above fail to settle it by the means indicated in that paragraph, they should obligate themselves to refer it to the Security Council. ~~The~~ If the Security Council *should in each case decide whether or not* deems that the continuance of the particular dispute is in fact likely to endanger the maintenance of international peace and security, *and, accordingly, whether the Security Council should deal with the dispute, and, if so, whether it should take action under Paragraph 5* it shall decide whether to take action under Paragraph 5 or whether itself to recommend such terms of settlement as it may consider appropriate."

(6) If a dispute is referred to the Security Council by the parties under this paragraph, would the veto be applicable to a decision by the Security Council under the second sentence of this paragraph that it deems the continuance of the particular dispute is in fact likely to endanger the maintenance of international peace and security?

(7) If the Security Council deems that the continuance of the particular dispute is in fact likely to endanger the maintenance of international peace and security, would the veto be applicable to a decision of the Security Council under the second sentence of this paragraph to take action under Paragraph 5?

(8) If the Security Council deems that the continuance of the particular dispute is in fact likely to endanger the maintenance of international peace and security, would the veto be applicable to a decision of the Security Council under the second sentence of this paragraph to recommend to the parties such terms of settlement as it considers appropriate?

Under Paragraph 5 of Chapter VIII (A):
"5. The Security Council should be empowered, at any stage of a dispute of the nature referred to in Paragraph 3 above, to recommend appropriate procedures or methods of adjustment."

(9) Would the veto be applicable to a decision of the Security Council, at any stage of a dispute, to recommend to the parties appropriate procedures or methods of adjustment?

Under Paragraph 6 of Chapter VIII (A):
"6. Justiciable disputes should normally be referred to the International Court of Justice. The Security Council should be empowered to refer to the Court, for advice, legal questions connected with other disputes."

(10) Would the veto be applicable to a decision of the Security Council under the first sentence of this paragraph that a dispute is of a justiciable character?

(11) Would the veto be applicable to a decision of the Security Council under the first sentence of this paragraph to refer a justiciable dispute to the International Court of Justice?

(12) Would the veto be applicable to a decision of the Security Council to deal with a justiciable dispute by some other means of adjustment?

(13) Would the veto be applicable to a decision of the Security Council to refer to the International Court of Justice a legal question connected with a nonjusticiable dispute?

Under Paragraph 1 of Chapter VIII (B) as proposed by the four sponsoring Governments:

"Section B. Determination of Threats to the Peace or Acts of Aggression and Action with Respect Thereto. 1. Should the Security Council deem that a failure to settle a dispute in accordance with procedures indicated in Paragraph 3 of Section A, or in accordance with its recommendations made under Paragraphs *4 or 5* of Section A, constitutes a threat to the maintenance of international peace and security, it should take any measures necessary for the maintenance of international peace and security in accordance with the purposes and principles of the Organization."

(14) Would the veto be applicable to a decision of the Security Council that it deemed that a failure would constitute a threat to the maintenance of peace and security?

(15) Would the veto be applicable to a decision of the Security Council that it should take any measures necessary for the maintenance of international peace and security?

Under new Paragraph 2 of Chapter VIII (B) as proposed by the four sponsoring Governments:

"2. In general the Security Council should determine the existence of any threat to the peace, breach of the peace or act of aggression and should make recommendations or decide upon the measures set forth in Paragraphs 3 and 4 of this Section to be taken to maintain or restore peace and security."

(16) Would the veto be applicable to a decision of the Security Council that it determined the existence of any threat to the peace, etc.?

Under new paragraph proposed by the four sponsoring Governments to be inserted between Paragraphs 2 and 3 of Chapter VIII (B):

"Before making the recommendations or deciding upon the measures for the maintenance or restoration of peace and security in accordance with the provisions of Paragraph 2, the Security Council may call upon the parties concerned to comply with such provisional measures as it may deem necessary or desirable in order to prevent an aggravation of the situation. Such provisional measures should be without prejudice to the rights, claims or positions of the parties concerned. Failure to comply with such provisional measures should be duly taken account of by the Security Council."

(17) Would the veto be applicable to a decision of the Security Council that it may call upon the parties, etc.?

(18) Would the veto be applicable to a decision of the Security Council that failure to comply should be duly taken account of, etc.?

Under the second paragraph of Chapter VI (C):
"Section C. Voting. 1. Each member of the Security Council should have one vote.

"2. Decisions of the Security Council on procedural matters should be made by an affirmative vote of seven members."

(19) In case a decision has to be taken as to whether a certain point is a procedural matter, is that preliminary question to be considered in itself as a procedural matter or is the veto applicable to such preliminary question?

Under the third paragraph of Chapter VI (C):
"3. Decisions of the Security Council on all other matters should be made by an affirmative vote of seven members including the concurring votes of the permanent members; provided that, in decisions under Chapter VIII, Section A, and under the second sentence of Paragraph 1 of Chapter VIII, Section C, a party to a dispute should abstain from voting."

(20) If a motion is moved in the Security Council on a matter, other than a matter of procedure, under the general words in Paragraph 3, would the abstention from voting of any one of the permanent members of the Security Council have the same effect as a negative vote by that member in preventing the Security Council from reaching a decision on the matter?

(21) If one of the permanent members of the Security Council is a party to a dispute, and in conformity with the proviso to Paragraph 3 has abstained from voting on a motion on a matter, other than a matter of procedure, would its mere abstention prevent the Security Council from reaching a decision on the matter?

(22) In case a decision has to be made under Chapter VIII, Section A, or under the second sentence of Chapter VIII, Section C, Paragraph 1, will a permanent member of the Council be entitled to participate in a vote on the question whether that permanent member is itself a party to the dispute or not?

(23) In view of questions raised by several delegations, the Greek Delegation would like to be informed whether, under Chapter 10, Paragraph 1, of the Dumbarton Oaks Proposals as amended by the four Governments, the recommendation of the Security Council to the Assembly in respect of the election of the Secretary General and his deputies is subject to veto.

(11) *Charter of the United Nations, Signed at the United Nations Conference on International Organization, San Francisco, California, June 26, 1945* [1]

WE THE PEOPLES OF THE UNITED NATIONS DETERMINED

to save succeeding generations from the scourge of war, which twice in our lifetime has brought untold sorrow to mankind, and

to reaffirm faith in fundamental human rights, in the dignity and worth of the human person, in the equal rights of men and women and of nations large and small, and

to establish conditions under which justice and respect for the obligations arising from treaties and other sources of international law can be maintained, and

to promote social progress and better standards of life in larger freedom,

AND FOR THESE ENDS

to practice tolerance and live together in peace with one another as good neighbors, and

to unite our strength to maintain international peace and security and

to ensure, by the acceptance of principles and the institution of methods, that armed force shall not be used, save in the common interest, and

to employ international machinery for the promotion of the economic and social advancement of all peoples,

---

[1] Department of State, *Bulletin*, XII, p. 1119–42; also, Publication 2353, Conf. Series 74.

The Charter, together with the *Statute of the International Court of Justice*, was ratified by the United States Senate on July 28, 1945 by a vote of 89 to 2. The two Senators who voted against ratification were William Langer of North Dakota and Henrik Shipstead of Minnesota.

The Charter was signed at San Francisco by the following 50 countries: Argentina, Australia, Belgium, Bolivia, Brazil, Byelorussia, Canada, Chile, China, Colombia, Costa Rica, Cuba, Czechoslovakia, Denmark, Dominican Republic, Ecuador, Egypt, El Salvador, Ethiopia, France, Greece, Guatemala, Haiti, Honduras, India, Iran, Iraq, Lebanon, Liberia, Luxembourg, Mexico, Netherlands, New Zealand, Nicaragua, Norway, Panama, Paraguay, Peru, Philippine Commonwealth, Saudi Arabia, Syria, Turkey, Ukraine, Union of South Africa, Union of Soviet Socialist Republics, United Kingdom, United States of America, Uruguay, Venezuela, Yugoslavia. On October 15, 1945 the representative of the Polish Provisional Government signed the Charter in Washington as an original Member.

For protocol of ratifications, see this volume, p. 385.

HAVE RESOLVED TO COMBINE OUR EFFORTS TO ACCOM-
PLISH THESE AIMS.

Accordingly, our respective Governments, through representatives
assembled in the city of San Francisco, who have exhibited their full
powers found to be in good and due form, have agreed to the present
Charter of the United Nations and do hereby establish an international
organization to be known as the United Nations.

CHAPTER I. PURPOSES AND PRINCIPLES

Article 1

The Purposes of the United Nations are:

1. To maintain international peace and security, and to that end:
to take effective collective measures for the prevention and removal of
threats to the peace, and for the suppression of acts of aggression or
other breaches of the peace, and to bring about by peaceful means, and
in conformity with the principles of justice and international law, adjustment or settlement of international disputes or situations which might
lead to a breach of the peace;

2. To develop friendly relations among nations based on respect for
the principle of equal rights and self-determination of peoples, and to
take other appropriate measures to strengthen universal peace;

3. To achieve international cooperation in solving international
problems of an economic, social, cultural, or humanitarian character,
and in promoting and encouraging respect for human rights and for
fundamental freedoms for all without distinction as to race, sex, language,
or religion; and

4. To be a center for harmonizing the actions of nations in the attainment of these common ends.

Article 2

The Organization and its Members, in pursuit of the Purposes stated
in Article 1, shall act in accordance with the following Principles.

1. The Organization is based on the principle of the sovereign equality
of all its Members.

2. All Members, in order to ensure to all of them the rights and
benefits resulting from membership, shall fulfil in good faith the obligations assumed by them in accordance with the present Charter.

3. All Members shall settle their international disputes by peaceful
means in such a manner that international peace and security, and
justice, are not endangered.

4. All Members shall refrain in their international relations from the
threat or use of force against the territorial integrity or political inde-

pendence of any state, or in any other manner inconsistent with the Purposes of the United Nations.

5. All Members shall give the United Nations every assistance in any action it takes in accordance with the present Charter, and shall refrain from giving assistance to any state against which the United Nations is taking preventive or enforcement action.

6. The Organization shall ensure that states which are not Members of the United Nations act in accordance with these Principles so far as may be necessary for the maintenance of international peace and security.

7. Nothing contained in the present Charter shall authorize the United Nations to intervene in matters which are essentially within the domestic jurisdiction of any state or shall require the Members to submit such matters to settlement under the present Charter; but this principle shall not prejudice the application of enforcement measures under Chapter VII.

CHAPTER II. MEMBERSHIP

Article 3

The original Members of the United Nations shall be the states which, having participated in the United Nations Conference on International Organization at San Francisco, or having previously signed the Declaration by United Nations of January 1, 1942, sign the present Charter and ratify it in accordance with Article 110.

Article 4

1. Membership in the United Nations is open to all other peace-loving states which accept the obligations contained in the present Charter and, in the judgment of the Organization, are able and willing to carry out these obligations.

2. The admission of any such state to membership in the United Nations will be effected by a decision of the General Assembly upon the recommendation of the Security Council.

Article 5

A Member of the United Nations against which preventive or enforcement action has been taken by the Security Council may be suspended from the exercise of the rights and privileges of membership by the General Assembly upon the recommendation of the Security Council. The exercise of these rights and privileges may be restored by the Security Council.

Article 6

A Member of the United Nations which has persistently violated the Principles contained in the present Charter may be expelled from the Organization by the General Assembly upon the recommendation of the Security Council.

CHAPTER III. ORGANS

Article 7

1. There are established as the principal organs of the United Nations: a General Assembly, a Security Council, an Economic and Social Council, a Trusteeship Council, an International Court of Justice, and a Secretariat.

2. Such subsidiary organs as may be found necessary may be established in accordance with the present Charter.

Article 8

The United Nations shall place no restrictions on the eligibility of men and women to participate in any capacity and under conditions of equality in its principal and subsidiary organs.

CHAPTER IV. THE GENERAL ASSEMBLY

COMPOSITION

Article 9

1. The General Assembly shall consist of all the Members of the United Nations.

2. Each Member shall have not more than five representatives in the General Assembly.

FUNCTIONS AND POWERS

Article 10

The General Assembly may discuss any questions or any matters within the scope of the present Charter or relating to the powers and functions of any organs provided for in the present Charter, and, except as provided in Article 12, may make recommendations to the Members of the United Nations or to the Security Council or to both on any such questions or matters.

Article 11

1. The General Assembly may consider the general principles of cooperation in the maintenance of international peace and security,

including the principles governing disarmament and the regulation of armaments, and may make recommendations with regard to such principles to the Members or to the Security Council or to both.

2. The General Assembly may discuss any questions relating to the maintenance of international peace and security brought before it by any Member of the United Nations, or by the Security Council, or by a state which is not a Member of the United Nations in accordance with Article 35, paragraph 2, and, except as provided in Article 12, may make recommendations with regard to any such questions to the state or states concerned or to the Security Council or to both. Any such question on which action is necessary shall be referred to the Security Council by the General Assembly either before or after discussion.

3. The General Assembly may call the attention of the Security Council to situations which are likely to endanger international peace and security.

4. The powers of the General Assembly set forth in this Article shall not limit the general scope of Article 10.

Article 12

1. While the Security Council is exercising in respect of any dispute or situation the functions assigned to it in the present Charter, the General Assembly shall not make any recommendation with regard to that dispute or situation unless the Security Council so requests.

2. The Secretary-General, with the consent of the Security Council, shall notify the General Assembly at each session of any matters relative to the maintenance of international peace and security which are being dealt with by the Security Council and shall similarly notify the General Assembly, or the Members of the United Nations if the General Assembly is not in session, immediately the Security Council ceases to deal with such matters.

Article 13

1. The General Assembly shall initiate studies and make recommendations for the purpose of:

a. promoting international cooperation in the political field and encouraging the progressive development of international law and its codification;

b. promoting international cooperation in the economic, social, cultural, educational, and health fields, and assisting in the realization of human rights and fundamental freedoms for all without distinction as to race, sex, language, or religion.

2. The further responsibilities, functions, and powers of the General Assembly with respect to matters mentioned in paragraph 1 (b) above are set forth in Chapters IX and X.

Article 14

Subject to the provisions of Article 12, the General Assembly may recommend measures for the peaceful adjustment of any situation, regardless of origin, which it deems likely to impair the general welfare or friendly relations among nations, including situations resulting from a violation of the provisions of the present Charter setting forth the Purposes and Principles of the United Nations.

Article 15

1. The General Assembly shall receive and consider annual and special reports from the Security Council; these reports shall include an account of the measures that the Security Council has decided upon or taken to maintain international peace and security.

2. The General Assembly shall receive and consider reports from the other organs of the United Nations.

Article 16

The General Assembly shall perform such functions with respect to the international trusteeship system as are assigned to it under Chapters XII and XIII, including the approval of the trusteeship agreements for areas not designated as strategic.

Article 17

1. The General Assembly shall consider and approve the budget of the Organization.

2. The expenses of the Organization shall be borne by the Members as apportioned by the General Assembly.

3. The General Assembly shall consider and approve any financial and budgetary arrangements with specialized agencies referred to in Article 57 and shall examine the administrative budgets of such specialized agencies with a view to making recommendations to the agencies concerned.

VOTING

Article 18

1. Each member of the General Assembly shall have one vote.

2. Decisions of the General Assembly on important questions shall be made by a two-thirds majority of the members present and voting. These questions shall include: recommendations with respect to the maintenance of international peace and security, the election of the non-permanent members of the Security Council, the election of the members of the Economic and Social Council, the election of members of the Trusteeship Council in accordance with paragraph 1 (c) of

Article 86, the admission of new Members to the United Nations, the suspension of the rights and privileges of membership, the expulsion of Members, questions relating to the operation of the trusteeship system, and budgetary questions.

3. Decisions on other questions, including the determination of additional categories of questions to be decided by a two-thirds majority, shall be made by a majority of the members present and voting.

Article 19

A Member of the United Nations which is in arrears in the payment of its financial contributions to the Organization shall have no vote in the General Assembly if the amount of its arrears equals or exceeds the amount of the contributions due from it for the preceding two full years. The General Assembly may, nevertheless, permit such a Member to vote if it is satisfied that the failure to pay is due to conditions beyond the control of the Member.

PROCEDURE

Article 20

The General Assembly shall meet in regular annual sessions and in such special sessions as occasion may require. Special sessions shall be convoked by the Secretary-General at the request of the Security Council or of a majority of the Members of the United Nations.

Article 21

The General Assembly shall adopt its own rules of procedure. It shall elect its President for each session.

Article 22

The General Assembly may establish such subsidiary organs as it deems necessary for the performance of its functions.

CHAPTER V.   THE SECURITY COUNCIL

COMPOSITION

Article 23

1. The Security Council shall consist of eleven Members of the United Nations. The Republic of China, France, the Union of Soviet Socialist Republics, the United Kingdom of Great Britain and Northern Ireland, and the United States of America shall be permanent members of the Security Council. The General Assembly shall elect six other Members of the United Nations to be non-permanent members of the Security Council, due regard being specially paid, in the first instance to the

contribution of Members of the United Nations to the maintenance of international peace and security and to the other purposes of the Organization, and also to equitable geographical distribution.

2. The non-permanent members of the Security Council shall be elected for a term of two years. In the first election of the non-permanent members, however, three shall be chosen for a term of one year. A retiring member shall not be eligible for immediate re-election.

3. Each member of the Security Council shall have one representative.

FUNCTIONS AND POWERS

Article 24

1. In order to ensure prompt and effective action by the United Nations, its Members confer on the Security Council primary responsibility for the maintenance of international peace and security, and agree that in carrying out its duties under this responsibility the Security Council acts on their behalf.

2. In discharging these duties the Security Council shall act in accordance with the Purposes and Principles of the United Nations. The specific powers granted to the Security Council for the discharge of these duties are laid down in Chapters VI, VII, VIII, and XII.

3. The Security Council shall submit annual and, when necessary, special reports to the General Assembly for its consideration.

Article 25

The Members of the United Nations agree to accept and carry out the decisions of the Security Council in accordance with the present Charter.

Article 26

In order to promote the establishment and maintenance of international peace and security with the least diversion for armaments of the world's human and economic resources, the Security Council shall be responsible for formulating, with the assistance of the Military Staff Committee referred to in Article 47, plans to be submitted to the Members of the United Nations for the establishment of a system for the regulation of armaments.

VOTING

Article 27

1. Each member of the Security Council shall have one vote.

2. Decisions of the Security Council on procedural matters shall be made by an affirmative vote of seven members.

3. Decisions of the Security Council on all other matters shall be made by an affirmative vote of seven members including the concurring

votes of the permanent members; provided that, in decisions under Chapter VI, and under paragraph 3 of Article 52, a party to a dispute shall abstain from voting.

PROCEDURE

Article 28

1. The Security Council shall be so organized as to be able to function continuously. Each member of the Security Council shall for this purpose be represented at all times at the seat of the Organization.
2. The Security Council shall hold periodic meetings at which each of its members may, if it so desires, be represented by a member of the government or by some other specially designated representative.
3. The Security Council may hold meetings at such places other than the seat of the Organization as in its judgment will best facilitate its work.

Article 29

The Security Council may establish such subsidiary organs as it deems necessary for the performance of its functions.

Article 30

The Security Council shall adopt its own rules of procedure, including the method of selecting its President.

Article 31

Any Member of the United Nations which is not a member of the Security Council may participate, without vote, in the discussion of any question brought before the Security Council whenever the latter considers that the interests of that Member are specially affected.

Article 32

Any Member of the United Nations which is not a member of the Security Council or any state which is not a Member of the United Nations, if it is a party to a dispute under consideration by the Security Council, shall be invited to participate, without vote, in the discussion relating to the dispute. The Security Council shall lay down such conditions as it deems just for the participation of a state which is not a Member of the United Nations.

CHAPTER VI. PACIFIC SETTLEMENT OF DISPUTES

Article 33

1. The parties to any dispute, the continuance of which is likely to endanger the maintenance of international peace and security, shall, first of all, seek a solution by negotiation, enquiry, mediation, concilia-

tion, arbitration, judicial settlement, resort to regional agencies or arrangements, or other peaceful means of their own choice.

2. The Security Council shall, when it deems necessary, call upon the parties to settle their dispute by such means.

Article 34

The Security Council may investigate any dispute, or any situation which might lead to international friction or give rise to a dispute, in order to determine whether the continuance of the dispute or situation is likely to endanger the maintenance of international peace and security.

Article 35

1. Any Member of the United Nations may bring any dispute, or any situation of the nature referred to in Article 34, to the attention of the Security Council or of the General Assembly.

2. A state which is not a Member of the United Nations may bring to the attention of the Security Council or of the General Assembly any dispute to which it is a party if it accepts in advance, for the purposes of the dispute, the obligations of pacific settlement provided in the present Charter.

3. The proceedings of the General Assembly in respect of matters brought to its attention under this Article will be subject to the provisions of Articles 11 and 12.

Article 36

1. The Security Council may, at any stage of a dispute of the nature referred to in Article 33 or of a situation of like nature, recommend appropriate procedures or methods of adjustment.

2. The Security Council should take into consideration any procedures for the settlement of the dispute which have already been adopted by the parties.

3. In making recommendations under this Article the Security Council should also take into consideration that legal disputes should as a general rule be referred by the parties to the International Court of Justice in accordance with the provisions of the Statute of the Court.

Article 37

1. Should the parties to a dispute of the nature referred to in Article 33 fail to settle it by the means indicated in that Article, they shall refer it to the Security Council.

2. If the Security Council deems that the continuance of the dispute is in fact likely to endanger the maintenance of international peace and security, it shall decide whether to take action under Article 36 or to recommend such terms of settlement as it may consider appropriate.

Article 38

Without prejudice to the provisions of Articles 33 to 37, the Security Council may, if all the parties to any dispute so request, make recommendations to the parties with a view to a pacific settlement of the dispute.

CHAPTER VII. ACTION WITH RESPECT TO THREATS TO THE PEACE, BREACHES OF THE PEACE, AND ACTS OF AGGRESSION

Article 39

The Security Council shall determine the existence of any threat to the peace, breach of the peace, or act of aggression and shall make recommendations, or decide what measures shall be taken in accordance with Articles 41 and 42, to maintain or restore international peace and security.

Article 40

In order to prevent an aggravation of the situation, the Security Council may, before making the recommendations or deciding upon the measures provided for in Article 39, call upon the parties concerned to comply with such provisional measures as it deems necessary or desirable. Such provisional measures shall be without prejudice to the rights, claims, or position of the parties concerned. The Security Council shall duly take account of failure to comply with such provisional measures.

Article 41

The Security Council may decide what measures not involving the use of armed force are to be employed to give effect to its decisions, and it may call upon the Members of the United Nations to apply such measures. These may include complete or partial interruption of economic relations and of rail, sea, air, postal, telegraphic, radio, and other means of communication, and the severance of diplomatic relations.

Article 42

Should the Security Council consider that measures provided for in Article 41 would be inadequate or have proved to be inadequate, it may take such action by air, sea, or land forces as may be necessary to maintain or restore international peace and security. Such action may include demonstrations, blockade, and other operations by air, sea, or land forces of Members of the United Nations.

Article 43

1. All Members of the United Nations, in order to contribute to the maintenance of international peace and security, undertake to make

available to the Security Council, on its call and in accordance with a special agreement or agreements, armed forces, assistance, and facilities, including rights of passage, necessary for the purpose of maintaining international peace and security.

2. Such agreement or agreements shall govern the numbers and types of forces, their degree of readiness and general location, and the nature of the facilities and assistance to be provided.

3. The agreement or agreements shall be negotiated as soon as possible on the initiative of the Security Council. They shall be concluded between the Security Council and Members or between the Security Council and groups of Members and shall be subject to ratification by the signatory states in accordance with their respective constitutional processes.

Article 44

When the Security Council has decided to use force it shall, before calling upon a Member not represented on it to provide armed forces in fulfillment of the obligations assumed under Article 43, invite that Member, if the Member so desires, to participate in the decisions of the Security Council concerning the employment of contingents of that Member's armed forces.

Article 45

In order to enable the United Nations to take urgent military measures, Members shall hold immediately available national air-force contingents for combined international enforcement action. The strength and degree of readiness of these contingents and plans for their combined action shall be determined, within the limits laid down in the special agreement or agreements referred to in Article 43, by the Security Council with the assistance of the Military Staff Committee.

Article 46

Plans for the application of armed force shall be made by the Security Council with the assistance of the Military Staff Committee.

Article 47

1. There shall be established a Military Staff Committee to advise and assist the Security Council on all questions relating to the Security Council's military requirements for the maintenance of international peace and security, the employment and command of forces placed at its disposal, the regulation of armaments, and possible disarmament.

2. The Military Staff Committee shall consist of the Chiefs of Staff of the permanent members of the Security Council or their representatives. Any Member of the United Nations not permanently represented

on the Committee shall be invited by the Committee to be associated with it when the efficient discharge of the Committee's responsibilities requires the participation of that Member in its work.

3. The Military Staff Committee shall be responsible under the Security Council for the strategic direction of any armed forces placed at the disposal of the Security Council. Questions relating to the command of such forces shall be worked out subsequently.

4. The Military Staff Committee, with the authorization of the Security Council and after consultation with appropriate regional agencies, may establish regional subcommittees.

Article 48

1. The action required to carry out the decisions of the Security Council for the maintenance of international peace and security shall be taken by all the Members of the United Nations or by some of them, as the Security Council may determine.

2. Such decisions shall be carried out by the Members of the United Nations directly and through their action in the appropriate international agencies of which they are members.

Article 49

The Members of the United Nations shall join in affording mutual assistance in carrying out the measures decided upon by the Security Council.

Article 50

If preventive or enforcement measures against any state are taken by the Security Council, any other state, whether a Member of the United Nations or not, which finds itself confronted with special economic problems arising from the carrying out of those measures shall have the right to consult the Security Council with regard to a solution of those problems.

Article 51

Nothing in the present Charter shall impair the inherent right of individual or collective self-defense if an armed attack occurs against a Member of the United Nations, until the Security Council has taken the measures necessary to maintain international peace and security. Measures taken by Members in the exercise of this right of self-defense shall be immediately reported to the Security Council and shall not in any way effect the authority and responsibility of the Security Council under the present Charter to take at any time such action as it deems necessary in order to maintain or restore international peace and security.

CHAPTER VIII. REGIONAL ARRANGEMENTS

Article 52

1. Nothing in the present Charter precludes the existence of regional arrangements or agencies for dealing with such matters relating to the maintenance of international peace and security as are appropriate for regional action, provided that such arrangements or agencies and their activities are consistent with the Purposes and Principles of the United Nations.

2. The Members of the United Nations entering into such arrangements or constituting such agencies shall make every effort to achieve pacific settlement of local disputes through such regional arrangements or by such regional agencies before referring them to the Security Council.

3. The Security Council shall encourage the development of pacific settlement of local disputes through such regional arrangements or by such regional agencies either on the initiative of the states concerned or by reference from the Security Council.

4. This Article in no way impairs the application of Articles 34 and 35.

Article 53

1. The Security Council shall, where appropriate, utilize such regional arrangements or agencies for enforcement action under its authority. But no enforcement action shall be taken under regional arrangements or by regional agencies without the authorization of the Security Council, with the exception of measures against any enemy state, as defined in Paragraph 2 of this Article, provided for pursuant to Article 107 or in regional arrangements directed against renewal of aggressive policy on the part of any such state, until such time as the Organization may, on request of the Governments concerned, be charged with the responsibility for preventing further aggression by such a state.

2. The term enemy state as used in Paragraph 1 of this Article applies to any state which during the Second World War has been an enemy of any signatory of the present Charter.

Article 54

The Security Council shall at all times be kept fully informed of activities undertaken or in contemplation under regional arrangements or by regional agencies for the maintenance of international peace and security.

CHAPTER IX. INTERNATIONAL ECONOMIC AND SOCIAL COOPERATION

Article 55

With a view to the creation of conditions of stability and well-being which are necessary for peaceful and friendly relations among nations based on respect for the principle of equal rights and self-determination of peoples, the United Nations shall promote:

a. higher standards of living, full employment, and conditions of economic and social progress and development;

b. solutions of international economic, social, health, and related problems; and international cultural and educational cooperation; and

c. universal respect for, and observance of, human rights and fundamental freedoms for all without distinction as to race, sex, language, or religion.

Article 56

All Members pledge themselves to take joint and separate action in cooperation with the Organization for the achievement of the purposes set forth in Article 55.

Article 57

1. The various specialized agencies, established by intergovernmental agreement and having wide international responsibilities, as defined in their basic instruments, in economic, social, cultural, educational, health, and related fields, shall be brought into relationship with the United Nations in accordance with the provisions of Article 63.

2. Such agencies thus brought into relationship with the United Nations are hereinafter referred to as specialized agencies.

Article 58

The Organization shall make recommendations for the coordination of the policies and activities of the specialized agencies.

Article 59

The Organization shall, where appropriate, initiate negotiations among the states concerned for the creation of any new specialized agencies required for the accomplishment of the purposes set forth in Article 55.

Article 60

Responsibility for the discharge of the functions of the Organization set forth in this Chapter shall be vested in the General Assembly and, under the authority of the General Assembly, in the Economic and Social Council. which shall have for this purpose the powers set forth in Chapter X.

CHAPTER X. THE ECONOMIC AND SOCIAL COUNCIL

COMPOSITION

Article 61

1. The Economic and Social Council shall consist of eighteen Members of the United Nations elected by the General Assembly.

2. Subject to the provisions of Paragraph 3, six members of the Economic and Social Council shall be elected each year for a term of three years. A retiring member shall be eligible for immediate re-election.

3. At the first election, eighteen members of the Economic and Social Council shall be chosen. The term of office of six members so chosen shall expire at the end of one year, and of six other members at the end of two years, in accordance with arrangements made by the General Assembly.

4. Each member of the Economic and Social Council shall have one representative.

FUNCTIONS AND POWERS

Article 62

1. The Economic and Social Council may make or initiate studies and reports with respect to international economic, social, cultural, educational, health, and related matters and may make recommendations with respect to any such matters to the General Assembly, to the Members of the United Nations, and to the specialized agencies concerned.

2. It may make recommendations for the purpose of promoting respect for, and observance of, human rights and fundamental freedoms for all.

3. It may prepare draft conventions for submission to the General Assembly, with respect to matters falling within its competence.

4. It may call, in accordance with the rules prescribed by the United Nations, international conferences on matters falling within its competence.

Article 63

1. The Economic and Social Council may enter into agreements with any of the agencies referred to in Article 57, defining the terms on which the agency concerned shall be brought into relationship with the United Nations. Such agreements shall be subject to approval by the General Assembly.

2. It may coordinate the activities of the specialized agencies through consultation with and recommendations to such agencies and through recommendations to the General Assembly and to the Members of the United Nations.

Article 64

1. The Economic and Social Council may take appropriate steps to obtain regular reports from the specialized agencies. It may make arrangements with the Members of the United Nations and with the specialized agencies to obtain reports on the steps taken to give effect to its own recommendations and to recommendations on matters falling within its competence made by the General Assembly.

2. It may communicate its observations on these reports to the General Assembly.

Article 65

The Economic and Social Council may furnish information to the Security Council and shall assist the Security Council upon its request.

Article 66

1. The Economic and Social Council shall perform such functions as fall within its competence in connection with the carrying out of the recommendations of the General Assembly.

2. It may, with the approval of the General Assembly, perform services at the request of Members of the United Nations and at the request of specialized agencies.

3. It shall perform such other functions as are specified elsewhere in the present Charter or as may be assigned to it by the General Assembly.

VOTING

Article 67

1. Each member of the Economic and Social Council shall have one vote.

2. Decisions of the Economic and Social Council shall be made by a majority of the members present and voting.

PROCEDURE

Article 68

The Economic and Social Council shall set up commissions in economic and social fields and for the promotion of human rights, and such other commissions as may be required for the performance of its functions.

Article 69

The Economic and Social Council shall invite any Member of the United Nations to participate, without vote, in its deliberations on any matter of particular concern to that Member.

Article 70

The Economic and Social Council may make arrangements for representatives of the specialized agencies to participate, without vote, in its deliberations and in those of the commissions established by it, and for its representatives to participate in the deliberations of the specialized agencies.

Article 71

The Economic and Social Council may make suitable arrangements for consultation with non-governmental organizations which are concerned with matters within its competence. Such arrangements may be made with international organizations and, where appropriate, with national organizations after consultation with the Member of the United Nations concerned.

Article 72

1. The Economic and Social Council shall adopt its own rules of procedure, including the method of selecting its President.
2. The Economic and Social Council shall meet as required in accordance with its rules, which shall include provisions for the convening of meetings on the request of a majority of its members.

CHAPTER XI. DECLARATION REGARDING NON–SELF–GOVERNING TERRITORIES

Article 73

Members of the United Nations which have or assume responsibilities for the administration of territories whose peoples have not yet attained a full measure of self-government recognize the principle that the interests of the inhabitants of these territories are paramount, and accept as a sacred trust the obligation to promote to the utmost, within the system of international peace and security established by the present Charter, the well-being of the inhabitants of these territories, and, to this end:

a. to ensure, with due respect for the culture of the peoples concerned, their political, economic, social, and educational advancement, their just treatment, and their protection against abuses;

b. to develop self-government, to take due account of the political aspirations of the peoples, and to assist them in the progressive development of their free political institutions, according to the particular circumstances of each territory and its peoples and their varying stages of advancement;

c. to further international peace and security;

d. to promote constructive measures of development, to encourage research, and to cooperate with one another and, when and where appropriate, with specialized international bodies with a view to the practical achievement of the social, economic, and scientific purposes set forth in this Article; and

e. to transmit regularly to the Secretary-General for information purposes, subject to such limitation as security and constitutional considerations may require, statistical and other information of a technical nature relating to economic, social, and educational conditions in the territories for which they are respectively responsible other than those territories to which Chapters XII and XIII apply.

Article 74

Members of the United Nations also agree that their policy in respect of the territories to which this Chapter applies, no less than in respect of their metropolitan areas, must be based on the general principle of good-neighborliness, due account being taken of the interests and well-being of the rest of the world, in social, economic, and commercial matters.

CHAPTER XII. INTERNATIONAL TRUSTEESHIP SYSTEM

Article 75

The United Nations shall establish under its authority an international trusteeship system for the administration and supervision of such territories as may be placed thereunder by subsequent individual agreements. These territories are hereinafter referred to as trust territories.

Article 76

The basic objectives of the trusteeship system, in accordance with the Purposes of the United Nations laid down in Article 1 of the present Charter, shall be:

a. to further international peace and security;

b. to promote the political, economic, social, and educational advancement of the inhabitants of the trust territories, and their progressive development towards self-government or independence as may be appropriate to the particular circumstances of each territory and its peoples and the freely expressed wishes of the peoples concerned, and as may be provided by the terms of each trusteeship agreement;

c. to encourage respect for human rights and for fundamental freedoms for all without distinction as to race, sex, language, or religion, and to encourage recognition of the interdependence of the peoples of the world; and *d.* to ensure equal treatment in social, economic, and commercial matters for all Members of the United Nations and their nationals, and also equal treatment for the latter in the administration of justice, without prejudice to the attainment of the foregoing objectives and subject to the provisions of Article 80.

Article 77

1. The trusteeship system shall apply to such territories in the following categories as may be placed thereunder by means of trusteeship agreements:

a. territories now held under mandate;

b. territories which may be detached from enemy states as a result of the Second World War; and

c. territories voluntarily placed under the system by states responsible for their administration.

2. It will be a matter for subsequent agreement as to which territories in the foregoing categories will be brought under the trusteeship system and upon what terms.

Article 78

The trusteeship system shall not apply to territories which have become Members of the United Nations, relationship among which shall be based on respect for the principle of sovereign equality.

Article 79

The terms of trusteeship for each territory to be placed under the trusteeship system, including any alteration or amendment, shall be agreed upon by the states directly concerned, including the mandatory power in the case of territories held under mandate by a Member of the United Nations, and shall be approved as provided for in Articles 83 and 85.

Article 80

1. Except as may be agreed upon in individual trusteeship agreements, made under Articles 77, 79, and 81, placing each territory under the trusteeship system, and until such agreements have been concluded, nothing in this Chapter shall be construed in or of itself to alter in any manner the rights whatsoever of any states or any peoples or the terms of existing international instruments to which Members of the United Nations may respectively be parties.

2. Paragraph 1 of this Article shall not be interpreted as giving grounds for delay or postponement of the negotiation and conclusion of agreements for placing mandated and other territories under the trusteeship system as provided for in Article 77.

Article 81

The trusteeship agreement shall in each case include the terms under which the trust territory will be administered and designate the authority which will exercise the administration of the trust territory. Such authority, hereinafter called the administering authority, may be one or more states or the Organization itself.

Article 82

There may be designated, in any trusteeship agreement, a strategic area or areas which may include part or all of the trust territory to which the agreement applies, without prejudice to any special agreement or agreements made under Article 43.

Article 83

1. All functions of the United Nations relating to strategic areas, including the approval of the terms of the trusteeship agreements and of their alteration or amendment, shall be exercised by the Security Council.

2. The basic objectives set forth in Article 76 shall be applicable to the people of each strategic area.

3. The Security Council shall, subject to the provisions of the trusteeship agreements and without prejudice to security considerations, avail itself of the assistance of the Trusteeship Council to perform those functions of the United Nations under the trusteeship system relating to political, economic, social, and educational matters in the strategic areas.

Article 84

It shall be the duty of the administering authority to ensure that the trust territory shall play its part in the maintenance of international peace and security. To this end the administering authority may make use of volunteer forces, facilities, and assistance from the trust territory in carrying out the obligations towards the Security Council undertaken in this regard by the administering authority, as well as for local defense and the maintenance of law and order within the trust territory.

Article 85

1. The functions of the United Nations with regard to trusteeship agreements for all areas not designated as strategic, including the approval of the terms of the trusteeship agreements and of their alteration or amendment, shall be exercised by the General Assembly.

2. The Trusteeship Council, operating under the authority of the General Assembly, shall assist the General Assembly in carrying out these functions.

CHAPTER XIII. THE TRUSTEESHIP COUNCIL

COMPOSITION

Article 86

1. The Trusteeship Council shall consist of the following Members of the United Nations:

a. those Members administering trust territories;

b. such of those Members mentioned by name in Article 23 as are not administering trust territories; and

c. as many other Members elected for three-year terms by the General Assembly as may be necessary to ensure that the total number of members of the Trusteeship Council is equally divided between those Members of the United Nations which administer trust territories and those which do not.

2. Each member of the Trusteeship Council shall designate one specially qualified person to represent it therein.

FUNCTIONS AND POWERS

Article 87

The General Assembly and, under its authority, the Trusteeship Council, in carrying out their functions, may:

a. consider reports submitted by the administering authority;

b. accept petitions and examine them in consultation with the administering authority;

c. provide for periodic visits to the respective trust territories at times agreed upon with the administering authority; and

d. take these and other actions in conformity with the terms of the trusteeship agreements.

Article 88

The Trusteeship Council shall formulate a questionnaire on the political, economic, social, and educational advancement of the inhabitants of each trust territory, and the administering authority for each trust territory within the competence of the General Assembly shall make an an annual report to the General Assembly upon the basis of such questionnaire.

VOTING

Article 89

1. Each member of the Trusteeship Council shall have one vote.

2. Decisions of the Trusteeship Council shall be made by a majority of the members present and voting.

PROCEDURE

Article 90

1. The Trusteeship Council shall adopt its own rules of procedure, including the method of selecting its President.
2. The Trusteeship Council shall meet as required in accordance with its rules, which shall include provision for the convening of meetings on the request of a majority of its members.

Article 91

The Trusteeship Council shall, when appropriate, avail itself of the assistance of the Economic and Social Council and of the specialized agencies in regard to matters with which they are respectively concerned.

CHAPTER XIV. THE INTERNATIONAL COURT OF JUSTICE

Article 92

The International Court of Justice shall be the principal judicial organ of the United Nations. It shall function in accordance with the annexed Statute, which is based upon the Statute of the Permanent Court of International Justice and forms an integral part of the present Charter.

Article 93

1. All Members of the United Nations are *ipso facto* parties to the Statute of the International Court of Justice.
2. A state which is not a Member of the United Nations may become a party to the Statute of the International Court of Justice on conditions to be determined in each case by the General Assembly upon the recommendation of the Security Council.

Article 94

1. Each Member of the United Nations undertakes to comply with the decision of the International Court of Justice in any case to which it is a party.
2. If any party to a case fails to perform the obligations incumbent upon it under a judgment rendered by the Court, the other party may have recourse to the Security Council, which may, if it deems necessary, make recommendations or decide upon measures to be taken to give effect to the judgment.

Article 95

Nothing in the present Charter shall prevent Members of the United Nations from entrusting the solution of their differences to other tribunals by virtue of agreements already in existence or which may be concluded in the future.

Article 96

1. The General Assembly or the Security Council may request the International Court of Justice to give an advisory opinion on any legal question.

2. Other organs of the United Nations and specialized agencies, which may at any time be so authorized by the General Assembly, may also request advisory opinions of the Court on legal questions arising within the scope of their activities.

CHAPTER XV. THE SECRETARIAT

Article 97

The Secretariat shall comprise a Secretary-General and such staff as the Organization may require. The Secretary-General shall be appointed by the General Assembly upon the recommendation of the Security Council. He shall be the chief administrative officer of the Organization.

Article 98

The Secretary-General shall act in that capacity in all meetings of the General Assembly, of the Security Council, of the Economic and Social Council, and of the Trusteeship Council, and shall perform such other functions as are entrusted to him by these organs. The Secretary-General shall make an annual report to the General Assembly on the work of the Organization.

Article 99

The Secretary-General may bring to the attention of the Security Council any matter which in his opinion may threaten the maintenance of international peace and security.

Article 100

1. In the performance of their duties the Secretary-General and the staff shall not seek or receive instructions from any government or from any other authority external to the Organization. They shall refrain from any action which might reflect on their position as international officials responsible only to the Organization.

2. Each Member of the United Nations undertakes to respect the exclusively international character of the responsibilities of the Secretary-General and the staff and not to seek to influence them in the discharge of their responsibilities.

Article 101

1. The staff shall be appointed by the Secretary-General under regulations established by the General Assembly.

2. Appropriate staffs shall be permanently assigned to the Economic and Social Council, the Trusteeship Council, and, as required, to other organs of the United Nations. These staffs shall form a part of the Secretariat.

3. The paramount consideration in the employment of the staff and in the determination of the conditions of service shall be the necessity of securing the highest standards of efficiency, competence, and integrity. Due regard shall be paid to the importance of recruiting the staff on as wide a geographical basis as possible.

CHAPTER XVI.　MISCELLANEOUS PROVISIONS

Article 102

1. Every treaty and every international agreement entered into by any Member of the United Nations after the present Charter comes into force shall as soon as possible be registered with the Secretariat and published by it.

2. No party to any such treaty or international agreement which has not been registered in accordance with the provisions of Paragraph 1 of this Article may invoke that treaty or agreement before any organ of the United Nations.

Article 103

In the event of a conflict between the obligations of the Members of the United Nations under the present Charter and their obligations under any other international agreement, their obligations under the present Charter shall prevail.

Article 104

The Organization shall enjoy in the territory of each of its Members such legal capacity as may be necessary for the exercise of its functions and the fulfillment of its purposes.

Article 105

1. The Organization shall enjoy in the territory of each of its Members such privileges and immunities as are necessary for the fulfillment of its purposes.

2. Representatives of the Members of the United Nations and officials of the Organization shall similarly enjoy such privileges and immunities as are necessary for the independent exercise of their functions in connection with the Organization.

3. The General Assembly may make recommendations with a view to determining the details of the application of Paragraphs 1 and 2 of this Article or may propose conventions to the Members of the United Nations for this purpose.

CHAPTER XVII. TRANSITIONAL SECURITY ARRANGEMENTS

Article 106

Pending the coming into force of such special agreements referred to in Article 43 as in the opinion of the Security Council enable it to begin the exercise of its responsibilities under Article 42, the parties to the Four-Nation Declaration, signed at Moscow, October 30, 1943, and France, shall, in accordance with the provisions of Paragraph 5 of that Declaration, consult with one another and as occasion requires with other Members of the United Nations with a view to such joint action on behalf of the Organization as may be necessary for the purpose of maintaining international peace and security.

Article 107

Nothing in the present Charter shall invalidate or preclude action, in relation to any state which during the Second World War has been an enemy of any signatory to the present Charter, taken or authorized as a result of that war by the Governments having responsibility for such action.

CHAPTER XVIII. AMENDMENTS

Article 108

Amendments to the present Charter shall come into force for all Members of the United Nations when they have been adopted by a vote of two thirds of the members of the General Assembly and ratified in accordance with their respective constitutional processes by two thirds of the Members of the United Nations, including all the permanent members of the Security Council.

Article 109

1. A General Conference of the Members of the United Nations for the purpose of reviewing the present Charter may be held at a date and place to be fixed by a two-thirds vote of the members of the General Assembly and by a vote of any seven members of the Security Council. Each Member of the United Nations shall have one vote in the conference.

2. Any alteration of the present Charter recommended by a two-thirds vote of the conference shall take effect when ratified in accordance with their respective constitutional processes by two thirds of the Members of the United Nations including all the permanent members of the Security Council.

3. If such a conference has not been held before the tenth annual session of the General Assembly following the coming into force of the present Charter, the proposal to call such a conference shall be placed on the agenda of that session of the General Assembly, and the conference shall be held if so decided by a majority vote of the members of the General Assembly and by a vote of any seven members of the Security Council.

CHAPTER XIX. RATIFICATION AND SIGNATURE

Article 110

1. The present Charter shall be ratified by the signatory states in accordance with their respective constitutional processes.

2. The ratifications shall be deposited with the Government of the United States of America, which shall notify all the signatory states of each deposit as well as the Secretary-General of the Organization when he has been appointed.

3. The present Charter shall come into force upon the deposit of ratifications by the Republic of China, France, the Union of Soviet Socialist Republics, the United Kingdom of Great Britain and Northern Ireland, and the United States of America, and by a majority of the other signatory states. A protocol of the ratifications deposited shall thereupon be drawn up by the Government of the United States of America which shall communicate copies thereof to all the signatory states.

4. The states signatory to the present Charter which ratify it after it has come into force will become original Members of the United Nations on the date of the deposit of their respective ratifications.

Article 111

The present Charter, of which the Chinese, French, Russian, English, and Spanish texts are equally authentic, shall remain deposited in the archives of the Government of the United States of America. Duly certified copies thereof shall be transmitted by that Government to the Governments of the other signatory states.

IN FAITH WHEREOF the representatives of the Governments of the United Nations have signed the present Charter.

DONE at the city of San Francisco the twenty-sixth day of June, one thousand nine hundred and forty-five.

(12) *Statute of the International Court of Justice* [1]

Article 1

THE INTERNATIONAL COURT OF JUSTICE established by the Charter of the United Nations as the principal judicial organ of the United Nations shall be constituted and shall function in accordance with the provisions of the present Statute.

CHAPTER I. ORGANIZATION OF THE COURT

Article 2

The Court shall be composed of a body of independent judges, elected regardless of their nationality from among persons of high moral character, who possess the qualifications required in their respective countries for appointment to the highest judicial offices, or are jurisconsults of recognized competence in international law.

Article 3

1. The Court shall consist of fifteen members, no two of whom may be nationals of the same state.

2. A person who for the purposes of membership in the Court could be regarded as a national of more than one state shall be deemed to be a national of the one in which he ordinarily exercises civil and political rights.

Article 4

1. The members of the Court shall be elected by the General Assembly and by the Security Council from a list of persons nominated by the national groups in the Permanent Court of Arbitration, in accordance with the following provisions.

2. In the case of Members of the United Nations not represented in the Permanent Court of Arbitration, candidates shall be nominated by national groups appointed for this purpose by their governments under the same conditions as those prescribed for members of the Permanent Court of Arbitration by Article 44 of the Convention of The Hague of 1907 for the pacific settlement of international disputes.

3. The conditions under which a state which is a party to the present Statute but is not a Member of the United Nations may participate in electing the members of the Court shall, in the absence of a special agreement, be laid down by the General Assembly upon recommendation of the Security Council.

[1] Department of State, *Bulletin*, XII, p. 1134.

Article 5

1. At least three months before the date of the election, the Secretary-General of the United Nations shall address a written request to the members of the Permanent Court of Arbitration belonging to the states which are parties to the present Statute, and to the members of the national groups appointed under Article 4, Paragraph 2, inviting them to undertake, within a given time, by national groups, the nomination of persons in a position to accept the duties of a member of the Court.

2. No group may nominate more than four persons, not more than two of whom shall be of their own nationality. In no case may the number of candidates nominated by a group be more than double the number of seats to be filled.

Article 6

Before making these nominations, each national group is recommended to consult its highest court of justice, its legal faculties and schools of law, and its national academies and national sections of international academies devoted to the study of law.

Article 7

1. The Secretary-General shall prepare a list in alphabetical order of all the persons thus nominated. Save as provided in Article 12, Paragraph 2, these shall be the only persons eligible.

2. The Secretary-General shall submit this list to the General Assembly and to the Security Council.

Article 8

The General Assembly and the Security Council shall proceed independently of one another to elect the members of the Court.

Article 9

At every election, the electors shall bear in mind not only that the persons to be elected should individually possess the qualifications required, but also that in the body as a whole the representation of the main forms of civilization and of the principal legal systems of the world should be assured.

Article 10

1. Those candidates who obtain an absolute majority of votes in the General Assembly and in the Security Council shall be considered as elected.

2. Any vote of the Security Council, whether for the election of judges or for the appointment of members of the conference envisaged

in Article 12, shall be taken without any distinction between permanent and non-permanent members of the Security Council.

3. In the event of more than one national of the same state obtaining an absolute majority of the votes both of the General Assembly and of the Security Council, the eldest of these only shall be considered as elected.

Article 11

If, after the first meeting held for the purpose of the election, one or more seats remain to be filled, a second and, if necessary, a third meeting shall take place.

Article 12

1. If, after the third meeting, one or more seats still remain unfilled, a joint conference consisting of six members, three appointed by the General Assembly and three by the Security Council, may be formed at any time at the request of either the General Assembly or the Security Council, for the purpose of choosing by the vote of an absolute majority one name for each seat still vacant, to submit to the General Assembly and the Security Council for their respective acceptance.

2. If the joint conference is unanimously agreed upon any person who fulfills the required conditions, he may be included in its list, even though he was not included in the list of nominations referred to in Article 7.

3. If the joint conference is satisfied that it will not be successful in procuring an election, those members of the Court who have already been elected shall, within a period to be fixed by the Security Council, proceed to fill the vacant seats by selection from among those candidates who have obtained votes either in the General Assembly or in the Security Council.

4. In the event of an equality of votes among the judges, the eldest judge shall have a casting vote.

Article 13

1. The members of the Court shall be elected for nine years and may be re-elected; provided, however, that of the judges elected at the first election, the terms of five judges shall expire at the end of three years and the terms of five more judges shall expire at the end of six years.

2. The judges whose terms are to expire at the end of the above-mentioned initial periods of three and six years shall be chosen by lot to be drawn by the Secretary-General immediately after the first election has been completed.

3. The members of the Court shall continue to discharge their duties until their places have been filled. Though replaced, they shall finish any cases which they may have begun.

4. In the case of the resignation of a member of the Court, the resignation shall be addressed to the President of the Court for transmission to the Secretary-General. This last notification makes the place vacant.

Article 14

Vacancies shall be filled by the same method as that laid down for the first election, subject to the following provision: the Secretary-General shall, within one month of the occurrence of the vacancy, proceed to issue the invitations provided for in Article 5, and the date of the election shall be fixed by the Security Council.

Article 15

A member of the Court elected to replace a member whose term of office has not expired shall hold office for the remainder of his predecessor's term.

Article 16

1. No member of the Court may exercise any political or administrative function, or engage in any other occupation of a professional nature.

2. Any doubt on this point shall be settled by the decision of the Court.

Article 17

1. No member of the Court may act as agent, counsel, or advocate in any case.

2. No member may participate in the decision of any case in which he has previously taken part as agent, counsel, or advocate for one of the parties, or as a member of a national or international court, or of a commission of enquiry, or in any other capacity.

3. Any doubt on this point shall be settled by the decision of the Court.

Article 18

1. No member of the Court can be dismissed unless, in the unanimous opinion of the other members, he has ceased to fulfill the required conditions.

2. Formal notification thereof shall be made to the Secretary-General by the Registrar.

3. This notification makes the place vacant.

Article 19

The members of the Court, when engaged on the business of the Court, shall enjoy diplomatic privileges and immunities.

Article 20

Every member of the Court shall, before taking up his duties, make a solemn declaration in open court that he will exercise his powers impartially and conscientiously.

Article 21

1. The Court shall elect its President and Vice-President for three years; they may be re-elected.

2. The Court shall appoint its Registrar and may provide for the appointment of such other officers as may be necessary.

Article 22

1. The seat of the Court shall be established at The Hague. This, however, shall not prevent the Court from sitting and exercising its functions elsewhere whenever the Court considers it desirable.

2. The President and the Registrar shall reside at the seat of the Court.

Article 23

1. The Court shall remain permanently in session, except during the judicial vacations, the dates and duration of which shall be fixed by the Court.

2. Members of the Court are entitled to periodic leave, the dates and duration of which shall be fixed by the Court, having in mind the distance between The Hague and the home of each judge.

3. Members of the Court shall be bound, unless they are on leave or prevented from attending by illness or other serious reasons duly explained to the President, to hold themselves permanently at the disposal of the Court.

Article 24

1. If, for some special reason, a member of the Court considers that he should not take part in the decision of a particular case, he shall so inform the President.

2. If the President considers that for some special reason one of the members of the Court should not sit in a particular case, he shall give him notice accordingly.

3. If in any such case the member of the Court and the President disagree, the matter shall be settled by the decision of the Court.

Article 25

1. The full Court shall sit except when it is expressly provided otherwise in the present Statute.

2. Subject to the condition that the number of judges available to constitute the Court is not thereby reduced below eleven, the Rules of the Court may provide for allowing one or more judges, according to circumstances and in rotation, to be dispensed from sitting.

3. A quorum of nine judges shall suffice to constitute the Court.

Article 26

1. The Court may from time to time form one or more chambers, composed of three or more judges as the Court may determine, for dealing with particular categories of cases; for example, labor cases and cases relating to transit and communications.

2. The Court may at any time form a chamber for dealing with a particular case. The number of judges to constitute such a chamber shall be determined by the Court with the approval of the parties.

3. Cases shall be heard and determined by the chamber provided for in this Article if the parties so request.

Article 27

A judgment given by any of the chambers provided for in Articles 26 and 29 shall be considered as rendered by the Court.

Article 28

The chambers provided for in Articles 26 and 29 may, with the consent of the parties, sit and exercise their functions elsewhere than at The Hague.

Article 29

With a view to the speedy despatch of business, the Court shall form annually a chamber composed of five judges which, at the request of the parties, may hear and determine cases by summary procedure. In addition, two judges shall be selected for the purpose of replacing judges who find it impossible to sit.

Article 30

1. The Court shall frame rules for carrying out its functions. In particular, it shall lay down rules of procedure.

2. The Rules of the Court may provide for assessors to sit with the Court or with any of its chambers, without the right to vote.

Article 31

1. Judges of the nationality of each of the parties shall retain their right to sit in the case before the Court.

2. If the Court includes upon the Bench a judge of the nationality of one of the parties, any other party may choose a person to sit as judge.

Such person shall be chosen preferably from among those persons who have been nominated as candidates as provided in Articles 4 and 5.

3. If the Court includes upon the Bench no judge of the nationality of the parties, each of these parties may proceed to choose a judge as provided in Paragraph 2 of this Article.

4. The provisions of this Article shall apply to the case of Articles 26 and 29. In such cases, the President shall request one or, if necessary, two of the members of the Court forming the chamber to give place to the members of the Court of the nationality of the parties concerned, and, failing such, or if they are unable to be present, to the judges specially chosen by the parties.

5. Should there be several parties in the same interest, they shall, for the purpose of the preceding provisions, be reckoned as one party only. Any doubt upon this point shall be settled by the decision of the Court.

6. Judges chosen as laid down in Paragraphs 2, 3, and 4 of this Article shall fulfil the conditions required by Articles 2, 17 (Paragraph 2), 20, and 24 of the present Statute. They shall take part in the decision on terms of complete equality with their colleagues.

Article 32

1. Each member of the Court shall receive an annual salary.

2. The President shall receive a special annual allowance.

3. The Vice-President shall receive a special allowance for every day on which he acts as President.

4. The judges chosen under Article 31, other than members of the Court, shall receive compensation for each day on which they exercise their functions.

5. These salaries, allowances, and compensation shall be fixed by the General Assembly. They may not be decreased during the term of office.

6. The salary of the Registrar shall be fixed by the General Assembly on the proposal of the Court.

7. Regulations made by the General Assembly shall fix the conditions under which retirement pensions may be given to members of the Court and to the Registrar, and the conditions under which members of the Court and the Registrar shall have their traveling expenses refunded.

8. The above salaries, allowances, and compensation shall be free of all taxation.

Article 33

The expenses of the Court shall be borne by the United Nations in such a manner as shall be decided by the General Assembly.

CHAPTER II. COMPETENCE OF THE COURT

Article 34

1. Only states may be parties in cases before the Court.

2. The Court, subject to and in conformity with its Rules, may request of public international organizations information relevant to cases before it, and shall receive such information presented by such organizations on their own initiative.

3. Whenever the construction of the constituent instrument of a public international organization or of an international convention adopted thereunder is in question in a case before the Court, the Registrar shall so notify the public international organization concerned and shall communicate to it copies of all the written proceedings.

Article 35

1. The Court shall be open to the states parties to the present Statute.

2. The conditions under which the Court shall be open to other states shall, subject to the special provisions contained in treaties in force, be laid down by the Security Council, but in no case shall such conditions place the parties in a position of inequality before the Court.

3. When a state which is not a Member of the United Nations is a party to a case, the Court shall fix the amount which that party is to contribute towards the expenses of the Court. This provision shall not apply if such state is bearing a share of the expenses of the Court.

Article 36

1. The jurisdiction of the Court comprises all cases which the parties refer to it and all matters specially provided for in the Charter of the United Nations or in treaties and conventions in force.

2. The states parties to the present Statute may at any time declare that they recognize as compulsory *ipso facto* and without special agreement, in relation to any other state accepting the same obligation, the jurisdiction of the Court in all legal disputes concerning:

a. the interpretation of a treaty;

b. any question of international law;

c. the existence of any fact which, if established, would constitute a breach of an international obligation;

d. the nature or extent of the reparation to be made for the breach of an international obligation.

3. The declarations referred to above may be made unconditionally or on condition of reciprocity on the part of several or certain states, or for a certain time.

4. Such declarations shall be deposited with the Secretary-General of the United Nations, who shall transmit copies thereof to the parties to the Statute and to the Registrar of the Court.

5. Declarations made under Article 36 of the Statute of the Permanent Court of International Justice and which are still in force shall be deemed, as between the parties to the present Statute, to be acceptances of the compulsory jurisdiction of the International Court of Justice for the period which they still have to run and in accordance with their terms.

6. In the event of a dispute as to whether the Court has jurisdiction, the matter shall be settled by the decision of the Court.

Article 37

Whenever a treaty or convention in force provides for reference of a matter to a tribunal to have been instituted by the League of Nations, or to the Permanent Court of International Justice, the matter shall, as between the parties to the present Statute, be referred to the International Court of Justice.

Article 38

1. The Court, whose function is to decide in accordance with international law such disputes as are submitted to it, shall apply:

a. international conventions, whether general or particular, establishing rules expressly recognized by the contesting states;

b. international custom, as evidence of a general practice accepted as law;

c. the general principles of law recognized by civilized nations;

d. subject to the provisions of Article 59, judicial decisions and the teachings of the most highly qualified publicists of the various nations, as subsidiary means for the determination of rules of law.

2. This provision shall not prejudice the power of the Court to decide a case *ex aequo et bono*, if the parties agree thereto.

CHAPTER III. PROCEDURE

Article 39

1. The official languages of the Court shall be French and English. If the parties agree that the case shall be conducted in French, the judgment shall be delivered in French. If the parties agree that the case shall be conducted in English, the judgment shall be delivered in English.

2. In the absence of an agreement as to which language shall be employed, each party may, in the pleadings, use the language which it prefers; the decision of the Court shall be given in French and English. In this case the Court shall at the same time determine which of the two texts shall be considered as authoritative.

3. The Court shall, at the request of any party, authorize a language other than French or English to be used by that party.

Article 40

1. Cases are brought before the Court, as the case may be, either by the notification of the special agreement or by a written application addressed to the Registrar. In either case the subject of the dispute and the parties shall be indicated.

2. The Registrar shall forthwith communicate the application to all concerned.

3. He shall also notify the Members of the United Nations through the Secretary-General, and also any other states entitled to appear before the Court.

Article 41

1. The Court shall have the power to indicate, if it considers that circumstances so require, any provisional measures which ought to be taken to preserve the respective rights of either party.

2. Pending the final decision, notice of the measures suggested shall forthwith be given to the parties and to the Security Council.

Article 42

1. The parties shall be represented by agents.

2. They may have the assistance of counsel or advocates before the Court.

3. The agents, counsel, and advocates of parties before the Court shall enjoy the privileges and immunities necessary to the independent exercise of their duties.

Article 43

1. The procedure shall consist of two parts: written and oral.

2. The written proceedings shall consist of the communication to the Court and to the parties of memorials, counter-memorials and, if necessary, replies; also all papers and documents in support.

3. These communications shall be made through the Registrar, in the order and within the time fixed by the Court.

4. A certified copy of every document produced by one party shall be communicated to the other party.

5. The oral proceedings shall consist of the hearing by the Court of witnesses, experts, agents, counsel, and advocates.

Article 44

1. For the service of all notices upon persons other than the agents, counsel, and advocates, the Court shall apply direct to the government of the state upon whose territory the notice has to be served.

2. The same provision shall apply whenever steps are to be taken to procure evidence on the spot.

Article 45

The hearing shall be under the control of the President or, if he is unable to preside, of the Vice-President; if neither is able to preside, the senior judge present shall preside.

Article 46

The hearing in Court shall be public, unless the Court shall decide otherwise, or unless the parties demand that the public be not admitted.

Article 47

1. Minutes shall be made at each hearing and signed by the Registrar and the President.
2. These minutes alone shall be authentic.

Article 48

The Court shall make orders for the conduct of the case, shall decide the form and time in which each party must conclude its arguments, and make all arrangements connected with the taking of evidence.

Article 49

The Court may, even before the hearing begins, call upon the agents to produce any document or to supply any explanations. Formal note shall be taken of any refusal.

Article 50

The Court may, at any time, entrust any individual, body, bureau, commission, or other organization that it may select, with the task of carrying out an enquiry or giving an expert opinion.

Article 51

During the hearing any relevant questions are to be put to the witnesses and experts under the conditions laid down by the Court in the rules of procedure referred to in Article 30.

Article 52

After the Court has received the proofs and evidence within the time specified for the purpose, it may refuse to accept any further oral or written evidence that one party may desire to present unless the other side consents.

Article 53

1. Whenever one of the parties does not appear before the Court, or fails to defend its case, the other party may call upon the Court to decide in favor of its claim.

2. The Court must, before doing so, satisfy itself, not only that it has jurisdiction in accordance with Articles 36 and 37, but also that the claim is well founded in fact and law.

Article 54

1. When, subject to the control of the Court, the agents, counsel, and advocates have completed their presentation of the case, the President shall declare the hearing closed.

2. The Court shall withdraw to consider the judgment.

3. The deliberations of the Court shall take place in private and remain secret.

Article 55

1. All questions shall be decided by a majority of the judges present.

2. In the event of an equality of votes, the President or the judge who acts in his place shall have a casting vote.

Article 56

1. The judgment shall state the reasons on which it is based.

2. It shall contain the names of the judges who have taken part in the decision.

Article 57

If the judgment does not represent in whole or in part the unanimous opinion of the judges, any judge shall be entitled to deliver a separate opinion.

Article 58

The judgment shall be signed by the President and by the Registrar. It shall be read in open court, due notice having been given to the agents.

Article 59

The decision of the Court has no binding force except between the parties and in respect of that particular case.

Article 60

The judgment is final and without appeal. In the event of dispute as to the meaning or scope of the judgment, the Court shall construe it upon the request of any party.

Article 61

1. An application for revision of a judgment may be made only when it is based upon the discovery of some fact of such a nature as to be a decisive factor, which fact was, when the judgment was given, unknown to the Court and also to the party claiming revision, always provided that such ignorance was not due to negligence.

2. The proceedings for revision shall be opened by a judgment of the Court expressly recording the existence of the new fact, recognizing that it has such a character as to lay the case open to revision, and declaring the application admissible on this ground.

3. The Court may require previous compliance with the terms of the judgment before it admits proceedings in revision.

4. The application for revision must be made at latest within six months of the discovery of the new fact.

5. No application for revision may be made after the lapse of ten years from the date of the judgment.

Article 62

1. Should a state consider that it has an interest of a legal nature which may be affected by the decision in the case, it may submit a request to the Court to be permitted to intervene.

2. It shall be for the Court to decide upon this request.

Article 63

1. Whenever the construction of a convention to which states other than those concerned in the case are parties is in question, the Registrar shall notify all such states forthwith.

2. Every state so notified has the right to intervene in the proceedings; but if it uses this right, the construction given by the judgment will be equally binding upon it.

Article 64

Unless otherwise decided by the Court, each party shall bear its own costs.

CHAPTER IV. ADVISORY OPINIONS

Article 65

1. The Court may give an advisory opinion on any legal question at the request of whatever body may be authorized by or in accordance with the Charter of the United Nations to make such a request.

2. Questions upon which the advisory opinion of the Court is asked shall be laid before the Court by means of a written request containing an exact statement of the question upon which an opinion is required, and accompanied by all documents likely to throw light upon the question.

Article 66

1. The Registrar shall forthwith give notice of the request for an advisory opinion to all states entitled to appear before the Court.

2. The Registrar shall also, by means of a special and direct communication, notify any state entitled to appear before the Court or inter-

national organization considered by the Court, or, should it not be sitting, by the President, as likely to be able to furnish information on the question, that the Court will be prepared to receive, within a time limit to be fixed by the President, written statements, or to hear, at a public sitting to be held for the purpose, oral statements relating to the question.

3. Should any such state entitled to appear before the Court have failed to receive the special communication referred to in Paragraph 2 of this Article, such state may express a desire to submit a written statement or to be heard; and the Court will decide.

4. States and organizations having presented written or oral statements or both shall be permitted to comment on the statements made by other states or organizations in the form, to the extent, and within the time limits which the Court, or, should it not be sitting, the President, shall decide in each particular case. Accordingly, the Registrar shall in due time communicate any such written statements to states and organizations having submitted similar statements.

Article 67

The Court shall deliver its advisory opinions in open Court, notice having been given to the Secretary-General and to the representatives of Members of the United Nations, of other states and of international organizations immediately concerned.

Article 68

In the exercise of its advisory functions the Court shall further be guided by the provisions of the present Statute which apply in contentious cases to the extent to which it recognizes them to be applicable.

CHAPTER V. AMENDMENT

Article 69

Amendments to the present Statute shall be effected by the same procedure as is provided by the Charter of the United Nations for amendments to that Charter, subject however to any provisions which the General Assembly upon recommendation of the Security Council may adopt concerning the participation of states which are parties to the present Statute but are not Members of the United Nations.

Article 70

The Court shall have power to propose such amendments to the present Statute as it may deem necessary, through written communications to the Secretary-General, for consideration in conformity with the provisions of Article 69.

(13) *Interim Arrangements Concluded by the Governments Repre-*
sented at the United Nations Conference on International Organ-
ization, San Francisco, June 26, 1945 [1]

THE governments represented at the United Nations Conference
on International Organization in the city of San Francisco.

Having determined that an international organization to be
known as the United Nations shall be established,

Having this day signed the Charter of the United Nations, and

Having decided that, pending the coming into force of the Charter
and the establishment of the United Nations as provided in the Charter,
a Preparatory Commission of the United Nations should be established
for the performance of certain functions and duties,

AGREE as follows:

1. There is hereby established a Preparatory Commission of the
United Nations for the purpose of making provisional arrangements for
the first sessions of the General Assembly, the Security Council, the
Economic and Social Council, and the Trusteeship Council, for the
establishment of the Secretariat, and for the convening of the International Court of Justice.

2. The Commission shall consist of one representative from each
government signatory to the Charter. The Commission shall establish
its own rules of procedure. The functions and powers of the Commission,
when the Commission is not in session, shall be exercised by an Executive
Committee composed of the representatives of those governments now
represented on the Executive Committee of the Conference. The Executive Committee shall appoint such committees as may be necessary to
facilitate its work, and shall make use of persons of special knowledge
and experience.

3. The Commission shall be assisted by an Executive Secretary, who
shall exercise such powers and perform such duties as the Commission
may determine, and by such staff as may be required. This staff shall
be composed so far as possible of officials appointed for this purpose by
the participating governments on the invitation of the Executive
Secretary.

4. The Commission shall:

a. convoke the General Assembly in its first session;

b. prepare the provisional agenda for the first sessions of the principal
organs of the Organization, and prepare documents and recommendations relating to all matters on these agenda;

c. formulate recommendations concerning the possible transfer of
certain functions, activities, and assets of the League of Nations which

[1] *Ibid.*, p. 1142.

it may be considered desirable for the new Organization to take over on terms to be arranged;

d. examine the problems involved in the establishment of the relationship between specialized intergovernmental organizations and agencies and the Organization;

e. issue invitations for the nomination of candidates for the International Court of Justice in accordance with the provisions of the Statute of the Court;

f. prepare recommendations concerning arrangements for the Secretariat of the Organization; and

g. make studies and prepare recommendations concerning the location of the permanent headquarters of the Organization.

5. The expenses incurred by the Commission and the expenses incidental to the convening of the first meeting of the General Assembly shall be met by the Government of the United Kingdom of Great Britain and Northern Ireland or, if the Commission so requests, shared by other Governments. All such advances from governments shall be deductible from their first contributions to the Organization.

6. The seat of the Commission shall be located in London. The Commission shall hold its first meeting in San Francisco immediately after the conclusion of the United Nations Conference on International Organization. The Executive Committee shall call the Commission into session again as soon as possible after the Charter of the Organization comes into effect and whenever subsequently it considers such a session desirable.

7. The Commission shall cease to exist upon the election of the Secretary-General of the Organization, at which time its property and records shall be transferred to the Organization.

8. The Government of the United States of America shall be the temporary depositary and shall have custody of the original document embodying these interim arrangements in the five languages in which it is signed. Duly certified copies thereof shall be transmitted to the governments of the signatory states. The Government of the United States of America shall transfer the original to the Executive Secretary on his appointment.

9. This document shall be effective as from this date, and shall remain open for signature by the states entitled to be the original Members of the United Nations until the Commission is dissolved in accordance with Paragraph 7.

In faith whereof, the undersigned representatives having been duly authorized for that purpose, sign this document in the English, French, Chinese, Russian, and Spanish languages, all texts being of equal authenticity.

Done in the City of San Francisco, this twenty-sixth day of June, 1945.

(14) *Tripartite Conference at Berlin, July 17–August 2, 1945* [1]

(Excerpts)

I

REPORT ON THE TRIPARTITE CONFERENCE OF BERLIN

O N JULY 17, 1945, the President of the United States of America, Harry S. Truman, the Chairman of the Council of People's Commissars of the Union of Soviet Socialist Republics, Generalissimo J. V. Stalin, and the Prime Minister of Great Britain, Winston S. Churchill, together with Mr. Clement R. Attlee, met in the Tripartite Conference of Berlin. They were accompanied by the Foreign Secretaries of the three governments, Mr. James F. Byrnes, Mr. V. M. Molotov, and Mr. Anthony Eden, the Chiefs of Staff, and other advisers.

There were nine meetings between July seventeenth and July twenty-fifth. The conference was then interrupted for two days while the results of the British general election were being declared.

On July twenty-eighth Mr. Attlee returned to the conference as Prime Minister, accompanied by the new Secretary of State for Foreign Affairs, Mr. Ernest Bevin. Four days of further discussion then took place. During the course of the conference there were regular meetings of the heads of the three governments accompanied by the Foreign Secretaries, and also of the Foreign Secretaries alone. Committees appointed by the Foreign Secretaries for preliminary consideration of questions before the conference also met daily.

The meetings of the conference were held at the Cecilienhof near Potsdam. The conference ended on August 2, 1945.

Important decisions and agreements were reached. Views were exchanged on a number of other questions and consideration of these matters will be continued by the Council of Foreign Ministers established by the conference.

President Truman, Generalissimo Stalin and Prime Minister Attlee leave this conference, which has strengthened the ties between the three governments and extended the scope of their collaboration and understanding, with renewed confidence that their governments and peoples, together with the other United Nations, will ensure the creation of a just and enduring peace.

II

ESTABLISHMENT OF A COUNCIL OF FOREIGN MINISTERS

The conference reached an agreement for the establishment of a Council of Foreign Ministers representing the five principal powers to continue the necessary preparatory work for the peace settlements and to take up other matters which from time to time may be referred to

[1] Released to the press, August 2, 1945, *ibid.*, XIII, p. 153.

the Council by agreement of the governments participating in the Council.

The text of the agreement for the establishment of the Council of Foreign Ministers is as follows:

1. There shall be established a Council composed of the foreign ministers of the United Kingdom, the Union of Soviet Socialist Republics, China, France and the United States.

2. (*i*) The Council shall normally meet in London, which shall be the permanent seat of the joint secretariat which the Council will form. Each of the foreign ministers will be accompanied by a high-ranking deputy, duly authorized to carry on the work of the Council in the absence of his foreign minister, and by a small staff of technical advisers.

(*ii*) The first meeting of the Council shall be held in London not later than September 1, 1945. Meetings may be held by common agreement in other capitals as may be agreed from time to time.

3. (*i*) As its immediate important task, the Council shall be authorized to draw up, with a view to their submission to the United Nations, treaties of peace with Italy, Rumania, Bulgaria, Hungary and Finland, and to propose settlements of territorial questions outstanding on the termination of the war in Europe. The Council shall be utilized for the preparation of a peace settlement for Germany to be accepted by the government of Germany when a government adequate for the purpose is established.

(*ii*) For the discharge of each of these tasks the Council will be composed of the members representing those states which were signatory to the terms of surrender imposed upon the enemy state concerned. For the purpose of the peace settlement for Italy, France shall be regarded as a signatory to the terms of surrender for Italy. Other members will be invited to participate when matters directly concerning them are under discussion.

(*iii*) Other matters may from time to time be referred to the Council by agreement between the member governments.

4. (*i*) Whenever the Council is considering a question of direct interest to a state not represented thereon, such state should be invited to send representatives to participate in the discussion and study of that question.

(*ii*) The Council may adapt its procedure to the particular problem under consideration. In some cases it may hold its own preliminary discussions prior to the participation of other interested states. In other cases, the Council may convoke a formal conference of the state chiefly interested in seeking a solution of the particular problem.

In accordance with the decision of the conference the three governments have each addressed an identical invitation to the governments of China and France to adopt this text and to join in establishing the Council.

The establishment of the Council of Foreign Ministers for the specific purposes named in the text will be without prejudice to the agreement of the Crimea Conference that there should be periodic consultation among the Foreign Secretaries of the United States, the Union of Soviet Socialist Republics and the United Kingdom.

The conference also considered the position of the European Advisory Commission in the light of the agreement to establish the Council of Foreign Ministers. It was noted with satisfaction that the Commission had ably discharged its principal tasks by the recommendations that it had furnished for the terms of Germany's unconditional surrender, for the zones of occupation in Germany and Austria, and for the inter-Allied control machinery in those countries. It was felt that further work of a detailed character for the coordination of allied policy for the control of Germany and Austria would in future fall within the competence of the Allied Control Council at Berlin and the Allied Commission at Vienna. Accordingly, it was agreed to recommend that the European Advisory Commission be dissolved.

. . . .

X

CONCLUSION OF PEACE TREATIES AND ADMISSION TO THE UNITED NATIONS ORGANIZATION

The conference agreed upon the following statement of common policy for establishing, as soon as possible, the conditions of lasting peace after victory in Europe:

The three governments consider it desirable that the present anomalous position of Italy, Bulgaria, Finland, Hungary and Rumania should be terminated by the conclusion of peace treaties. They trust that the other interested Allied governments will share these views.

For their part the three governments have included the preparation of a peace treaty for Italy as the first among the immediate important tasks to be undertaken by the new Council of Foreign Ministers. Italy was the first of the Axis powers to break with Germany, to whose defeat she has made a material contribution, and has now joined with the Allies in the struggle against Japan. Italy has freed herself from the Fascist regime and is making good progress towards the reestablishment of a democratic government and institutions. The conclusion of such a peace treaty with a recognized and democratic Italian government will make it possible for the three governments to fulfill their desire to support an application from Italy for membership of the United Nations.

The three governments have also charged the Council of Foreign Ministers with the task of preparing peace treaties for Bulgaria, Finland, Hungary and Rumania. The conclusion of peace treaties with recognized democratic governments in these states will also enable the three governments to support applications from them for membership of the

United Nations. The three governments agree to examine each separately in the near future, in the light of the conditions then prevailing, the establishment of diplomatic relations with Finland, Rumania, Bulgaria and Hungary to the extent possible prior to the conclusion of peace treaties with those countries.

The three governments have no doubt that in view of the changed conditions resulting from the termination of the war in Europe, representatives of the Allied press will enjoy full freedom to report to the world upon developments in Rumania, Bulgaria, Hungary and Finland.

As regards the admission of other states into the United Nations Organization, Article 4 of the Charter of the United Nations declares that:

"1. Membership in the United Nations is open to all other peace-loving states who accept the obligations contained in the present Charter and, in the judgment of the Organization, are able and willing to carry out these obligations;

"2. The admission of any such state to membership in the United Nations will be effected by a decision of the General Assembly upon the recommendation of the Security Council."

The three governments, so far as they are concerned, will support applications for membership from those states which have remained neutral during the war and which fulfill the qualifications set out above.

The three governments feel bound however to make it clear that they for their part would not favor any application for membership put forward by the present Spanish Government, which, having been founded with the support of the Axis powers, does not, in view of its origins, its nature, its record and its close association with the aggressor states, possess the qualifications necessary to justify such membership.

XI

TERRITORIAL TRUSTEESHIPS

The conference examined a proposal by the Soviet Government concerning trusteeship territories as defined in the decision of the Crimea Conference and in the Charter of the United Nations Organization.

After an exchange of views on this question it was decided that the disposition of any former Italian territories was one to be decided in connection with the preparation of a peace treaty for Italy and that the question of Italian territory would be considered by the September Council of Ministers of Foreign Affairs.

· · · · · · · ·

Approved: J. V. STALIN
HARRY S. TRUMAN
C. R. ATTLEE

(15) *Protocol of Deposit of Ratifications of the Charter of the United Nations, Washington, D. C., October 24, 1945* [1]

WHEREAS, paragraph 3 of Article 110 of the Charter of the United Nations, signed at San Francisco on June 26, 1945, provides as follows:

"3. The present Charter shall come into force upon the deposit of ratifications by the Republic of China, France, the Union of Soviet Socialist Republics, the United Kingdom of Great Britain and Northern Ireland, and the United States of America, and by a majority of the other signatory states. A protocol of the ratifications deposited shall thereupon be drawn up by the Government of the United States of America which shall communicate copies thereof to all the signatory states.";

WHEREAS, the Charter of the United Nations has been signed by the Plenipotentiaries of fifty-one states;

WHEREAS, instruments of ratification of the Charter of the United Nations have been deposited by

the Republic of China on September 28, 1945,

France on August 31, 1945,

the Union of Soviet Socialist Republics on October 24, 1945,

the United Kingdom of Great Britain and Northern Ireland on October 20, 1945, and

the United States of America on August 8, 1945;

   and by

Argentina on September 24, 1945,

Brazil on September 21, 1945,

the Byelorussian Soviet Socialist Republic on October 24, 1945,

Chile on October 11, 1945,

Cuba on October 15, 1945,

Czechoslovakia on October 19, 1945,

Denmark on October 9, 1945,

the Dominican Republic on September 4, 1945,

Egypt on October 22, 1945,

El Salvador on September 26, 1945,

Haiti on September 27, 1945,

Iran on October 16, 1945,

Lebanon on October 15, 1945,

Luxembourg on October 17, 1945,

New Zealand on September 19, 1945,

Nicaragua on September 6, 1945,

Paraguay on October 12, 1945,

the Philippine Commonwealth on October 11, 1945,

[1] *Ibid.*, p. 679; for dates of ratifications of other Members, see p. 299.

Poland on October 24, 1945,

Saudi Arabia on October 18, 1945,

Syria on October 19, 1945,

Turkey on September 28, 1945,

the Ukrainian Soviet Socialist Republic on October 24, 1945,

Yugoslavia on October 19, 1945;

AND WHEREAS, the requirements of paragraph 3 of Article 110 with respect to the coming into force of the Charter have been fulfilled by the deposit of the aforementioned instruments of ratification;

Now, THEREFORE, I, James F. Byrnes, Secretary of State of the United States of America, sign this Protocol in the English language, the original of which shall be deposited in the archives of the Government of the United States of America and copies thereof communicated to all the states signatory of the Charter of the United Nations.

DONE at Washington this twenty-fourth day of October, one thousand nine hundred forty-five.

JAMES F. BYRNES
Secretary of State
of the United States of America

BIBLIOGRAPHY

OFFICIAL DOCUMENTS

Charter of the United Nations. Report to the President on the Results of the San Francisco Conference by the Chairman of the United States Delegation, the Secretary of State, June 26, 1945. Washington, D. C., Department of State Publication 2349, Conference Series 71, 266 p.

Charter of the United Nations together with the Statute of the International Court of Justice, Signed at the United Nations Conference on International Organization, San Francisco, California, June 26, 1945. Washington, D. C., Department of State Publication 2353, Conference Series 74, 58 p.

Constitution of the Food and Agriculture Organization of the United Nations. *First Report to the Governments of the United Nations by the Interim Commission on Food and Agriculture.* Appendix I. Washington, D. C., August 1, 1944, p. 41.

Dumbarton Oaks Documents on International Organization. Washington, D. C., Department of State Publication 2192, Conference Series 56, 1944, 22 p.

Facsimile of the Charter of the United Nations, Statute of the International Court of Justice and Interim Arrangements in Five Languages. Signed at the United Nations Conference on International Organization, San Francisco, California, June 26, 1945. Washington, D. C., Department of State Publication 2368, Conference Series 76, 234 p.

Food and Agriculture Organization. *First Report to the Governments of the United Nations by the Interim Commission on Food and Agriculture.* Washington, D. C., August 1, 1944, 55 p.

Inter-Allied Committee. *Report on the Future of the Permanent Court of International Justice.* London, H. M. Stationery Office, 1944, Brit. Parl. Papers, Cmd. 6531.

Inter-American Juridical Committee. *Recommendations and Reports, Official Documents, 1942–1944.* Rio de Janeiro, Imprensa nacional, 1945, 161 p.

International Civil Aviation Conference, Chicago, Illinois, November 1 to December 7, 1944. Final Act and Related Documents. Washington, D. C., Department of State Publication 2282, Conference Series 64, 284 p.

International Institute of Intellectual Cooperation. N. Y., Columbia Univ. Press, 1934, 192 p.

International Labor Organization. *Constitution of the International Labor Organization, together with Documents Effecting Membership of the United States.* Washington, D. C., Washington Branch, International Labor Office, 1941, 29 p.

International Labour Conference, 26th Sess., Philadelphia, 1944. *Director's Report.* Report VII of Conference, Montreal, International Labour Office, 1944, 91 p.

——. *Future Policy, Programme and Status of the International Labour Organisation.* Report I. Montreal, I.L.O., 1944.

——. *Minimum Standards of Social Policy in Dependent Territories.* Report V. Montreal, I.L.O., 1944, 109 p.

International Labour Conference, 26th Sess., Philadelphia, 1944. *Record of Proceedings.* Montreal, I.L.O., 1944, 647 p. (Includes Declaration Concerning the Aims and Purposes of the I.L.O. known as "The Philadelphia Charter," p. 621.)

——. *Social Policy in Dependent Territories.* Montreal, I.L.O., 1944, Studies and Reports, Series B, No. 38, 185 p.

——. 27th Sess., Paris, 1945. *Director's Report.* Report I. Montreal, I.L.O., 1945, 163 p.

——. *The Maintenance of High Level of Employment during the Period of Industrial Rehabilitation and Reconversion.* Report II. Montreal, I.L.O., 1945, 181 p.

——. *Matters Arising out of the Work of the Constitutional Committee. Part I. The Relationship of the I.L.O. to Other International Bodies.* Report IV (1). Montreal, I.L.O., 1945, 165 p.

——. *Minimum Standards of Social Policy in Dependent Territories (Supplementary Provisions).* Report V and Report V (Supplement). Montreal, I.L.O., 1945, 110 p. and 8 p.

League of Nations. *Commercial Policy in the Inter-War Period: International Proposals and National Policies.* Part I. An Historical Survey; Part II. An Analysis of the Reasons for the Success or Failure of International Proposals. Geneva, League of Nations Series. 1942. II. A. 6. (N. Y., Columbia Univ. Press, agents.) 164 p.

——. *Commercial Policy in the Post-War World.* Geneva, League of Nations Series. 1945. II. A. 7. (N. Y., Columbia Univ. Press, agents.) 124 p.

——. *Committees of the League of Nations. Report by the Secretary-General.* Geneva, League of Nations Series. 1934. General. 4. (N. Y., Columbia Univ. Press, agents.) 105 p.

——. *Covenant of the League of Nations* in *Report on the Work of the League, 1942–1943 . . .* Geneva, League of Nations Series. 1943. General. 1, Appendix 1. (N. Y., Columbia Univ. Press, agents.) p. 87–99.

——. *The Development of International Cooperation in Economic and Social Affairs* (The Bruce Report). Report of the Special Committee. Geneva, League of Nations Series. 1939. General. 3. (N. Y., Columbia Univ. Press, agents.) 22 p.

——. *Economic Stability in the Post-War World.* Report of the Delegation on Economic Depressions, Part II. Geneva, League of Nations Series. 1945. II. A. 2. (N. Y., Columbia Univ. Press, agents.) 341 p.

——. *Essential Facts About the League of Nations.* 10th ed. (rev.) Geneva, Information Section, 1939. (N. Y., Columbia Univ. Press, agents.) 359 p.

——. *Handbook of International Organisations (Associations, Bureaux, Committees, etc.).* Geneva, 1938. League of Nations Series. 1937. XII. B. 4. (N. Y., Columbia Univ. Press, agents.) 491 p.

——. *The Mandates System: Origin — Principles — Application.* Geneva, League of Nations Series. 1945. VI. A. 1. (N. Y., Columbia Univ. Press, agents.) 120 p.

——. *Monthly Summary,* 1921–1940. A record of all League meetings and an account of League activities. (N. Y., Columbia Univ. Press, agents.)

——. *Official Journal,* Vol. I, No. 1, February 1920– Vol. 21, No. 2/3, January/March 1940. *Special Supplements,* 1920–   . (Contains the complete Minutes of the Council since the 16th sess., the text of the Reports and Resolutions adopted by the Council, as well as the principal official documents received or despatched by the Secretariat of the League.) (N. Y., Columbia Univ. Press, agents.)

——. *Powers and Duties Attributed to the League of Nations by International*

Treaties. Geneva, League of Nations Series. 1944. V. 1. (N. Y., Columbia Univ. Press, agents.) 48 p.

——. *Records of the Assembly,* 1920–40. (Verbatim minutes, speeches, and Resolutions and Recommendations adopted.) (N. Y., Columbia Univ. Press, agents.)

——. *Report of the Committee Appointed to Study the Constitution, Procedure and Practice of Committees of the League of Nations.* Geneva, League of Nations Series. 1935. General. 2. (N. Y., Columbia Univ. Press, agents.)

——. *Report on the Work of the League, by the Secretary-General,* 1920–1943/44. Geneva, League of Nations, 1920–1945. (N. Y., Columbia Univ. Press, agents.)

——. *Resolutions Adopted by the Assembly during its First–Twentieth Sessions, 1920–1939.* Geneva, League of Nations, 1920–1939. (N. Y., Columbia Univ. Press, agents.)

——. *Ten Years of World Co-operation.* Geneva, Secretariat of the League of Nations, 1930. (N. Y., Columbia Univ. Press, agents.) 467 p.

——. *The Transition from War to Peace Economy. Report of the Delegation on Economic Depressions.* Part I. Geneva, League of Nations Series. 1943. II. A. 3. (N. Y., Columbia Univ. Press, agents.) 118 p.

Permanent Court of International Justice. *Acts and Documents Concerning the Organisation of the Court.* Series D. Fourth Addendum to No. 2. *Elaboration of the Rules of Court of March 11th, 1936.* March 1943. Leyden, Sijthoff. (N. Y., Columbia Univ. Press, agents.)

——. *Collection of Texts Governing the Jurisdiction of the Court.* 4th ed. Jan. 1932. Series D. No. 6. 8 Addenda to June 1939. Leyden, Sijthoff. (N. Y., Columbia Univ. Press, agents.)

——. *The Statute and Rules of Court and Other Constitutional Documents, Rules or Regulations.* 3rd ed. March 1936. Series D. No. 1, Leyden, Sijthoff. (N. Y., Columbia Univ. Press, agents.)

United Kingdom Government. *A Commentary on the Dumbarton Oaks Proposals for the Establishment of a General International Organization.* London, H. M. Stationery Office, November 1944, Cmd. 6571.

United Nations Conference on Food and Agriculture, Hot Springs, Virginia, May 18–June 3, 1943. Final Act and Section Reports. Washington, D. C., Department of State Publication 1948, Conference Series 52, 61 p.

United Nations Conference on International Organization, San Francisco, 1945. *Documents. . . .* Published in cooperation with the Library of Congress by the United Nations Information Organizations, New York. 15 vols. and Index vol. Approx. 12,000 p.

United Nations Educational, Scientific and Cultural Organization. "Constitution of the United Nations Educational, Scientific and Cultural Organization." Washington, D. C., Department of State, *Bulletin,* XIII (November 18, 1945), p. 802.

United Nations Monetary and Financial Conference, Bretton Woods, New Hampshire, July 1 to July 22, 1944. Final Act and Related Documents. Washington, D. C., Department of State Publication 2187, Conference Series 55, 122 p.

United Nations Organization. *Report by the Executive Committee to the Preparatory Commission of the United Nations.* London, 1945. PC/EX/113 Rev. 1. 12 November, 1945. 144 p.

United Nations Relief and Rehabilitation Administration. *Reports of President to Congress on United States Participation in Operations of UNRRA under the Act of March 28, 1944.* Washington, D. C., Govt. Printing Office, 1944–.

United Nations Relief and Rehabilitation Administration. *First Session of the Council of the United Nations Relief and Rehabilitation Administration. Selected Documents, Atlantic City, New Jersey, November 10–December 1, 1943.* Washington, D. C., Department of State Publication 2040, Conference Series 53, 215 p.

——. *Journal, Second Session of the Council and Related Documents of the First Session, Montreal, Canada, September 15 to 27, 1944.* Washington, D. C., 1944, 182 p.

——. *UNRRA — Organization, Aims, Progress.* Washington, D. C., 1944, 34 p.

U. S. Congress. Senate. Committee on Foreign Relations. *The Charter of the United Nations. Hearings before the Committee on Foreign Relations, United States Senate, 79th Cong., 1st sess. on the Charter of the United Nations for the Maintenance of International Peace and Security, submitted by the President of the United States on July 2, 1945.* (Revised), July 9–13, 1945. Washington, D. C., 1945, 723 p.

DOCUMENTARY COLLECTIONS

Documents on American Foreign Relations, 1938–39, 1939–40, 1940–41, 1941–42, 1942–43, 1943–44. Vols. I–III edited by S. Shepard Jones and Denys P. Myers; IV by Leland M. Goodrich with collaboration of Jones and Myers; V–VI by Leland M. Goodrich and Marie J. Carroll. Boston, World Peace Foundation, 1939–45.

HABICHT, MAX. *Post-War Treaties for the Settlement of International Disputes.* Cambridge, Harvard Univ. Press, 1931, 1109 p.

HARLEY, JOHN EUGENE. *Documentary Textbook on International Relations.* Los Angeles, Suttonhouse, 1934, 848 p.

HOLBORN, LOUISE W., ed. *War and Peace Aims of the United Nations.* September 1, 1939–December 31, 1942. Boston, World Peace Foundation, 1943, 730 p. (Vol. II covering period January 1, 1943–June 30, 1945 now in preparation.)

HUDSON, MANLEY O. *International Legislation.* Washington, D. C., Carnegie Endowment for International Peace, 1931–1941, 7 vols.

——. *The World Court: 1921–1938.* Boston, World Peace Foundation, 1938, 345 p.

——. *World Court Reports.* Washington, D. C., Carnegie Endowment for International Peace, 1934–43, 4 vols.

SCHNAPPER, M. B., ed. *United Nations Agreements.* Washington, D. C., American Council on Public Affairs, 1944, 376 p.

The Royal Institute of International Affairs, *Documents on International Affairs.* N. Y., Oxford Univ. Press, 1929–39, 13 vols.

The United Nations in the Making: Basic Documents. Boston, World Peace Foundation, 1945. 2d ed. 136 p.

United Nations Information Office. *War and Peace Aims. Extracts from Statements of United Nations Leaders.* Vol. I. December 6, 1942; II. July 7, 1943; III. January 1, 1944; IV. July 15, 1944; V. January 15, 1945; VI. July 15, 1945 (Special Supplements to the "United Nations Review," Nos. 1–6). N. Y. (610 Fifth Ave.)

U. S. Department of State. *Toward the Peace.* Washington, D. C., Department of State Publication 2298 (Revision of War Documents, Publication 2162), 1945, 38 p.

BOOKS

BAILEY, STANLEY H. *The Anti-Drug Campaign.* London, King, 1936, 263 p.

BASDEVANT, SUZANNE. *Les fonctionnaires internationaux.* Paris, 1931.

BENEŠ, EDVARD and others. *International Security.* Chicago, Univ. of Chicago Press, 1939, 152 p.

BEAUCOURT, A. *Les commissions internationales d'enquête.* Arras, 1909.

BOGGS, MARION W. *Attempts to Define and Limit "Aggressive" Armament in Diplomacy and Strategy.* Columbia, Mo., Univ. of Missouri, 1941, 113 p.

BOURQUIN, M., ed. *Collective Security.* A Record of the Seventh and Eighth International Studies Conferences, 1934 and 1935. Paris, International Institute of Intellectual Co-operation, 1936.

BRIERLY, J. L. *The Outlook for International Law.* Oxford, Clarendon Press, 1944, 142 p.

BURTON, MARGARET E. *The Assembly of the League of Nations.* Chicago, Univ. of Chicago Press, 1941, 441 p.

BUSTAMANTE, ANTONIO S. DE. *The World Court.* N. Y., Macmillan, 1925, 379 p.

CARR, EDWARD H. *Conditions of Peace.* N. Y., Macmillan, 1942, 282 p.

CECIL OF CHELWOOD, ROBERT CECIL, 1ST VISCOUNT. *A Great Experiment.* N. Y., Oxford Univ. Press, 1941, 390 p.

CONDLIFFE, JOHN B. *Agenda for a Postwar World.* N. Y., Norton, 1942, 232 p.

——. *Reconstruction of World Trade.* N. Y., Norton, 1940, 427 p.

—— and STEVENSON, A. *The Common Interest in International Economic Organisation.* Montreal, International Labour Office, 1944, Studies and Reports, Series B, No. 39, 135 p.

CONWELL-EVANS, T. P. *The League Council in Action.* N. Y. and London, Oxford Univ. Press, 1929, 292 p.

CORBETT, PERCY. *Post-War Worlds.* N. Y., American Council, Institute of Pacific Relations, Inquiry Series, 1942, 211 p.

CORWIN, EDWARD S. *The Constitution and World Organization.* Princeton, Princeton Univ. Press, 1944.

CORY, H. M. *Compulsory Arbitration of International Disputes.* N. Y., Columbia Univ. Press, 1932.

CURTIS, LIONEL. *World War: Its Cause and Cure.* London, Oxford Univ. Press, 1945, 274 p.

DAVIS, HARRIET EAGER, ed. *Pioneers in World Order; An American Appraisal of the League of Nations.* N. Y., Columbia Univ. Press, 1944, 272 p.

DILLON, C. H. *International Labor Conventions.* Chapel Hill, Univ. of North Carolina Press, 1942, 272 p.

DULLES, JOHN FOSTER. *War, Peace and Change.* N. Y., Harper, 1939, 170 p.

DUMBAULD, E. *Interim Measures of Protection in International Controversies.* N. Y., Van Riemsdyck, 1932, 204 p.

DUNN, FREDERICK S. *Peaceful Change: A Study of International Procedures.* N. Y., Council on Foreign Relations, 1937, 156 p.

EAGLETON, CLYDE. *Analysis of the Problem of War,* N. Y., Ronald, 1937, 132 p.

——. *International Government.* N. Y., Ronald, 1932, 672 p.

EISENLOHR, LOUISE E. S. *International Narcotics Control.* N. Y., Macmillan, 1935, 295 p.

ÉLES, GEORGES TIBÈRE. *Le principe de l'unanimité dans la Société des Nations et les exceptions à ce principe.* Paris, Pedone, 1935, 279 p.

FACHIRI, ALEXANDER P. *The Permanent Court of International Justice.* N. Y., Oxford Univ. Press, 1932, 416 p.

FEIS, HERBERT. *The Sinews of Peace.* N. Y., Harper, 1944, 271 p.

FINER, HERMAN. *The United Nations Economic and Social Council.* Boston, World Peace Foundation, America Looks Ahead Series, No. 12, 1945.

FLEMING, DENNA FRANK. *The United States and the League of Nations, 1918–1920.* N. Y., G. P. Putnam's Sons, 1932, 559 p.

——. *The United States and the World Court.* N. Y., Doubleday, Doran, 1945, 206 p.

——. *The United States and World Organization, 1920–1933.* N. Y., Columbia Univ. Press, 1938, 569 p.

FOX, W. T. R. *The Super-Powers: The United States, Britain and the Soviet Union—Their Responsibility for Peace.* N. Y., Harcourt, Brace, 1944, 184 p.

GERIG, BENJAMIN. *The Open Door and the Mandates System.* London, G. Allen & Unwin, 1930.

GONSIOROWSKI, M. *Société des Nations et problème de la paix.* Paris, 1927, 2 vols.

GREAVES, HAROLD R. G. *The League Committees and World Order.* London, 1931.

HAMBRO, CARL J. *How to Win the Peace.* Phila., Lippincott, 1942, 384 p.

HAMBRO, EDVARD. *L'exécution des sentences internationales.* Liége, 1936.

HANSEN, ALVIN H. *America's Role in the World Economy.* N. Y., Norton, 1945, 197 p.

HILL, MARTIN. *The Economic and Financial Organization of the League of Nations, A Survey of Twenty-five Years' Experience.* Washington, D. C., Carnegie Endowment for International Peace, 1945, 153 p.

HILL, NORMAN L. *The Public International Conference: Its Function, Organization and Procedure.* Stanford Univ., Calif., Stanford Univ. Press, 1929, 267 p.

HINDMARSH, ALBERT E. *Force in Peace.* Cambridge, Harvard Univ. Press, 1933, 249 p.

HOLCOMBE, ARTHUR N. *Dependent Areas in the Post-War World.* Boston, World Peace Foundation, America Looks Ahead Series, No. 4, 1941, 108 p.

HOOVER, CALVIN. *International Trade and Domestic Employment.* N. Y., McGraw-Hill, 1945.

HOOVER, HERBERT, and GIBSON, HUGH. *The Problems of a Lasting Peace.* N. Y., Doubleday, Doran, 295 p.

HOWARD-ELLIS, CHARLES. *The Origin, Structure and Working of the League of Nations.* London, G. Allen & Unwin; Boston, Houghton Mifflin, 1928, 528 p.

HUDSON, MANLEY O. *By Pacific Means.* New Haven, Yale Univ. Press, 1935, 200 p.

——. *International Tribunals, Past and Future.* Washington, D. C., The Brookings Institution and the Carnegie Endowment for International Peace, 1944, 287 p.

——. *The Permanent Court of International Justice, 1920–1942: A Treatise.* N. Y., Macmillan, 1943, 807 p.

JESSUP, PHILIP C. *International Security.* N. Y., Council on Foreign Relations, 1935.

JOYCE, JAMES AVERY, ed. *World Organization — Federal or Functional.* A Round Table Discussion by David Mitrany, Patrick Ransome, George Catlin, Edvard Hambro, C. B. Purdom and H. G. Wells. London, (November) 1944, C. A. Watts & Co. Ltd., 54 p.

KEETON, GEORGE WILLIAMS. *National Sovereignty and International Order.* London, Peace Book Co., 1939, 191 p.

KELSEN, HANS. *Law and Peace in International Relations.* Cambridge, Harvard Univ. Press, 1942, 181 p.

——. *Legal Technique in International Law.* N. Y., Columbia Univ. Press, 1939, 178 p.

——. *Peace Through Law.* Chapel Hill, Univ. of North Carolina Press, 1944, 155 p.

LAUTERPACHT, HERSH. *The Development of International Law by the Permanent Court of International Justice.* N. Y., Longmans, 1934.

——. *The Function of Law in the International Community.* London and N. Y., Oxford Univ. Press, 1933.

——. *An International Bill of the Rights of Man.* N. Y., Columbia Univ. Press, 1945, 224 p.

LORWIN, LEWIS L. *Postwar Plans of the United Nations.* N. Y., Twentieth Century Fund, 1943.

MAANEN-HELMER, ELIZABETH VAN. *The Mandates System in Relation to Africa and the Pacific Islands.* London, 1929.

MACARTNEY, C. A. *National States and National Minorities.* N. Y., Oxford Univ. Press, 1934, 553 p.

MADARIAGA, SALVADOR DE. *Disarmament.* N. Y., Coward, McCann, 1929.

——. *Theory and Practice in International Relations.* Phila., Univ. of Pennsylvania Press, 1937, 105 p.

——. *The World's Design.* London, G. Allen & Unwin, 1938, 291 p.

MAHAIM, ERNEST. *The Historical and Social Importance of International Labor Legislation: The Origins of the International Labor Organization.* N. Y., Carnegie Endowment for International Peace, Columbia Univ. Press, 1943.

MANNING, C. A. W., ed. *Peaceful Change.* N. Y., Macmillan, 1937.

MARBURG, THEODORE. *Development of the League of Nations Idea.* N. Y., Macmillan, 1932, 2 vols.

MARRIOTT, SIR JOHN A. R. *Commonwealth or Anarchy? A Survey of Projects of Peace from the Sixteenth to the Twentieth Century.* N. Y., Columbia Univ. Press, 1939, 227 p.

MARSTON, F. S. *The Peace Conference of 1919: Organization and Procedure.* N. Y., Oxford Univ. Press, 1944.

McCLURE, WALLACE M. *World Prosperity as Sought through the Economic Work of the League of Nations.* N. Y., Macmillan, 1933, 613 p.

MILLER, DAVID HUNTER. *The Drafting of the Covenant.* N. Y., G. P. Putnam's Sons, 1928, 2 vols.

MILLSPAUGH, ARTHUR C. *Peace Plans and American Choices: The Pros and Cons of World Order.* Washington, D. C., The Brookings Institution, 1942, 107 p.

MITRANY, D. *The Progress of International Government.* New Haven, Yale Univ. Press, 1933, 176 p.

MORLEY, FELIX. *The Society of Nations, Its Organization and Constitutional Development.* Washington, D. C., The Brookings Institution, 1932, 678 p.

MUNCH, P. *Les origines et l'œuvre de la Société des Nations.* Copenhagen, Glydendalske Boghandel-Nordesk Forlag, 1923, 2 vols.

MYERS, DENYS P. *Handbook of the League of Nations.* Boston, World Peace Foundation, 1935, 411 p.

NIEMEYER, GERHART. *Law Without Force.* N. J., Princeton Univ. Press, 1941, 480 p.

OTTLIK, GEORGES. *Annuaire de la Société des Nations.* Geneva, 1920–1938, Librairie Payot & Cie.

PASTUHOV, VLADIMIR D. *A Guide to the Practice of International Conferences.* Washington, D. C., Carnegie Endowment for International Peace (Studies in the Administration of International Law and Organization, No. 4), 1945, 266 p.

——. *Memorandum on the Composition, Procedure, and Functions of Committees of the League of Nations.* Washington, D. C., Carnegie Endowment for International Peace, 1943, 96 p., mimeographed.

PHELAN, EDWARD J. *Yes and Albert Thomas.* London, Cresset Press Ltd., 1936, 271 p.

PHILIPSE, A. H. *La rôle du Conseil de la Société des Nations dans le règlement pacifique des différends internationaux.* The Hague, 1928.

POLITIS, NICOLAS. *La justice internationale.* Paris, 1924.

——. *La morale internationale.* Neuchâtel, Éditions de la Baconnière, 1943. N. Y., Brentano, 1944, 194 p.

POTTER, PITMAN B. *Introduction to the Study of the International Organization.* N. Y., Macmillan, 1922; 4th ed., 1935.

PRÉVOST, MARCEL-HENRI. *Les commissions de l'Assemblée de la Société des Nations.* Paris, Pedone, 1936, 278 p.

Problems of Peace. N. Y., Oxford Univ. Press, 1932–38, 8 vols.

RALSTON, JACKSON H. *International Arbitration from Athens to Locarno.* Stanford Univ., Calif., Stanford Univ. Press, 1929.

——. *A Quest for International Order.* Washington, D. C., Byrne, 1941, 205 p.

RANSHOFEN-WERTHEIMER, EGON F. *The International Secretariat. A Great Experiment in International Administration.* Washington, D. C., Carnegie Endowment for International Peace (Studies in the Administration of International Law and Organization), 1945, 478 p.

RAPPARD, WILLIAM E. *The Quest for Peace.* Cambridge, Harvard Univ. Press, 1940, 516 p.

RAY, JEAN. *La politique et la jurisprudence de la Société des Nations.* Paris, Sirey, 1931–35, 4 vols. Supplements to "Commentaire du Pacte de la Société des Nations.

REINSCH, PAUL S. *Public International Unions; Their Work and Organization, a Study in International Administrative Law.* Boston, World Peace Foundation, 1911, 191 p.

REMLINGER, EUGÈNE. *Les avis consultatifs de la Cour Permanente de Justice Internationale.* Paris, Pedone, 1938, 123 p.

REVES, EMERY. *The Anatomy of Peace.* N. Y., Harper, 1945, 275 p.

RICHES, CROMWELL A. *Majority Rule in International Organization; A Study of the Trend from Unanimity to Majority Decision.* Baltimore, Johns Hopkins Press, 1940, 322 p.

——. *The Unanimity Rule and the League of Nations.* Baltimore, Johns Hopkins Press, 1933, 224 p.

ROBBINS, L. C. *The Economic Causes of War.* N. Y., Macmillan, 1940, 124 p.

ROGERS, JAMES GRAFTON. *World Policing and the Constitution.* Boston, World Peace Foundation, America Looks Ahead Series, No. 11, 1945, 123 p.

Royal Institute of International Affairs, London. *The Colonial Problem.* N. Y., Oxford Univ. Press, 1937, 448 p.

——. *International Sanctions.* (Report by a Group.) N. Y., Oxford Univ. Press, 1938, 247 p.

SALTER, SIR J. ARTHUR. *Allied Shipping Control; An Experiment in International Administration.* London, Oxford Univ. Press, 1921, 372 p.

SCHÜCKING, W., and WEHBERG H. *Die Satzung des Volkerbundes.* Berlin, 1931, 3d ed.

SHOTWELL, JAMES T. *The Great Decision.* N. Y., Macmillan, 1944, 268 p.
——. *On the Rim of the Abyss.* N. Y., Macmillan, 1936, 400 p.
——, ed. *The Origins of the International Labour Organization.* N. Y., Columbia Univ. Press, 1934, 2 vols.
——. *War as an Instrument of National Policy and Its Renunciation in the Pact of Paris.* N. Y., Harcourt, Brace, 1929.
SMUTS, FIELD MARSHAL JAN C. *The League of Nations: A Practical Suggestion.* London, 1918. (Reprinted in D. H. Miller, *The Drafting of the Covenant,* 2 vols. N. Y., G. P. Putnam's Sons, 1918.)
STALEY, EUGENE. *World Economic Development: Effects on Advanced Industrial Countries.* Montreal, International Labour Office, 1944, Studies and Reports, Series B, No. 36.
——. *World Economy in Transition.* N. Y., Council on Foreign Relations, 1939, 340 p.
STONE, JULIUS. *International Guarantees of Minority Rights.* N. Y., Oxford Univ. Press, 1932, 288 p.
STRUPP, KARL. *Legal Machinery for Peaceful Change.* London, Constable, 1937, 86 p.
SWARZENBERGER, GEORG. *The League of Nations and World Order.* London, Constable, 1936, 191 p.
TAYLER, WILLIAM LONSDALE. *Federal States and Labor Treaties.* N. Y., the Author, 1935, 171 p.
TOBIN, HAROLD J. *The Termination of Multipartite Treaties.* N. Y., Columbia Univ. Press, 1933, 321 p.
VINER, JACOB. "The International Economic Organization of the Future." In *Toward World Organization,* N. Y., Harper, 1943.
WALLACE, B. B., and EDMINISTER, L. R. *International Control of Raw Materials.* Washington, D. C., 1930.
WEBSTER, CHARLES K. *The League of Nations in Theory and Practice.* Boston, Houghton Mifflin, 1933, 320 p.
WEHBERG, HANS. *Theory and Practice of International Policing.* New Commonwealth International Monographs. London, Constable, 1935, 100 p.
WELLES, SUMNER. *The Time for Decision.* N. Y., Harper, 1944, 431 p.
WHEELER-BENNETT, JOHN W. *The Pipe Dream of Peace.* (The World Disarmament Conference.) N. Y., Morrow, 1935, 302 p.
WHITTON, JOHN B., ed. *The Second Chance. America and the Peace.* Princeton, N. J., Princeton Univ. Press, 1944, 235 p.
WILCOX, FRANCIS O. *The Ratification of International Conventions.* N. Y., Macmillan, 1936.
WILD, PAYSON S., JR. *Sanctions and Treaty Enforcement.* Cambridge, Harvard Univ. Press, 1934, 231 p.
WILLIAMS, SIR JOHN FISCHER. *Chapters on Current International Law and the League of Nations.* London and N. Y., Oxford Univ. Press, 1929.
——. *Some Aspects of the Covenant of the League of Nations.* London and N. Y., Oxford Univ. Press, 1934, 322 p.
WILSON, FLORENCE. *The Origins of the League Covenant; Documentary History of Its Drafting.* London, Hogarth Press, 1928, 260 p.
WILSON, FRANCIS G. *Labor in the League System.* Stanford Univ., Calif., Stanford Univ. Press, 1934, 384 p.
WOOLF, LEONARD S. *International Government.* London, G. Allen & Unwin, Ltd, 1916.
World Organization: A Balance Sheet of the First Great Experiment. Washington, D. C., American Council on Public Affairs, 1942, 426 p.

WRIGHT, QUINCY. *Mandates Under the League of Nations.* Chicago, Univ. of Chicago Press, 1930.

WYNNER, EDITH, and LLOYD, GEORGIA. *Searchlight on Peace Plans.* N. Y., E. P. Dutton, 1944, 532 p.

YEPES, JESÚS MARIA and PEREIRA DA SILVA, FERNANDO CORREIA. *Commentaire théorètique et pratique de Pacte de la Société des Nations et des Statuts de l'Union Panaméricaine.* Paris, Pedone, 1934–39, 3 vols.

YORK, ELIZABETH. *Leagues of Nations: Ancient, Mediaeval and Modern.* London, Swarthmore Press, 1919.

ZIMMERN, SIR ALFRED E. *The League of Nations and the Rule of Law.* N. Y., Macmillan, 1936, 527 p.

ARTICLES AND PAMPHLETS

Academy of Political Science, Columbia Univ., N. Y. "Shaping the Economic Future," *Proceedings*, XXI, no. 2 (January 1945), **139 p.**

——. "World Organization — Economic, Political and Social," *ibid.*, no. 3 (May 1945), **191 p.**

BIDWELL, PERCY W. "Controlling Trade After the War," *Foreign Affairs*, vol. 21 (January 1943), p. 297–311.

Bishops' Statement on International Order. Issued November 16, 1944, by the Catholic Bishops of the United States. Washington, D. C., National Catholic Welfare Conference (1312 Mass. Ave., N. W.).

BONN, M. J. "How Sanctions Failed," *Foreign Affairs*, vol. 15 (January 1937), p. 350–61.

BORCHARD, EDWIN M. "The Place of Law and Courts in International Relations," *American Journal of International Law*, XXXVII (1943), p. 46.

BONNET, HENRI. *The United Nations: What They Are and What They May Become.* Chicago, World Citizens Assoc., 1941.

BRECHT, ARNOLD. "Distribution of Powers between an International Government and the Governments of National States," *American Political Science Review*, vol. 37 (October 1943), p. 862–72.

BRIERLY, J. L. "International Law: Its Actual Part in World Affairs," London, *International Affairs* (published by Royal Institute of International Affairs), XX (1944), p. 381.

CALDERWOOD, HOWARD B. "The General Committee and Other Auxiliary Committees of the League Assembly," *American Journal of International Law*, XXXVIII (1944), p. 74–94.

CANYES, MANUEL S. "The Inter-American System and the Conference of Chapultepec," *American Journal of International Law*, XXXIX (1945), p. 504–18.

CARR, WILLIAM G. *Only by Understanding: Education and International Organization.* N. Y., Foreign Policy Assn., Headline Series, No. 52 (May–June 1945), **96 p.**

Catholic Association for International Peace. *A Peace Agenda for United Nations.* Washington, D. C., 1943, **40 p.**

——. *World Society.* Washington, D. C., 1941, 48 p.

CECIL OF CHELWOOD, ROBERT CECIL, 1ST VISCOUNT. "Dumbarton Oaks Scheme," *Contemporary Review*, vol. 166 (December 1944), p. 321–5.

CHAMBERLAIN, JOSEPH P. "International Organization." N. Y., *International Conciliation*, no. 385 (December 1942), p. 459.

Chapultepec, Act of. Inter-American Conference, Mexico City, March 6, 1945. *International Conciliation*, no. 410 (April 1945), sec. 2, p. 335.

Commission on a Just and Durable Peace of the Federal Council of Churches. *A Message to the Churches from the National Study Conference on the Churches and a Just and Durable Peace.* Cleveland, Ohio, January 16–19, 1945. (Contains Nine Proposals for Amendment of Dumbarton Oaks Proposals.) N. Y., The Commission etc. (297 Fourth Ave.) 16 p.; *International Conciliation*, no. 409 (March 1945), sec. 1, p. 142–166.

Commission to Study the Organization of Peace. *Fourth Report: Fundamentals of International Organization. General Statement.* Part I. *Security and World Organization.* N. Y., November 1943.

——. "The General International Organization. Its Framework and Functions." Statement of the Commission to Study the Organization of Peace. *International Conciliation*, no. 403 (September 1944), p. 547.

——. *Human Rights and the World Order*, by Quincy Wright. N. Y., 1943, 32 p.

——. *Second Report: The Transitional Period*, 1942; *International Conciliation*, no. 379 (April 1942), p. 149.

CONWELL-EVANS, T. P. "Old and New Security League," *Nineteenth Century*, vol. 137 (January 1945), p. 43–8.

CORBETT, PERCY E. "World Order — An Agenda for Lawyers," *American Journal of International Law*, XXXVII (1943), p. 207.

CORDIER, ANDREW W. "A General Peace and Security Organization: Analysis of Its Major Functions," Department of State, *Bulletin*, XII (February 18, 1945), p. 253–5.

CULBERTSON, ELY. *Our Fight for Total Peace: World Problems of 1945 and New Solutions.* N. Y., Fight for Total Peace, Inc., 1945, 60 p.

DEAN, VERA MICHELES. *After Victory . . . Questions and Answers on World Organization.* N. Y., Foreign Policy Assoc., Headline Series, No. 50 (January 1945).

——. "The San Francisco Conference — with Text of Charter," *Foreign Policy Reports*, XXI, no. 9 (July 15, 1945).

A Design for a Charter of the General International Organization (Envisaged in the Moscow Declaration of October 30, 1943 and in the Resolution Adopted by the Senate of the United States on November 5, 1943). August 1, 1944. *International Conciliation*, no. 402 (August 1944), p. 519.

DULLES, JOHN FOSTER. "The United Nations: A Prospectus — The General Assembly," *Foreign Affairs*, vol. 24 (October 1945), p. 1–11.

EAGLETON, CLYDE. "Covenant of the League of Nations and Charter of the United Nations: Points of Difference," Department of State, *Bulletin*, XIII (August 19, 1945), p. 263.

——. "The United Nations: The Charter Adopted at San Francisco," *American Political Science Review*, XXXIX (October 1945), p. 934.

ENGEL, S. "League Reform, An Analysis of Official Proposals and Discussions," 1936–1939. Geneva, *Geneva Studies*, XI, Nos. 3–4, August 1940 (N. Y., Columbia Univ. Press, agents).

FAGLEY, REV. RICHARD M., OPHER, RABBI AHRON, and CONWAY, REV. EDWARD A., S. J. *The San Francisco Charter, Goals and Achievements.* N. Y., Church Peace Union, 1945.

FENWICK, CHARLES G. "Failure of the League of Nations," *American Journal of International Law*, XXX (1936), p. 506–9.

"First Conference of FAO" (Food and Agriculture Organization), Department of State, *Bulletin*, XIII (September 2, 1945), p. 323–4.

FISHER, ALLAN G. B. "International Economic Collaboration and the Economic and Social Council," London, *International Affairs* (published by Royal Institute of International Affairs), XXI, no. 4 (October 1945).

Fox, WILLIAM T. R. "The United Nations: Collective Enforcement of Peace and Security," *American Political Science Review*, vol. XXXIX (October 1945), p. 970.

FULBRIGHT, J. WILLIAM. "Power Adequate to Enforce Peace," *New York Times Magazine*, October 17, 1943, p. 9.

GILCHRIST, HUNTINGTON. "The United Nations: Colonial Questions at the San Francisco Conference," *American Political Science Review*, XXXIX (October 1945), p. 982.

GOODRICH, LELAND M. "The Nature of the Advisory Opinions of the Permanent Court of International Justice," *American Journal of International Law*, XXXII (1938), p. 738.

——. "The United Nations: Pacific Settlement of Disputes," *American Political Science Review*, XXXIX (October 1945), p. 956.

GRAHAM, R. A., LUCEY, W. L., and BURKE, J. L. *Hope for Peace at San Francisco? What Catholics Should Think of the World Organization.* N. Y., The America Press, 1945, **42 p.**

HACKWORTH, GREEN H. "The International Court of Justice," Department of State, *Bulletin*, XIII (August 12, 1945), p. 216.

HANNA, J. "The Adjustment of the International Opium Administration to an Eventual Dissolution of the League of Nations," N. Y., *Columbia Law Review*, vol. 45, no. 3 (May 1945), p. 392–411.

HANSEN, ALVIN H. "World Institutions for Stability and Expansion," *Foreign Affairs*, vol. 22 (January 1944), p. 248.

HIGHLEY, ALBERT E. "The First Sanctions Experiment. A Study of League Procedures." Geneva, *Geneva Studies*, IX, No. 4, July 1938 (N. Y., Columbia Univ. Press, agents.).

HILL, NORMAN L. "International Commissions of Inquiry and Conciliation," *International Conciliation*, no. 278 (March 1932), p. 87.

HOCKING, WILLIAM E. "The Working of the Mandates," *Yale Review*, Winter 1930, p. 244–68.

HOLMES, OLIVE. "The Mexico City Conference and Regional Security," *Foreign Policy Reports*, XXI, No. 4 (May 1, 1945).

HUDSON, MANLEY O. "Amendment of the Covenant of the League of Nations with a View to its Separation from the Treaties of Peace," *American Journal of International Law*, XXXIII (1939), p. 138–46.

——. "The New World Court," *Foreign Affairs*, vol. 24, no. 1 (October 1945), p. 75–85.

International Consultative Group of Geneva. "Causes of the Peace Failure, 1919–1939," *International Conciliation*, no. 363 (October 1940), p. 333–69.

The International Court of the United Nations Organization: A Consensus of American and Canadian Views. Canadian Bar Association, Committee on Legal Problems of International Organization for the Maintenance of Peace and American Bar Association Committee on Proposals for the Organization of the Nations for Peace, Justice and Law, 1945.

"The International Law of the Future; Postulates, Principles and Proposals," *International Conciliation*, no. 399 (April 1944), p. 251.

JENKS, C. WILFRED. "Some Problems of an International Civil Service," *Public Administration Review*, vol. III (Spring 1943), p. 94.

JESSUP, PHILIP C. "The Court as an Organ of the United Nations," N. Y., *Foreign Affairs*, vol. 23, no. 2 (January 1945), p. 233.

——. "The International Court of Justice of the United Nations — with Texts of Statute," *Foreign Policy Reports*, XXI, no. 11 (August 15, 1945).

JOHNSTONE, W. C. "The Future of the Japanese Mandated Islands," *Foreign Policy Reports*, XXI, no. 13 (September 15, 1945).

KANE, R. KEITH. "The United Nations: A Prospectus — The Security Council," *Foreign Affairs*, vol. 24, no. 1 (October 1945), p. 12–25.

KAPP, KARL W. "The League of Nations and Raw Materials, 1919–1939." Geneva, *Geneva Studies*, XII, No. 3, September 1941 (N. Y., Columbia Univ. Press, agents), 64 p.

KELSEN, HANS. "Compulsory Adjudication of International Disputes," *American Journal of International Law*, XXXVII (1943), p. 397.

——. "The Old and the New League: The Covenant and the Dumbarton Oaks Proposals," *American Journal of International Law*, XXXIX (January 1945), p. 45.

——. "The Principle of Sovereign Equality of States as a Basis for International Organization," *Yale Law Journal*, March 1944.

KIRK, GRAYSON. "Postwar Security for the United States," *The American Political Science Review*, XXXVIII (1944), p. 945.

—— and CHAMBERLAIN, LAWRENCE H. "The Organization of the San Francisco Conference," N. Y., *Political Science Quarterly*, LX (September 1945), p. 321–43.

KUHN, ARTHUR K. "Post-War Development of International Courts," *American Journal of International Law*, XXXVII (1944), p. 276.

KUNZ, JOSEF L. "The International Law of the Future," *The American Political Science Review*, XXXVIII (1944), p. 354.

MAHONY, THOMAS H. *The United Nations Charter*. A Report of the Post-War World Committee of The Catholic Association for International Peace. Washington, D. C., 1945 (Pamphlet Series no. 36), 24 p.

MANNING, C. A. W. "Failure of the League of Nations," London, *Agenda*, vol. 1, January 1942, p. 59–72.

MITRANY, D. *A Working Peace System*. London, Royal Institute of International Affairs, 1943, 56 p.

MORGENTHAU, HENRY, JR. "Bretton Woods and International Cooperation," *Foreign Affairs*, vol. 23 (1945), p. 182.

National Catholic Welfare Conference. *The Bishops Speak Out on World Peace*. Washington, D. C., 1945, 4 p.

The Pattern for Peace. Catholic, Jewish and Protestant Declaration on World Peace. Released October 7, 1943. N. Y., Church Peace Union (70 Fifth Ave.).

POTTER, PITMAN B. "The League of Nations and Other International Organizations; An Analysis of the Evolution and Position of the League in Cooperation among States." Geneva, *Geneva Special Studies*, V, No. 6, 1934 (N. Y., Columbia Univ. Press, agents), 22 p.

——. "Permanent Delegations to the League of Nations," *American Political Science Review*, XXV (February 1931).

——. "The United Nations Charter and the Covenant of the League of Nations," *American Journal of International Law*, XXXIX (July 1945), p. 546.

PREUSS, LAWRENCE. "The International Court of Justice and the Problem of Compulsory Jurisdiction," Department of State, *Bulletin*, XIII (September 30, 1945), p. 471.

PRINCE, CHARLES. "Current Views of the Soviet Union on the International Organization of Security, Economic Cooperation and International Law: A Summary," *American Journal of International Law*, XXXIX (July 1945), p. 450–85.

RANSHOFEN-WERTHEIMER, EGON F. "International Administration: Lessons from the Experience of the League of Nations," *American Political Science Review*, XXXVII (October 1943), p. 872–87.

——. "International Reorganization," Washington, D. C., *American Society of International Law, Proceedings*, April 1941.

——. "The Position of the Executive and Administrative Heads of the United Nations International Organizations," *American Journal of International Law*, XXXIX (April 1945), p. 323–30.

The Royal Institute of International Affairs, London. *The International Secretariat of the Future*. Lessons from Experience by a Group of Former Officials of the League of Nations. N. Y., Oxford Univ. Press, Post-War Problems, 1944, 64 p.

STONE, J. "The Rule of Unanimity: The Practice of the Council and Assembly of the League of Nations," *British Yearbook of International Law*, XIV (1933), p. 18.

SWEETSER, ARTHUR. "The League of Nations and Associated Agencies," *International Conciliation*, no. 397 (February 1944), p. 140–9.

——. "Non-political Achievements of the League," *Foreign Affairs*, vol. 19 (October 1940), p. 179–92.

TEAD, ORDWAY. "The Importance of Administration in International Action," *International Conciliation*, no. 407 (January 1945), p. 7–40.

THOMPSON, C. MILDRED. "United Nations Plans for Post-War Education," *Foreign Policy Reports*, XX, no. 24 (March 1, 1945).

TOBIN, HAROLD J. "The Problem of Permanent Representation at the League of Nations," *Political Science Quarterly*, December 1933.

TOLLEY, HOWARD R., and STINEBOWER, LEROY D. "Food for the Family of Nations: The Purpose and Structure of the Proposed Food and Agriculture Organization of the United Nations." Department of State, *Bulletin*, XII (February 18, 1945), p. 225–30.

Universities Committee on Post-War International Problems. *The Dumbarton Oaks Proposals: Economic and Social Cooperation*. Boston, Problem Analysis XIX (February 1945), 38 p.

——. *The Dumbarton Oaks Proposals: The Enforcement of Peace*. Boston, Problem Analysis XVIII (December 1944), 39 p.

——. *Peaceful Settlement of International Disputes*. Boston, Problem Analysis XVII (September 1944), 34 p.

VAN ZANDT, J. PARKER. "The Chicago Civil Aviation Conference — with Texts of Convention on International Civil Aviation and International Air Transport Agreement," *Foreign Policy Reports*, XX, no. 23 (February 15, 1945).

VAN ZEELAND, PAUL. "The Large Role of the Small Nations," *New York Times Magazine*, September 24, 1944, p. 9.

WARNER, EDWARD. "The Chicago Air Conference," *Foreign Affairs*, vol. 23, no. 3 (April 1945), p. 406–21.

WILCOX, FRANCIS O. "The United Nations: The Yalta Voting Formula," *American Political Science Review*, XXXIX (October 1945), p. 943.

WOLFERS, ARNOLD. "The Small Powers and the Enforcement of Peace," *Yale Review*, Winter 1944.

LIST OF REFERENCES TO ARTICLES

LIST OF REFERENCES TO ARTICLES

INDEX

CHARTER OF THE UNITED NATIONS
COMMENTARY AND DOCUMENTS

WORLD PEACE FOUNDATION

40 Mt. Vernon Street, Boston, Massachusetts

Founded in 1910

THE World Peace Foundation is a non-profit organization which was founded in 1910 by Edwin Ginn, the educational publisher, for the purpose of promoting peace, justice and good-will among nations. For many years the Foundation has sought to increase public understanding of international problems by an objective presentation of the facts of tional relations. This p complished principally through its publications and by the maintenance of a Reference Service which furnishes on request information on current international problems. Recently increased attention has been focused on American foreign relations by study groups organized for the consideration of actual problems of policy.